The Official RED BOOK®

A Guide Book of
United States Paper Money

Complete Source for History, Grading, and Prices

Written and compiled by

Arthur L. and Ira S. Friedberg

Introduction and Narrative by

Q. David Bowers

Whitman Publishing, LLC
PUBLISHING SINCE 1934

www.whitman**books**.com

© 2006 by Whitman Publishing, LLC
3101 Clairmont Road • Suite C • Atlanta GA 30329

ISBN 079481786-6

Printed in China

The Official RED BOOK™ Series Includes:

- *A Guide Book of Morgan Silver Dollars*
- *A Guide Book of Double Eagle Gold Coins*
- *A Guide Book of United States Type Coins*
- *A Guide Book of Modern United States Proof Coin Sets*
- *A Guide Book of Indian and Flying Eagle Cents*
- *A Guide Book of United States Nickel Five-Cent Pieces*
- *A Guide Book of United States Commemorative Coins*
- *A Guide Book of United States Barber Silver Coins*
- *A Guide Book of United States Liberty Seated Silver Coins*

TABLE OF CONTENTS

About the Authors 4

Foreword by Dennis Tucker 6

Introduction by Q. David Bowers.. 8

Acknowledgements and Credits.. 47

One Dollar Notes 50

Two Dollar Notes 84

Five Dollar Notes 102

Ten Dollar Notes 150

Twenty Dollar Notes.. 206

Fifty Dollar Notes 258

One Hundred Dollar Notes.. 302

Five Hundred Dollar Notes 340

One Thousand Dollar Notes 354

Five Thousand Dollar Notes 366

Ten Thousand Dollar Notes 368

Fractional Currency... 378

Encased Postage.. 392

Treasury Notes of the War of 1812 400

Error Notes... 408

Appendix A: The Signatures of United States Currency...................... 418

Appendix B: Friedberg Numbers by Page... 420

Appendix C: Glossary 426

A full-color gallery of select notes is located after page 432.

Arthur Friedberg and Ira Friedberg

Arthur and Ira Friedberg have been professional numismatists for more than thirty years. Their firm, The Coin & Currency Institute, Inc., is a founding member of the elite International Association of Professional Numismatists (I.A.P.N.).

In June, 2001 in Rome, Italy, Arthur Friedberg was elected president of the Association, marking the first time in the fifty-year history of the organization an American has occupied that office. He is also a life member of the American Numismatic Association and has been a member of the prestigious Professional Numismatists Guild since 1977.

Both brothers joined Coin & Currency (a family firm) after college. Arthur graduated in 1972 with a BA in history from The George Washington University in Washington, DC He later earned an MBA from New York University, in 1976. Ira received his BS in Journalism from Boston University in 1975. Within a short time they co-authored revisions of *Gold Coins of the World* (now in its seventh edition) and *Paper Money of the United States* (now in its 17th edition). They also wrote the new editions of *Appraising and Selling Your Coins*, the 24th edition of which was released in 1996 by a division of Random House, and which has more than a quarter of a million copies in print. They also published and edited the revisions to R.S. Yeoman's classics, *Modern World Coins* and *Current Coins of the World*, new editions of which are now being prepared by Whitman Publishing LLC for release beginning in 2006. Arthur is a contributor to the *Standard Catalog of World Coins* and has written numerous articles for *The Numismatist*, the journal of the American Numismatic Association.

Arthur Friedberg has been a consultant to the Money and Medal Programme of the Food and Agriculture Organization of the United Nations in Rome, Italy; and has testified as an expert on commemorative coin matters before the United States Senate Banking Committee. He has also been retained by advertising agencies, law firms, insurance companies, and others to provide advice on coins and on international and domestic numismatic marketing.

In 1993 the Friedbergs were awarded the Prix d'Honneur of the I.A.P.N. for *Gold Coins of the World* as the best book of the preceding year. They have also been presented the Medal of Merit of the American Numismatic Association (1992) for "distinguished service to the hobby." Arthur received the first place Heath Literary Award (1994) as author of the article judged best in *The Numismatist* during 1993, and the Swiss Vrenelli Prize (1999) for "outstanding contributions to numismatics."

Q. David Bowers

Q. David Bowers, born in 1938, became interested in coin collecting in 1952 and became a dealer in 1953. Since that time he has gone from one numismatic endeavor and success to another, including serving as president of the Professional Numismatists Guild (1977-1979) and the American Numismatic Association (1983-1985). Bowers is the recipient of the highest awards given by each of these groups: the Founders Award by the PNG, and the Farran Zerbe Award by the ANA. A 1960 graduate of the Pennsylvania State University, with a degree in Finance, he was given the Alumnus Achievement Award in 1976 by its College of Business Administration.

At present Bowers is numismatic director of Whitman Publishing, LLC, and is also a principal in the well-known rare coin firm American Numismatic Rarities, LLC, of Wolfeboro, New Hampshire.

He is the author of more than 40 books, many of which have won the highest honors given by the Numismatic Literary Guild ("Book of the Year Award"), the Professional Numismatists Guild ("Friedberg Award"), and other organizations. His column, "The Joys of Collecting," has appeared in Coin World weekly for more than 40 years—the longest-running feature by any numismatic author in the history of the hobby. Further contributions to the hobby include compiling or contributing to hundreds of important auction catalogs (including the Louis E. Eliasberg, Sr. Collection, the Norweb Collection, the Harry W. Bass, Jr. Collection, and the Childs Collection), and editing and contributing to hobby periodicals.

Dave is a fellow of the American Numismatic Society, the American Antiquarian Society, and the Massachusetts Historical Society. In 1999, he was named as one of only six living people in the roster of 18 "Numismatists of the Century" in a poll conducted by *COINage* magazine.

In the field of currency Dave is a columnist for *Paper Money*, the magazine of the Society of Paper Money Collectors. He has collected, studied, and enjoyed paper money since the 1950s, with historical and technical information being a particular focus of activity. Currently, he is doing research for a book covering obsolete notes of 1782 to 1866 and, separately, on paper money of New Hampshire, a comprehensive study being conducted with David M. Sundman as co-author.

Invited to contribute the collecting, historical, and technical text to the present volume, Dave complied with enthusiasm, drawing upon his experience in combination with extensive historical files and other information.

FOREWORD

Until recent years there has been a certain stability to the designs of American banknotes—a sedate, familiar sameness that hardly encouraged the uninitiated to pay much attention to the currency in their wallets. The turn of the new century, though, has brought bold and colorful changes to those longstanding designs. To curtail any confusion, Treasury publicity campaigns introduced the world to the refreshingly new notes as they were updated—notes which, up to that point, had always been static, unchanging… or had they?

In fact, of course, United States paper money hasn't always been the same, though the thirsty man struggling to slide his $1 bill into a vending machine might rarely stop to think about it. Our currency has varied dramatically over the nearly 150 years since it was federalized. Far from merely acting as a medium of exchange, American banknotes have been mirrors to the life and times of the nation: their designs reflecting cultural, social, and political changes; showing the viewer—through portrait, vignette, repetition, and emphasis—what "the United States" is.

Christopher Columbus arrived in the New World in 1492; an American family of 1892 would observe his triumph on the $5 note that paid for their groceries. George Washington crossed the Delaware in the dead of winter, 1776; one hundred years later, an American businessman would see the great general in action on the $50 bill. The landing of the Pilgrims in 1620, Benjamin Franklin's famous kite experiment, the signing of the Declaration of Independence—all would be honored on the paper that changed hands every day, from New York City to Peoria to Los Angeles. As the nation expanded westward, exotic new sights would make their way onto its banknotes: Indian chiefs, bison, and railroad locomotives. Military might and commercial strength would be seen in the battleships and steamships of the day. Famous statesmen—and the occasional not-so-famous politician or Army officer—would be immortalized in green paper and black ink. The ideals of freedom, independence, and hard work would take shape in American eagles, the steadfast Miss Liberty, and scenes of industry and farming, art and invention.

So, then: static and unchanging, the paper money of the United States? Never. It's as rich as the nation's own history.

There was a time when the federal government was not the sole issuer of our currency, when state-chartered banks (and even private agencies) issued their own paper money to aid commerce. There was a time when the states were not united, when the Demand Notes of 1861 were issued to raise money to fight the Civil War. And there was a time when the Treasury partnered with private companies in New York to print the money that circulated east to west, north to south. The story of those times and more—of Legal Tender Notes (financially weak but artistically strong), beautiful and historic National Bank Notes, Silver Certificates marked HAWAII, fractional currency worth 3¢, Watermelon Notes and Buffalo bills—is told in this remarkable work, *A Guide Book of United States Paper Money*. Numismatic historian Q. David Bowers expands on the original classic text written by the Friedberg family (father Robert, then brothers Arthur and Ira). He sets each series of bills in its historical context, and explains the people, events, and forces that combined to make our currency. Inside these pages you'll find large- and small-size notes, encased postage, errors, fractional currency, and more—pieces ranging from the commonplace to the ultra rare.

Beyond immersing yourself in the history and romance of United States paper money, you'll benefit from a unique combination of features in this book.

The Friedberg numbering system: This system has been used to catalog paper money collections ever since Robert Friedberg compiled the first edition of his standard reference book in the early 1950s. His numbering system has been the hobby standard for more than fifty years; "What's the Friedberg number?" is the first question you'll hear when you tell a collector about your latest purchase or get ready to sell. Each note in the *Guide Book of United States Paper Money* is identified by its unique number.

An intuitive, updated layout: The notes are laid out in a new format: by types (Silver Certificate, Federal Reserve Note, etc.) within each denomination, rather than by denominations within each type. This makes it easy for the novice collector to identify an unknown note, by going directly to its face value and then skimming to match it to its photograph. The more experienced collector or dealer who wants to look up a note by its Friedberg number will find a valuable reference in Appendix B, which matches each note to the page it's on.

Current market price valuations: Knowledge is power in the marketplace, and, armed with the pricing information that accompanies each note in this book, you're on your way to becoming a smarter buyer, seller, and collector. These valuations have been compiled by leading experts in the field—people who make their living in collectable currency and understand the market from real-world analysis, auction and show attendance, and day-to-day trading.

Advice on the hobby: Dave Bowers shares a longtime collector's insight on how to build your own collection: what features to look for, how to grade your notes, practices to beware of, various ways to collect currency, how to watch the market, and where the hobby is heading.

Hundreds of photographs: Detailed text descriptions are combined with high-resolution black and white images of hundreds of different notes, face and back, making identification easy and convenient. An eight-page spread of beautiful full-color photographs explores the richness and diversity of select United States notes through the centuries.

Adding up this wealth of information, it's easy to see that *A Guide Book of United States Paper Money* is an engaging welcome for the newcomer, a valuable resource for the established collector or dealer, and an indispensable addition to any numismatic reference library.

Dennis Tucker, Publisher
February 2005

ESERVE BANK NOTE

DOLLARS.

ARTS OF THE UNITED STATES IN PAYMENT OF ALL
TED STATES EXCEPT DUTIES ON IMPORTS AND
ANDS OWING BY THE UNITED STATES TO INDIVID
THE UNITED STATES EXCEPT INTEREST ON PU

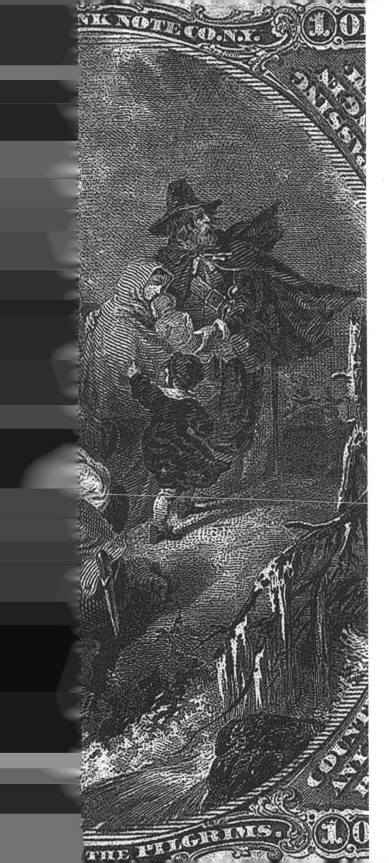

INTRODUCTION

INFORMATION ABOUT PAPER MONEY

By Q. David Bowers

The United States did not issue paper money on a widespread basis until 1861. However, the federal government was an important stockholder in the federally chartered Bank of the United States (1791 to 1811) and its successor, the star-crossed Second Bank of the United States (1816 to 1836). Both of these banks issued large quantities of paper money, including bills payable at many different branches. All such currency is very rare today, and that identified with certain of the branch offices ranges from extremely rare to unknown.

From 1812 to 1815, the Treasury Department issued interest-bearing notes in five different series, to the total face value of $36,000,000, from plates by Murray, Draper, Fairman & Co., Philadelphia. Denominations ranged from $5 to $1,000, and early issues named a specific payee and place of redemption.

The standard issues of federal money commenced with the Demand Notes of 1861, issued to finance the Civil War. At first, the Civil War was envisioned to be brief, with the North prevailing. In April 1861, President Abraham Lincoln called for three-month enlistments, surely enough time to conclude the rebellion. Reality proved to be different. In ensuing years, many different series of currency were produced, based upon their backing or stated obligation, in values from $1 to $10,000. Legal Tender bills, introduced in 1862, were not specifically redeemable in coin, but later Silver Certificates, Gold Certificates, and Coin Notes (also called Treasury Notes) were. Large-size bills were issued until 1929, in which year the change was made to the small size still in use today. In the 20th century, Federal Reserve Notes in several variations were introduced. In time, the different classes of currency were terminated, and today just the Federal Reserve Notes remain, made in denominations of $1, $2 (occasionally), $5, $10, $20, $50, and $100. Recently, the designs of bills have undergone changes, with modification of the portraits to larger sizes and with the addition of security features.

Currency was printed by private contractors in New York City in the early years, the most important being the American Bank Note Co. The Continental Bank Note Co. and the National Bank Note Co. also had contracts, and, later, a small amount of work was done by the Columbian Bank Note Co. (Washington, DC). For security purposes, some bills were printed on the face by one firm, on the back by another, and the seal and serial numbers were added at the Treasury Department in Washington. Beginning in the mid-1870s, production was transferred to the Bureau of Engraving and Printing, sometimes with the use of older plates. Today, currency is produced in Washington plus a satellite printing facility in Fort Worth, Texas. Bills bear imprints for the 12 Federal Reserve Banks, creating many different varieties each time there is a signature combination or design change.

DIFFERENT ISSUES, TYPES, AND SERIES

Interest Bearing Notes
(Authorized 1861 to 1865)

Large-Size

Interest Bearing Notes (as they are called today), in effect loan certificates, were authorized under the Act of March 2, 1861, in a time of great controversy between the North and the South, but before the Civil War erupted. These were to yield 6% annual interest and to be redeemed in 60 days. No specimens are known to exist today.

Under several acts from 1863 to 1865, bills of $10 to $5,000 were authorized, for periods of one and two years, at 6% interest, and three-year notes at 7.3%, the last issued in denominations from $50 upward. The bills of 7.3% had daily interest printed on them, of one cent per day for the $50, and proportionately for higher values. These had five printed coupons past the right border of the note, each one removable and exchangeable for six months' interest, after which the bill itself would be turned in to get the final interest plus principal.

Interest Bearing Notes, some imprinted as "Treasury Notes," were very popular as a way to earn interest and help alleviate the ever-depreciating value of Legal Tender and state bank bills.

Figure I

The American Bank Note Company, located in the Merchants' Exchange, New York City, as it appeared in 1861. This firm printed the lion's share of federal currency on contract from 1861 through the mid-1870s, after which the Treasury did its own work at the Bureau of Engraving and Printing. Through 1865, the company also printed bills for hundreds of state-chartered banks.

Figure II

Above is the printing room. Artisans inked the steel plates with rollers, then printed sheets of bills (usually four notes to a sheet) on hand-operated "spider" presses, using dampened paper. Afterward, the notes were dried, bundled, and shipped to the Treasury Department in Washington, where the seals and serial numbers were imprinted.

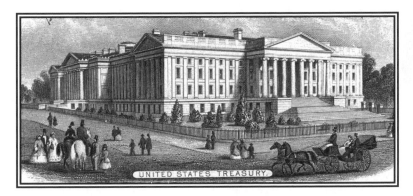

Figure III

The Treasury Building, Washington, DC, as it appeared in the 1860s. Within this Greek Revival structure the Currency Bureau, established by Spencer M. Clark, imprinted seals and serial numbers on currency printed in New York City by the American, Continental, and National Bank Note companies. The Currency Bureau also printed Fractional Currency. Treasury officials had their offices in the building.

Banks were large purchasers of these, listing them as "bonds" in their reports to stockholders. Nearly all were redeemed in due course, with the result that any example is a great rarity today. Certain of the large denominations are not known to exist.

Demand Notes
(Authorized 1861)

Large-Size

By July 1861, the easy win envisioned by the North had not come to pass, and both the Yankees and Confederates (Rebels, as they were called) were coming to realize that the war was going to last for more than just a few months. On the 21st of July, the Battle of Bull Run would settle the question with an overwhelming victory, albeit a short-lived one, for the South. In the meantime, the Union was in desperate need of funds to finance its side of the war.

A partial solution was provided by a $250,000,000 loan, mostly bonds, but including $50,000,000 in currency to be known as Demand Notes, authorized by the acts of July 17 and August 5, supplemented early the next year, on February 12, by an additional $10,000,000. The reverses of the notes, $5, $10, and $20, were printed in green ink, quickly giving rise to the popular term *greenback*, although this was more widely applied to the later Legal Tender Notes issued in far greater quantities.

The Demand Notes were payable at five different federal depositories, located in New York City, Philadelphia, Boston, Cincinnati, and St. Louis. The first bills were paid out in August 1861, and used to pay government salaries in Washington. Soon thereafter, notes were given to Union soldiers, defense contractors, and others to whom the government was obligated. Merchants and commercial interests in the larger eastern cities were very skeptical of these new, unfamiliar notes and in many instances declined to receive them. Some railroads would not accept them either, and various banks in New York City united in their opposition of the paper. This played some havoc with government employees and soldiers who had such bills to spend.

To remedy the stalemate, a circular letter was sent by the Treasury Department to the assistant U.S. treasurers in Boston, New York City, Cincinnati, Philadelphia, and St. Louis, directing them to redeem Demand Notes in gold coins, if requested. This seemed to settle the situation and from then until December 28, 1861, Demand Notes and gold $5, $10, and $20 coins had equivalent values. This circular letter was to become very important after December 28, 1861, after which time banks stopped paying out gold coins at par, and the bills of state-chartered banks began to depreciate. By then, $33,460,000 in Demand Notes had been paid out. By April 1, 1862, the entire $60,000,000 worth had been printed and issued.

Apparently, the earliest bills were personally signed by L[ucius] E. Chittenden, register of the Treasury, and F[rancis] E[lias] Spinner, treasurer. This soon proved unfeasible, as per this account published in 1883:

> In 1861 the New York bank note companies printed our first greenbacks, and the Treasurer and Register signed them with their own proper hands. But the infant army, that financial Oliver Twist, was always clamoring for "more." Spinner was no Briareus the hundred-handed, and Chittenden could not devote more than 24 hours a day to his own autographs. So Congress authorized them to sign by proxy.

> Then the issue grew till 70 clerks at $1,200 a year were kept busy in writing their own in lieu of these officers' names. But so many different hands destroyed all the value of signatures. They were no more protection against fraud than the type in which this is printed, and the Secretary was in sore perplexity.

> There was a keen-eyed Superintendent of Constructing the Public Buildings, named S.M. Clark. A Vermont Yankee, and true to his nativity, he had done a little of everything, and could make anything. Just now he was at leisure; the nation needed no new edifices till arms should decide whether it was a nation. He proposed facsimiles of the signatures, and also of the Treasury Seal, to be engraved and printed on the notes in peculiar ink, and by a peculiar process.

Figure IV

Figure V

Figure VI

$1 National Bank Note, Series of 1875, Friedberg-385 (Figure IV). This note bears the imprint SERIES 1875 vertically at the left—the hallmark of all notes of the new series, issued when the Treasury Department began printing bills for its own account in Washington, DC, but using plates made by the private companies (in this instance, the American Bank Note Co.). The bank serial number (1089); the Treasury seal; the charter number (1564); and the Treasury serial number (A908493) are all in bright red. The bill is signed by Jno. A. Butler (John A. Butler) and W. Harris (William Harris), who also signed the bank stock certificate shown (Figure V). Also illustrated is a $1 bill from its predecessor, the state-chartered West River Bank, circa 1860 (Figure VI).

Chase, under sanction of Congress, adopted the suggestion. Then Spinner was the hundred-handed. He could sign with a rapidity limited only by the capacity of lightning presses. Notes came to the department in sheets of four each. Seventy-five girls, everyone armed with her shears, trimmed and separated them by hand. Clark declared this ought to be done by machinery, and that he could make the machines himself. Fogies pooh-poohed. Cut bank notes apart, and trim their edges by steam? Utterly impossible! Beside, it would be too expensive, and would take bread from these worthy women. But the Secretary said, "Go ahead"; so the Yankee coaxed his brains, and in two months brought in two trial machines, worked by a crank.

The clerk, to whom they were referred, inspected and reported them failures. So Chase ordered them removed from the building but what inventor ever acquiesced in the slaughter of his own progeny? This one implored the Secretary, "Come and examine for yourself." Chase did examine, and found that these marvelous automata, with cunning fingers of steel, not only did the work perfectly, but also reduced its cost more than four-fifths. He instantly rescinded the order, placed Clark in charge of the cutting and trimming, and assigned him rooms for the purpose. That was the origin of the Printing and Engraving Bureau of the Treasury Department.

On the 29th of August 1862, Clark began, assisted by one man and four women. Now, this Bureau has more than a score of subordinate superintendents, hundreds of employees, and has turned out sixty millions of dollars in a single day.[1]

The multi-talented Spencer M. Clark was also a controversial figure. It should be noted that while the above described corps of ladies with pen and ink added their own signatures above "for the" treasurer or register, certain of them became adept at copying the signature of F.E. Spinner and added it to some notes, especially certain proof impressions of the later Fractional Currency issues.

Demand Notes became highly prized, and, after Legal Tender Notes were issued (discussed below; these were first paid out in April 1862 and were not redeemable in gold or usable at par for customs duties), Demand Notes sold for a sharp premium, especially after the coin-hoarding panic of July 1862.

Almost immediately after the Legal Tender Notes were circulated, the Treasury Department began retiring as many Demand Notes as it could, these in addition to those it exchanged for gold coins in the first few months of 1862. Within a year after they were issued, Demand Notes were rare, although legal authorization for current production remained in effect. By early August 1862, it took $115.25 in Legal Tender bills to buy $100 worth of gold coins, but only $100 in Demand Notes. By July 1, 1880, all but $60,535 of the Demand Notes had been redeemed.

Today, Demand Notes are very rare—so much so that they are seldom collected except by advanced specialists. Among the branch depositories, no bills with the St. Louis imprint are known today.

Legal Tender or United States Notes
(Authorized 1862)
Series of 1862 to 1923 Legal Tender Notes
Large-Size

Legal Tender Notes, as they are generally called, were mostly imprinted with "United States Note" at the border. These were born of necessity, for in January 1862, gold coins disappeared from circulation, and a widely accepted high-denomination monetary medium was needed, other than Interest Bearing Notes and Demand Notes. The situation was becoming increasingly uncomfortable. No prospect for victory was in sight for the Union, and losses increased on a daily basis. Banks, manufacturers, and merchants became increasingly worried. On January 15, 1862, the *London Post* commented:

Figure VII

Figure VIII

The National Bank Note Company, Wall Street, New York City. Its headquarters has a large sign above the second story, to the right. Founded in 1859, this firm printed many larger-denomination bills in the Original Series.

These vignettes (Figure VIII) by the National Bank Note Co. were used on certain currency of the 1860s, as shown in *Heath's Infallible Counterfeit Detector*, Banking and Counting House Edition, 1867.

The monetary intelligence from America is of the most important kind. National bankruptcy is not an agreeable prospect, but it is the only one presented by the existing state of American finance. What a strange tale does not the history of the United States for the past twelve months unfold? What a striking moral does it not point? Never before was the world dazzled by a career of more reckless extravagance. Never before did a flourishing and prosperous state make such gigantic strides towards affecting its own ruin.

On January 29, 1862, in a letter to the Committee of Ways and Means, Secretary of the Treasury Salmon P. Chase stated, in part:

It is not unknown to the Committee that I have felt, nor do I wish to conceal, that I now feel a great aversion to making anything but coin legal tender in payment of debts. It has been my anxious wish to avoid the necessity of such legislation. It is, however, at present impossible, in consequence of the large expenditures entailed by the war, and the suspension [of the payment of gold coins] of the banks, to procure sufficient coin for disbursement; and it has, therefore, become indispensably necessary that we should resort to the issue of United States Notes.

The making them a legal tender might, however, still be avoided, if the willingness manifested by the people generally, the railroad companies, and by many of the banking institutions, to receive and pay them as money in all transactions, were absolutely or practically universal; but, unfortunately there are some people and some institutions which refuse to receive and pay them. Such discriminations would, if possible be prevented; and the provision making the notes a legal tender, in a great measure at least, prevents it, by putting all citizens in this respect on the same level, both of rights and duties.

Chase went on to say that such was a temporary measure, and that he hoped to "secure the earliest possible return to a sound currency of coin and promptly convertible notes," the last referring to the success enjoyed by the Demand Notes redeemable in gold.

The first Legal Tender Notes were dated March 10, 1862, and were issued in denominations of $5 to $1,000, followed by those dated August 1, 1862, of the values of $1 and $2. A $3 value was contemplated, this being a popular denomination with state banks, but was never issued. Eventually, $5,000 bills were made. However, most circulation consisted of lower denominations from $1 to $20. The American Bank Note Co. of New York was the primary printing contractor for these bills, with the National Bank Note Co. of the same city doing the balance.

These notes were legal tender for all debts, public and private, except for import duties and payment on the public debt. They were not exchangeable at par for silver or gold coins. The prospect for these paper bills was uncertain, and the memory of worthless bills of failed and broken banks was fresh in the memory of many.

Because there was no time set for their redemption in gold or silver coins, and as they had no backing other than the good faith of the government, Legal Tender bills depreciated from the very beginning. Soon, a double system of pricing arose in the marketplace—a larger price if paid in Legal Tender bills, or smaller if coins were tendered in payment. Indeed, at the outset, there were many merchants who would not accept Legal Tender Notes at all and demanded coins. Not even the Philadelphia Mint would accept Legal Tender Notes in payment at par for the Proof coins it struck for collectors, a situation that endured for many years. To buy such pieces, numismatists had to buy older silver and gold coins from an exchange broker and submit them to the Mint in payment.[2]

The early $1 bills of the Legal Tender type bore the portrait of Secretary of the Treasury Chase, who was living at the time, not unusual as other living men were portrayed on certain higher denomination bills. The total issue of this $1 style amounted to 28,351,348 notes. Smaller quantities were printed of other denominations, but their total face value was higher. On the Legal Tender bills, the portrait of George Washington was instituted on the $1 beginning with the Series of 1869. Since that time, the Father of Our Country has been featured more or less continuously on notes of this denomination issued in various categories (today on Federal Reserve Notes).

On July 11, 1864, it took $256 in Legal Tender Notes to buy $100 worth of gold coins, this being the highest differential in history. However, in the Confederacy, the situation was even worse, and it took $2,174 in Confederate bills to buy $100 in Federal coins (which remained highly regarded) in the South).

On the West Coast, the State Legislature of California had decreed in 1850 that paper money of any kind was not to be used in commerce. This would prevent problems with unsound banks, such as many Forty-Niners had experienced back East before going westward to seek their fortunes. Accordingly, in 1862, when Legal Tender bills were first issued, and continuing for years afterward, they were of no use at face value in commerce in such places as San Francisco and Sacramento. Instead, silver and gold coins were the media of exchange, and anyone wanting to spend a Legal Tender bill had to accept a deep discount equal to the premium charged for gold and silver in the East.

The federal government did not countenance this arrangement and in the West paid the wages of Army and Navy personnel and other federal employees in Legal Tender bills. The recipients had no choice but to take large losses when they spent the notes. For a long time, it took $20 in such bills to buy merchandise priced at $12 to $15 in terms of gold coins. On August 25, 1864, in San Francisco, the employees in the office of the Assessor of Internal Revenue went on strike seeking payment of their wages in gold coins or, alternatively, higher wages if they continued to be paid in Legal Tender Notes.[3]

Finally, on December 17, 1878, the difference in value of gold coins vs. paper, which had been narrowing since the Civil War, ended, and Legal Tender and all other federal bills could be readily exchanged for gold and silver. In practice, few citizens did this. With the assurance that Legal Tender Notes could be redeemed for gold, just about everyone was content to keep using paper.

Over a long period of time, most of the smaller Legal Tender Note denominations were printed in large quantities, making types easy to collect today. Favorite designs include the Pioneer Family on Series 1869 to 1907 notes, some earlier examples of which were printed on blue-tinted paper (notes of the Series of 1869 are, in fact, called "Rainbow Notes" because of their bright coloring); the Bison Note (always called a "bison," correctly, by numismatists, and never a "buffalo") of the Series of 1901; and, for those who can afford one, the imposing spread-eagle on the $100 bills of the 1860s.

Series of 1928 to 1966 Legal Tender Notes

Small-Size

Small-size Legal Tender Notes have been made of the Series of 1928 (issued in 1929) to 1966. Printed with a distinctive red Treasury seal, denominations are $1, $2, $5, and $100, the last being a latecomer and first produced in the Series of 1966. The designs follow closely those of the small-size Silver Certificates.

Interestingly, the only $1 bills in this class are the Series of 1928. The others, including the not particularly popular $2, were made in larger quantities and through the 1960s. Under the Act of May 3, 1878, circulation of Legal Tender Notes was to be maintained at $346,861,016, which the Treasury adheres to today through the use of an adequate remaining supply of Series 1966 and 1966-A $100 bills (a technical and legislative curiosity). No new bills have been printed for many years.

Today, Legal Tender Notes are primarily collected by types. The varieties are not extensive, and forming a set of signature combinations is feasible. As is the case with all small-size notes, those with a star at the serial number, indicating a replacement bill, are avidly sought and sell for significant premiums.

Compound Interest Treasury Notes
(Authorized 1863 and 1864)

Large-Size

Authorized by acts of Congress on March 3, 1863, and June 30, 1864, Compound Interest Treasury Notes were in essence loans to the federal government. Made in denominations of $10, $20, $50, $100, $500, and $1,000, each featured on the reverse a schedule of the accumulating interest, compounded at 6%. These bills were to be held for three years, at the end of which the principal and interest would be paid. For a $10 note, this amounted to a total of $11.94.

Interest began to accrue beginning with the imprinted date on the face of the note, known to be as early as June 10, 1864, and as late as October 16, 1865. Each bill had "gold" lettering, in bronzing powder (also used on certain Fractional Currency bills) stating COMPOUND INTEREST TREASURY NOTE, and numerals of the denomination.

As these bills did not accrue interest after the expiration date, most were redeemed at the end of three years. Interest on the bills authorized in 1863 ceased on June 10, 1867, and interest on those authorized in 1864 ceased on May 16, 1868, although any bill issued after May 16, 1865, would still have some time to run.

Today, such bills are very rare, and the $500 and $1,000 values are unknown.

National Bank Notes
(Authorized 1863)

In 1861, John Sherman of Ohio, who had served in Congress since 1854, took Salmon P. Chase's seat in the Senate when the latter was named by President Abraham Lincoln to be secretary of the Treasury.[4] John Sherman served as 32nd secretary of the Treasury, 1877 to 1881, and before and after that time, he was in the Senate. He was the author of the 1890 Sherman Silver Purchase Act, which provided most of the silver to coin Morgan dollars through and including 1904 (and also spawned the Coin or Treasury Notes of 1890).

Sherman, with his background in finance, realized that the banks of the United States could be a great asset in the war effort. At the time, most of them issued their own currency, primarily from the presses of the American Bank Note Co. Sherman envisioned a National Currency, as it was called, backed by interest-bearing bonds of the United States, to be issued by the various banks. Accordingly, millions of dollars in new bonds could be sold this way. The bills were to have the name of the bank and its location, and also the seal, authorization, and appropriate signatures of the Treasury Department.

Under this proposal, the state-chartered banks could convert (the term used in much Treasury Department correspondence) to a National Bank association (another term), through forming a new corporate entity. Sherman felt that a bond-backed currency was far preferable to seemingly limitless issues of paper money without backing, such as more Legal Tender Notes. Should a National Bank fail, its bills would still be good, as the Treasury Department would have securities to redeem them. There would be no uncertainty. State banks were not forced to convert but were just given the opportunity, providing they were in sound financial condition.

After much discussion and modification, on February 25, 1863, the "Loan Bill," better known as the National Banking Act, passed Congress. Under its provisions, all banks granted charters by the national government were allowed to deposit government bonds with the treasurer of the United States, after which they could issue notes in an amount limited to 90% of the par value of bonds so given.

Secretary Chase sent a notice soliciting designs for bills for denominations of $5 upward (it was not until later than the $1 and $2 denominations were considered):

To Artists, Engravers, and Others

Designs for National Currency Notes are hereby invited, of the denominations of $5, $10, $20, $50, $100, $500, and $1,000, to be issued under the Act of Congress authorizing a National Currency, approved February 25, 1863.

The designs must be national in their character: and none will be considered that have been used, in whole or in part, upon any currency, bond, certificate, or other representative of value, and completed bills must all be of the uniform size of seven inches by three inches.

Designs must be for both the obverse and reverse of the note, and be susceptible of receiving upon their obverse the following legend: 'National Currency, secured by the Bonds of the United States, deposited with the Treasurer of the United States,' as well as the signatures of the Treasurer of the United States and the Register of the Treasury, together with the promise to pay of the association issuing the notes, signed by the President and Cashier thereof, and their place of redemption.

The reverse must be susceptible of receiving the following legend: 'This note is receivable at par in all parts of the United States in payment of taxes, excises, and all other dues to the United States, except for duties on imports; and also for all salaries and other debts and demands owing by the United States to individuals, corporations, and associations, within the United States, except interest on public debt.'

And, also, to have suitable tablets for imprinting the following synopsis of Sec. 57 and 58 of the Act authorizing a National Currency, approved February 25, 1863:

'Every person making or engraving, or aiding to make or engrave, or passing or attempting to pass, any imitation or alteration of this note; and every person having in possession a plate or impression made in imitation of it, or any paper made in imitation of that on which the note is printed, is, by the Act of Congress approved 25th February, 1863, guilty of felony, and subject to fine not exceeding one thousand dollars, or imprisonment not exceeding fifteen years at hard labor, or both.'

Designs will be received until the 28th day of March, 1863, and must in all cases be accompanied by models or illustrative drawings, and the Department reserves the right to reject any or all that may be offered. For such designs or parts of designs as may be accepted, suitable compensation will be paid, not exceeding in the aggregate two hundred dollars for each note; and the accepted designs will then become the exclusive property of the United States. The designs not accepted will be returned to the parties submitting them.

Proposals will also be received for furnishing dies in accordance with the designs; stating the cost of the completed dies, and the date at which they can be furnished; the Secretary reserving the right to accept designs or parts of designs, and causing them to be engraved by other parties than those submitting the designs, if he deems it for the interest of the government to do so. In all cases the dies, and all transfers or copies thereof, to be the exclusive property of the United States. In the selection of designs, special attention will be given to security against counterfeiting, and against alterations, as well as to suitableness for use as currency.

Proposals and designs must be enclosed in sealed envelopes, and directed to the Secretary of the Treasury, and plainly endorsed, 'Designs and Proposals for National Currency,' and will be opened on the 28th day of March, 1863, at 12 o'clock, M.

Provision was made under the 1863 legislation for issuing denominations of $5, $10, $20, $50, $100, $500, and $1,000. A secondary act, June 3, 1864, included other provisions, including for issuing $1, $2, and $3 denominations, but with no more than one-sixth of a bank's bills being of these low values. The $3 was never employed, but the others were.

Banks could not use their former names but were required to take a numerical designation, the First National Bank for the first application approved from a town or city, Second National Bank for the next, and so on. This worked well for First National Banks, but in the larger cities, many bank officers balked at becoming Second, Third, Fourth, or any other later number, as these might reflect a lower status than being named First.

However, many banks complied, and in New York City, the Tenth National Bank was a reality before Congress changed the rules, in 1864, to permit other designations, but with National a part of the title, soon after which the Irving National Bank, Central National Bank, National Currency Bank, and other institutions were formed in the same city. The only exception to the "National" word requirement was the Bank of North America, Philadelphia, for which Congress granted an exemption, as it was the oldest commercial bank in the United States. The capitalized word "The" was included in the bank name of most bills, such as The National Bank of Commerce of New London (CT). In most instances, it was small, often in all caps as THE. Sometimes it was in large type, the same font as for the bank name. In describing bills in numismatic texts, "the" is usually not capitalized.

Each bank was given a charter number, awarded in sequence. By the end of the National Bank Note-issuing era, in 1935, the numbers had reached 14,348. Not all of these banks exercised the privilege to issue currency, but the majority did.

DIFFERENT ISSUES, TYPES, AND SERIES

The First National Bank of Portsmouth, New Hampshire, was first to submit an application, but due to an omission in filling out the form, it was returned, after which it was sent back in proper order, and charter 19 was awarded to it. Number 1 went to the First National Bank of Philadelphia, controlled by financier Jay Cooke, who had endeared himself to the Treasury Department by selling many government bonds. Cooke would remain prominent in government securities until his company collapsed in 1873. In the meantime, not by intention but by mistake, the First National Bank of Davenport, Iowa, became the first to open for business. The Treasury Department had instructed new banks to commence trade on Monday, July 1, 1863, but in Davenport, the notice arrived on the preceding Saturday, June 29, was not read carefully, and the doors were immediately opened to the public. Still another "first" was claimed by the First National Bank of Washington, DC, charter number 26, which was actually the first to issue currency. Bills were delivered to the bank on December 21, 1863, in the form of four-subject $5-$5-$5-$5 sheets, printed in New York by the Continental Bank Note Co., and with Treasury seals and serial numbers imprinted in red by the Currency Bureau under the direction of Spencer M. Clark, operating in the basement of the Treasury Building in Washington.

In time, National Banks were chartered in all states and in several territories that later became states. Bills of the large-size format were issued in denominations of $1, $2, $5, $10, $20, $50, $100, $500, and $1,000. The $1 and $2 issues were discontinued in January 1, 1879. From 1929 to 1935, small-size bills were printed for values from $5 to $100. The majority of bills of both sizes were in lower denominations, through $20.

From the first bills of 1863 through July 1875, National Bank Notes were printed in New York City by the American Bank Note Co., National Bank Note Co., and Continental Bank Note Co. In these times, the face of each note required one printing while the back, with black and green ink, required two. Certain of the black printing on the back of $5 bills was done in Washington by the Columbian Bank Note Co. The bills were then sent to the Currency Bureau within the Treasury Building in Washington, in sheets of four subjects (two for certain high denominations). There they were imprinted with the Treasury seal in red, the bank serial number in red, and the Treasury serial number in red (or, on some notes, in blue).

The sheets were then shipped to the banks, where they were cut apart. The $5 bills, printed by the Continental Bank Note Co., had closer spacing between the notes than did those of other denominations printed elsewhere and thus, when cut apart, had very tight margins. The Act of March 3, 1875, provided that only part of the three-part printing (black face, separate black and green impressions for the back) be done privately, and the balance be done by the Treasury Department. In 1877, new bids were solicited for the printing of National Bank Notes and Legal Tender Notes. On September 25, 1877, submissions were reviewed from seven private companies as well as the Bureau of Engraving and Printing. The contract went to the Bureau, which afterward produced all notes. Certain plates bearing the names of private companies were re-entered with the imprint of the Bureau.

All large-size National Bank Notes include a day, month, and year date on the face, this being when the plate was prepared. It has no relation to the establishment of the bank. In instances of charter renewals, subsequent plates were often given a date of 20 years later.

It has been the standard custom for many years for collectors, dealers, auction sale cataloguers, and authors of important reference books (and less important ones as well) to group the large-size bills under names of "First Charter," "Second Charter," and "Third Charter" periods which correspond to the following series of notes, although this has no basis in either Treasury documents or in history. As the book *Paper Money of the United States* has used these terms since 1953 and they are accepted nomenclature, in the interest of tradition, they are continued here:

- "First Charter Period" Original Series and also Series of 1875
- "Second Charter Period" Series of 1882
- "Third Charter Period" Series of 1902

"First Charter Period"

Original Series and Series of 1875 National Bank Notes

February 25, 1863, to July 11, 1882: Currency associated with this span is of two types: Original (without a series year imprint) and Series of 1875 (with imprint stating such), the last observing the changeover of certain aspects of printing from the New York City bank note firms to the Bureau of Engraving and Printing. All the designs are the same as used on Original Series notes. The main difference is the bold overprint SERIES 1875 on the later notes.

Notes of the Original Series and Series of 1875 types were issued by banks that were chartered from 1863 through and including early 1882. The banks chartered in 1863 were given a life of 19 years, after which their charters expired. Congress failed to pass legislation on a timely basis to simply renew the charters, with the result that these early banks had to liquidate their corporation, immediately form another, and get a new charter number! Later banks, including those chartered from 1864 through early 1882, were able to renew and keep their charter numbers. The renewal periods were for 20 years. Any bank renewing before the summer of 1882 kept on using bills of the Series of 1875 designs, and this series imprint, for the next 20 years. In the meantime, any banks chartered before summer 1882, but not yet up for renewal, kept using Series of 1875 until their charter needed renewal. Some of these charter expirations and renewal expirations lasted into early 1902, this being the term of 20 years. Hence, there is the curious situation that such a bank would receive from the Bureau of Engraving and Printing new Series of 1875 bills in 1900, 1901, and early 1902, even though in the meantime Series of 1882 bills were used by other banks. This scenario is, of course, very confusing to just about everyone!

By July 1, 1882, $358,742,034 worth of Original Series and Series of 1875 notes had reached circulation. After that time, production diminished, but, as noted, for some banks, it continued as late as 1902.

Original Series and Series of 1875 notes were issued in denominations of $1, $2, $5, $10, $20, $50, $100, $500, and $1,000. Each note bore the name of the issuing bank, two serial numbers (a federal serial number of many digits plus a bank serial number, often of low digits from 1 through several thousand). Each note had as part of its back design a representation of the appropriate seal of its state. Notes issued for territories had a generic motif.

In practice, most banks issuing Original Series and Series of 1875 notes ordered from the Treasury Department currency of the $1 denomination through $20, with $5 notes being the most popular. Higher values were not made in quantity. Today, any note of $50 is rare, and any note of $100 and upward is particularly so. Congress mandated that as of January 1, 1879, all currency be exchangeable with gold coins at par (in practice, parity was achieved in the marketplace two weeks earlier, on December 17, 1878). After January 1879, no more $1 and $2 bills of the Series of 1875 were printed for any bank (although higher denominations were). As a result, these two denominations are slightly scarcer among Series of 1875 notes in collections today.

The bills of the Original Series and Series of 1875 are much more ornate, with historical scenes and other motifs, than are later issues. Today, numismatists consider them to be the *creme de la creme* of the National Bank Note series. In the planning stages, it seemed that the Continental Bank Note Co.; New York, would provide most of the large "scenic" vignettes for the backs of the notes. This style, designated as the "unit system," was advocated by W.L. Ormsby, founder of that firm, as the best protection against counterfeiting. However, extreme political maneuvering took place in which John Cisco, Treasury representative in New York City; Ormsby; principals of the American Bank Note Co., and others were involved, with Secretary Salmon P. Chase being kept advised by Cisco. Ormsby had criticized the Treasury Department earlier, and in 1863, when new contracts were about to be awarded, his competitors made sure that Chase was aware of this. Through information, not by personal encounter, Chase considered Ormsby to be *persona non grata*. In order to get government business, Ormsby resigned from the management of Continental, but remained at work in the company making bank note plates, supervising the siderographic process. When matters were settled, Chase awarded the American Bank Note Co. the $10, $20, $50, and $100 issues, Continental the $5 (which, as it turned out, was the denomination made in the largest quantity), and National the $500 and $1,000. Not making matters easy to sort out for the historian is the fact that

Continental did business on several upstairs floors in a large building at 114 Greenwich Street rented from Cisco! Such were the intrigues of government contracts.

Later, beginning in 1865, plates for the $1 bills were made by American and, on the same four-subject plate, National added the "Lazy 2" $2 bill, a most curious situation. Because of this, on the same plate, there are style differences in the script between the two denominations, such as inconsistent abbreviating or spelling out in full the names of certain months. No one knows how the actual printing of notes was distributed between the two companies.

Today, notes of the Original Series and Series of 1875 are usually collected by basic design types (one of each denomination, typically $1 to $20, sometimes higher), or by location (one from each state or territory), or, as a specialty, by banks within a given state. The elusive quality of certain Western and territorial notes of these designs has given some of them an aura of fame and great value. Only a tiny fraction of the notes originally issued still exist at the present time. For many issues, especially from smaller banks, such grades as G, VG, or F may represent the highest condition known for some varieties. For some banks that in their day issued thousands of bills, none are known today of these or any later series. In New Hampshire, for example, this is true for the Carroll County National Bank (of Sandwich), Conway National Bank, and National Bank of the Commonwealth (Manchester).

"Second Charter Period"
Series of 1882 National Bank Notes

July 12, 1882, to April 11, 1902: The first use of Series of 1882 bills for banks extended from July 12, 1882, to April 11, 1902, and notes of these designs were issued as late as 1922. The scenario for this late use is provided by banks chartered close to, but before, April 11, 1902. Accordingly, a bank chartered very early in 1902 would be given the current Series of 1882 designs, and would be provided with these for the next 20 years.

By this time, the Treasury Department had gained experience with National Bank Notes. There had been little call for Original Series or Series of 1875 $500 or $1,000 notes, and these were discontinued. Thus, the denominations produced of the Series of 1882 were of the $5, $10, $20, $50, and $100 values.

Designs varied and fell into three classifications: "Brown Backs," with the back printed in brown, with the bank's charter number in large blue-green numerals at the center; "Date Backs," inscribed 1882-1908 and issued under special legislation; and "Value Backs," with the denomination spelled out at the center, such as TWENTY DOLLARS. Each note depicts the appropriate state seal of its issuing bank.

The basic face designs were continued from the Original Series and Series of 1875 notes except for the $5 denomination. Notes of the latter were redesigned at the Bureau of Engraving and Printing, under the direction of George W. Casilear, chief of the engraving department. Much experimentation was done with the lettering at the center, including the bank name, town, and state, creating some varieties highly interesting from a numismatic viewpoint today. Peter Huntoon has delved deeply into National Bank Note production and styles and has unearthed much information, particularly about the interesting $5 varieties of 1882. One of the more ornate representations has been called the "circus poster" style by collectors for a long time.

As a class, Series of 1882 notes are more plentiful than the earlier series bills, as the economy had expanded by that era, and more banks had been chartered. As is the case with other National Bank Notes, they are collected by types, states, or towns within states.

"Third Charter Period"
Series of 1902 National Bank Notes

April 12, 1902, to April 11, 1922: The first use of Series of 1902 notes extended from April 12, 1902, to April 11, 1922, with notes issued through 1929 (for later charter extensions), when the new small-size notes replaced all large-size currency.

Denominations were the same as before: $5, $10, $20, $50, and $100. No longer were state or territorial seals included. Several variations of seals and imprints were made, including the Red Seal, Date Back (with blue seal), and Plain Back (with blue seal). Generally, Plain Back bills are by far the most plentiful today as a type. Within any type there are bank imprints and denominations that range from common to extremely rare or unknown.

The Series of 1902 notes are the most plentiful of all today, and for some states with many banks—such as New York and Pennsylvania—many different large-size National Bank Notes can be collected from a wide variety of institutions and towns. Notes from some areas such as Alaska, New Mexico, and Arizona territories and from Puerto Rico (a protectorate) are scarce and expensive, as are certain high denominations. Many of these bills have rubber-stamped signatures of officers, the ink of which has lightened or faded.

With so many different banks issuing multiple denominations, designs, and varieties of National Bank Notes over a long period of years, the panorama of collecting possibilities is immense. For a long time, I have enjoyed the *history* of these banks and have collected information concerning them, my interest extending through the later era as well, to 1935. This is a fascinating field and one open to anyone who cares to delve into old newspapers, financial accounts, and other sources.

Series of 1929 Types 1 and 2 National Bank Notes
Small-Size

National Bank Notes in small-size format were printed in sheets of six notes. These are all Series of 1929, with the Treasury signatures of E.E. Jones and W.O. Woods, who served together from January 22, 1929, to May 31, 1933. However, such bills continued to be issued until May 1935. Each also bore the name and location of each bank and the printed signatures of that bank's cashier and president. These bills were produced in denominations of $5, $10, $20, $50, and $100, with the $50 and $100 values usually in small quantities.

There were two "types" produced, today designated as:

1929 Type 1 (Printed from May 1929 to May 1933) Bank charter number in black, twice on the face. • The six notes on each sheet had the same serial number, six digits, with prefixes A through F, and each with the suffix A. Accordingly, the second sheet printed for a certain bank would have these serials: A000002A • B000002A • C000002A • D000002A • E000002A • F000002A

1929 Type 2 (Printed from May 1933 to May 1935) Bank charter number in black, twice on the face, and also in brown, twice. • The six notes on each sheet had different serial numbers, in sequence, each with the prefix A but with no suffix. Accordingly, the second sheet printed would have these serials: A000007 • A000008 • A000009 • A0000010 • A0000011 • A000012

Today, bills of the Type 1 are typically much more plentiful in numismatic hands than are those of Type 2 and therefore are less expensive. However, among certain banks, there are exceptions. While most banks issued both types, some used just Type 1 and others just Type 2.

As to values, those from more populous states are relatively inexpensive, while those from such states as Arizona and Nevada are considerably more costly. Within any state, there can be "rare banks" for which the bills are very valuable.

National Gold Bank Notes
(Authorized 1870)
Large-Size

As described above under the narrative for Legal Tender Notes, on the West Coast such bills did not trade at par. Merchants, banks, and others would accept them only at deep discounts. National Bank Notes, issued in the East since 1863, were traded at similar reductions.

Figure IX

Figure X

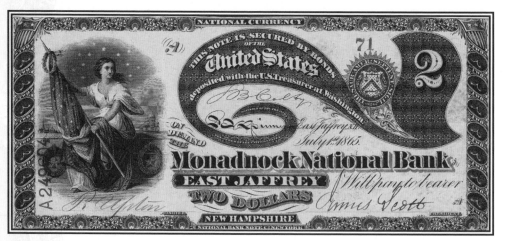

Figure XI

Banks and their stories… It has been fine sport to collect notes and also gather postcards, engravings, and other information about the issuing bank. The most ornate such structure in the state of New Hampshire—the Monadnock National Bank of East Jaffrey—is shown as it appeared in the late 19th century, along with a "Lazy 2" bill from the bank (Figures IX and XI).

In time, the tradition was lost, the top part of the bank was torn away, and the interior and exterior were heavily remodeled, yielding the building as it appears today (Figure X, a photo by Q. David Bowers, 2003).

Figure xii

Figure xiii

Figure xiv

Banks and their stories… Tracking down bank buildings often ends in disappointment. However, sometimes, as with the Winchester (NH) National Bank, the building still stands. The $10 note is the Series of 1902 Plain Back style (Friedberg-613), with Lyons and Roberts printed signatures plus the rubber-stamped signatures (allowable procedure by this time, but not in the early years) of the bank officers. The bank serial number (12912); Treasury serial number (V676984H); Treasury seal; and bank charter number (887) are all printed in blue. (Clark Collection)

Constructed in the Greek Revival style in the late 1840s, this brick building successively housed the Winchester Bank, then the Winchester National Bank. The photographs shown here are by Underwood & Underwood (1912) and by Q. David Bowers (2003). Today, the building remains an architectural gem, but it is no longer used for banking. Instead, it is a storage facility for a convenience store.

DIFFERENT ISSUES, TYPES, AND SERIES

Samuel Bowles, a newspaper editor from Springfield, Massachusetts, was on the West Coast shortly after the Civil War and wrote:

> Paper money has been kept out [of California] by the force of a very obstinate public opinion and the instrumentality of state legislation. Our national currency of greenbacks are seen here simply as merchandise; you buy and sell them at the brokers.... Of course, being made a 'legal tender' by United States law, it is competent to pay a debt here with them, but no man who should do this once...could henceforth have any credit in the mercantile community. All large and long credits are now coupled with an express stipulation that they are on a specie footing, and a law of the state, known as the 'Specific Contract Act,' protects such arrangements.

This unusual East Coast vs. West Coast arrangement is very significant in the history of American paper money and is directly responsible for a later class of currency, authorized in 1870, known as Gold Bank Notes.

By 1870, no National Banks had been established in California, as their bills would not have been useful in commerce. To remedy this, Congress took an unusual step. The Act of July 12, 1870, provided for the establishment of special institutions, to be known as National Gold Banks, to issue bills *redeemable at par in gold coins*.

Nine such institutions were established in California and issued bills from $5 to $500, although not all denominations were utilized by each bank. These found immediate acceptance in commerce in California and were equal in value to gold coins. Bills of the First National Gold Bank of San Francisco, the National Gold Bank of D.O. Mills & Co., Sacramento, and others, traded at a premium in terms of Legal Tender bills or National Bank bills from the Midwest and East.

The record of high and low exchange rates for the year 1873 reveals that the exchange value of Legal Tender bills, in terms of gold coins or National Gold Bank Notes, ranged from a low of $106.12 in November to a high of $119.12 in April. This reveals that in April 1873 it would have taken over $1,190 in Legal Tender bills, plus an exchange fee, to buy $1,000 in federal gold coins or National Gold Bank Notes.

The face designs of the National Gold Bank issues are similar to that used on regular National Bank Notes. The reverse vignette is a collage, almost photographic in its clarity, of a large group of various United States gold coins, the obverse of an 1871 double eagle being the most prominent. A special, light yellow-gold paper was used to print the bills.

As time passed, the difference in exchange value between Legal Tender Notes and gold coins narrowed. Congress mandated that they be exchangeable at par beginning on January 1, 1879. However, the market anticipated this, and parity was achieved on December 17, 1878. Afterward, the need for National Gold Bank Notes became redundant. Such bills, typically showing extensive use in circulation, were withdrawn. Today, all range from scarce to very rare. When seen, they are nearly always in lower grades such as VG.

Silver Certificates
(Authorized 1878)
Series of 1878 to 1923
Large-Size

Silver Certificates were born under the Bland-Allison Act of February 28, 1878, the same legislation that created what we now know as the Morgan silver dollar. Soon, Series of 1878 and Series of 1880 notes were made, but in relatively small numbers, in denominations from $10 to $1,000. Boldly emblazoned on the back of each is the word SILVER, in letters so large that it can be read from across the room. This was a strong signal to the silver-mining interests of the West that, indeed, their senators and congressmen were acting in the interests of this important industry—in an era when prices of the metal continued to drift lower. These and later bills were not officially legal tender, but were specifically payable in silver dollars—no problem, for from the beginning of Morgan dollar coinage, large quantities piled up in government storage facilities. The silver dollars were legal tender, so in a way, the bills were also, *de facto*. The government was very precise in the wording of its various note issues and what they represented. That is why so many different classes were created, often circulating at the same time.

The Act of August 4, 1886, authorized more Silver Certificates, after which this class of note was made in very large quantities, including the new $1, $2, and $5 denominations. Vast quantities of Morgan dollars, put up in cloth bags of 1,000 coins each, continued to accumulate as backing for these bills. In 1918, the Pittman Act provided for the melting of over 350,000,000 of these silver dollars, not even close to the entire supply in existence, but enough to sharply deplete stocks held by the government. In October 1921, *The Numismatist* included this:

> When all those dollars were melted the United States had to call in all the Silver Certificates—the $1, $2, and $5 bills, to speak in common lingo—representing the dollars that were deposited in the vaults of the mints. Under the law of the land the Treasury must hold a silver dollar for each dollar Silver Certificate issued. So with the melting of the silver dollars the Silver Certificates had to be recalled.

> To cover that loss in currency, the government issued short-term certificates of indebtedness bearing 2% interest. The silver dollars now being coined [the new Morgan dollars of 1921] allow for the issuance of new Silver Certificates, which are being used in calling in those certificates of indebtedness.[5]

In the 1920s, Silver Certificates were issued only in lower denominations. In 1929, this class of note was continued in small size.

Today, Silver Certificates are very popular to collect. It is delightful that the most beautiful designs, in the opinion of many, are those that were used on the smaller denominations of $1, $2, and $5, these also being the values made in the largest quantities. In particular, the "Educational" notes, the Series of 1896, are elegant—with the faces depicting allegorical scenes of goddesses known as *History Instructing Youth* ($1), *Science Presenting Steam and Electricity to Commerce and Manufacture* ($2), and *Electricity as the Dominant Force in the World* ($5). This was indeed the age of electricity, and the world was changing as a result. Most towns and cities were wired for electricity, and at expositions of the era electrical illumination at night was a main emphasis. On the back of each Educational bill were portraits of two prominent Americans.

Elsewhere in the Silver Certificate series, the Series of 1886 $1 bills depict Martha Washington, the Series 1886 $5 shows on the reverse five Morgan silver dollars all arranged in a tidy row, the Series 1899 $5 has a realistic portrait of an Indian chief, the Series of 1923 $5 has Lincoln in a "porthole" (surrounded by a heavy circular frame), and the Series of 1886 $10 has the image of Vice President Thomas A. Hendricks (who died on November 25, 1885) in a distinctively shaped frame, creating what today is known as the "Tombstone Note."

Series of 1928 to 1953

Small-Size Silver Certificates

Silver Certificates of the small size were produced in denominations of $1, $5, and $10. The earliest issues, the $1 bills, were imprinted as the Series of 1928, although the small-size format was not actually introduced until July 10, 1929. The 1928 Series alone is payable in "one silver dollar." Later, $1 bills as well as all those of the other denominations are payable "in silver" or in "silver coin," but have no mention of silver dollars. Save for certain World War II issues, all have the Treasury seal in blue.

Except for the backs of the $1 bills of Series 1928 through 1934, the small-size bills of these denominations appear quite similar to bills of the same denomination in other series produced through the early years of the 21st century. In the small-size notes, most series were given letter suffixes, changed whenever the signature combination changed. The series date was changed only when there was a modification of the design, these typically being of a trivial nature. Thus, for $1 bills these were made (early changes only):

Series 1928: Tate-Mellon signatures. • **Series 1928-A:** Woods-Mellon • **Series 1928-B:** Woods-Mills • **Series 1928-C:** Woods-Woodin • **Series 1928-D:** Julian-Woodin • **Series 1928-E:** Julian-Morgenthau

Series 1934: Julian-Morgenthau (different arrangement of lettering and seal on face)

This sequence was continued through and including **Series 1957-B:** Granahan-Dillon.

Certain varieties of Series 1935-A were made with a bright red R or S overprint in the field, to the extent of 1,184,000 of each. These were in connection with printing on two different types of paper. These were placed in circulation and observed for their characteristics of wear, although quite a few were bought up by numismatists.

Other collectable varieties are provided by the overprint HAWAII on the face and back of $1 Series 1934-A (and, in small-size Federal Reserve Notes, the $5 1934 and 1934-A, $10 1934-A, and $20 1934 and 1934-A). These bills have brown seals. These were distributed in the Hawaiian Islands after the United States declared war on Japan in 1941. If the islands fell into the hands of the Japanese, these bills could be repudiated, preventing the enemy from using them on world markets.

Related are bills distinguished by a yellow seal. These were for the Allied troops in the North African campaign and elsewhere. Denominations included $1 Silver Certificate Series 1935-A, as well as Federal Reserve Notes ($5 1934-A and $10 1934 and 1934-A).

There are no "impossible" rarities among the small-size Silver Certificates, although some are elusive in Uncirculated grade. The best-known is the 1928-E $1. The $10 note of the Series of 1933, with a printing of only 216,000 pieces, is arguably the rarest small-size note. The star note of this issue is unique.

Coin Notes (Treasury Notes)
(Authorized 1890)
Series of 1890 and 1891
Large-Size Coin Notes

The Coin Notes, payable "in coin," also called Treasury Notes, Series of 1890, are considered by numismatists to be among the most beautiful of all United States currency, this with reference to the ornate engraving on the back of each. The entire area of the back is filled with designs and lettering, with no open or white space. As gorgeous as these may seem to viewers today, in 1890, they were viewed as susceptible to counterfeiting, and their use was discontinued soon afterward. This was based on the old theory (prominent in the history of the Bank of England, for example) that bills should have open areas, as they would be less confusing to the public, and counterfeits could be more easily detected.[6]

The Series of 1891 bills, with ample open spaces on the back, solved the "problem." However, it seems to me that the later Series of 1896 "Educational" Series Silver Certificates had very little white space on their backs.

The Series of 1890 and 1891 bills were issued to buy silver bullion under the Sherman Silver Purchase Act of 1890. For a time, it seemed that Morgan dollars would no longer be made; the production of Silver Certificates was halted, and these bills took their place. As only "coin" was specified, it was left to the discretion of the secretary of the Treasury as to whether gold or silver should be paid out. In practice, most people wanted gold, causing some anxiety among Treasury officials, who nonetheless paid gold coins out.

Soon, silver dollars were again aplenty in current production. Silver Certificates were issued in large quantities, and the Coin Notes were discontinued. Treasury documents reveal that Coin Notes were an annoyance to that department, perhaps because of the uncertainty as to the class of coins needed to be held in reserve for their redemption. A special effort was made to retire them quickly.

Series of 1890 notes with beautifully engraved backs were made in the intermittent denominations of $1, $2, $5, $10, $20, $100, and $1,000. The $1, $2, $5, $10, and $20 values each have their

Figure xv

Figure xvi

Figure xvii

Series of 1880 $10 Silver Certificate, Friedberg-289 (Figure XVI). This is one of many different varieties and denominations among Silver Certificates. These were issued in denominations from $1 to $1,000 and, typically, were specifically payable in silver dollars, such as the 1878-S Morgan dollar shown in Figure XV (the first year of issue of the design that was used through 1904, then again in 1921). During this era there was a glut of silver, and to help provide a market for the metal Uncle Sam minted hundreds of millions of silver dollars, putting many into storage and issuing Silver Certificates in their place. Undoubtedly, the bold "SILVER" lettering on the back of note was pleasing to silver-mine owners!

Panoramic view of the aptly-named Silverton, Colorado (Figure XVII). Silverton was one of many silver-mining towns in that state. During the late 19th century there was an oversupply of this precious metal, as new mines and districts were developed.

denominations spelled out in full, as, for example, TWENTY. The rare $100 and extremely rare $1,000 notes each have the 0's in the fanciful form of delicious green "watermelons," hence "Watermelon Note" and "Grand Watermelon Note" as their nicknames.

Federal Reserve Notes
(Authorized 1913)
Series of 1914 and 1918 Federal Reserve Notes
Large-Size

The Federal Reserve Act of December 23, 1913, set up a system of 12 regional banks, still in operation today. These are located in Boston, New York City, Philadelphia, Cleveland, Richmond, Atlanta, Chicago, St. Louis, Minneapolis, Kansas City, Dallas, and San Francisco. Bills issued with the imprints of the banks were named by city and also by a letter, sequentially as per the list above, from Boston (A) to San Francisco (L). Each note bears the appropriate letter as the serial number prefix as well.

These bills, also designated as National Currency, were redeemable in dollars, including "in gold on demand at the Treasury Department of the United States in the City of Washington, District of Columbia, or in gold or lawful money at any Federal Reserve Bank." Accordingly, in a way, these can be considered as Gold Coin Notes.

Denominations of $5, $10, $20, $50, $100, $500, $1,000, $5,000, and $10,000 were produced, in different combinations of bank and Treasury officials' signatures and with red or blue seals. The face designs feature portraits of government officials in history, plus lettering, etc., while the reverses have scenic motifs. Today, examples of the values from $5 to $100, by design types, are easily found on the market. Higher denominations are rare. Certain bank and signature combinations are very rare, but there is little interest in systematically collecting them, so premiums for such are not great.

Series of 1963 to Date Federal Reserve Notes
Small-Size

These are the bills of our current era, taking the place of other classes. Each bears a seal with the name, location, and identifying letter of one of the 12 Federal Reserve Banks.

Today, they are printed in denominations of $1, $2 (intermittently and not beginning until the Series of 1976, in connection with the Bicentennial), $5, $10, $20, $50, and $100. In the 1930s and 1940s values of $500, $1,000, $5,000, and $10,000 were made. These higher denominations are all collectors' items, and there is a surprising demand even for the $10,000 due to its novelty. Early series bills were payable in gold, a provision later removed.

The designs were more or less similar to other small-size bills until the late 1990s, when significant changes began to be made to the portraits on the face and the buildings on the back of each denomination, along with improvements for security, including microscopic printing and anti-copying features. Bills printed before the design revision were with eight-digit serials, prefixed by a letter (A to L) for the bank, and with the various letter suffixes to expand the number of notes beyond what eight digits allow for. The redesigned bills omit printed mention of specific Federal Reserve Bank branches, but have a designation such as G7 (Chicago) or L12 (San Francisco), which numismatists can decipher, but not obvious to the general public. In addition, eight-digit serials with double-letter prefixes and single-letter suffixes, not specifically relating to a branch, are used.

Today, these bills, especially the smaller denominations, are very popular. The smaller denominations are generally very available and quite affordable in Uncirculated grade. They are widely collected on a systematic basis, by bank and by Treasury signature combinations (each bill has two printed signatures, the secretary of the Treasury (instead of the register, beginning in 1933), and the treasurer). Treasurer Kathryn O'Hay Granahan and Secretary Joseph Barr were in office together only from December 23, 1968, to January 20, 1969. When $1 bills of this combination were released, there was great excitement across America, when the rumor spread that these would become very rare and valuable. Large quantities were hoarded, and dealers were bombarded with calls and visitors seeking to cash in. However, the plates with these signatures were continued in use for a long time afterward, hundreds of millions were printed, and most of the Granahan-Barr bills are very common.

Federal Reserve Bank Notes
(Authorized 1913)
Series of 1915 and 1918 Federal Reserve Bank Notes
Large-Size

The Federal Reserve Bank Notes closely follow the concept of Federal Reserve Notes (without "Bank" in the title), as delineated above. They are also inscribed as National Currency. Among Federal Reserve Bank Notes, the Series of 1915 includes $5, $10, and $20 denominations, and the Series of 1918 includes these plus the $1, $2, and $50. The $50 was made only for the St. Louis Federal Reserve Bank and is a numismatic classic. Treasury records show that only 33 of these are outstanding, while in numismatic hands over 50 different have been identified by their serial numbers. This discrepancy is due to the occasional practice of the Treasury to write off certain bills as presumed lost or destroyed. While such records are valuable to numismatic researchers, they must be reviewed carefully. Each Federal Reserve Bank Note has the city name boldly at the center, as, for example, PHILADELPHIA. The back designs of the $1, with an eagle clutching a flag, and the $2, with a dreadnought-type battleship, have been collectors' favorites for a long time. The denominations of $5 to $50 use the same back motifs as on the Federal Reserve Notes.

The Federal Reserve Bank Notes were produced with two Treasury signatures and two bank signatures. Sometimes this can become expansive. For example, the San Francisco Federal Reserve Bank $1 bills are found with Teehee and Burke of the Treasury and in two varieties of bank signatures, Clerk and Lynch. Then for the same bank come the Elliott-Burke Treasury combination with Clerk-Lynch of the bank and now also with Ambrose-Calkins, for a total of four varieties. However, these can be interesting to collect.

Of nearly $762,000,000 face value in these bills issued, all but about $2,000,000 worth are said to have been redeemed. This reflects that while people often kept gold coins as souvenirs in the early 20th century, paper did not have the same attraction. Accordingly, in proportion, many paper issues are quite scarce today.

Series of 1929
Small-Size

Federal Reserve Bank Notes in small-size format were printed in sheets of six notes, all Series of 1929, with the Treasury signatures of E.E. Jones and W.O. Woods, who served together from January 22, 1929, to May 31, 1933. These are similar in many respects to National Bank Notes, but have the name of the Federal Reserve Bank, its location and district letter (A to L), and the printed signatures of Treasury officials and of the cashier and governor or other bank officers. Not all 12 banks issued notes of each denomination.

These bills were printed in six subject sheets, each with the same eight-digit number, a prefix letter from A through L designating the district, and a uniform suffix letter of A, yielding a series such as, for a San Francisco bill, L00345232A.

Today, these are mainly collected by design types, not by bank varieties. There are many that are scarce or rare in Uncirculated grades, but as collector specialists may be rarer than the notes are, the differentials are not great.

Fractional and Postage Currency
Five Issues 1862 to 1876

In the summer of 1862, the Union position in the Civil War was becoming increasingly uncertain, and in the South, the citizens of the Confederacy were experiencing shortages and problems.[7] Coins had been hoarded since late in 1861, and by July 1862, not even copper-nickel Indian cents were anywhere to be seen! It was impossible to find a coin to buy a newspaper, get a haircut, or take a ride

Figure xviii

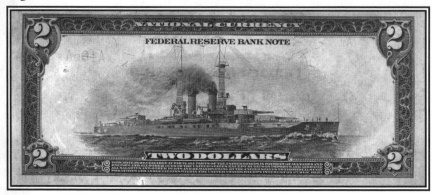

Figure xix

Figure xx

Federal Reserve Bank Notes, Series of 1918. These are among the most popular of all large-size currency issues. The $1 (Friedberg-708 shown here, Figure XVIII) depicts on the face the portrait of Washington, the name of the Federal Reserve Bank and city, and signatures of two Treasury and two bank officials. The $2 (F-747 shown, Figure XIX) is the famous "Battleship Note," depicting a dreadnaught at full steam on a run at sea.

Federal Reserve district map, from the *American Monthly Review of Reviews* (December, 1914) (Figure XX). Each of the 12 Federal Reserve districts has its own bank. These are identified by numbers and sequential letters. Hence, 1, or the Boston district, is also A, while 12, or San Francisco, is L. On the notes such are expressed as A-1, B-2, C-3, etc., to L-12.

on a horse-drawn car. Bridging the gap, many merchants, towns, and others issued tickets imprinted with various values from 1¢ onward, and paper money scrip notes, with 3¢ and 5¢ being the most popular, but with other values up to a dollar or more. In time, many merchants issued bronze tokens, the size of a cent, which served for that value, and several dozen advertised on encased postage stamps.

In the meantime, both the Confederate and Union governments were issuing more and more paper money. On February 25, 1862, the first Legal Tender bills were authorized. By June 1862, over $100,000,000 worth of these greenbacks flooded the North. Silver and gold coins sold at increasing premiums, with changing rates published in the daily papers. In New York City on July 11, 1862, it took $130 in greenbacks to buy $100 in federal coins.

Horace Greeley, proprietor of the *New York Tribune*, suggested on July 9, 1862, that ordinary postage stamps could be used as change, these being conveniently pasted onto the bottom of a small piece of paper, the top being folded over. The idea achieved some popularity, but mostly by taking loose postage stamps and putting them into small envelopes imprinted on the front with a value such as 25¢. Others took postage stamps and pasted them to small pieces of cardboard. The idea caught on, and the Treasury Department began experimenting with such.

On July 14, 1862, Secretary of the Treasury Salmon P. Chase sent a memorial to Congress petitioning that government stamps be made official as legal tender for small transactions. In the meantime, Treasurer Francis E. Spinner had pasted postage stamps onto sheets of Treasury Department letterhead paper, cut down, and bearing his signature, together with stamps amounting to 5¢, 10¢, 25¢, and 50¢. He contacted the local post office and made an arrangement that stamps that were damaged should be redeemed at face value for new ones.

In response to Chase's request, the Act of July 17, 1862, provided for the use of postage stamps for monetary transactions, including authority that by August 1 stamps would be exchangeable for Legal Tender "greenback" notes at all Treasury offices. They were also receivable for government obligations in amounts of under $5, but they were not given official legal tender status, despite the request of Chase.

In August 1862, Postage Currency fractional bills were issued, featuring the same designs as postage stamps, but in the shape of small pieces of paper money with additional inscriptions and with perforated edges. At first these were distributed to Army paymasters, then in September to the general public.

These notes were made in denominations of 5¢, 10¢, 25¢, and 50¢. Similar to stamps, the Postage Currency notes were issued in perforated sheets, to be torn apart by the recipients. By early 1863, about $100,000 of these notes reached circulation per day, but the demand remained unsatisfied.[8] A lively trade developed in the making and selling of small cardboard and leather wallets for the storage of these little bills.

The Act of March 3, 1863, provided for a new small denomination series, Fractional Currency. Distribution of such notes—5¢, 10¢, 25¢, and 50¢—began in October of the same year. In late autumn 1864, a new Fractional Currency denomination, the 3¢ note, reached circulation, but it never became popular. In the summer of 1869, another Fractional Currency denomination, 15¢, was added to the Fractional Currency lineup, but it, too, was never widely used. Face and back colors varied over a period of time, as did the sizes. Fractional bills were created in the following issues from 1862 to 1876:

1st Issue: August 21, 1862, to May 27, 1863 (Postage Currency)

The designs copied contemporary postage stamps. Early printings were issued with perforated issues. Later printings of the series had straight issues (as on all later issues as well). Denominations of 5¢ (with the design of a 5¢ stamp), 10¢ (10¢ stamp), 25¢ (five 5¢ stamps in a row), and 50¢ (five 10¢ stamps in a row).

2nd Issue: October 20, 1863, to February 23, 1867 (Fractional Currency)

Denominations of 5¢, 10¢, 25¢, and 50¢. All have the portrait of Washington within an overprinted oval applied with bronzing powder (a messy process that caused problems in production).

3rd Issue: December 5, 1864, to August 16, 1869 (Fractional Currency)

Denominations of 3¢, 5¢, 10¢, 25¢, and 50¢: The 3¢ denomination was made for just a short time, as the law of March 3, 1865, authorizing the nickel three-cent coin, prohibited any further issue of Fractional Currency of this value. Spencer M. Clark, superintendent of the Currency Bureau, had his own portrait, captioned CLARK, placed on the 5¢ note of this issue. Most people thought that William Clark, of 1804-1806 Lewis and Clark Expedition fame, was the one being honored! The 5¢ Fractional Currency bill is believed to have inspired the Act of April 7, 1866, specifying: "No portrait or likeness of any living person hereafter engraved, shall be placed upon any of the bonds, securities, notes, fractional or Postage Currency of the United States." The 10¢ note, or at least we suppose it is a 10-cent note, simply says 10, with no mention of cents, sort of a numismatic precursor to the later famous 1883 CENTS-less Liberty Head nickel.

The Treasury tapped into collector interest for Fractional Currency and issued this notice:

Specimen Currency: The Treasury Department is now ready to supply applicants with sets of specimen Fractional Currency of all the descriptions ever issued, including two varieties of fifty-cent notes and one of the ten-cent notes, which are signed by the Register and Treasurer. The sets of full notes may be purchased for $5.75, while a set of half notes, or those having the face and back separate, will be sold for $4. The latter variety will be printed on Confederate bank-note paper, bearing the letters C.S.A. in watermark, which was manufactured in London for the Treasury Department of the Confederate States, so-called, and was found on board a blockade runner captured by one of the vessels composing the blockade squadron. A large quantity was obtained and sent to the Treasury Department, where it has been used for various purposes.

This paper had been seized on April 27, 1862, from the *Bermuda*, on the way back from England.

4th Issue: July 14, 1869, to February 16, 1875 (Fractional Currency)

Denominations of 5¢, 10¢, 15¢, 25¢, and 50¢. This series included the 15¢ denomination, never popular, and was also the first to have the Treasury seal imprinted. Some were printed on paper with blue tinting, also used on certain National Bank and Legal Tender bills of the era, giving them a special elegance.

5th Issue: February 26, 1874, to February 15, 1876 (Fractional Currency)

Denominations of 10¢, 25¢, and 50¢. This was in the twilight era of such notes, and many undistributed pieces were sold by banks to numismatists, as the collecting of such bills had become popular.

Fractional Currency Shields: To aid in the identification of counterfeits and to provide bills for display to banks and others interested, the Treasury Department created Fractional Currency Shields. These consisted of a shield outline printed in gray (a few in green or pink which are much rarer) surmounted by an eagle and stars. On the shield, 39 specimens of Fractional Currency, consisting of 20 faces and 19 backs, were pasted by hand. These were of the 1st, 2nd, and 3rd issues. Mounted under glass in a wooden frame with a gilt inner strip, and backed by thin wooden slats, these were sold for $4.50 each, beginning in 1867. In January 1868, Philadelphia dealer E.L. Mason, Jr., offered them for $6 each, stating they had just been released.[9] In 1869, U.S. Treasurer F.E. Spinner stated that the remaining examples in Washington had been destroyed. However, it seems that a few were kept on hand and later augmented with a few later Fractional Currency notes, sometimes with a postage stamp or two. As to how many were issued, I am not aware of any specific records. Estimates have ranged from about 200 to 400. Most of these have water stains along the bottom, from slight flooding in the Treasury Department basement where they were stored. Among any and all numismatic items produced in American history, the Fractional Currency Shield is no doubt the most "displayable" in its original form. Indeed, these are one of only a few such 19th-century items originally intended for this purpose.

Specimens: Specimen impressions of Fractional Currency bills, face or back designs, printed on one side, in either wide-margin or narrow-margin versions, were very popular with stamp collectors as well as numismatists, and large quantities were sold through dealers in these fields.

The counterfeiting of Postage and Fractional Currency was a problem from the early days onward. Certain innovations such as imprinted bronze ovals and surcharges were supposed to deter such activity. These two accounts from *Banker's Magazine*, July 1864, reflect the situation:

Seizure of Counterfeit Postage Currency. William H. Diamond, mail agent on the Hudson River Railroad, was arrested in Troy, N.Y., on a charge of circulating counterfeit Fractional Currency. Marshal Lowell has for some time known that counterfeit Postage Currency and Treasury Notes were brought to Albany and Troy by some unknown persons and delivered to confederates, to be scattered broadcast over the rural districts.

Suspicion finally fell upon this mail agent, a man who has held the position for four or five years, and been regarded as above reproach. Each embarked upon the train at New York City—pursuer and pursued. Nothing occurred until the cars reached the depot, when the arrest was made. On searching Diamond he was found to have a large quantity of counterfeit Postage Currency—fresh, clean and tolerably well executed—tied to the buttons of his suspenders. He acknowledged that he had been a common carrier of this bogus stuff for some time past, but denied having circulated any of it directly. It was his habit, it seems, to receive orders and deliver the currency—and a large amount of altered and counterfeit Treasury Notes were to have been brought up on this particular trip.

Officer Lowell telegraphed for officers Kipp and Hurlbut to be present at the depot and assist him in the arrest; but the dispatch did not reach them in time. Leaving the prisoner in jail, Mr. Lowell started for his home in Syracuse at noon today.

A Legal Problem. The law authorizing the issue of Fractional Currency does not provide against having counterfeit currency in possession. —United States Commissioner's Office. [Before Commissioner Osborn] Lemuel Kenney, who was arrested some weeks ago, charged with having in his possession a large amount of counterfeit Postage Currency, was this morning discharged.

Without going into the facts of the case, the commissioner decided that the Act of July, 1862, authorizing this currency, has not provided against keeping or holding in possession counterfeits; therefore, as there was no charge made that the prisoner sold or passed any of it, he could not be held for simply having it in possession. A careful examination of the law shows that this curious defect really does exist in the law as it now stands. Mr. Corsen and John Sedgwick, Esq., appeared for the prisoner, and Assistant District Attorney Bell for the government.

Postage Currency and Fractional Currency notes tended to become dirty and tattered quickly and could not be counted easily. The public referred to them derisively as "stamps."

It is a curious sidelight on the collecting of United States paper money that in the 1860s and 1870s the acquisition of regular and specimen Fractional Currency notes was a passion for many, and all dealers with storefront shops maintained good stocks of them. However, so far as is known, no one at all collected such interesting things (to a later generation) as $1 and $2 National Bank Notes!

PRINTED FEATURES OF NOTES

The sizes of most federal notes 1861 and later can be divided into two categories. Large-size bills measure about 7 by 3 inches, although there are some variations. The width of the margins can vary considerably, especially among National Bank bills, and affects the size. Small-size bills, issued since 1929, measure about 6 by 2.5 inches.

The majority of bills from the 1861 Demand Note "greenbacks" to the present day are printed in green on the back. This arose from the promotion of this color by the American Bank Note Company, proprietors of the "Patented Green Tint" (introduced in 1857 on state bank bills), and the assertion that of all colors it was most resistant to counterfeiting by photographic means. Green proved to be popular, and today greenbacks remain part of the American idiom. Certain Gold Certificates of large sizes were printed in yellow on the back, some Silver Certificates were in brown, and there are a few other scattered exceptions.

Most large-size bills were printed in sheets of four subjects, with National Bank bills often having two denominations to a sheet, such as $1-$1-$1-$2 or $10-$10-$10-$20. Certain large-size high denominations were printed two to a sheet. Small-size bills have been printed in sheets of 6, 12, 18 (starting in 1952), and today, 32 subjects.

Very early federal notes and nearly all National Bank Notes of the 19th century bear inked signatures. Some of the later Nationals have rubber-stamped signatures or, in a few instances, signatures printed on the original plates. Treasury signatures have been printed on notes since the early 1860s.

Over a period of time, federal currency has included these characteristics:

Type of note: Federal currency has been issued by classes of issue. Notes have appropriate imprints as part of the designs, as LEGAL TENDER, SILVER CERTIFICATE, NATIONAL CURRENCY, FEDERAL RESERVE NOTE, etc.

Inscriptions and obligations: The inscription UNITED STATES OF AMERICA appears on the various notes, and since autumn 1957, IN GOD WE TRUST has been imprinted, following Congressional authorization in 1955. The lettering of each bill typically includes a "promise to pay," or "redeemable in," or some other inscription. Some have legal tender provisions, comments about customs duties, and warnings against counterfeiting. Generally, earlier types have more extensive inscriptions than do those of later years.

Series: Most currency bears a designation as to the dated series within its type. Generally, a series designation or date was made when there was a change in design or some other aspect of a note, such as Series of 1875 or Series of 1880. Among small-size bills, the series designation at first changed only when there was a significant change in the design. A change in signatures resulted in the addition of an alphabetic suffix (Series 1969-A, 1969-B, etc.). Beginning in 1974, the series year changed with the appointment of a new secretary of the Treasury. Commencing with the Series of 1990, a new series year has been added each time there is a change in signatures. The series date remains constant and is sometimes used over a span of succeeding years until a new series is instituted. Accordingly, the year of issue of a bill is usually later than the series date imprinted on it.

Denominations: The value of the note is prominent, usually expressed in some or all corners as a numeral such as 5 or 10, with added lettering, as FIVE or TEN (continuing the examples), and sometimes with one or more Roman numerals, as V or X. On some bills, the denomination appears many times in smaller letters and numbers, such as part of the border design.

Seals: The Treasury seal, in various sizes and colors, with scales of justice and a key, is a standard feature of notes. The Great Seal (pyramid, all-seeing eye) appears on most small-size $1 bills. State seals are on the backs of early National Bank Notes (through and including the Series of 1882).

Vignettes or illustrations: Illustrations on bills range from the marvelously ornate, such as the faces of the Series of 1896 Silver Certificates ("Educational" Series) and the backs of the 1890 Coin Notes, to simple portraits and buildings, as on small-size bills. While present-day collectors probably prefer bills with lavish embellishments, as with the Treasury Notes of 1890, the Treasury Department has consistently taken the stance that to deter counterfeiting, bills should have ample open or plain space on both sides. Some vignettes and portraits found on currency were also used elsewhere, such as on postage stamps and fiscal paper.

Plate letters and numbers: Letters identify the position of a note on the face of large-size bills, and for most types a tiny numeral designates the back plate position. Small-size bills have a combination letter and number on the face, such as H22, and a number on the reverse, such as 78.

Serial numbers: Serial numbers were printed separately, occasionally in two places, and often in a color. The colors vary, depending on the note: red, blue, brown, gold, yellow, and many shades of green. Many serial numbers were given a letter prefix, such as A324422, or a suffix letter, or both a letter prefix and suffix. These suffixes permitted the numbers to be lower. In instances, after 1908, in which some notes in a series were misprinted or otherwise had to be destroyed and replaced, the serial numbers on the face of the replacement notes are preceded or followed by a star. These are called "star notes" today and form a separate specialty for many numismatists. Some earlier currency such as the Coin or Treasury Notes and the Series of 1890 and 1891 have stars following the serial numbers as part of the design.

Signatures of Treasury officials: Most large-size bills include the signatures of the register of the Treasury and the treasurer of the United States. Certain early bills have inked signatures, most done by a corps of secretaries. Some early bills are countersigned by other Treasury officials, such as at branch offices. Federal Reserve Notes from 1914 onward and all small-size bills have the printed signatures of the treasurer of the United States and the secretary of the Treasury. Federal Reserve Bank Notes (Series of 1929) also bear printed signatures of officials of that branch, and National Bank Notes have signatures of bank officers.

Imprint of printers and engravers: Certain early federal bills bore the names of the private companies that printed them. Later large-size bills have the imprint of the Bureau of Engraving and Printing (in several forms). On small-size bills, the Bureau is not mentioned, but since the opening of the Fort Worth branch printing facility, starting with the Series of 1988-A, a small "FW" appears on notes printed there.

Overprints: Some series of bills are overprinted, such as bronze printing on Compound Interest Treasury Notes, the HAWAII overprint on certain small-size bills $1 to $20, and others.

National Bank Note features: National Bank Notes, issued from 1863 to 1935, have distinctive features, including the name of the bank, location, and state, and, for all except the earliest issues, the charter number of the bank. In addition to the signatures of federal officials, each National Bank Note has a space for the signature of the cashier and president. In early years, these were inked in. Sometimes, an assistant cashier or a vice president would sign, making an appropriate notation of such. Some later of the large-size issues were rubber stamped with one or both signatures, and a few were printed in the plate. Bills of the series through and including 1882 have a representation of the state seal on the back. All small-size Nationals 1929-1935 have printed signatures. In addition to the federal serial number, each large-size bill has a bank serial number, numerals only (no letter prefixes or suffixes). Some large-size Nationals from the late 19th and early 20th centuries have a regional letter such as N (for Northeast) or S (for South), to aid in sorting the bills when they were redeemed by the Treasury Department. Small-size Nationals have their own serial numbering system, with prefix letters and, for 1929 Type 1, suffix letters, as explained earlier.

SOME WAYS TO COLLECT

Large-size United States bills from 1861 to 1929 and small-size bills from 1929 to date, are much easier to collect than are obsolete notes issued by state-chartered banks. As a class, most types of lower-denomination large-size and small-size bills in the larger classes (Legal Tender Notes, Silver Certificates, various Federal Reserve Bank issues) are plentiful, although certain varieties and signature combinations can be rare. Unfortunately, because the Treasury Department did not grant permission to depict bills until it was given to Robert Friedberg for the first edition of *Paper Money of the United States* in 1953, old auction catalogs that listed notes were sadly lacking in illustrations of the bills. As a result, many of these are next to useless for research today, beyond the most basic of information.

Today, with capable catalogers drawing on standard reference books and databases, plus illustrating the notes, most such problems have been overcome. Still, very little is ever said of the history and romance surrounding early bills. Sometimes when information is not known, it is guessed at, and wildly. I find it particularly interesting to see identifications of the signatures of cashiers and presidents on National Bank bills and then comparing them with the often vastly different *real* names as listed in Treasury reports and bank journals.

Counterfeits and alterations are not much of a problem in the collecting of federal currency, for it is a federal offense to issue false notes, the penalties are severe, and few false bills remained in circulation for very long. This situation is vastly different from the field of obsolete notes, where such items abound and, in fact, are collected with enthusiasm.

SOME WAYS TO COLLECT

Most numismatists specialize in a particular area of paper money, such as National Bank Notes, Silver Certificates, small-size $1 bills by types, small-size Federal Reserve Notes by bank and signature combinations, or something else of interest. Here are some possibilities:

Large-size types, lower denominations: A collection of the $1, $2, and $5 values makes a very nice display. A good way to start is with $1 and $2 denominations, for certain of the rare series (Demand Notes, Gold Certificates) are not represented. Afterward, your collection can be expanded to include $5 bills. This is an ideal way to acquaint yourself with the panorama of designs, denominations, and changes over the years.

Large-size types, expanded: As preceding, but higher denominations such as $10 and $20 can be included, after which point the going becomes difficult, especially for the earlier types. Perhaps just selected types of certain $50 and $100 bills can be included. As to $500, $1,000, or even higher values, these are so rare and so expensive that only a few have been fortunate enough to collect them over the years.

Types within special series: Collecting one of each major type of Silver Certificate or one of each Demand Note. It might seem logical that many collectors of Morgan and Peace silver dollars would also desire Silver Certificates, most of which are specifically payable in silver dollars, but this is not the case. The paper and coin specialties seldom meet.

Systematic by varieties, large size: Collecting by varieties involves going beyond basic types and collecting different signature combinations, Treasury seal variations, and others. Not many people do this for large-size bills, with the result that such popular types as the 1890 Coin Notes, 1899 "Indian" $5 bills, and others are more or less priced generically—with little premium added for rarer signature or seal varieties. Federal Reserve Bank Notes, Series of 1918, can be collected with different combinations of Federal Reserve Banks, each of the two Treasury signatures, and each of two bank signatures, offering many variables. Lower denominations, especially the $1 bills, are quite inexpensive and furnish many different varieties. Certain terms of combined service for the register of the Treasury and the treasurer of the United States were very short, the briefest being just 18 days, from June 1, 1893, to the 18th, for William S. Rosecrans and Daniel N. Morgan. While at first it might seem that short terms together would have created extremely rare and valuable bills, this is not necessarily the case, as printing quantities were sometimes extensive during a short term and sparse during a long one, and in other instances, plates with those signatures were used long after one or both persons left office.

Small-size by types: While few people can afford or have the interest in collecting small-size bills from $1 to $100 by all combinations or, for that matter, the rare $500, $1,000, $5,000, and $10,000 bills, quite a few numismatists desire to get one each of as many different types as they can. Changes in types were not frequent, and except for the higher values, such a display can be acquired in high grades for modest outlay.

Systematic by varieties, small size: Small-size bills can be collected by denominations, signatures, and Federal Reserve Banks. Lower denominations, especially the $1 bills, are quite inexpensive and furnish many different varieties. Such a collection can be kept current by adding new bills each time there is a signature combination or other change. This field has been the focus of interest for many numismatists.

Interesting serial numbers: This is a particularly popular pursuit, especially for small-size bills of small denominations. The eight serial numbers can yield all sorts of possibilities. The beginning and ending letters are of interest as well, especially if both are A, but most attention is paid to the numerals. Low serials such as 00000001 (especially), 00001492, 00001776, and others sell for premiums. "Lucky" 7's are popular, and 77777777 would be worth passing around at a show for collectors to see, while having a bunch of 7's together, mixed with other numbers, is interesting, too, as 83777779, ideal for "liar's poker," a game played at coin shows in which the winner has the best "poker hand" as reflected in a bill taken from supposedly random examples in a wallet. Numbers that are symmetrical are called "radar" (spelled the same way in each direction) or, more formally, palindromic, notes, such as 12344321 or 44888844. Ascending or descending runs such as 12345678 or 98765432 are also desirable.

Figure XXI

Figure XXII

The Bureau of Engraving and Printing Building, Washington, DC, 1879 (Figure XXI). All operations for processing paper money were moved from the Treasury Building to this facility once it was completed in July 1880.

From time to time the Bureau made specimen or presentation books containing vignettes, including some used on paper money, bonds, and other security printing. Shown here is *Concordia* (Figure XXII), created at the American Bank Note Company and used on $1 Original Series National Bank notes, later at the Bureau on Series of 1875 notes of the same design.

SOME WAYS TO COLLECT

Star notes: Small-size (in particular) notes with a star by the serial number are another popular collectable. When a note is found defective after printing, it is replaced with a star note. On Federal Reserve Notes, the star is after the serial number. On all other issues, the star comes before it. A star note is also used for the 100,000,000th note in a series because numbering machines cannot print over eight digits. Star notes are indicated in small-size notes by placing the star after the catalog number. The use of the star on large-size notes for this purpose did not begin until 1908. Prior to that, the star was merely a part of the design, as on Treasury Notes. The star notes form an avidly collected series. Values are sometimes dramatically high for with-star varieties that are inexpensive without this feature.

Currency errors: All sorts of interesting misprints and errors exist, the most dramatic of which is the double-denomination bill, such as with $5 on one side and $10 on the other, the result of a wrong sheet being fed into the press, or a $10-$10-$10-$20 or other multi-denomination sheet being fed upside down (with the first $10 obverse getting a $20 reverse and the $20 getting a $10 reverse). However, the thrust of activity is with more available errors, such as mismatched serial numbers, upside-down serial numbers or seals, missing seals or serials, or bold creases showing white areas without ink.

National Bank Notes: These are collected with wild, unbridled passion by some. The standard work is *National Bank Notes* by Don C. Kelly, built upon many years of effort, most notably the early work of John Hickman and Dean Oakes. With such bills, as with real estate, the three aspects of value for a National Bank bill within a given denomination are location, location, and location! A bill from Carson City, Nevada, a "rare town" as well as being a state capital (a specialty for many), is worth an eyetooth, while a common one from the National Park Bank of New York City might merit an unstifled yawn. Also interesting are the unusual names of some banks and municipalities, which often draw an interest and price far exceeding rarity. Among the most prominent examples of this is the legendary charter number 9216, the First National Bank of Intercourse, PA, which issued $5, $10, and $20 bills in both large- and small-size versions. Nationals, as they are called, are usually collected by states—in one of several different ways: a note from each town in the state, or from each bank in each town, or of each denomination of each type series of each bank. This can be a very serious pursuit, and anyone wanting to collect 19th-century notes from rare locations, or rare states, or, the ultimate, rare territories (before they achieved statehood), should be prepared to spend a lot of money, but not in a hurry, as many varieties are seldom seen. However, the challenge is enjoyable, and those who specialize in Nationals are a special breed. Condition, while important in Nationals, is sometimes disregarded, as many banks are represented only by low-grade notes.

Sheets: While sheets of large-size bills are sometimes seen, especially for National Banks of the Series of 1902, they are not common and cannot be collected systematically. Sheets of small-size Nationals, six subjects, are more available but are scarce. Many of the latter are from the estate of Col. E.H.R. Green, who had thousands, acquiring them in the early 1930s via a mail soliciting campaign to banks. Sheets for regular bills of the past several decades are plentiful, as the Treasury Department has made them available to collectors, charging a small premium for the service. Sometimes, modern sheets are cut down to a lesser number of bills, but I see no point in paying a premium for such things. Full sheets are interesting, but a bit clumsy to store or display.

Other specialties: Military payment certificates (MPCs) issued to soldiers in the 20th century have been an enthusiastically collected area. Produced in large numbers for use in soldiers' pay, most were quickly redeemed. Today, many varieties are quite scarce.

Notes with so-called courtesy autographs by Treasury officials form an interesting pursuit for many. Among 19th-century bills, those autographed by Daniel N. Morgan (register of the Treasury from June 1, 1893, to June 30, 1897) are particularly numerous. Morgan was an enthusiastic collector and asked visitors to his office to sign an autograph book he kept on hand.

Bills created as souvenirs are also popular to collect, with among the best known being the "short snorters" of World War II. These consist of multiple bills taped together end-to-end and signed by soldier or sailor buddies.

GRADE CATEGORIES FOR U.S. PAPER MONEY

Gem Uncirculated (Gem Unc) • **(Unc-65)** • A note that is flawless, with the same freshness, crispness, and bright color as when first printed. It must be perfectly centered, with full margins, and free of any marks, blemishes, or traces of handling.

Choice Uncirculated (Ch Unc) • **(Unc-63)** • An Uncirculated note that is fresher and brighter than the norm for its particular issue. Almost as nice as Gem Uncirculated but not quite there. Must be reasonably well centered.

Uncirculated (Unc) • **(Unc-60)** • A note that shows no trace of circulation. It might not have perfect centering and might have one or more pinholes, counting smudges, or other evidence of improper handling, while still retaining its original crispness. Sometimes large-size notes will be encountered which are obviously Uncirculated, but which have some tiny pinholes. It was customary in the old days to spindle or pin new notes together, and that is why so many Uncirculated notes might show tiny pinholes. Such imperfections do not generally impair the choice appearance of a new note, and such notes are to be regarded as being in Uncirculated condition, although they generally command slightly lower prices than notes in perfect condition.

About Uncirculated (AU) • **(AU-50, AU-55, and AU-58)** • A bright, crisp note that appears new but upon close examination shows a trace of very light use, such as a corner fold or faint crease. About Uncirculated is a borderline condition, applied to a note that may not be quite Uncirculated, but yet is obviously better than an average Extremely Fine note. Such notes command a price only slightly below a new note and are highly desirable.

Extremely Fine (EF) • **(EF-40 and EF-45)** • A note that shows some faint evidence of circulation, although it will still be bright and retain nearly full crispness. It may have two or three minor folds or creases but no tears or stains and no discolorations.

Very Fine (VF) • **(VF-20, VF-25, VF-30, and VF-35)** • A note that has been in circulation, but not actively or for long. It still retains some crispness and is still choice enough in its condition to be altogether desirable. It may show folds or creases, or some light smudges from the hands of a past generation. Sometimes, Very Fine notes are the best available in certain rare issues, and they should accordingly be cherished just as much as Uncirculated notes.

Fine (F) • **(F-12 and F-15)** • A Fine note shows evidence of much more circulation and has lost its crispness and very fine detail, and creases are more pronounced, although the note is still not seriously soiled, or stained.

Very Good (VG) • **(VG-8 and VG-10)** • A note that has had considerable wear or circulation and may be limp, soiled, or dark in appearance, and might even have a small tear or two on an edge.

Good (G) • **(G-4)** • A note that is badly worn, with margin or body tears, frayed margins, and missing corners.

Commentary: In general, discriminating collectors will not acquire Fine or lower grade notes because they have lost their aesthetic appeal, but this applies only to common notes. However, a really rare note has a ready market in even Good condition, because it may not otherwise exist, or if it is choice, will have an extremely high price commensurate with its great rarity.

Third party grading: Third party comercial grading services for paper money are operated by PCGS and PMG. In addition, several other services are operated by paper money dealers. These services place notes in holders and add information as to their opinions concerning the grade.

In recent times, the 1 to 70 point American Numismatic Association Grading System for coins has been adopted by many paper money enthusiasts, and commercial grading services employ these designations. For many collectors, it has become convenient shorthand for many numismatic series. Increasingly, we are all seeing VF-20 and EF-40 for Very Fine and Extremely Fine. Mint State doesn't make much sense for paper money, as it was printed, not minted! Accordingly, Uncirculated-60 or -63 is used. On the other hand, it is common to describe postage stamps as Mint, and they were not minted either!

Being somewhat traditional in my outlook, perhaps even old-fashioned, I think it desirable to include information beyond a simple grading word or adjective, especially for a rare or valuable note. Also, for some notes the margins can vary, although virtually nothing about this important aspect is included in any reference book I have ever seen. For example, every Original Series and

GRADE CATEGORIES FOR U.S. PAPER MONEY

Series of 1875 National Bank bill of the $5 denomination has very tiny margins (except for the top margin of a note with plate letter A and the bottom margin for a note with plate letter D). Accordingly, such a note with plate letter B or C can have very tiny top and bottom margins, but wide left and right margins, and still be a Gem Uncirculated note. On the other hand, Silver Certificates of the Series of 1923, Federal Reserve Bank Notes, and most others were printed with ample margins separating the notes on a sheet. This aspect has not been widely studied, but should be, especially when certain bills are implied to be sub par if they have closely trimmed margins. My information is from studying many sheets of proof impressions kindly made available by the Smithsonian Institution.

For United States paper money, a high-grade note is always more valuable than a low-grade one. For most basic types of large-size bills of the denominations $1 to $5, Uncirculated examples turn up with frequency on the market. Values of $10 to $20 are considerably scarcer, and in many instances, $50 and $100 bills are very rare in this preservation. Demand Notes, Compound Interest Notes, and certain of the early National Bank Notes are quite scarce in Uncirculated grade, no matter what the denomination, and for some varieties, all known specimens show extensive circulation.

There has been a "grade-flation" in currency over the years. In the 1960s and early 1970s, for a bill to qualify as Uncirculated it had to be crisp and without a hint of a fold. Today, United States paper money with some such evidence is often called Uncirculated by some sellers, and those without have graduated to choice and gem Uncirculated. It is important to inspect any note carefully for such small imperfections and miscategorizations before purchasing.

"IMPROVING" CURRENCY

Many bills have been improved, some desirably so, by "laundering" to remove dirt and grease, then drying between pieces of tissue paper. Some collectors and dealers have added starch in an effort to restore crispness. Still other bills have had holes or tears repaired. Such improvements are generally accepted and should always be mentioned when offered for sale whether by an auctioneer or a dealer. Anything else is a misrepresentation. Reality is reality, and in the marketplace today, there are many bills which under careful examination show slight traces of having been folded (such as lightness or microscopic irregularity at the fold marks), but which are as crisp as a new note. Indeed, bills in grades such as VG and Fine, normally quite limp, are often with stiffness. My advice is that if a bill is very rare, this is okay, if you examine and recognize it. But for regular low-denomination notes, I would prefer bills that have not been treated.

As you might expect, for most numismatic rules there are exceptions. Accordingly, I cannot help but wonder what the American Numismatic Association or the Professional Currency Dealers Association would have to say if today a currency dealer utilized the apparatus described below!

In July 1910 *The Numismatist* included this item:

Experiments at the Treasury in Washington for the cleansing of paper money have been so successful that the time does not seem far distant when laundered and unlaundered will be used in reference to U.S. paper money. The process includes washing and resizing and makes the laundered notes as crisp as when new.

The process is simple, a machine is being perfected to do the work, and, it is said, that it is the purpose of the government to encourage clearing houses in the large cities to install "money laundries" for the convenience of the local banks. We will be able to have our "filthy lucre" cleansed at home.

Mehl's Numismatic Monthly, February 1911, printed an article by Thomas D. Gannaway, of the Treasury Department, first printed in the *National Monthly*:

The Government Money Laundry

Ever hear of our money laundry at Washington? The government maintains such a laundry, wherein soiled and dirty green backs are washed and ironed. The "life" of this paper currency is thus prolonged and the country is saved considerable expense each year because of this laundering process, which has now passed the experimental stage.

Arrangements are now under way for the installation of improved machinery and when this is in operation the money laundry will be equipped to turn out more and even better work than is the case today.

It actually costs Uncle Sam $13.50 per thousand notes (regardless of denomination) to manufacture and put them into circulation. This is equal to an annual interest of almost 1 percent on the $1 notes, which have an average life of only 14 months. The life of small notes is very much shorter than that of the large denominations, because of the greater amount of handling, therefore the greater part of the expense of our paper currency circulation is incurred with the smaller denominations.

This is better understood when we learn that the $1, $2, and $5 notes, excluding National bank currency, compose about 90% of the number of notes in circulation. The larger denominations are fit for circulation much longer after they are first issued than the smaller ones; hence, they do not have to be redeemed so soon thereafter.

A very large portion of the notes which come back to the Treasury Department for redemption, are not worn out, but are merely soiled from rough usage. As a result of the clamor for economy in public expenditures and also for clean paper currency, the Director of the Bureau of Engraving and Printing, Joseph E. Ralph, conceived the idea of putting these soiled notes through a laundering process, and then back into circulation. The more he studied the scheme, the more feasible it appeared to him. He submitted his plan to the Secretary of the Treasury and the latter appointed a committee.... These men have been experimenting with the laundering process for about seven months, and, as a result of these experiments, have proved, beyond reasonable doubt, that it is feasible and worthy of general adoption by the government. The process of washing the money is very simple, being almost identical to that used by the steam laundries in washing clothes....

One of the most feasible plans is to put the notes into a wire contrivance, which holds them in such manner as to prevent any friction whatever, and also prevents them from piling together. This contrivance consists of a number of wire trays with a single layer of notes in each and then stacked together and placed inside of a cylindrical tub filled with suds made with a soap especially prepared for this work by chemist Smith, who has charge of the practical part of the work. The soap is composed principally of potash and some high-grade oils. Mr. Smith is now trying to manufacture a soap, which will cleanse the money and at the same time bleach it.

After the trays of money have been placed in the suds, which has been heated to a temperature of 130 degrees to 140 degrees F., the tub is closed and started to revolving. A greater temperature than 140 degrees F. has proved to be injurious to the money. This process is kept going for 10 to 15 minutes, during which time the dirt has been removed from the notes. They are then taken out and rinsed the same way in clear water for about five minutes to remove all the suds. Next the money is put into a germicide bath of the nature of formaldehyde, thereby killing all germs, which may be lurking around on it. It is taken from this and bleached and partially dried. The next step is to put it through the sizing tub, or vat as it may be called. This vat contains a 10% solution of glue with a little alum in it. There are a number of small endless belts, which pass over rollers at the top of either end of the vat and under one in the solution. The money is fed in between these belts at one end of the vat and they carry it, down through the solution and drop, it out at the other end.

It is then taken to the ironing machine. Here it is placed in stacks containing about 40 notes each, with a piece of Fuller board separating, the notes from each other. This Fuller, or pressboard, is a thin, flexible substance resembling a thin piece of sole leather. These stacks are taken one at a time and fed through between two heavy steel rollers, which are held together with a thirty-ton pressure. Each stack of notes is put through two of these machines, which completes the ironing.

"IMPROVING" CURRENCY

After the bills are washed and ironed they are placed in the drying room, for the purpose of getting rid of every particle of moisture. The yellow ink used on the Gold Certificates is of such a character that the potash dissolves it and it is washed out, hence these certificates can not yet be laundered. So it is with the signatures of the bank officers on the National Bank Notes. The committee hopes to overcome this difficulty. As it is at present they can only launder Silver Certificates and Treasury Notes, but these all compose a very large percentage of our paper money.

During the year 1909, excluding National Bank Notes, there were 187,784,000 one-dollar, two-dollar and five-dollar notes issued, and in the same period of time there were 177,412,809 notes of the same denominations destroyed. At the close of the year 1909 there were 222,365,692 notes of these three denominations still in circulation. The cost to the government for manufacturing and issuing these 187,784,000 notes was $2,535,084. The cost of destroying the 177,412,809 notes was $309,308.18, making a grand total of $2,925,392.18 for maintaining the circulation of notes of only three denominations for one year. It is estimated that it will not cost more than one-tenth of 1% per note to launder them. It is claimed that laundering the notes will add at least eight months or 56 per cent to their life, thereby diminishing the annual redemption by 56 per cent. The redeeming and issuing of the 177,412,809 notes in 1909, cost the government $2,787,151.23. With the new process 56% of this, or $1,560,806.93, less $298,053.52, the cost of laundering and reissuing of the 56 per rent of the redemptions for 1909, would be saved. This would leave a net saving of $1,262,753.41 in one year on the circulation of $1, $2 and $5 notes, National Bank Notes excluded.

A good deal of space in the press has been devoted to the discussion of the money laundry, even though much of it had to be drawn from imagination. What is said about the laundry tub for the permanent plant has to be of a very uncertain character, as it has not yet been ordered made; in fact, the committee has not decided what style it will use. But they are satisfied it will not be like the experimental one. As to the ironing machines and the sizing machine, they will be of about the same design as the experimental ones, but only about one-third as large. These have already been ordered made and will soon be ready for installation.

Of course, today "money laundering" has an entirely different meaning—not at all numismatic—involving the altering of bank and commercial transactions to make income from illegal or questionable operations appear to be legitimate. The preceding article is interesting for some of the other information it gives concerning paper money production costs, use of bills, and their service length.

MORE ABOUT GRADING

Returning to the grading of currency, there have been some interesting comments about bills that were illustrated and described as damaged (as with pin holes) in one auction catalog, but later re-emerged in another sale, in a higher grade and without damage, after being given disclosed "improvements."

Similar to the situation for rare coins, it is important to be aware of the technicalities of grading beyond the designations you might see in a catalog or other offering. Examining notes and talking with collectors and dealers will be useful. My own preference in selecting a note for my reference collection is to be sure it is an attractive example of its type and grade. If it is Uncirculated, that is nice, but I am not into such divisions as Uncirculated, choice Uncirculated, gem Uncirculated, super-gem Uncirculated, and so on. For me, an attractive example will fill the bill (pun). Collecting paper money is an enjoyable pursuit, but it is important to be aware.

These comments reflect my observations of certain United States paper money series 1861 to date:

Denominations: In any series, it is a general rule that lower denominations are more readily available than higher. The lower denominations are also more often seen in Uncirculated and other high grades, whereas a $50 or $100 bill might be rare or unknown in such preservation.

Printing quantities: Quantities produced can be a guide to availability, but only in part, as such factors as redemption policies, areas of distribution, and the finding of hoards affect the equation.

Hoards: Every once in a while, in an old bank vault or other location, a cache of bills comes to light. Often, these are Uncirculated and serially numbered. Although details are rarely announced, for fear of disturbing the market, the existence of such can be deduced if serial number sequences of bills in Uncirculated grade are seen. In addition, nearly all paper money dealers know which notes are available from groups and hoards and which are not, and are often willing to share information. Often, hoard notes are particularly choice and, further, offer the opportunity to acquire examples that might not otherwise be available, at least not easily.

Numismatic popularity: Certain series have been popular with numismatists for a long time, and in such instances, many Uncirculated notes exist from the early days of interest. This is nowhere more true than with Fractional Currency bills, which were avidly collected in the 1870s, in an era when no one collected large-size notes. Accordingly, most standard varieties, plus proofs, of Fractional Currency are plentiful today. Most lower-denomination small-size bills from the Series of 1928 (first issued in 1929) through the 1940s were saved by collectors and dealers, including quantities of popular varieties such as the $1 HAWAII overprints. These used to be plentiful on the market. After about 1953, the collecting of small-size notes became very popular, and quantities of most bills exist for lower denominations since that time. Higher values such as $20, $50, and $100 can be rare for certain varieties.

Souvenirs and keepsakes: Relatively few 19th-century bills of denominations $1 and upward were saved as souvenirs or given as gifts. Recipients preferred gold dollars, quarter eagles, and other coins, which displayed an immediate aspect of permanent value. The worth of paper money remained in serious question for a long time. Sometimes bank officers would keep a few National Bank Notes with their signatures, accounting for a disproportionate amount of serial number 1 bills surviving today.

Proofs and vignettes: Proof impressions were printed by the thousands of many Fractional Currency bills. These can be collected as a specialty on their own. Proofs of regular United States bills, often on heavy paper or cardboard and with wide margins, were made in very small quantities and were not widely distributed, but examples become available from time to time. Most are rare and expensive. Many individually printed vignettes from large-size National Bank and other 19th-century bills are on the market, these showing portraits, battle scenes, or another topic, on light card stock. These are interesting to collect in connection with the bills themselves. Some are from large presentation books of specimen notes distributed by the Treasury Department in the 1870s and 1880s with nicely imprinted covers. Much rarer are specially made books of Fractional Currency proofs.

END NOTES

1. *American Journal of Numismatics*, July 1883, pp. 18, 19.

2. For many auctions of rare coins during this period, bids were called in terms of payment in specie. Accordingly, "prices realized" must be interpreted with care, as practices varied.

3. Langley's *San Francisco Directory*, 1864-5, p. 17 (chronicle of events).

4. Quoted information from Sherman is from *John Sherman's Recollections of Forty Years in the House, Senate and Cabinet*, 1895, *passim*.

5. Also see Frank Clark, "1882 $20 Gold Certificates and Patent Lettering," *The Rag Picker*, official publication of the Paper Money Collectors of Michigan, July-September 2003 (copy courtesy of David M. Sundman).

6. When Jacob Perkins endeavored to introduce his Patent Stereotype Steel Plate for the use of the Bank of England, 1820, Sir William Congreve, present supplier of bills to the bank and an inventor of some repute, conducted an "investigation" of the design-filled Perkins plate and persuaded the bank to reject it.

7. Certain remarks are adapted from the writer's contributed (by invitation) introduction to part of the John J. Ford, Jr., sale of encased postage stamps, Stack's, 2004.

8. Neil Carothers, *Fractional Money*, 1930, 177-178.

9. Mason's *Coin and Stamp Collectors' Magazine*, January 1868.

ACKNOWLEDGEMENTS AND CREDITS

Special thanks to the following for their contributions to the *Guide Book of United States Paper Money*.

- **Mark Abramson** corresponded concerning interesting serial numbers on notes.

- **Wynn Bowers** assisted with proofreading.

- **Jason Bradford** of PCGS provided information on third-party grading of banknotes.

- **Edward A. and Joanne Dauer** contributed images of various notes, including the "Grand Watermelon" $1,000 and the Series of 1863 $100 Legal Tender Note.

- **Tom Denly** of Denly's of Boston was the main coordinator of pricing information, and provided many valuable editorial suggestions. He was essential to the success of the project.

- **Martin Gengerke** of R.M. Smythe shared information and photographs.

- **Stephen Goldsmith** of R.M. Smythe provided the use of his staff's time in gathering data.

- Certain information from **Don C. Kelly** concerning National Bank Notes was useful in the writing stage.

- **Peter Huntoon** provided information on various historical and technical aspects.

- **Scott Lindquist** of R.M. Smythe was instrumental in compiling valuations for small-size notes.

- **Harry E. Jones** of Jones Rare Currency contributed text and images for the "Error Notes" section.

- **Glen Jorde** of PMG provided information on third-party grading of banknotes.

- **Donald H. Kagin** contributed images and information to the book.

- **Marc Michaelsen** of R.M. Smythe assisted with pricing of high-denomination small-size notes.

- **Susan Novak** worked with David Bowers in gathering information from Treasury Department documents.

- **The Smithsonian Institution** provided information and proof impressions of National Bank Notes.

- **Sergio Sanchez** of Sergio Sanchez Jr. Rare Coins and Currency helped with pricing large-size notes.

- **David M. Sundman** of Littleton Coin Company made generous contributions to the book's historical and technical information, and shared illustrations.

Various other contributors to the original Friedberg book are acknowledged in *Paper Money of the United States, 17th ed.*

Certain illustrations and historical information are used on a non-exclusive basis and are from the archives of Q. David Bowers, LLC. Certain illustrations from the files of Littleton Coin Co. are also used on a non-exclusive basis.

AUTHENTICATION

EXPERT GRADING

ENCAPSULATION

Certification. Standardization. Protection.

Professional and impartial paper money grading and encapsulation gives you a collecting environment that is stable, liquid and free of fraud.

Paper Money Guaranty (PMG), the newest independent member of the Certified Collectibles Group (CCG), combines accurate, impartial and knowledgeable graders with proven processes and standards for the care and evaluation of your notes.

IMAGING

Many of these standards have been established for years at our sister company, Numismatic Guaranty Corporation (NGC), the largest, most respected company in the authentication and grading of rare coins. And, as with coins, each of our paper money experts is prohibited from buying and selling notes to ensure impartiality.

INTEGRITY

Most importantly, behind it all is the passion and respect for the hobby that we bring to work with us each and every day.

To learn more about PMG, contact your local dealer, visit www.PMGnotes.com, or contact Glen Jorde, Grading Finalizer, at 877-PMG-5570.

IMPARTIALITY

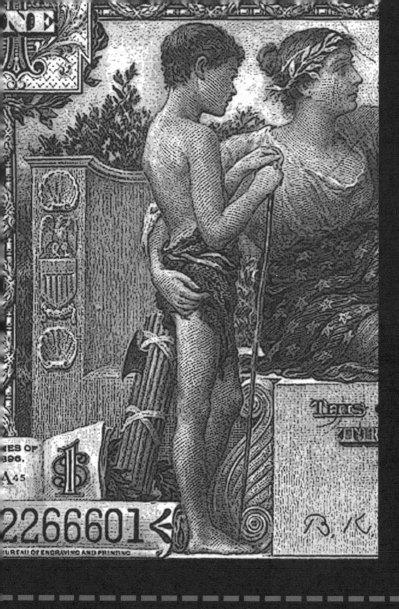

"One dollar notes are wonderfully diverse in their designs, quite affordable, and provide a panorama of collecting opportunities…"

ONE DOLLAR NOTES

COLLECTING ONE DOLLAR NOTES

Made in large quantities ever since the first Legal Tender Notes of 1862, bills of the $1 denomination have been plentiful in commerce ever since. Every once in a while a movement starts to eliminate the paper dollar by creating a coin substitute. The theory is that a dollar bill, which may last only 18 months in active circulation, could be replaced with a metal dollar that would last 10 years or more. The Susan B. Anthony dollar launched in 1979 was not a success in commerce, nor was the Sacagawea dollar of 2000. In the meantime, the paper dollar continues to be as useful and popular as ever.

From a collecting viewpoint, $1 bills are wonderfully diverse in their designs and, for most early large-size types, are quite affordable. Current $1 notes are made in a wide variety of Federal Reserve Bank imprints and signature combinations, providing a panorama of collecting opportunities.

Large-Size $1 Notes

$1 Legal Tender Notes, Large-Size: The first federal $1 bills are the Legal Tender Notes, Series of 1862, each with a bright green reverse (which popularized the term "greenback," although it was not the first use of this color). The various private printing and engraving firms advanced the notion that green was less susceptible to counterfeiting than were other colors. There was much publicity given to this color, sometimes called "Canada green," beginning in the late 1850s, for use on bills of state-chartered banks printed by Rawdon, Wright, Hatch & Edson (the largest of eight firms that combined to form the American Bank Note Co. in 1858). For federal paper money the idea was promoted by the American Bank Note Company and quickly found acceptance. Ever since then most bills of all denominations have had backs of green.

There is a general uniformity of color and appearance, but differences in motifs, across all denominations in the Series of 1862 Legal Tender bills. The Legal Tender $1 notes were made in large quantities and are readily collectable as a basic type today. The bold signature of F.E. Spinner printed on the notes has always been popular—the most dramatic of any Treasury individual.

The next major type, the Series of 1869 Legal Tender Notes, features George Washington, whose visage still greets us on $1 bills today. The Series of 1869 evolved into others, through and including the Series of 1917, with variations in the Treasury seal, signatures, and other elements. Generally these Legal Tender bills are collected as a single note of the 1869 to 1917 design, and less often by signature combination or Treasury seal variations. A signature combination might be rare but the premium charged for it modest, as this method of collecting is not presently in the limelight.

Large-size Legal Tender Notes were imprinted LEGAL TENDER, TREASURY NOTE, and, finally, UNITED STATES NOTE, culminating in the Series of 1923 with the signatures of Speelman and White (Friedberg-40). These are plentiful today.

$1 National Bank Notes, Large-Size: $1 National Bank Notes of the Original Series were first made in 1865, although other denominations had been distributed as early as December 1863. Such bills across all denominations were designated as National Currency, but collectors today prefer the term "Nationals" or "National Bank Notes." These were printed on sheets of four subjects (typically $1-$1-$1-$2, the last being the "Lazy 2" variety). They were made by the American Bank Note Co., then shipped to the Treasury Department, where serial numbers and the Treasury seal were imprinted. Each note was given a bank serial number in red and, in a separate process, a Treasury serial number (usually in red, but sometimes in blue early in the Original Series). Certain later Original Series and all Series of 1875 $1 notes have the bank's charter number printed in bold red.

Then came the Series of 1875, with a vertically oriented imprint to this effect on the left side of the face, reflecting that the notes were printed in Washington by the Treasury Department, but still bearing the American Bank Note Company name on the printing plates. Production of $1 and $2 National Bank bills stopped in 1879.

These $1 bills, nicknamed "aces," of the Original Series and Series of 1875, play to a wide audience and are usually collected by the place of issue, sometimes by states and other times by towns and cities. Only rarely are they collected by signature combinations. Most Original Series bills have the Colby-Spinner names; fewer have Allison-Spinner. Those fewer still with the Jeffries-Spinner pairing are very valuable. The most extreme price differences are seen when the issuing location is rare; for example, such states as South Carolina and Wyoming. Those from Utah Territory, Alabama, West Virginia, and a few other places are quite scarce and bring strong premiums. Most plentiful are those from the eastern states with large populations, such as New York and Massachusetts. A crisp, bright Unc.-60 Series of 1875 $1 bill from a New York City bank (for which many examples exist) will be valued at just a fraction of the price of a F-12 bill from a "rare bank" in a western territory. All bets are off when it comes to grades of rare notes. For many such, preservations of Fair and Good are the order of the day, there being no finer known of their particular variety. National Bank notes are truly the *crème de la crème* of large-size $1 issues.

$1 Silver Certificates, Large-Size: Silver Certificates of the $1 denomination start with the Series of 1886. This type depicts Martha Washington—the first time that a First Lady of the United States appeared on federal paper money. (Females of various kinds, ranging from goddesses to women in historical panoramas, had been used for a long time, including on notes issued by state-chartered banks.)

Foremost in popularity among Silver Certificates (as among all federal currency) are the Series of 1896 "Educational" bills, made in three denominations: $1, $2, and $5. The $1 has the panorama *History Instructing Youth*, a vista from a perspective in or near the Lee mansion across the Potomac River from Washington. On its face, a goddess points out the Washington Monument to a young boy. Soon, the Series of 1896 bills were replaced by the Series of 1899, with a small but bold "black eagle" on the face, made in many signature combinations and produced until the advent of the Series of 1923. More than just a few such bills were saved with low serial numbers, furnishing an interesting opportunity to collect them today. Two varieties exist bearing the Vernon-McClung signature combination: the usual, with the series date below the serial number (Friedberg-229); and a rarity, with the date to the right of the Treasury seal (Friedberg-229a).

Series of 1923 Silver Certificates, with Washington in a reprise appearance on the face, were made in three signature combinations, but are usually collected by single examples for type.

$1 Treasury or Coin Notes, Large-Size: Treasury Notes (also called Coin Notes) of the Series of 1890 have on the back the word ONE against an extremely rich background, beautiful to behold, especially on high-grade examples. As a class these bills are rare, creating one of the more elusive types within the denomination.

The Treasury Department wanted open areas on the back, feeling that the "busy" space made counterfeiting easier, so the Series of 1891 was created. While lacking in artistic effect, it perhaps foiled counterfeiters (although the writer has not come across any notice that the Series of 1890 bills were a real problem in this regard).

The face of each of the notes, Series of 1890 and Series of 1891, features the portrait of Edwin M. Stanton, secretary of war under presidents Lincoln and Johnson—one of many individuals, once prominent but relatively little remembered today, who can be seen on large-size federal paper money.

$1 Federal Reserve Bank Notes, Large-Size: $1 Federal Reserve Bank Notes, Series of 1918, featuring the city location of a Federal Reserve Bank on the face and a patriotic eagle grasping a flag on the reverse, were produced in many different combinations (Friedberg-708 through -746), and are quite popular today. They can be collected either as a single note to illustrate the type, or one note from each of the 12 banks, or else by signature combinations. The rarest of the varieties is Friedberg-735, with the Teehee-Burke signatures of Treasury officials and Cook-Young for the Minneapolis Federal Reserve Bank.

Small-Size $1 Notes

Small-size $1 notes are the most popular collected today. The face value is low, and most were made in sufficient quantities that examples are readily available, although certain early issues are scarce in Uncirculated grade. Indeed, more varieties are being made now than ever before in the past—a rather interesting situation. With the Federal Reserve Banks in the equation, many different collecting possibilities are presented each time there is a new signature or other change!

COLLECTING ONE DOLLAR NOTES

In the pages that follow, a star beside a small-sized note refers to a "star note"—one printed to replace another made in error and then destroyed. Collecting star notes has become a passion in its own right, and certain of these command substantial premiums.

$1 Legal Tender Notes, Small-Size: These notes begin with the Series of 1928, each of which has a red Treasury seal. These have the combined signatures of W.O. Woods and W.H. Woodin—William H. Woodin being President Franklin D. Roosevelt's first secretary of the Treasury and one of the most prominent numismatists of his era. Often, collectors simply call these bills "1928 Red Seals."

$1 Silver Certificates, Small-Size: Then follow the $1 Silver Certificates, commencing with the Series of 1928, distinguished by blue seals. A number of different signature combinations are known, the most famous of which is the 1928-E combining Julian and Morgenthau, a classic for a long time. The $1 Silver Certificates were produced for many years, through and including several variations of the Series of 1957.

Along the way the curious and historically significant Friedberg-2300 and -2306 bills with the HAWAII overprint and others with the yellow seal (for use by Allied troops in the North Africa and related campaigns) reflect the uncertain outcome of two theaters in World War II. The thought was that if such bills fell into enemy hands, they could be repudiated. These varieties have always been popular with numismatists. Other varieties of 1935-A include those with bright red "R" or "S" control letters printed on the face, said by some to be for "Regular" and "Synthetic" (or "Special"), representing two different types of paper intended to be tested in circulation to determine durability.

$1 Federal Reserve Notes, Small-Size: The new era of small-size $1 Federal Reserve Notes commenced with the Series of 1963, with notes issued by the 12 different Federal Reserve Banks and bearing appropriate designations. Each has a green Treasury seal. All these notes are highly collectable today and are available in approximate proportion to the numbers actually printed.

It will be seen that the Series of 1963-B, combining the signatures of Granahan and Barr (famous at one time because they held office only a few weeks together), were actually made in large quantities and are not particularly valuable today. At one time they were a nationwide sensation featured in the popular media.

Beginning with the Series of 1988-A, certain bills were printed in Fort Worth, Texas (known as the Western Facility), identified by a small FW on the face. In theory, for each new signature combination there could be 12 different varieties from the Bureau of Engraving and Printing, plus 12 star note varieties, plus the same numbers from Fort Worth, yielding 48 different in total! $1 bills furnish an affordable denomination; but to collect $50 or $100 bills in such varieties would be beyond the reach of most numismatists.

The beat goes on, and as these words are being written, new changes are being planned, including an eventual redesign of the face of the $1 to incorporate security features now seen on higher denominations. While as recently as the early 1960s the collecting of a full set of date and signature combinations of $1 was easy enough to do (star notes were not in the limelight), today the panorama has extended from horizon to horizon, and hundreds of varieties beckon. What fun!

$1 National Bank Notes, or "aces," of the Original Series and the Series of 1875 were produced only from 1865 to 1878 (Friedberg-380 to -386). Although signatures of Treasury officials vary, such bills are usually collected by state, town, or bank. Shown on this page are four *crème de la crème* bills.

The Citizens National Bank of Washington City is one of just a handful of $1 National Bank Notes known from the District of Columbia. This Original Series bill is from a plate dated June 15, 1874, just before the Series of 1875 commenced.

The Missoula National Bank $1 note bears the imprint of Montana territory, a part of the rare territorial series.

This Deseret National Bank $1 from Salt Lake City, Utah Territory, bears the signature of Mormon Church leader Brigham Young as president.

Rather ratty and decrepit is this $1 Original Series bill from the First National Bank of Franklin, Pennsylvania. Its claim to numismatic desirability is that it is the only such bill known to have survived from 6,000 issued, according to Don C. Kelly in *National Bank Notes*.

Legal Tender Notes

Face of Notes 16-17a.
Bust of Treasury Secretary Salmon P. Chase.

Back of Notes 16-17a.

Series of 1862, with signatures of Chittenden and Spinner and a small red seal

No.		VG-8	F-12	VF-20	EF-40	Unc-63
16.	National Bank Note Co. twice above lower border	$190.00	$325.00	$600.00	$800.00	$1,900.00
16a.	As above, with American Bank Note Co. monogram near center at right edge of face	400.00	650.00	1,250.00	1,750.00	4,000.00
17.	National Bank Note Co. and American Bank Note Co. above lower border, no monogram	Rare	—	—	—	—
17a.	As above, with American Bank Note Co. monogram near center at right edge of face	190.00	340.00	625.00	850.00	2,000.00

Legal Tender Notes

Face of Note 18.
Bust of George Washington in center; Christopher Columbus making sight of land at left.

Back of Note 18.

No.	Series	Signatures	Seal	VG-8	F-12	VF-20	EF-40	Unc-63
18.	1869	Allison Spinner	Large Red	$200.00	$425.00	$700.00	$950.00	$1,950.00

Legal Tender Notes

Face of Note 19-39.

Vignettes as above. Treasury seal at left, red floral ornament around "ONE DOLLAR" at right.

Back of Notes 19-39.

No.	Series	Signatures		Seal	VG-8	F-12	VF-20	EF-40	Unc-63
19.	1874	Allison	Spinner	Small Red, Rays	$140.00	$175.00	$250.00	$400.00	$1,100.00
20.	1875	Allison	New	Small Red, Rays	140.00	175.00	250.00	400.00	1,100.00
21.		Same but Series A			350.00	500.00	700.00	1,400.00	5,000.00
22.		Same but Series B			350.00	500.00	700.00	1,400.00	7,500.00
23.		Same but Series C			500.00	700.00	900.00	1,500.00	4,500.00
24.		Same but Series D			450.00	600.00	800.00	1,500.00	10,000.00
25.		Same but Series E			500.00	750.00	950.00	1,800.00	8,500.00
26.	1875	Allison	Wyman	Small Red, Rays	130.00	175.00	250.00	375.00	1,050.00
27.	1878	Allison	Gilfillan	Small Red, Rays	130.00	175.00	250.00	375.00	975.00

Large seal in place of floral ornament at right; red serial numbers

No.	Series	Signatures		Seal	VG-8	F-12	VF-20	EF-40	Unc-63
28.	1880	Scofield	Gilfillan	Large Brown	125.00	175.00	250.00	325.00	875.00
29.	1880	Bruce	Gilfillan	Large Brown	125.00	175.00	250.00	325.00	875.00
30.	1880	Bruce	Wyman	Large Brown	125.00	175.00	250.00	325.00	875.00

As above, except serial numbers are blue

No.	Series	Signatures		Seal	VG-8	F-12	VF-20	EF-40	Unc-63
31.	1880	Rosecrans	Huston	Large Red	300.00	500.00	900.00	1,400.00	3,000.00
32.	1880	Rosecrans	Huston	Large Brown	450.00	650.00	1,200.00	1,750.00	4,000.00
33.	1880	Rosecrans	Nebeker	Large Brown	550.00	750.00	1,450.00	2,000.00	5,000.00

Small seal is moved to left side of note; blue serial numbers

No.	Series	Signatures		Seal	VG-8	F-12	VF-20	EF-40	Unc-63
34.	1880	Rosecrans	Nebeker	Small Red, Scalloped	100.00	140.00	185.00	300.00	850.00
35.	1880	Tillman	Morgan	Small Red, Scalloped	100.00	140.00	185.00	300.00	850.00

Legal Tender Notes

Serial numbers are red, no longer in ornamental frames

No.	Series	Signatures		Seal	VG-8	F-12	VF-20	EF-40	Unc-63
36.	1917	Teehee	Burke	Small Red, Scalloped	$75.00	$80.00	$90.00	$100.00	$275.00
37.	1917	Elliott	Burke	Small Red, Scalloped	75.00	80.00	90.00	100.00	275.00
37a.	1917	Burke	Elliott (Signatures Reversed)		400.00	500.00	600.00	800.00	1,700.00
38.	1917	Elliott	White	Small Red, Scalloped	75.00	80.00	90.00	100.00	275.00
39.	1917	Speelman	White	Small Red, Scalloped	70.00	80.00	90.00	100.00	275.00

Face of Note 40.
Bust of George Washington.

Back of Note 40.

No.	Series	Signatures		Seal	VG-8	F-12	VF-20	EF-40	Unc-63
40.	1923	Speelman	White	Small Red, Scalloped	$90.00	$110.00	$175.00	$250.00	$525.00

National Bank Notes
"First Charter Period" (Original Series and Series of 1875)

Face of Notes 380-386.
Concordia, *by T.A. Liebler and Charles Burt—two maidens before an altar in an allegorical representation of Union and Peace.*

Back of Notes 350-386.
Landing of the Pilgrims, *engraved by Charles Burt.*

No.	Series	Signatures		Seal		VG-8	F-12	VF-20	EF-40	Unc-63
380.	Original	Colby	Spinner	Red, Rays		$950.00	$1,000.00	$1,350.00	$2,000.00	$3,252.00
381.	Original	Jeffries	Spinner	Red, Rays		2,250.00	3,500.00	4,250.00	5,500.00	12,500.00
382.	Original	Allison	Spinner	Red, Rays		950.00	1,000.00	1,350.00	2,000.00	3,250.00
383.	1875	Allison	New	Red, Scalloped		950.00	1,000.00	1,350.00	2,000.00	3,250.00
384.	1875	Allison	Wyman	Red, Scalloped		950.00	1,000.00	1,350.00	2,000.00	3,250.00
385.	1875	Allison	Gilfillan	Red, Scalloped		950.00	1,000.00	1,350.00	2,000.00	3,250.00
386.	1875	Scofield	Gilfillan	Red, Scalloped		950.00	1,000.00	1,350.00	2,000.00	3,250.00

These are the only National Bank Notes of the one dollar denomination.

Silver Certificates

Face of Notes 215-221.
Bust of Martha Washington.

Back of Notes 215-221.

No.	Series	Signatures		Seal	VG-8	F-12	VF-20	EF-40	Unc-63
215.	1886	Rosecrans	Jordan	Small Red, Plain	$225.00	$265.00	$400.00	$650.00	$1,600.00
216.	1886	Rosecrans	Hyatt	Small Red, Plain	225.00	300.00	450.00	700.00	1,750.00
217.	1886	Rosecrans	Hyatt	Large Red	225.00	265.00	400.00	650.00	1,600.00
218.	1886	Rosecrans	Huston	Large Red	225.00	265.00	400.00	650.00	1,600.00
219.	1886	Rosecrans	Huston	Large Brown	225.00	265.00	400.00	650.00	1,750.00
220.	1886	Rosecrans	Nebeker	Large Brown	225.00	265.00	400.00	650.00	1,750.00
221.	1886	Rosecrans	Nebeker	Small Red, Scalloped .	225.00	265.00	400.00	650.00	1,600.00

Silver Certificates

Face of Notes 222-223. Bust of Martha Washington.

Back of Notes 222-223.

No.	Series	Signatures		Seal	VG-8	F-12	VF-20	EF-40	Unc-63
222.	1891	Rosecrans	Nebeker	Small Red, Scalloped	$250.00	$300.00	$400.00	$675.00	$1,900.00
223.	1891	Tillman	Morgan	Small Red, Scalloped	225.00	275.00	375.00	625.00	1,700.00

Face of Notes 224-225.
Allegory of History instructing Youth before a vista of Washington, DC The Constitution is at right.

Silver Certificates

Back of Notes 224-225.

Busts of Martha and George Washington. This is the first of the three notes issued in the Educational Series.

No.	Series	Signatures		Seal	VG-8	F-12	VF-20	EF-40	Unc-63
224.	1896	Tillman	Morgan	Small Red, Rays ...	$315.00	$400.00	$500.00	$700.00	$2,000.00
225.	1896	Bruce	Roberts	Small Red, Rays ...	315.00	400.00	500.00	700.00	2,000.00

Face of Notes 226-236. Large eagle standing before Capitol building. Small busts of Lincoln and Grant in oval frames below. Known as the "Black Eagle" note.

Back of Notes 226-236.

Silver Certificates

No.	Series	Signatures		Seal	VG-8	F-12	VF-20	EF-40	Unc-63
226.	1899 . . .	Lyons	Roberts	Blue. Date above serial no.	$85.00	$100.00	$125.00	$200.00	$475.00
226a.	1899 . . .	Lyons	Roberts	Blue. Date below serial no.	80.00	100.00	125.00	180.00	450.00
227.	1899 . . .	Lyons	Treat	Blue. Date below serial no.	80.00	100.00	125.00	180.00	450.00
228.	1899 . . .	Vernon	Treat	Blue. Date below serial no.	80.00	100.00	125.00	180.00	450.00
229.	1899 . . .	Vernon	McClung	Blue. Date below serial no.	80.00	100.00	125.00	180.00	450.00
229a.	1899 . . .	Vernon	McClung	Blue. Date to right of seal	1,250.00	2,250.00	3,000.00	5,000.00	9,000.00
230.	1899 . . .	Napier	McClung	Blue. Date to right of seal	80.00	100.00	125.00	180.00	450.00
231.	1899 . . .	Napier	Thompson . . .	Blue. Date to right of seal	175.00	275.00	400.00	500.00	1,750.00
232.	1899 . . .	Parker	Burke	Blue. Date to right of seal	80.00	100.00	125.00	180.00	450.00
233.	1899 . . .	Teehee	Burke	Blue. Date to right of seal	80.00	100.00	125.00	180.00	450.00
234.	1899 . . .	Elliott	Burke	Blue. Date to right of seal	80.00	100.00	125.00	180.00	450.00
235.	1899 . . .	Elliott	White	Blue. Date to right of seal	80.00	100.00	125.00	180.00	450.00
236.	1899 . . .	Speelman	White	Blue. Date to right of seal	80.00	100.00	125.00	180.00	450.00

Face of Notes 237-239. Gilbert Stuart portrait of George Washington.

Back of Notes 237-239.

No.	Series	Signatures		Seal	VG-8	F-12	VF-20	EF-40	Unc-63
237.	1923	Speelman	White	Blue	$35.00	$40.00	$50.00	$55.00	$125.00
238.	1923	Woods	White	Blue	35.00	40.00	50.00	55.00	125.00
239.	1923	Woods	Tate	Blue	60.00	75.00	100.00	160.00	500.00

Treasury or Coin Notes

Face of Notes 347-349. Bust of Secretary of War (1862-1868) Edwin M. Stanton.

Back of Notes 347-349.

No.	Series	Signatures		Seal	VG-8	F-12	VF-20	EF-40	Unc-63
347.	1890	Rosecrans	Huston	Large Brown ...	$275.00	$525.00	$900.00	$1,350.00	$4,000.00
348.	1890. ...	Rosecrans	Nebeker	Large Brown ...	275.00	525.00	900.00	1,350.00	5,000.00
349.	1890	Rosecrans	Nebeker	Small Red	275.00	525.00	900.00	1,350.00	4,000.00

LARGE-SIZE ONE DOLLAR NOTES

Treasury or Coin Notes

Face of Notes 350-352. Bust of Secretary of War (1862-1868) Edwin M. Stanton.

Back of Notes 350-352.

No.	Series	Signatures		Seal	VG-8	F-12	VF-20	EF-40	Unc-63
350.	1891	Rosecrans	Nebeker	Small Red	$175.00	$225.00	$300.00	$450.00	$1,200.00
351.	1891	Tillman	Morgan	Small Red	175.00	225.00	300.00	450.00	1,000.00
352.	1891	Bruce	Roberts	Small Red	175.00	225.00	300.00	450.00	1,000.00

Federal Reserve Bank Notes

Face of Notes 708-746. Bust of George Washington.

Federal Reserve Bank Notes

Back of Notes 708-746.

No.	Issuing Bank	Series	Government Signatures		Bank Signatures		VG-8	F-12	VF-20	EF-40	Unc-63
708.	Boston	1918	Teehee	Burke	Bullen	Morss	$95.00	$110.00	$125.00	$150.00	$400.00
709.	Boston	1918	Teehee	Burke	Willett	Morss	95.00	140.00	160.00	225.00	575.00
710.	Boston	1918	Elliott	Burke	Willett	Morss	95.00	110.00	125.00	150.00	400.00
711.	New York	1918	Teehee	Burke	Sailer	Strong	95.00	110.00	125.00	150.00	400.00
712.	New York	1918	Teehee	Burke	Hendricks	Strong	95.00	110.00	125.00	150.00	400.00
713.	New York	1918	Elliott	Burke	Hendricks	Strong	95.00	110.00	125.00	150.00	400.00
714.	Philadelphia	1918	Teehee	Burke	Hardt	Passmore	95.00	110.00	125.00	175.00	575.00
715.	Philadelphia	1918	Teehee	Burke	Dyer	Passmore	95.00	110.00	125.00	150.00	400.00
716.	Philadelphia	1918	Elliot	Burke	Dyer	Passmore	95.00	110.00	125.00	175.00	575.00
717.	Philadelphia	1918	Elliott	Burke	Dyer	Norris	95.00	110.00	125.00	150.00	400.00
718.	Cleveland	1918	Teehee	Burke	Baxter	Fancher	95.00	110.00	125.00	150.00	400.00
719.	Cleveland	1918	Teehee	Burke	Davis	Fancher	95.00	110.00	125.00	175.00	575.00
720.	Cleveland	1918	Elliott	Burke	Davis	Fancher	95.00	110.00	125.00	150.00	400.00
721.	Richmond	1918	Teehee	Burke	Keesee	Seay	95.00	110.00	125.00	150.00	400.00
722.	Richmond	1918	Elliott	Burke	Keesee	Seay	95.00	110.00	125.00	175.00	575.00
723.	Atlanta	1918	Teehee	Burke	Pike	McCord	95.00	110.00	125.00	150.00	400.00
724.	Atlanta	1918	Teehee	Burke	Bell	McCord	95.00	110.00	125.00	200.00	625.00
725.	Atlanta	1918	Teehee	Burke	Bell	Wellborn	95.00	110.00	125.00	200.00	625.00
726.	Atlanta	1918	Elliott	Burke	Bell	Wellborn	95.00	110.00	125.00	150.00	400.00
727.	Chicago	1918	Teehee	Burk	McCloud	McDougal	95.00	110.00	125.00	150.00	400.00
728.	Chicago	1918	Teehee	Burke	Cramer	McDougal	95.00	110.00	125.00	150.00	400.00
729.	Chicago	1918	Elliott	Burke	Cramer	McDougal	95.00	110.00	125.00	150.00	400.00
730.	St. Louis	1918	Teehee	Burke	Attebery	Wells	95.00	110.00	125.00	150.00	400.00
731.	St. Louis	1918	Teehee	Burke	Attebery	Biggs	95.00	110.00	125.00	175.00	575.00
732.	St. Louis	1918	Elliott	Burke	Attebery	Biggs	95.00	110.00	125.00	175.00	575.00
733.	St. Louis	1918	Elliott	Burke	White	Biggs	95.00	110.00	125.00	150.00	400.00
734.	Minneapolis	1918	Teehee	Burke	Cook	Wold	95.00	110.00	125.00	150.00	400.00
735.	Minneapolis	1918	Teehee	Burke	Cook	Young	225.00	350.00	750.00	1,350.00	3,500.00
736.	Minneapolis	1918	Elliott	Burke	Cook	Young	95.00	110.00	125.00	150.00	400.00
737.	Kansas City	1918	Teehee	Burke	Anderson	Miller	95.00	110.00	125.00	150.00	400.00
738.	Kansas City	1918	Elliott	Burke	Anderson	Miller	95.00	110.00	125.00	150.00	400.00
739.	Kansas City	1918	Elliot	Burke	Helm	Miller	95.00	110.00	125.00	150.00	400.00
740.	Dallas	1918	Teehee	Burke	Talley	Van Zandt	95.00	110.00	125.00	175.00	575.00
741.	Dallas	1918	Elliott	Burke	Talley	Van Zandt	200.00	350.00	600.00	900.00	2,000.00
742.	Dallas	1918	Elliott	Burke	Lawder	Van Zandt	95.00	110.00	125.00	175.00	575.00
743.	San Francisco	1918	Teehee	Burke	Clerk	Lynch	95.00	110.00	125.00	150.00	400.00
744.	San Francisco	1918	Teehee	Burke	Clerk	Calkins	95.00	110.00	125.00	175.00	575.00
745.	San Francisco	1918	Elliott	Burke	Clerk	Calkins	95.00	110.00	125.00	175.00	575.00
746.	San Francisco	1918	Elliott	Burke	Ambrose	Calkins	95.00	110.00	125.00	150.00	400.00

SMALL-SIZE ONE DOLLAR NOTES

Legal Tender Notes (Red Seal)

Face of Note 1500.

Back of Notes 1500.

No.	Series	Signatures		Quantity Printed	VF-20	Unc-63
1500.	1928	Woods	Woodin	1,872,012	$100.00	$325.00
1500*.	1928	Woods	Woodin	8,000	5,000.00	25,000.00

Silver Certificates (Blue Seal)

Face of Notes 1600-1605.

Back of Notes 1600-1605.

No.	Series	Signatures		Quantity Printed	VF-20	Unc-63
1600.	1928 ...	Tate	Mellon	638,296,908	$25.00	$60.00
1600*.	1928 ...	Tate	Mellon		85.00	500.00
1601.	1928-A .	Woods	Mellon	2,267,809,500	25.00	55.00
1601*.	1928-A .	Woods	Mellon		40.00	375.00
1602.	1928-B .	Woods	Mills	674,597,808	25.00	60.00
1602*.	1928-B .	Woods	Mills		200.00	1,000.00
1603.	1928-C .	Woods	Woodin	5,364,348	200.00	600.00
1603*.	1928-C .	Woods	Woodin	....	4,500.00	30,000.00

Silver Certificates (Blue Seal)

No.	Series	Signatures		Quantity Printed	VF-20	Unc-63
1604.	1928-D ..	Julian	Woodin	14,451,372	$60.00	$450.00
1604*.	1928-D ..	Julian	Woodin		4,000.00	15,000.00
1605.	1928-E ..	Julian	Morgenthau	3,519,324	500.00	2,250.00
1605*.	1928-E ..	Julian	Morgenthau		14,500.00	55,000.00

Face of Note 1606.

Back of Note 1606.

No.	Series	Signatures		Quantity Printed	VF-20	Unc-63
1606.	1934	Julian	Morgenthau	682,176,000	$20.00	$75.00
1606*.	1934	Julian	Morgenthau	7,680,000	75.00	650.00

Face of Notes 1607-1616.

Back of Notes 1607-1616.

No.	Series	Signatures		Quantity Printed	VF-20	Unc-63
1607.	1935	Julian	Morgenthau	1,681,552,000	$3.50	$25.00
1607*.	1935	Julian	Morgenthau		60.00	400.00
1608.	1935-A ..	Julian	Morgenthau	6,111,832,000	3.50	10.00
1608*.	1935-A ..	Julian	Morgenthau		5.00	55.00

SMALL-SIZE ONE DOLLAR NOTES

Silver Certificates (Blue Seal)

No.	Series	Signatures	Quantity Printed	VF-20	Unc-63
1609.	1935-A ..	Julian Morgenthau (R)	1,184,000	$75.00	$350.00
1609*.	1935-A ..	Julian Morgenthau (R)	12,000	1,500.00	5,000.00
1610.	1935-A ..	Julian Morgenthau (S)	1,184,000	70.00	300.00
1610*.	1935-A ..	Julian Morgenthau (S)	12,000	1,500.00	5,000.00

Notes issued for Hawaii after the attack on Pearl Harbor

Face of Note 2300.

Back of Note 2300. Silver Certificate Surcharged HAWAII *on both sides,*
with signatures of Julian and Morgenthau, and with a brown Seal (not blue).

No.	Denomination	Series	Quantity Printed	VF-20	Unc-63
2300.	One Dollar	1935-A	35,052,000	$40.00	$150.00
2300*.	One Dollar	1935-A	....	500.00	2,500.00

Notes issued for the Armed Forces in Europe and North Africa

Face of Note 2306. Silver Certificates with signatures of Julian and Morgenthau
and with blue serial numbers and a yellow seal (not blue).

Back of Note 2306.

Notes issued for the Armed Forces in Europe and North Africa

No.	Denomination	Series	Design No.	Quantity Printed	VF-20	Unc-63
2306.	One Dollar	1935-A	197	26,916,000	$32.50	$150.00
2306*.	One Dollar	1935-A	197		500.00	2,500.00

Regular Issue Silver Certificates (continued from note 1610)

No.	Series	Signatures		Quantity Printed	VF-20	Unc-63
1611.	1935-B	Julian	Vinson	806,612,000	$3.50	$20.00
1611*.	1935-B	Julian	Vinson		40.00	200.00
1612.	1935-C	Julian	Snyder	3,088,108,000	3.00	15.00
1612*.	1935-C	Julian	Snyder		15.00	65.00
1613W.	1935-D	Clark	Snyder		3.00	12.50
1613W*.	1935-D	Clark	Snyder	4,656,968,000	15.00	70.00
1613N.	1935-D	Clark	Snyder		3.00	12.50
1613N*.	1935-D	Clark	Snyder		10.00	50.00
1614.	1935-E	Priest	Humphrey	5,134,056,000	3.00	12.50
1614*.	1935-E	Priest	Humphrey		5.00	17.50
1615.	1935-F	Priest	Anderson	1,173,360,000	3.00	12.50
1615*.	1935-F	Priest	Anderson	53,200,000	5.00	17.50
1616.	1935-G	Smith	Dillon	194,600,000	3.00	12.50
1616*.	1935-G	Smith	Dillon	8,640,000	7.50	30.00

*NOTE: The Series 1935-D notes were produced with backs of two different widths, with the wide variety 1/16 inch larger than the narrow one. Notes with the wide design have a four-digit plate number of 5015.

Face of Notes 1617-1621.

Back of Notes 1617-1621.

No.	Series	Signatures		Quantity Printed	VF-20	Unc-63
1617.	1935-G	Smith	Dillon	31,320,000	$5.00	$40.00
1617*.	1935-G	Smith	Dillon	1,080,000	30.00	200.00
1618.	1935-H	Granahan	Dillon	30,520,000	3.50	17.50
1618*.	1935-H	Granahan	Dillon	1,436,000	5.00	35.00
1619.	1957	Priest	Anderson	2,609,600,000	3.00	9.00
1619*.	1957	Priest	Anderson	307,640,000	4.00	15.00
1620.	1957-A	Smith	Dillon	1,594,080,000	3.00	9.00
1620*.	1957-A	Smith	Dillon	94,720,000	4.00	15.00
1621.	1957-B	Granahan	Dillon	718,400,000	3.00	9.00
1621*	1957-B	Granahan	Dillon	49,280,000	4.00	15.00

SMALL-SIZE ONE DOLLAR NOTES

Federal Reserve Notes (Green Seal)

Face of Notes 1900-.

Back of Notes 1900-.

Series of 1963
Signatures of Granahan and Dillon

No.	Issuing Bank	Quantity Printed	VF-20	Unc-63
1900-A.	Boston	87,680,000		$5.00
1900-A*.	Boston	6,400,000	$4.00	15.00
1900-B.	New York	219,200,000		5.00
1900-B*.	New York	15,360,000	4.00	8.00
1900-C.	Philadelphia	23,680,000		5.00
1900-C*.	Philadelphia	10,880,000	4.00	8.00
1900-D.	Cleveland	108,320,000		5.00
1900-D.*	Cleveland	8,320,000	4.00	8.00
1900-E.	Richmond	159,520,000		5.00
1900-E*.	Richmond	12,160,000	4.00	8.00
1900-F.	Atlanta	221,120,000		5.00
1900-F*.	Atlanta	19,200,000	4.00	8.00
1900-G.	Chicago	279,360,000		5.00
1900-G*.	Chicago	19,840,000	4.00	8.00
1900-H.	St. Louis	99,840,000		5.00
1900-H*.	St. Louis	9,600,000	4.00	9.50
1900-I.	Minneapolis	44,800,000		5.00
1900-I*.	Minneapolis	5,120,000	4.00	15.00
1900-J.	Kansas City	88,960,000		5.00
1900-J*.	Kansas City	8,960,000	4.00	8.00
1900-K.	Dallas	85,760,000		5.00
1900-K*.	Dallas	8,960,000	4.00	8.00
1900-L.	San Francisco	199,999,999		5.00
1900-L*.	San Francisco	14,720,000	9.00	30.00

Series of 1963-A
Signatures of Granahan and Fowler

No.	Issuing Bank	Quantity Printed	VF-20	Unc-63
1901-A.	Boston	319,840,000	$2.00	$4.50
1901-A*.	Boston	19,840,000	4.00	8.00
1901-B.	New York	657,600,000	2.00	4.50

Federal Reserve Notes (Green Seal)

No.	Issuing Bank	Quantity Printed	VF-20	Unc-63
1901-B*.	New York	47,680,000	$4.00	$8.00
1901-C.	Philadelphia	375,520,000		4.50
1901-C*.	Philadelphia	26,240,000	4.00	8.00
1901-D.	Cleveland	337,120,000		4.50
1901-D*.	Cleveland	21,120,000	4.00	8.00
1901-E.	Richmond	532,000,000		4.50
1901-E*.	Richmond	41,600,000	4.00	8.00
1901-F.	Atlanta	636,480,000		4.50
1901-F*.	Atlanta	40,960,000	4.00	8.00
1901-G.	Chicago	784,480,000		4.50
1901-G*.	Chicago	52,640,000	4.00	8.00
1901-H.	St. Louis	264,000,000		4.50
1901-H*.	St. Louis	17,920,000	4.00	8.00
1901-I.	Minneapolis	112,160,000		4.50
1901-I*.	Minneapolis	7,040,000	4.00	12.00
1901-J.	Kansas City	219,200,000		4.50
1901-J*.	Kansas City	14,720,000	4.00	8.00
1901-K.	Dallas	288,960,000		4.50
1901-K*.	Dallas	19,184,000	4.00	8.00
1901-L.	San Francisco	576,800,000		4.50
1901-L*.	San Francisco	43,040,000	4.00	8.00

Series of 1963-B
Signatures of Granahan and Barr

No.	Issuing Bank	Quantity Printed	VF-20	Unc-63
1902-B.	New York	123,040,000		$5.50
1902-B*.	New York	3,680,000	$3.00	13.00
1902-E.	Richmond	93,600,000		5.50
1902-E*.	Richmond	3,200,000	3.00	13.00
1902-G.	Chicago	91,040,000		5.50
1902-G*.	Chicago	2,400,000	3.00	18.00
1902-J.	Kansas City	44,800,000		5.50
1902-L.	San Francisco	106,400,000		5.50
1902-L*.	San Francisco	3,040,000	3.00	22.00

Series of 1969
Signatures of Elston and Kennedy (with new Treasury seal)

No.	Issuing Bank	Quantity Printed	VF-20	Unc-63
1903-A.	Boston	99,200,000		$4.50
1903-A*.	Boston	5,120,000	$4.25	7.00
1903-B.	New York	269,120,000		4.50
1903-B*.	New York	14,080,000	4.25	7.00
1903-C.	Philadelphia	68,480,000		4.50
1903-C*.	Philadelphia	3,776,000	4.25	7.00
1903-D.	Cleveland	120,480,000		4.50
1903-D*.	Cleveland	5,760,000	4.25	7.00
1903-E.	Richmond	250,560,000		4.50
1903-E*.	Richmond	10,880,000	4.25	7.00
1903-F.	Atlanta	185,120,000		4.50
1903-F*.	Atlanta	7,680,000	4.25	7.00
1903-G.	Chicago	359,520,000		4.50
1903-G*.	Chicago	12,160,000	4.25	7.00
1903-H.	St. Louis	74,880,000		4.50
1903-H*.	St. Louis	3,840,000	3.75	7.00
1903-I.	Minneapolis	48,000,000		4.50
1903-I*.	Minneapolis	1,920,000	6.00	15.00
1903-J.	Kansas City	95,360,000		4.50
1903-J*.	Kansas City	5,760,000	3.75	7.00
1903-K.	Dallas	113,440,000		4.50
1903-K*.	Dallas	5,120,000	3.75	7.00
1903-L.	San Francisco	226,240,000		4.50
1903-L*.	San Francisco	9,600,000	3.75	7.00

SMALL-SIZE ONE DOLLAR NOTES

Federal Reserve Notes (Green Seal)

Series of 1969-A
Signatures of Kabis and Kennedy

No.	Issuing Bank	Quantity Printed	VF-20	Unc-63
1904-A.	Boston	40,480,000		$4.50
1904-A*.	Boston	1,120,000	$4.50	7.50
1904-B.	New York	122,400,000		4.50
1904-B*.	New York	6,240,000	4.50	7.50
1904-C.	Philadelphia	44,960,000		4.50
1904-C*.	Philadelphia	1,760,000	4.50	7.50
1904-D.	Cleveland	30,080,000		4.50
1904-D*.	Cleveland	1,280,000	4.50	7.50
1904-E.	Richmond	66,080,000		4.50
1904-E*.	Richmond	3,200,000	4.50	7.50
1904-F.	Atlanta	70,560,000		4.50
1904-F*.	Atlanta	2,400,000	4.50	7.50
1904-G.	Chicago	75,680,000		4.50
1904-G*.	Chicago	4,480,000	4.50	7.50
1904-H.	St. Louis	41,420,000		4.50
1904-H*.	St. Louis	1,280,000	4.50	9.00
1904-I.	Minneapolis	21,760,000		4.50
1904-I*.	Minneapolis	640,000	7.00	20.00
1904-J.	Kansas City	40,480,000		4.50
1904-J*.	Kansas City	1,120,000	5.00	8.50
1904-K.	Dallas	27,520,000		4.50
1904-L.	San Francisco	51,840,000		4.50
1904-L*.	San Francisco	3,840,000	4.50	7.50

Series of 1969-B
Signatures of Kabis and Connally

No.	Issuing Bank	Quantity Printed	VF-20	Unc-63
1905-A.	Boston	94,720,000		$4.50
1905-A*.	Boston	1,920,000	$3.00	8.00
1905-B.	New York	329,440,000		4.50
1905-B*.	New York	7,040,000	3.00	7.00
1905-C.	Philadelphia	133,280,000		4.50
1905-C*.	Philadelphia	3,200,000	3.00	8.00
1905-D.	Cleveland	91,520,000		4.50
1905-D*.	Cleveland	4,480,000	3.00	8.00
1905-E.	Richmond	180,000,000		4.50
1905-E*.	Richmond	3,840,000	3.00	8.00
1905-F.	Atlanta	200,000,000		4.50
1905-F*.	Atlanta	3,840,000	3.00	8.00
1905-G.	Chicago	204,480,000		4.50
1905-G*.	Chicago	4,480,000	3.00	8.00
1905-H.	St. Louis	59,520,000		4.50
1905-H*.	St. Louis	1,920,000	3.00	8.00
1905-I.	Minneapolis	33,920,000		4.50
1905-I*.	Minneapolis	640,000	7.00	25.00
1905-J.	Kansas City	67,200,000		4.50
1905-J*.	Kansas City	2,560,000	3.00	8.00
1905-K.	Dallas	116,640,000		4.50
1905-K*.	Dallas	5,120,000	3.00	8.00
1905-L.	San Francisco	208,960,000		4.50
1905-L*.	San Francisco	5,760,000	3.00	8.00

Series of 1969-C
Signatures of Banuelos and Connally

No.	Issuing Bank	Quantity Printed	VF-20	Unc-63
1906-B.	New York	49,920,000		$6.00
1906-D.	Cleveland	15,520,000		7.00
1906-D*.	Cleveland	480,000	$12.00	20.00

Federal Reserve Notes (Green Seal)

No.	Issuing Bank	Quantity Printed	VF-20	Unc-63
1906-E.	Richmond	61,600,000		$6.00
1906-E*.	Richmond	480,000	$5.00	35.00
1906-F.	Atlanta	60,960,000		6.00
1906-F*.	Atlanta	3,680,000	5.00	20.00
1906-G.	Chicago	137,120,000		6.00
1906-G*.	Chicago	1,748,000	5.00	20.00
1906-H.	St. Louis	23,680,000		6.00
1906-H*.	St. Louis	640,000	5.00	20.00
1906-I.	Minneapolis	25,600,000		6.00
1906-I*.	Minneapolis	640,000	5.00	35.00
1906-J.	Kansas City	38,560,000		6.00
1906-J*.	Kansas City	1,120,000	5.00	30.00
1906-K.	Dallas	29,440,000		6.00
1906-K*.	Dallas	640,000	12.00	40.00
1906-L.	San Francisco	101,280,000		6.00
1906-L*.	San Francisco	2,400,000	50.00	180.00

Series of 1969-D
Signatures of Banuelos and Shultz

No.	Issuing Bank	Quantity Printed	VF-20	Unc-63
1907-A.	Boston	187,040,000		$5.50
1907-A*.	Boston	1,120,000	$4.00	14.00
1907-B.	New York	468,480,000		5.50
1907-B*.	New York	4,480,000	4.00	8.00
1907-C.	Philadelphia	218,560,000		5.50
1907-C*.	Philadelphia	4,320,000	4.00	9.00
1907-D.	Cleveland	161,440,000		5.50
1907-D*.	Cleveland	2,400,000	4.00	9.00
1907-E.	Richmond	374,240,000		5.50
1907-E*.	Richmond	8,480,000	4.00	9.00
1907-F.	Atlanta	377,440,000		5.50
1907-F*.	Atlanta	5,280,000	4.00	9.00
1907-G.	Chicago	378,080,000		5.50
1907-G*.	Chicago	5,270,000	4.00	9.00
1907-H.	St. Louis	168,480,000		5.50
1907-H*.	St. Louis	1,760,000	4.00	11.00
1907-I.	Minneapolis	83,200,000		5.50
1907-J.	Kansas City	185,760,000		5.50
1907-J*.	Kansas City	3,040,000	4.00	9.00
1907-K.	Dallas	158,240,000		5.50
1907-K*.	Dallas	6,240,000	4.00	9.00
1907-L.	San Francisco	400,640,000		5.50
1907-L*.	San Francisco	6,400,000	4.00	9.00

Series of 1974
Signatures of Neff and Simon

No.	Issuing Bank	Quantity Printed	VF-20	Unc-63
1908-A.	Boston	269,760,000		$4.50
1908-A*.	Boston	2,400,000	$4.00	7.00
1908-B.	New York	740,320,000		4.50
1908-B*.	New York	8,800,000	4.00	7.00
1908-C.	Philadelphia	308,800,000		4.50
1908-C*.	Philadelphia	1,600,000	4.00	20.00
1908-D.	Cleveland	240,960,000		4.50
1908-D*.	Cleveland	960,000	13.00	25.00
1908-E.	Richmond	644,000,000		4.50
1908-E*.	Richmond	4,960,000	4.00	7.00
1908-F.	Atlanta	599,680,000		4.50
1908-F*.	Atlanta	5,632,000	4.00	7.00
1908-G.	Chicago	473,600,000		4.50

SMALL-SIZE ONE DOLLAR NOTES

Federal Reserve Notes (Green Seal)

No.	Issuing Bank	Quantity Printed	VF-20	Unc-63
1908-G*.	Chicago	4,992,000	$4.00	$7.00
1908-H.	St. Louis	291,520,000		4.50
1908-H*.	St. Louis	2,880,000	4.00	12.00
1908-I.	Minneapolis	144,160,000		4.50
1908-I*.	Minneapolis	480,000	17.50	35.00
1908-J.	Kansas City	223,520,000		4.50
1908-J*.	Kansas City	2,144,000	4.00	10.00
1908-K.	Dallas	330,560,000		4.50
1908-K*.	Dallas	1,216,000	4.00	10.00
1908-L.	San Francisco	736,960,000		4.50
1908-L*.	San Francisco	3,520,000	4.00	7.00

Series of 1977
Signatures of Morton and Blumenthal

No.	Issuing Bank	Quantity Printed	VF-20	Unc-63
1909-A.	Boston	188,160,000		$4.50
1909-A*.	Boston	3,072,000	$8.00	15.00
1909-B.	New York	635,520,000		4.50
1909-B*.	New York	10,112,000	4.00	7.00
1909-C.	Philadelphia	216,960,000		4.50
1909-C*.	Philadelphia	4,480,000	4.00	7.00
1909-D.	Cleveland	213,120,000		4.50
1909-D*.	Cleveland	3,328,000	4.00	7.00
1909-E.	Richmond	418,560,000		4.50
1909-E*.	Richmond	6,400,000	4.00	7.00
1909-F.	Atlanta	565,120,000		4.50
1909-F*.	Atlanta	8,960,000	4.00	7.00
1909-G.	Chicago	615,680,000		4.50
1909-G*.	Chicago	9,472,000	4.00	7.00
1909-H.	St. Louis	199,680,000		4.50
1909-H*.	St. Louis	2,048,000	4.00	7.00
1909-I.	Minneapolis	115,200,000		4.50
1909-I*.	Minneapolis	2,944,000	4.00	7.00
1909-J.	Kansas City	223,360,000		4.50
1909-J*.	Kansas City	3,840,000	4.00	7.00
1909-K.	Dallas	289,280,000		4.50
1909-K*.	Dallas	4,608,000	4.00	7.00
1909-L.	San Francisco	516,480,000		4.50
1909-L*.	San Francisco	8,320,000	4.00	7.00

Series of 1977-A
Signatures of Morton and Miller

No.	Issuing Bank	Quantity Printed	VF-20	Unc-63
1910-A.	Boston	204,800,000	$2.00	$4.50
1910-A*.	Boston	2,432,000	3.50	25.00
1910-B.	New York	592,000,000	2.00	4.50
1910-B*.	New York	9,472,000	3.50	7.00
1910-C.	Philadelphia	196,480,000	2.00	4.50
1910-C*.	Philadelphia	2,688,000	3.50	7.00
1910-D.	Cleveland	174,720,000	2.00	4.50
1910-D*.	Cleveland	2,560,000	3.50	7.00
1910-E.	Richmond	377,600,000	2.00	4.50
1910-E*.	Richmond	6,400,000	3.50	7.00
1910-F.	Atlanta	396,160,000	2.00	4.50
1910-F*.	Atlanta	5,376,000	3.50	7.00
1910-G.	Chicago	250,680,000	2.00	4.50
1910-G*.	Chicago	2,560,000	3.50	7.00
1910-H.	St. Louis	103,680,000	2.00	4.50
1910-H*.	St. Louis	1,664,000	3.50	7.00
1910-I.	Minneapolis	38,400,000	2.00	4.50
1910-I*.	Minneapolis	384,000	3.50	7.00
1910-J.	Kansas City	266,880,000	2.00	4.50
1910-J*.	Kansas City	4,864,000	3.50	7.00

Federal Reserve Notes (Green Seal)

No.	Issuing Bank	Quantity Printed	VF-20	Unc-63
1910-K.	Dallas	313,600,000		$4.50
1910-K*.	Dallas	6,016,000	$3.50	7.00
1910-L.	San Francisco	432,280,000		4.50
1910-L*.	San Francisco	5,888,000	3.50	7.00

Series of 1981
Signatures of Buchanan and Regan

No.	Issuing Bank	Quantity Printed	VF-20	Unc-63
1911-A.	Boston	308,480,000	$1.75	$4.50
1911-A*.	Boston	3,200,000	5.00	9.00
1911-B.	New York	963,840,000	1.75	4.50
1911-B*.	New York	11,776,000	5.00	9.00
1911-C.	Philadelphia	359,680,000	1.75	4.50
1911-C*.	Philadelphia	1,536,000	15.00	125.00
1911-D.	Cleveland	295,680,000	1.75	4.50
1911-D*.	Cleveland	1,792,000	7.50	13.00
1911-E.	Richmond	603,520,000	1.75	4.50
1911-E*.	Richmond	3,840,000	5.00	9.00
1911-F.	Atlanta	741,760,000	1.75	4.50
1911-F*.	Atlanta	3,200,000	5.00	9.00
1911-G.	Chicago	629,760,000	1.75	4.50
1911-G*.	Chicago	5,184,000	5.00	9.00
1911-H.	St. Louis	163,840,000	1.75	4.50
1911-H*.	St. Louis	1,056,000	7.50	13.00
1911-I.	Minneapolis	105,600,000	1.75	4.50
1911-I*.	Minneapolis	1,152,000	7.50	13.00
1911-J.	Kansas City	302,080,000	1.75	4.50
1911-J*.	Kansas City	3,216,000	5.00	9.00
1911-K.	Dallas	385,920,000	1.75	4.50
1911-K*.	Dallas	1,920,000	5.00	9.00
1911-L.	San Francisco	677,760,000	1.75	4.50
1911-L*.	San Francisco	4,992,000	5.00	9.00

Series of 1981-A
Signatures of Ortega and Regan

No.	Issuing Bank	Quantity Printed	VF-20	Unc-63
1912-A.	Boston	204,800,000		$4.50
1912-B.	New York	537,600,000		4.50
1912-B*.	New York	9,216,000	$5.00	15.00
1912-C.	Philadelphia	99,200,000		4.50
1912-D.	Cleveland	188,800,000		4.50
1912-E.	Richmond	441,600,000		4.50
1912-E*.	Richmond	6,400,000	5.00	15.00
1912-F.	Atlanta	483,200,000		4.50
1912-G.	Chicago	482,000,000		4.50
1912-G*.	Chicago	3,200,000	5.00	15.00
1912-H.	St. Louis	182,400,000		4.50
1912-I.	Minneapolis	122,400,000		4.50
1912-J.	Kansas City	176,000,000		4.50
1912-K.	Dallas	188,800,000		4.50
1912-K*.	Dallas	3,200,000	300.00	750.00
1912-L.	San Francisco	659,000,000		4.50
1912-L*.	San Francisco	3,200,000	5.00	15.00

Series of 1985
Signatures of Ortega and Baker

No.	Issuing Bank	Quantity Printed	Unc-63
1913-A.	Boston	553,600,000	$4.50
1913-B.	New York	1,795,200,000	4.50
1913-C.	Philadelphia	422,400,000	4.50
1913-D.	Cleveland	636,800,000	4.50
1913-E.	Richmond	1,190,400,000	4.50

SMALL-SIZE ONE DOLLAR NOTES

Federal Reserve Notes (Green Seal)
Series of 1985
Signatures of Ortega and Baker

No.	Issuing Bank	Quantity Printed	VF-20	Unc-63
1913-E*.	Richmond	6,400,000	$6.00	$11.00
1913-F.	Atlanta	1,414,400,000		4.50
1913-G.	Chicago	1,190,400,000		4.50
1913-G*.	Chicago	5,120,000	5.00	9.00
1913-H.	St. Louis	400,000,000		4.50
1913-H*.	St. Louis	640,000	450.00	750.00
1913-I.	Minneapolis	246,400,000		4.50
1913-I*.	Minneapolis	3,200,000	6.00	11.00
1913-J.	Kansas City	390,400,000		4.50
1913-K.	Dallas	697,600,000		4.50
1913-K*.	Dallas	3,200,000	5.00	9.00
1913-L.	San Francisco	1,881,600,000		4.50
1913-L*.	San Francisco	9,600,000	5.00	9.00

Series of 1988
Signatures of Ortega and Brady

No.	Issuing Bank	Quantity Printed	VF-20	Unc-63
1914-A.	Boston	214,400,000		$4.50
1914-A*.	Boston	3,200,000		12.00
1914-B.	New York	921,600,000		4.50
1914-B*.	New York	2,560,000		12.00
1914-C.	Philadelphia	96,000,000		4.50
1914-D.	Cleveland	195,200,000		4.50
1914-E	Richmond	728,800,000		4.50
1914-E*.	Richmond	2,688,000		12.00
1914-F.	Atlanta	390,400,000		4.50
1914-F*.	Atlanta	3,840,000	$400.00	900.00
1914-G.	Chicago	416,400,000		4.50
1914-H.	St. Louis	396,800,000		4.50
1914-I.	Minneapolis	246,400,000		4.50
1914-J.	Kansas City	390,400,000		4.50
1914-J*.	Kansas City	3,200,000		12.00
1914-K.	Dallas	80,000,000		4.50
1914-K*.	Dallas	1,248,000		12.00
1914-L.	San Francisco	585,600,000		4.50
1914-L*.	San Francisco	3,200,000		12.00

Series of 1988-A
Signatures of Villalpando and Brady
Printed in Washington, DC, on sheet-fed presses

No.	Issuing Bank	Quantity Printed	Unc-63
1915-A.	Boston	582,400,000	$4.50
1915-B.	New York	2,161,344,000	4.50
1915-B*.	New York	12,800,000	7.00
1915-C.	Philadelphia	472,320,000	4.50
1915-D.	Cleveland	454,400,00	4.50
1915-D*.	Cleveland	6,400,000	7.00
1915-E.	Richmond	1,593,600,000	4.50
1915-E*.	Richmond	10,880,000	7.00
1915-F.	Atlanta	1,747,200,000	4.50
1915-F*.	Atlanta	12,800,000	7.00
1915-G.	Chicago	1,728,000,000	4.50
1915-G*.	Chicago	19,200,000	15.00
1915-H.	St. Louis	410,400,000	4.50
1915-H*.	St. Louis	3,200,000	50.00
1915-I.	Minneapolis	76,800,000	4.50
1915-I*.	Minneapolis	5,760,000	15.00
1915-J.	Kansas City	96,000,000	4.50
1915-K.	Dallas	211,200,000	4.50
1915-L.	San Francisco	280,600,000	4.50

Federal Reserve Notes (Green Seal)

Notes printed at the Fort Worth, Texas facility may be identified by a small "FW" on the right face, next to the plate. Check letter-number.

No.	Issuing Bank	Quantity Printed	Unc-63
1916-F.	Atlanta	533,000,000	$4.50
1916-G.	Chicago	748,800,000	4.50
1916-G*.	Chicago	6,400,000	10.00
1916-H.	St. Louis	326,400,000	4.50
1916-I.	Minneapolis	844,800,000	4.50
1916-I*.	Minneapolis	7,680,000	15.00
1916-J.	Kansas City	300,800,000	4.50
1916-K.	Dallas	761,000,000	4.50
1916-K*.	Dallas	3,200,000	15.00
1916-L.	San Francisco	2,009,600,000	4.50
1916-L*.	San Francisco	19,200,000	7.00

Series of 1988-A
Signatures of Villalpando and Brady
Printed in Washington, DC, on a web-fed press

Notes printed by this method may be identified by the absence of the check letter-number on the face and the placement of a check number only (no letter) on the back, to the right of "In God We Trust."

SMALL-SIZE ONE DOLLAR NOTES

Federal Reserve Notes (Green Seal)

No.	Issuing Bank	Quantity Printed	VF-20	Unc-63
1917-A.	Boston	64,000,000		
	Blocks AE, AF, AG		$5.00	$35.00
1917-B.	New York	1,920,000		
	Block BL		300.00	1,300.00
1917-C.	Philadelphia	12,800,000		
	Block CA			35.00
1917-E.	Richmond	38,400,000	5.00	40.00
	Blocks EI, EK		5.00	35.00
1917-F.	Atlanta	89,600,000		
	Block FL		15.00	125.00
	Block FM		15.00	125.00
	Block FN		15.00	125.00
	Block FU		5.00	30.00
	Block FV		5.00	35.00
1917-F*.	Atlanta	640,000	600.00	1,250.00
1917-G.	Chicago	19,200,000		
	Block GP		10.00	70.00
	Block GQ		25.00	125.00

Series of 1993
Signatures of Withrow and Bentsen
Printed in Washington, DC

No.	Issuing Bank	Quantity Printed	VF-20	Unc-63
1918-A.	Boston	140,800,000		$2.50
1918-B.	New York	716,800,000		2.50
1918-B*.	New York	2,240,000		5.00
1918-C.	Philadelphia	70,400,000		2.50
1918-C*.	Philadelphia	640,000	$40.00	175.00
1918-D.	Cleveland	108,800,000		2.50
1918-E.	Richmond	524,800,000		2.50
1918-F.	Atlanta	787,200,000		2.50
1918-F*.	Atlanta	16,000,000		7.00
1918-G.	Chicago	96,000,000		2.50
1905-H.	St. Louis	76,800,000		2.50
1918-L.	San Francisco	128,000,000		2.50

Series of 1993
Signatures of Withrow and Bentsen
Printed at the Western Facility (Fort Worth, Texas)

No.	Issuing Bank	Quantity Printed	VF-20	Unc-63
1919-G.	Chicago	646,400,000		$2.50
1919-G*.	Chicago	8,960,000		6.00
1919-H.	St. Louis	121,600,000		2.50
1919-I.	Minneapolis	25,600,000	$20.00	100.00
1919-K.	Dallas	620,800,000		2.50
1919-K*.	Dallas	19,200,000		7.50
1919-L.	San Francisco	1,171,200,000		2.50

Series of 1993
Signatures of Withrow and Bentsen
Printed in Washington, DC, on a web-fed press

No.	Issuing Bank	Quantity Printed	Unc-63
1920-B.	New York	12,800,000	
	Block BH		$15.00
1920-C.	Philadelphia	12,800,000	
	Block CA		15.00

Federal Reserve Notes (Green Seal)
Series of 1995
Signatures of Withrow and Rubin
Printed in Washington, DC

No.	Issuing Bank	Quantity Printed	VF-20	Unc-63
1921-A.	Boston	1,134,745,600		$2.50
1921-A*.	Boston	12,160,000		4.00
1921-B.	New York	2,062,080,000		2.50
1921-B*.	New York	9,600,000		4.00
1921-C.	Philadelphia	428,800,000		2.50
1921-C*.	Philadelphia	9,600,000		4.00
1921-D.	Cleveland	1,452,800,000		2.50
1921-D*.	Cleveland	7,040,000		4.00
1921-E.	Richmond	1,831,400,000		2.50
1921-E*.	Richmond	7,040,000		4.00
1921-F.	Atlanta	1,279,360,000		2.50
1921-F*.	Atlanta	19,840,000		4.00
1921-G	Chicago	38,400,000		3.00
1921-H.	St. Louis	76,800,000		2.50
1921-I.	St. Louis	76,800,000		2.50
1921-J.	Kansas City	83,200,000		2.50
1922-L.	San Francisco	44,800,000		2.50

Series of 1995
Signatures of Withrow and Rubin
Printed at the Western Facility (Fort Worth, Texas)

No.	Issuing Bank	Quantity Printed	VF-20	Unc-63
1922-C.	Philadelphia	76,800,000		$2.50
1922-C*.	Philadelphia	3,200,000		4.00
1922-D.	Cleveland	134,400,000		2.50
1922-F.	Atlanta	452,480,000		2.50
1922-F*.	Atlanta	3,584,000		4.00
1922-G.	Chicago	1,459,200,000		2.50
1922-G*.	Chicago	10,240,000		4.00
1922-H.	St. Louis	921,600,000		2.50
1922-I.	Minneapolis	1,310,720,000		2.50
1922-I*.	Minneapolis	14,080,000		4.00
1922-J.	Kansas City	262,400,000		2.50
1922-J*.	Kansas City	6,400,000		4.00
1922-K.	Dallas	1,273,600,000		2.50
1922-K*.	Dallas	1,440,000		10.00
1922-L.	San Francisco	2,252,800,000		2.50
1922-L*.	San Francisco	6,400,000		6.00

Series of 1995
Signatures of Withrow and Rubin
Printed in Washington, DC, on a web-fed press

No.	Issuing Bank	Quantity Printed	VF-20	Unc-63
1923-A.	Boston	18,560,000		
	Blocks AC, AD		$3.00	$12.50
1923-B.	New York	12,800,000		
	Block BH		3.00	12.50
1923-D.	Cleveland	6,400,000		
	Block DC		2.00	10.00
1923-F.	Atlanta	12,800,000		
	Block FD		3.00	12.50

SMALL-SIZE ONE DOLLAR NOTES

Federal Reserve Notes (Green Seal)

Series of 1999
Signatures of Withrow and Summers
Printed in Washington, DC

No.	Issuing Bank	Quantity Printed	Unc-63
1924-A.	Boston	556,800,000	$2.00
1924-A*.	Boston	3,840,000	3.00
1924-B.	New York	1,491,600,000	2.00
1924-B*.	New York	10,240,000	3.00
1924-C.	Philadelphia	1,062,400,000	2.00
1924-C*.	Philadelphia	13,760,000	3.00
1924-D.	Cleveland	268,800,000	2.00
1924-D*.	Cleveland	640,000	30.00
1924-E.	Richmond	748,800,000	2.00
1924-E*.	Richmond	7,040,000	6.00
1924-F.	Atlanta	780,800,000	2.00

Series of 1999
Signatures of Withrow and Summers
Printed at the Western Facility (Fort Worth, Texas)

No.	Issuing Bank	Quantity Printed	Unc-63
1925-F.	Atlanta	1,062,400,000	$2.00
1925-F*.	Atlanta	640,000	50.00
1925-G.	Chicago	864,000,000	2.00
1925-H.	St. Louis	89,600,000	2.00
1925-H*.	St. Louis	7,040,000	6.00
1925-I.	Minneapolis	12,800,000	2.00
1925-J.	Kansas City	339,200,000	2.00
1925-J*.	Kansas City	57,600,000	6.00
1925-K.	Dallas	934,400,000	3.00
1925-L.	San Francisco	1,920,000,000	2.00
1925-L*.	San Francisco	19,840,000	6.00

Series of 2001
Signatures of Marin and O'Neill
Printed in Washington, DC

No.	Issuing Bank	Quantity Printed	VF-20	Unc-63
1926-A.	Boston	448,000,000		$2.00
1926-A*.	Boston	3,520,000		4.00
1926-B.	New York	678,400,000		2.00
1926-C.	Philadelphia	550,400,000		2.00
1926-C*.	Philadelphia	6,400,000		4.00
1926-D.	Cleveland	307,200,000		2.00
1926-E.	Richmond	70,400,000		2.00
1926-F.	Atlanta	499,200,000		2.00
1926-F*.	Atlanta	3,520,000		4.00
1926-H.	St. Louis	147,200,000		2.00
1926-H*.	St. Louis	640,000	$20.00	60.00
1926-I.	Minneapolis	6,400,000		10.00
1926-J.	Kansas City	19,200,000		2.00

Series of 2001
Signatures of Marin and O'Neill
Printed at the Western Facility (Fort Worth, Texas)

No.	Issuing Bank	Quantity Printed	Unc-63
1927-F.	Atlanta	38,400,000	$2.00
1927-G.	Chicago	371,200,000	2.00
1927-G*.	Chicago	4,680,000	40.00
1927-H.	St. Louis	128,000,000	7.00

Federal Reserve Notes (Green Seal)

No.	Issuing Bank	Quantity Printed	Unc-63
1927-I.	Minneapolis	57,600,000	$3.00
1927-J.	Kansas City	160,000,000	2.00
1927-K.	Dallas	300,800,000	2.00
1927-K*.	Dallas	3,200,000	9.00
1927-L.	San Francisco	1,158,500,000	2.00
1927-L*.	San Francisco	3,200,000	3.00

Series of 2003
Signatures of Marin and Snow
Printed in Washington, DC

No.	Issuing Bank	Quantity Printed	Unc-63
1928-A.	Boston		Current
1928-A*.	Boston		$4.00
1928-B.	New York		Current
1928-B*.	New York		5.00
1928-C.	Philadelphia		Current
1928-D.	Cleveland		Current
1928-D.*	Cleveland	320,000	25.00
1928-E.	Richmond	268,800,000	Current
1928-E*.	Richmond	320,000	25.00
1928-F.	Atlanta	153,600,000	Current
1928-F*.	Atlanta	320,000	25.00

Series of 2003
Signatures of Marin and Snow
Printed at the Western Facility (Fort Worth, Texas)

No.	Issuing Bank	Quantity Printed	Unc-63
1929-F.	Atlanta	294,400,000	Current
1929-F*.	Atlanta		—
1929-G.	Chicago		Current
1929-G.*	Chicago		$4.00
1929-H.	St. Louis		25.00
1929-I.	Minneapolis	12,800,000	Current
1929-J.	Kansas City	32,000,000	Current
1929-K.	Dallas	102,400,000	Current
1929-L.	San Francisco	57,600,000	Current
1929-L.*	San Francisco		25.00

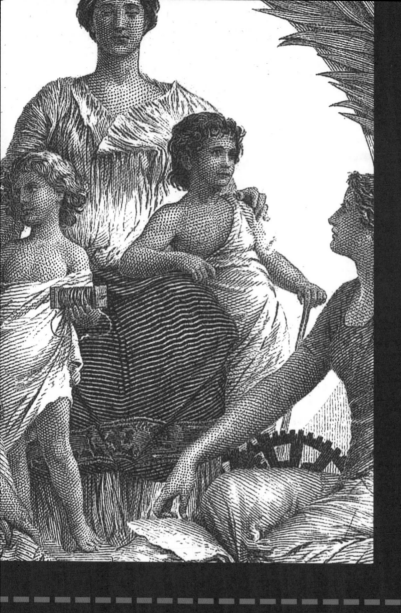

"Collecting $2 bills is a short, sweet, and interesting pursuit...."

$2

B

McPHERSON

COLLECTING TWO DOLLAR NOTES

Collecting $2 bills is a short, sweet, and interesting pursuit. There are some scarce issues, to be sure, but the overall number of varieties is rather small—no $2 equivalent to the lengthy runs of $1 notes discussed earlier. Across the board, notes of the $2 value are more difficult to find than those of $1.

The vista of federal currency is always changing, and who knows what will come up next? For a long time the $2 bill was considered to be as dead as a dodo bird, but, lo and behold! to help celebrate the 1976 Bicentennial the Treasury Department brought the denomination out of hiding and created a new version, illustrating on the back John Trumbull's well-known painting, the *Signing of the Declaration of Independence* (sometimes designated as the *Presentation of the Declaration of Independence*). This motif is one of the most familiar in American history, never mind just numismatics. However, within the realm of our hobby, it is depicted on the reverse of a handsome Washington medal by C.C. Wright and, separately, on many different varieties of obsolete bank notes (either a section of the Trumbull scene or just a small part of it). The $100 National Bank Notes of the Original Series and Series of 1875 use the same illustration.

Large-Size $2 Notes

$2 Legal Tender Notes, Large-Size: The first $2 bills are of the Legal Tender type, also called United States Notes, part of the "greenback" issues launched in 1862. On the face is the portrait of Alexander Hamilton. Some have the imprint of the National Bank Note Company, while others were made by the American Bank Note Company.

Thomas Jefferson made his debut on the $2 bill in the Series of 1869, establishing what proved to be an enduring connection. After some absence he popped up again on the Federal Reserve Bank Notes of 1918, and, later, on small-size bills.

$2 National Bank Notes, Large-Size: $2 National Bank notes bear the single most famous design in that particular specialty: the so-called "Lazy Two" or "Lazy Deuce." The large numeral 2 is seen on its side. The concept of a "lazy" numeral was not new to paper money, and several antecedents can be found on obsolete currency issued by state banks, but none as well-known as here. To the left is a female goddess designated as *Stars and Stripes*. (All nomenclature used here for National Bank Note designs is from Treasury records and differs in some instances from that used in popular numismatic texts.) On the back is a state seal, the vignette, *Introducing Tobacco From America*, and an eagle, amid ornate designs and lettering.

These bills were at the tag end of a $1-$1-$1-$2 sheet of four subjects, meaning that in each instance (with some minor exceptions) $2 bills were produced in quantities just one-third of the $1. The $2 bill bears the imprint of the National Bank Note Company, while the $1s on the sheet have the American Bank Note Company name. Similar to the $1 bills, the $2 issues were made in the Original Series and also the Series of 1875, the last with a vertical imprint in red, left of center. Today, all examples range from scarce to rare, and some are very rare. $1 and $2 National Bank bills were not made after January 1879, while in contrast, $5 to $100 values were produced for decades afterward. Typical collectable conditions run from Fair to Good to VG to Fine. Generally, anything that is nice VF or better is an exception to the rule, although now and again some Uncirculated pieces come to light, including a few issues from hoards.

Similar to the situation for $1 National Bank bills, the $2 issues are valued today not as much by signature combinations (although some are rare), but by issuing locations. Thus $2 notes from the Territories of Utah, Montana, or New Mexico are worth many multiples of what a comparable—condition $2 bill might sell for if issued in Boston, New York, or Philadelphia. Within any state, populous or sparsely settled, there are some "rare banks." Increasingly, specialists in states seek these, and a Lazy 2 note that is one of a kind or one of just a handful can bring a sharp premium.

$2 Silver Certificates, Large-Size: Silver Certificates in the $2 denomination begin with the Series of 1886, depicting on the face General Winfield Scott Hancock of the United States Army, a man once well known, but today relegated to obscurity, save for the interest of historians and players of trivia games. He lasted through several signature combinations, after which he was replaced by another obscure individual (at least from the viewpoint of being recognized today): William Windom, a native of Ohio, who later served as a senator from Minnesota, then as secretary of the Treasury.

Soon, the Series of 1896 did away with Windom and introduced one of the most elegant of all American designs—*Science Presenting Steam and Electricity to Commerce and Manufacture*, illustrated by the goddess Science, two other goddesses, and two youth, representative of ornate art, architecture, and design in the fading years of the Victorian era, just as Art Nouveau (not represented on currency) was coming into vogue. On the reverse two prominent Americans are depicted: Robert Fulton of steamboat fame, and Samuel F.B. Morse, well known as an artist but better known as inventor of the telegraph. These bills are part of the $1-$2-$5 suite of "Educational" notes that are often collected as a set.

$2 Treasury or Coin Notes, Large-Size: The Series of 1890 Treasury Note or Coin Note follows suit with others in the series, from the $1 to the $1,000 "Grand Watermelon." The back is completely filled with ornate engraving, in this case dominated by the large word TWO gracefully curved. These are scarce today in all grades and particularly so if Uncirculated.

Afterward came the Series of 1891 Treasury Note or Coin Note modified with generous amounts of open space on the back, said to deter counterfeiting, although the annals of banking and finance do not reveal that counterfeiting of Series of 1891 notes was ever much of a problem. The ways of government selection and emphasis are sometimes beyond understanding to the historian, and numismatists can shed a tear that the back design of the Series of 1890 was not continued longer. The faces of the Series of 1890 and 1891 notes are somewhat similar, each featuring General James B. McPherson, a military personality best known today to Civil War historians.

$2 Federal Reserve Bank Notes, Large-Size: Next in the large-size $2 series is the famous and very popular "Battleship Note," descriptive of the Federal Reserve Bank bills of the $2 denomination issued in the Series of 1918. Depicted is a dreadnought fighting ship—generic, not a specific vessel (named after states, dreadnaughts were objects of great pride, and it was not desired to show a specific one). Similar to the $1 bills, the $2 notes were released through the Federal Reserve Banks, 12 in number, each identified on the face, and each collectible separately for that reason. Numismatists who want to go further in a systematic collection can endeavor to assemble signature combinations, the most elusive of which seems to be the Atlanta note with the Teehee-Burke and Pike-McCord signature combinations. However, the greatest demand is from collectors who simply want a single example to illustrate the type.

Small-Size $2 Notes

$2 Legal Tender Notes, Small-Size: Rounding out the $2 denomination are small-size bills, commencing with the Legal Tender Notes (Series of 1928 through 1963). Never made in large quantities, today the issues are generally scarcer than are those of the $1 series. Star notes in particular are elusive, as this specialty was not widely popular until recent decades, by which time many early bills had become lost.

$2 Federal Reserve Notes, Small-Size: The Series of 1976 inaugurated this type and was produced for the Bicentennial celebration, although there was absolutely no call for this denomination for use in commerce. Then, surprise, came the Series of 1995 and the Series of 2003. Although the use of a single $2 bill would be more efficient in terms of printing and distribution than two $1 bills, they have not been popular in circulation, simply because cash-register drawers do not have a space for them, and they must be tucked in another location, an annoyance for those involved. No matter; numismatists love them dearly, and it is likely that they will remain popular for a long time.

LARGE-SIZE TWO DOLLAR NOTES

Legal Tender Notes

Face of Notes 41-41a. Profile bust of the first secretary of the Treasury, Alexander Hamilton.

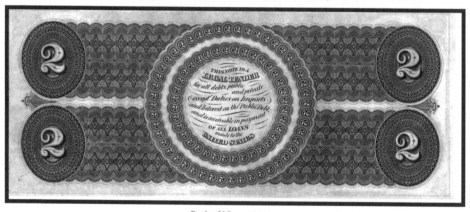

Back of Notes 41-41a.

Series of 1862 with signatures of Chittenden and Spinner and with small red seal

No.		VG-8	F-12	VF-20	F-12	Unc-63
41.	National Bank Note Company vertically at left	$375.00	$600.00	$1,100.00	$1,650.00	$3,500.00
41a.	American Bank Note Company vertically at left	400.00	625.00	1,100.00	1,650.00	3,500.00

Face of Note 42. U.S. Capitol building in center, with bust of Thomas Jefferson at left.

Legal Tender Notes

Back of Note 42.

No.	Series	Signatures	Seal	VG-8	F-12	VF-20	EF-40	Unc-63
42.	1869	Allison Spinner	Large Red	$300.00	$600.00	$1,000.00	$1,750.00	$4,000.00

Face of Notes 43-60 (similar to Note 42 with variations in coloring and seals).

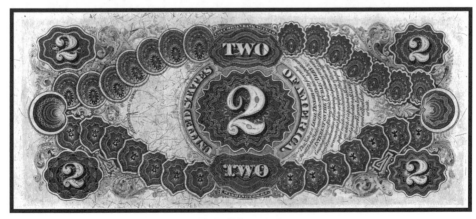

Back of Notes 43-60.

LARGE-SIZE TWO DOLLAR NOTES

Legal Tender Notes (United States Notes)

Red floral ornament around "Washington, DC" at right; seal at left

No.	Series	Signatures		Seal	VG-8	F-12	VF-20	EF-40	Unc-63
43.	1874	Allison	Spinner	Small Red with Rays	$200.00	$400.00	$675.00	$1,250.00	$2,000.00
44.	1875	Allison	New	Small Red with Rays	200.00	400.00	650.00	750.00	2,400.00
45.				Same but Series A.	400.00	600.00	1,200.00	1,800.00	4,000.00
46.				Same but Series B.	375.00	550.00	1,100.00	1,650.00	3,600.00
47.	1875	Allison	Wyman	Small Red with Rays	250.00	425.00	750.00	850.00	3,000.00
48.	1878	Allison	Gilfillan	Small Red with Rays	200.00	400.00	575.00	725.00	1,500.00
49.	1878	Scofield	Gilfillan	Small Red with Rays	2,500.00	9,500.00	12,500.00	16,500.00	30,000.00

Large seal replaces floral ornament at right; red serial numbers

No.	Series	Signatures		Seal	VG-8	F-12	VF-20	EF-40	Unc-63
50.	1880	Scofield	Gilfillan	Large Brown	$150.00	$225.00	$325.00	$500.00	$1,000.00
51.	1880	Bruce	Gilfillan	Large Brown	150.00	225.00	325.00	500.00	1,000.00
52.	1880	Bruce	Wyman	Large Brown	150.00	225.00	325.00	500.00	1,000.00

Same, except serial numbers are blue

No.	Series	Signatures		Seal	VG-8	F-12	VF-20	EF-40	Unc-63
53.	1880	Rosecrans	Huston	Large Red	$600.00	$850.00	$1,500.00	$3,000.00	$8,000.00
54.	1880	Rosecrans	Huston	Large Brown	750.00	1,000.00	2,000.00	4,250.00	12,000.00
55.	1880	Rosecrans	Nebeker	Small Red, Scalloped	200.00	250.00	325.00	400.00	1,700.00
56.	1880	Tillman	Morgan	Small Red, Scalloped	200.00	250.00	325.00	400.00	1,050.00

Same, except serial numbers are red

No.	Series	Signatures		Seal	VG-8	F-12	VF-20	EF-40	Unc-63
57.	1917	Teehee	Burke	Small Red, Scalloped	$80.00	$90.00	$140.00	$180.00	$450.00
58.	1917	Elliott	Burke	Small Red, Scalloped	80.00	90.00	140.00	180.00	450.00
59.	1917	Elliott	White	Small Red, Scalloped	80.00	90.00	140.00	180.00	450.00
60.	1917	Speelman	White	Small Red, Scalloped	75.00	85.00	125.00	160.00	350.00

National Bank Notes

Stars and Stripes—*woman unfurling flag. The famous "Lazy Deuce,"
called such because of the horizontal position of the large numeral 2.*

National Bank Notes

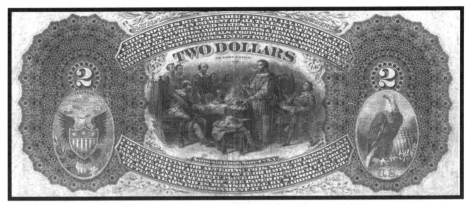

Sir Walter Raleigh showing the King of England corn and smoking tobacco.

No.	Series	Signatures		Seal	VG-8	F-12	VF-20	EF-40	Unc-63
387.	Original ..	Colby	Spinner	Red with Rays	$3,000.00	$3,500.00	$4,500.00	$6,000.00	$10,000.00
388.	Original ..	Jeffries	Spinner	Red with Rays	4,500.00	7,500.00	9,000.00	12,000.00	None Known
389.	Original ..	Allison	Spinner	Red with Rays	3,000.00	3,500.00	4,500.00	6,000.00	10,000.00
390.	1875	Allison	New	Red with Scallops	3,000.00	3,500.00	4,500.00	6,000.00	10,000.00
391.	1875	Allison	Wyman	Red with Scallops	3,000.00	3,500.00	4,500.00	6,000.00	10,000.00
392.	1875	Allison	Gilfillan	Red with Scallops	3,000.00	3,500.00	4,500.00	7,000.00	12,000.00
393.	1875	Scofield	Gilfillan	Red with Scallops	3,000.00	3,500.00	4,500.00	7,000.00	12,000.00

Silver Certificates

Bust of Civil War General Winfield Scott Hancock.

Back of Notes 240-244.

Silver Certificates

No.	Series	Signatures		Seal	VG-8	F-12	VF-20	EF-40	Unc-63
240.	1886	Rosecrans	Jordan	Small Red	$325.00	$500.00	$900.00	$1,250.00	$2,200.00
241.	1886	Rosecrans	Hyatt	Small Red	325.00	500.00	900.00	1,250.00	2,750.00
242.	1886	Rosecrans	Hyatt	Large Red	300.00	500.00	900.00	1,250.00	2,200.00
243.	1886	Rosecrans	Huston	Large Red	300.00	500.00	900.00	1,250.00	2,200.00
244.	1886	Rosecrans	Huston	Large Brown	300.00	500.00	900.00	1,250.00	2,800.00

Face of Notes 245-246. Bust of Treasury Secretary (1881-84, 1889-91) William Windom.

Back of Notes 245-246.

No.	Series	Signatures		Seal	VG-8	F-12	VF-20	EF-40	Unc-63
245.	1891	Rosecrans	Nebeker	Small Red	$300.00	$500.00	$850.00	$1,400.00	$3,500.00
246.	1891	Tillman	Morgan	Small Red	300.00	500.00	850.00	1,400.00	3,500.00

Silver Certificates

Face of 247-248. Allegory of Science (in background) presenting the youthful Steam and Electricity to the more mature Commerce and Manufacture. The second note in the Educational Series.

Back of Notes 247-248. Busts of the inventors Robert Fulton and Samuel F.B. Morse in oval frames.

No.	Series	Signatures	Seal	VG-8	F-12	VF-20	EF-40	Unc-63
247.	1896	Tillman Morgan	Small Red	$375.00	$550.00	$1,150.00	$1,900.00	$3,500.00
248.	1896	Bruce Roberts	Small Red	375.00	550.00	1,150.00	1,900.00	4,000.00

Silver Certificates

Face of Notes 249-258.

Bust of George Washington in ornate oval frame between women representing Agriculture and Mechanics.

Back of Notes 249-258.

No.	Series	Signatures		Seal	VG-8	F-12	VF-20	EF-40	Unc-63
249.	1899	Lyons	Roberts	Blue	$240.00	$265.00	$300.00	$400.00	$950.00
250.	1899	Lyons	Treat	Blue	240.00	265.00	300.00	400.00	1,000.00
251.	1899	Vernon	Treat	Blue	240.00	265.00	300.00	400.00	950.00
252.	1899	Vernon	McClung	Blue	240.00	265.00	300.00	400.00	950.00
253.	1899	Napier	McClung	Blue	240.00	265.00	300.00	400.00	950.00
254.	1899	Napier	Thompson	Blue	325.00	450.00	600.00	750.00	2,000.00
255.	1899	Parker	Burke	Blue	240.00	265.00	300.00	400.00	950.00
256.	1899	Teehee	Burke	Blue	240.00	265.00	300.00	400.00	950.00
257.	1899	Elliott	Burke	Blue	240.00	265.00	300.00	400.00	950.00
258.	1899	Speelman	White	Blue	240.00	265.00	300.00	400.00	950.00

Treasury or Coin Notes

Face of Notes 353-355. Bust of General James McPherson.

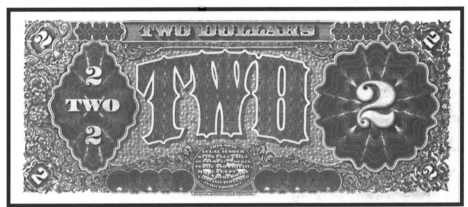

Back of Notes 353-355.

No.	Series	Signatures		Seal	VG-8	F-12	VF-20	EF-40	Unc-63
353.	1890	Rosecrans	Huston	Large Brown	$375.00	$900.00	$2,000.00	$3,500.00	$7,000.00
354.	1890	Rosecrans	Nebeker	Large Brown	375.00	900.00	2,000.00	3,500.00	12,000.00
355.	1890	Rosecrans	Nebeker	Small Red	375.00	900.00	2,000.00	3,500.00	7,000.00

Face of Notes 356-358. Bust of General James McPherson.

LARGE-SIZE TWO DOLLAR NOTES

Treasury or Coin Notes

Back of Notes 356-358.

No.	Series	Signatures		Seal	VG-8	F-12	VF-20	EF-40	Unc-63
356.	1891	Rosecrans	Nebeker	.... Small Red	$225.00	$375.00	$800.00	$1,200.00	$2,500.00
357.	1891	Tillman	Morgan	.... Small Red	225.00	375.00	800.00	1,200.00	2,500.00
358.	1891	Bruce	Roberts	.... Small Red	225.00	375.00	800.00	1,200.00	2,500.00

Federal Reserve Bank Notes

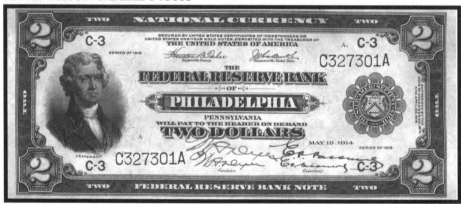

Face of Notes 747-780.
Bust of Thomas Jefferson.

Back of Notes 747-780.
An early 20th-century battleship

Federal Reserve Bank Notes

No.	Issuing Bank	Series	Signatures		Government Signatures		VG-8	F-12	VF-20	EF-40	Unc-63
747.	Boston	1918	Teehee	Burke	Bullen	Morss	$265.00	$375.00	$450.00	$600.00	$1,400.00
748.	Boston	1918	Teehee	Burke	Willett	Morss	275.00	400.00	500.00	700.00	1,750.00
749.	Boston	1918	Elliott	Burke	Willett	Morss	265.00	375.00	450.00	600.00	1,400.00
750.	New York	1918	Teehee	Burke	Sailer	Strong	265.00	375.00	450.00	600.00	1,400.00
751.	New York	1918	Teehee	Burke	Hendricks	Strong	265.00	375.00	450.00	600.00	1,400.00
752.	New York	1918	Elliott	Burke	Hendricks	Strong	265.00	375.00	450.00	600.00	1,400.00
753.	Philadelphia	1918	Teehee	Burke	Hardt	Passmore	265.00	375.00	450.00	600.00	1,400.00
754.	Philadelphia	1918	Teehee	Burke	Dyer	Passmore	275.00	400.00	500.00	700.00	1,750.00
755.	Philadelphia	1918	Elliott	Burke	Dyer	Passmore	400.00	600.00	1,000.00	2,500.00	7,000.00
756.	Philadelphia	1918	Elliott	Burke	Dyer	Norris	265.00	375.00	450.00	600.00	1,400.00
757.	Cleveland	1918	Teehee	Burke	Baxter	Fancher	265.00	375.00	450.00	600.00	1,400.00
758.	Cleveland	1918	Teehee	Burke	Davis	Fancher	275.00	400.00	500.00	700.00	1,750.00
759.	Cleveland	1918	Elliott	Burke	Davis	Fancher	265.00	375.00	450.00	600.00	1,400.00
760.	Richmond	1918	Teehee	Burke	Keesee	Seay	275.00	400.00	500.00	700.00	1,750.00
761.	Richmond	1918	Elliott	Burke	Keesee	Seay	275.00	400.00	500.00	700.00	1,750.00
762.	Atlanta	1918	Teehee	Burke	Pike	McCord	265.00	375.00	450.00	1,700.00	5,000.00
763.	Atlanta	1918	Teehee	Burke	Bell	McCord	400.00	600.00	700.00	1,000.00	2,700.00
764.	Atlanta	1918	Elliott	Burke	Bell	Wellborn	400.00	600.00	700.00	1,000.00	2,700.00
765.	Chicago	1918	Teehee	Burke	McCloud	McDougal	265.00	375.00	450.00	600.00	1,400.00
766.	Chicago	1918	Teehee	Burke	Cramer	McDougal	265.00	375.00	450.00	600.00	1,400.00
767.	Chicago	1918	Elliott	Burke	Cramer	McDougal	265.00	375.00	450.00	600.00	1,400.00
768.	St. Louis	1918	Teehee	Burke	Attebery	Wells	265.00	375.00	450.00	600.00	1,400.00
769.	St. Louis	1918	Teehee	Burke	Attebery	Biggs	400.00	600.00	700.00	1,000.00	2,700.00
770.	St. Louis	1918	Elliott	Burke	Attebery	Biggs	400.00	600.00	700.00	1,000.00	2,700.00
771.	St. Louis	1918	Elliott	Burke	White	Biggs	275.00	400.00	500.00	700.00	1,750.00
772.	Minneapolis	1918	Teehee	Burke	Cook	Wold	265.00	375.00	450.00	600.00	1,400.00
773.	Minneapolis	1918	Elliott	Burke	Cook	Young	275.00	400.00	500.00	700.00	1,750.00
774.	Kansas City	1918	Teehee	Burke	Anderson	Miller	265.00	375.00	450.00	600.00	1,400.00
775.	Kansas City	1918	Elliott	Burke	Helm	Miller	265.00	375.00	450.00	600.00	1,400.00
776.	Dallas	1918	Teehee	Burke	Talley	Van Zandt	265.00	375.00	450.00	600.00	1,400.00
777.	Dallas	1918	Elliott	Burke	Talley	Van Zandt	275.00	400.00	500.00	700.00	1,750.00
778.	San Francisco	1918	Teehee	Burke	Clerk	Lynch	275.00	400.00	500.00	700.00	1,750.00
779.	San Francisco	1918	Elliott	Burke	Clerk	Calkins	275.00	400.00	500.00	700.00	1,750.00
780.	San Francisco	1918	Elliott	Burke	Ambrose	Calkins	265.00	375.00	450.00	600.00	1,400.00

SMALL-SIZE TWO DOLLAR NOTES

Legal Tender Notes

Face of Notes 1501-1508.

Back of Notes 1501-1508.

SMALL-SIZE TWO DOLLAR NOTES

Legal Tender Notes

No.	Series	Signatures		Quantity Printed	VF-20	Unc-63
1501.	1928	Tate	Mellon	55,889,424	$15.00	$125.00
1501*.	1928	Tate	Mellon		225.00	1,500.00
1502.	1928-A ..	Woods	Mellon	46,859,136	65.00	350.00
1502*.	1928-A ..	Woods	Mellon		1,750.00	8,000.00
1503.	1928-B ..	Woods	Mills	9,001,632	125.00	1,200.00
1503*.	1928-B ..	Woods	Mills		10,000.00	60,000.00
1504.	1928-C ..	Julian	Morgenthau	86,584,008	25.00	150.00
1504*.	1928-C ..	Julian	Morgenthau		650.00	1,500.00
1505.	1928-D ..	Julian	Morgenthau	146,381,364	10.00	55.00
1505*.	1928-D ..	Julian	Morgenthau		100.00	700.00
1506.	1928-E ..	Julian	Vinson	5,261,016	25.00	85.00
1506*.	1928-E ..	Julian	Vinson		2,000.00	9,000.00
1507.	1928-F ..	Julian	Snyder	43,349,292	12.50	50.00
1507*.	1928-F ..	Julian	Snyder		85.00	500.00
1508.	1928-G ..	Clark	Snyder	52,208,000	10.00	45.00
1508*.	1928-G ..	Clark	Snyder		55.00	450.00

Face of Notes 1509-1512.

Back of Notes 1509-1512.

No.	Series	Signatures		Quantity Printed	VF-20	Unc-63
1509.	1953	Priest	Humphrey	45,360,000	$6.50	$12.00
1509*.	1953	Priest	Humphrey	2,160,000	10.00	45.00
1510.	1953-A	Priest	Anderson	18,000,000	6.50	12.00
1510*.	1953-A	Priest	Anderson	720,000	12.00	65.00
1511.	1953-B	Smith	Dillon	10,800,000	6.50	12.00
1511*.	1953-B	Smith	Dillon	720,000	12.00	55.00
1512.	1953-C	Granahan	Dillon	5,760,000	6.50	12.00
1512*.	1953-C	Granahan	Dillon	360,000	12.00	65.00

Legal Tender Notes

Face of Notes 1513-1514.

Back of Notes 1513-1514.

No.	Series	Signatures		Quantity Printed	VF-20	Unc-63
1513.	1963	Granahan	Dillon	15,360,000	$6.50	$12.00
1513*.	1963	Granahan	Dillon	640,000	10.00	30.00
1514.	1963-A	Granahan	Fowler	3,200,000	6.50	12.00
1514*.	1963-A	Granahan	Fowler	640,000	15.00	55.00

Federal Reserve Notes (Green Seal)

Face of Notes 1935-1937.

Back of Notes 1935-1937.

SMALL-SIZE TWO DOLLAR NOTES

Federal Reserve Notes (Green Seal)

Series of 1976
Signatures of Neff and Simon

No.	Issuing Bank	Quantity Printed	EF-40	Unc-63
1935-A .	Boston	29,440,000		$9.00
1935-A*.	Boston	1,280,000	5.00	15.00
1935-B .	New York	67,200,000		9.00
1935-B*.	New York	2,560,000	5.00	15.00
1935-C.	Philadelphia	33,280,000		9.00
1935-C*.	Philadelphia	1,280,000	5.00	15.00
1935-D.	Cleveland	31,360,000		6.00
1935-D*.	Cleveland	1,280,000	5.00	20.00
1935-E.	Richmond	56,960,000		9.00
1935-E*.	Richmond	640,000	15.00	75.00
1935-F.	Atlanta	60,800,000		8.00
1935-F*.	Atlanta	1,280,000	5.00	20.00
1935-G.	Chicago	84,480,000		9.00
1935-G*.	Chicago	1,280,000	10.00	50.00
1935-H.	St. Louis	39,040,000		10.00
1935-H*.	St. Louis	1,280,000	5.00	20.00
1935-I.	Minneapolis	23,680,000		15.00
1935-I*.	Minneapolis	640,000	75.00	200.00
1935-J.	Kansas City	24,960,000		20.00
1935-J*.	Kansas City	640,000	50.00	175.00
1935-K.	Dallas	41,600,000		12.50
1935-K*.	Dallas	1,280,000	5.00	25.00
1935-L.	San Francisco	82,560,000		12.50
1935-L*.	San Francisco	1,920,000	7.00	40.00

Series of 1995
Signatures of Withrow and Rubin

No.	Issuing Bank	Quantity Printed	EF-40	Unc-63
1936-A*.	Boston	9,999		$55.00
1936-B*.	New York	9,999		55.00
1936-C*.	Philadelphia	9,999		55.00
1936-D*.	Cleveland	9,999		55.00
1936-E*.	Richmond	9,999		55.00
1936-F.	Atlanta	153,600,000		5.00
1936-F*.	Atlanta	640,000		10.00
1936-G*.	Chicago	9,999		55.00
1936-H*.	St. Louis	9,999		55.00
1936-I*.	Minneapolis	9,999		55.00
1936-J*.	Kansas City	9,999		55.00
1936-K*.	Dallas	9,999		55.00
1936-L*.	San Francisco	9,999		55.00

Series of 2003
Signatures of Marin and Snow.
Printed at the Western Facility (Fort Worth, Texas)

No.	Issuing Bank	Quantity Printed	EF-40	Unc-63
1937-A*.	Boston	8,000		$95.00
1937-B*.	New York	8,000		95.00
1937-C*.	Philadelphia	8,000		95.00
1937-D*.	Cleveland	8,000		95.00
1937-E*.	Richmond	8,000		95.00
1937-F*.	Atlanta	8,000		95.00
1937-G*.	Chicago	8,000		95.00
1937-H*.	St. Louis	8,000		95.00
1937-I.	Minneapolis	124,600,000		4.00
1937-I.*	Minneapolis	3,840,000		50.00
1937-J*.	Kansas City	8,000		95.00
1937-L*.	Dallas	8,000		95.00
1937-L*.	San Francisco	8,000		95.00

"Few denominations can equal the beauty and appeal of the $5 series of notes, popular both in commerce and among collectors. Many of their designs stand out in artistry and historical significance…"

FIVE DOLLAR NOTES

COLLECTING FIVE DOLLAR NOTES

Of all large-currency series, few can equal the appeal, beauty, and collecting possibilities of $5 notes. Among National Bank Notes the Series of 1882 issues are remarkable for their typographical diversity. The National Gold Bank Notes, circulated only in California, also make their debut. The Silver Certificate types stand tall and proud with regard to artistry and include issues that have been numismatic favorites for a long time. Further, the $5 was one of the more popular denominations for use in commerce, resulting in a fairly good supply of bills today.

Large-Size $5 Notes

$5 Demand Notes of 1861, Large-Size: Printed by the American Bank Note Co., these were the first federal "greenback" notes. The face shows the statue *Freedom* (mounted on top of the United States Capitol) by Thomas Crawford and a portrait of Alexander Hamilton. The original intent was for these to be hand-signed by the treasurer of the United States and by the secretary of the Treasury. This procedure proved to be impractical, and other government employees did the signing, with the added notation "for the," to reflect they were acting on behalf of the senior officials. Today, all Demand Notes are exceedingly rare. Fortunate is the collector who can acquire a representative example for a type set.

$5 Legal Tender Notes, Large-Size: The earliest readily collectable bills of the $5 denomination are the United States Notes, or Legal Tender Notes, of the Series of 1862 and 1863. These "greenbacks," with the same general face motifs as the $5 Demand Notes, exist in several varieties. They include imprints of the American Bank Note Company and the National Bank Note Co., both in New York City. The plates were produced and printing accomplished there, after which the bills were sent to the Treasury Department to be imprinted with serial numbers and the Treasury seal. Most numismatists endeavor to acquire a single Series of 1862 note or the related design, Series of 1863, for type. However, there are differences, including the design and wording of the lettering on the reverse. As they are not expensive, these may be worth collecting.

Next in the line-up of United States Notes is the Series of 1869 featuring Andrew Jackson, who later was transplanted to the $10 series, then to the $20 small-size currency of today. At the center is a famous engraving of a pioneer family, complete with dog, in the outer reaches of the wilderness (ready to make a new life?). Bills of this type with various signature combinations and in different series, including later different series depending on the seals and other differences, are plentiful today. Examples for type can be easily obtained.

$5 National Bank Notes, Large-Size: National Bank Notes of the $5 denomination form a wonderful possibility for collecting, extending as they do from the very earliest period of the 1860s through 1929. They are also the most plentiful in survival today.

The first notes, the Original Series ("First Charter"), were printed by the Continental Bank Note Co., New York. This company was organized by W.L. Ormsby but run by others, due to political problems between Ormsby (an inventive genius) and the Treasury Department.

The notes were printed in sheets of four each ($5-$5-$5-$5, plate letters A through D). The separation between notes was very small—significantly narrower than on bills produced in other denominations by other firms. Accordingly, it is perfectly normal and proper for a given $5 of the early period to have very tight margins. Although most contract work for notes of various denominations in the National Bank Note series went to the American Bank Note Co., Continental scored a coup in that more were printed of the $5 denomination than any other value.

The face depicts two scenes: *Discovery of Land by Columbus*, and *Introduction of the Old World to the New* (these being the official descriptions used by the Treasury Department). The latter shows a mythical scene of an Indian, presumably Pocahontas, being presented to European royalty. The reverse depicts the *Landing of Columbus*. Spencer M. Clark of the Treasury Department wished to have panoramic or scenic illustrations on the back of National Bank Notes, the idea being directly taken from W.L. Ormsby, who forwarded the thought as part of his "Unit System" in his 1852 book, *Bank Note Engraving*. However, Ormsby was persona non grata with government officials in the 1860s; he was not credited for the idea (which is more or less common sense anyway) and, somehow, certain writers have suggested that Clark was the innovator. The use of full scenes, ornately done and usually from early paintings, did not last long, and later depictions of historical events on currency tended to be rather simple, with much white space. The Series of 1875 $5 bills have designs the same as the first, except for a vertical imprint at the left and a few other imprint differences.

A few Original Series and Series of 1875 $5 notes were prepared apparently as an experiment for several banks around the country. On these notes the charter number appears in black italic type, engraved directly on the face plate instead of overprinted with block red numerals. Today, these "Black Charter" notes are a very rare type, with fewer than 50 reported examples (on eight different banks known).

A particularly interesting era in the large-size $5 National Bank note series is the Series of 1882 ("Second Charter"). Now with facilities set up in the Bureau of Engraving and Printing building in Washington, DC, the Treasury Department decided not to adapt face and back plates created by the Continental Bank Note Company for the Original Series and Series of 1875 notes. The Treasury allowed its own engravers to come up with new ideas. This procedure was quite unlike what was done with the other National Bank currency in the Series of 1882, which simply copied the designs used earlier and in many instances was printed from old plates that had been altered (*re-entered* is the term).

For the Series of 1882 $5 bills, the portrait of recently martyred President James A. Garfield formed a logical illustration for the left side of the face, with the bank imprint at the center. The possibility of creating imprints provided a rich panorama of artistic expression at the BEP, and today certain of the styles have been given interesting nicknames, such as "circus poster" and "theater marquee." Students of the series, most notably Peter Huntoon, have enjoyed researching the specific years in which certain lettering arrangements were utilized. For many banks, Series of 1882 bills were continued well into the 20th century.

The backs of the Series of 1882 notes were made in three styles, the best known of which are the Brown Back bills with the engraving in brown, except for a blue-green design at the center prominently showcasing the charter number of the bank. The charter number was bold on both sides so that when bills were redeemed by the Treasury Department, clerks could easily classify them. Scarcer among the Series of 1882 issues are the Date Back bills bearing the twin dates 1882 and 1908, and, in particular, the Value Backs with the inscription FIVE DOLLARS. The backs of these last two are rather plain. That matters not to enthusiastic collectors, though Value Backs are somewhat unappreciated in the marketplace.

The Series of 1902, sometimes called the "Third Charter Period," represents the last major design in the $5 series. These notes were produced in several interesting variations. The first had the Treasury seal in bright red on the face, creating the Red Seal notes that are especially popular with collectors today. These are somewhat scarce. The second-issue notes (with a blue seal), the Date Back issues, have the dates 1902 and 1908 imprinted at the top part of the back, and were made in relatively small quantities. Most plentiful are the third issue, called the Plain Back, also with a blue seal. These were produced extensively until the small-size notes replaced them. The signatures of many of the third issue of the Series of 1902 notes were rubber-stamped by secretaries for the bank officers. These stamped impressions often fade, and sometimes they disappear completely. In contrast, the hand-signed notes of an earlier time tend to preserve well.

Although it is easy to collect large-size $5 National Bank bills by type, most collectors desire to acquire one from each different state that issued them, or perhaps each different town or each different bank within a state. Such interest can be very intense, especially if a bank is "rare" and few bills are known. It is often the case that the only known $5 National Bank bills from a given bank are in lower grades, this being particularly true of the earlier issues. Don C. Kelly, in his *National Bank Notes*, records the bank names, types, serial numbers, and plate letters of all bills known to him, of all denominations from $1 to $1,000, a compilation done with the assistance of many dealers and collectors.

$5 National Gold Bank Notes, Large-Size: Produced only in the Series of 1872, 1873, and 1874, and distributed only by banks in California, these are all rare today. They circulated extensively, with none known to have been saved at the time by numismatists. Interestingly, the *American Journal of Numismatics*, the quarterly publication of the hobby, took no particular notice of them (or of other currency) during this time. Because of this, large-size bills of this type are quite rare today.

COLLECTING FIVE DOLLAR NOTES

The National Gold Bank Notes depict on the face the same design used by the Continental Bank Note Co. for the Original Series and Series of 1875 bills, depicting *Columbus in Sight of Land* and *America Presented to the Old World*. The reverse is entirely different and displays a montage of United States gold coins of different denominations, with an 1871 $20 prominent. This same design was also used on higher-denomination National Gold Bank Notes.

$5 Silver Certificates, Large-Size: These commence with the Series of 1886, the famous "Silver Dollar Note" with five Morgan silver dollars arrayed across the back, one displaying the date 1886, all in green. An ornate background and border completes the scene. On the face is the portrait of Ulysses S. Grant, hero of the Civil War, the late president who served two terms and died in 1885. The same face design was continued later with different signature combinations as the Series of 1891.

Completing the "Educational" series of bills (also including the $1 and $2) is the $5 entry for the Series of 1896, illustrating an allegorical motif, *Electricity Presenting Light to the World*. This is Neoclassicism at its height: an elegant scene that stands as one of the most popular currency motifs in the view of collectors today. The uncovered bosoms of certain of the figures in the scene caused several Boston society ladies to rally against the design, and some banks to resist taking them—the origin of the term "banned in Boston," and the reason that the Series of 1899 Silver Certificates soon replaced them. The reverse of the Series of 1896 $5 depicted two prominent Americans, U.S. Grant and General Philip Sheridan. Such bills were produced in three signature combinations, but are mainly collected simply for type.

The next entry in the $5 Silver Certificates is the Series of 1899 type, featuring on the face the portrait of an Indian chief, said to be Running Antelope. He is depicted in natural style, quite unlike the Indian Head cent of the time, which showed a *female* wearing a war bonnet (a male type of head-dress). These "Indian Chief" notes, as they are called, were produced for a long period of years and in substantial quantities.

The last type among $5 Silver Certificates is a numismatic favorite. Abraham Lincoln is depicted at the center, surrounded by a heavy circular frame, giving rise to the nickname "Porthole Note." The reverse shows the United States Seal. By this time the era of elegance was gone, and it was Treasury policy to feature large amounts of white space.

$5 Treasury or Coin Notes, Large-Size: Next under our observation are the Treasury Notes, or Coin Notes, Series of 1890—another high spot in artistry. The face depicts General George H. Thomas, little remembered today, but one of several Civil War heroes used on currency in the late 19th century. The beauty part of the note is the reverse, where the word FIVE appears in very ornate green letters, with appropriate decorations surrounding. These notes, while scarce, are available today and are usually collected by type.

The Treasury Department desired more open space on the back of the notes, creating the Series of 1891. The reverse is styled differently, and, in the opinion of numismatists, not as attractively. These notes were continued in production for many years, through the early 20th century. The last signature combination in the series is that of Lyons and Roberts, two men who were in office jointly from 1898 to 1905.

$5 Federal Reserve Notes, Large-Size: The Federal Reserve Notes, Series of 1914, with red seals and with the Burke-McAdoo signature combination, are rather simple in their appearance and are usually collected singly for the type, although it is possible to acquire them by Federal Reserve Banks as well. The related blue seal notes can be collected by banks as well as by many signature combinations.

$5 Federal Reserve Bank Notes, Large-Size: Federal Reserve Bank Notes, Series of 1915 and 1918 (dates vary), each feature the Federal Reserve city spelled out in large letters on the face. These are more popular, but not in the same league as the $1 (green eagle holding flag) and $2 (battleship) bills in the same series. These notes can be acquired by Federal Reserve city as well as by signature combinations. None were issued by the Richmond Federal Reserve Bank. Among those produced, bills from Boston are considered to be the scarcest.

Small-Size $5 Notes

Small-size $5 notes are especially popular today. The face value is relatively low, and most were made in sufficient quantities that examples are readily available, although certain early issues are scarce in Uncirculated grades. A portrait of Abraham Lincoln appears on the face, and the back shows a front view of the Lincoln Memorial. These motifs were used on all series of small-size $5 bills. Indeed, more varieties are being made now than ever before in the past—a rather interesting situation in this and other modern series. How lucky we all are that the Federal Reserve Banks have entered into the equation, creating many different varieties each time there is a signature change or other difference! As is true for small-size bills of other values, in the following charts you will note a star beside each of these small-sized notes, referring to bills that were printed to replace those made in error and destroyed. The collecting of these has become a passion in its own right, and certain star notes command substantial premiums.

$5 Legal Tender Notes, Small-Size: Small-size Legal Tender or United States Notes begin with the Series of 1928 and continue for years thereafter, through the Series of 1963. This relatively brief series can be collected by varieties, with certain star notes being very elusive, especially in higher grades.

$5 National Bank Notes, Small-Size: The Series of 1929 National Bank Notes remained in use through early 1935. There are two styles, Type 1 (generally more plentiful) and Type 2, each printed in six-subject sheets. Each has a brown Treasury seal and brown serial numbers. Sheets of Type 1 bills each had the same serial number on a given sheet, prefixed by a letter, A through F, such as A000001A to F000001A. Sheets of Type 2 bills were numbered continuously, with a sheet starting with A000001 and ending with A000006. The same numbering system was used in higher-denomination small-size National Bank Notes. Signatures of the bank cashier and president were printed directly on each note at the BEP. These $5 bills are widely collected today, usually by geographical location.

$5 Silver Certificates, Small-Size: The small-size $5 Silver Certificates commence with the Series of 1934. These were continued through Series 1953.

$5 Federal Reserve Bank Notes, Small-Size: Federal Reserve Bank Notes of the Series of 1929, brown seal, are collectable from each of the Federal Reserve districts. These bills, different from the later Federal Reserve Notes, have the inscription NATIONAL CURRENCY at the top margin of the face. Related notes were made in $10, $20, $50, and $100 denominations. Printed signatures on these and other notes include two of Treasury officials and two of bank officials. Production lasted for only a short time.

$5 Federal Reserve Notes, Small-Size: The small-size $5 Federal Reserve Notes commenced with the Series of 1928. Such bills have been issued by the 12 Federal Reserve Banks since that time. Each bears identification as to the bank letter and number, such as 7-G for Chicago. Each has a green Treasury seal.

In addition to the regular issues, certain Series of 1934 and 1934-A notes have the HAWAII overprint or a yellow seal, for use during World War II (see related commentary under $1 Silver Certificates, Small-Size).

Starting with the Series of 1999, the face and back designs were modified. Lincoln's portrait was changed and enlarged, and anti-counterfeiting security features were added to the design and paper. By this time the widespread use of color copying machines had spawned a new generation of note imitations.

Although the $5 denomination is not as widely collected as the $1, there is still a large group of numismatists who seek the different bank and signature combinations as they are issued. Star or replacement notes form a specialty as well. Today, many collectors routinely acquire both a regular and a star note.

Demand Notes of 1861

Face of Notes 1-5a.
Statue of Freedom *from atop Capitol building in Washington, DC*
At right, bust of Alexander Hamilton in oval frame.

Back of Notes 1-5a.

No.	Payable at		VG-8	F-12	VF-20
1.	New York		$1,500.00	$2,500.00	$4,750.00
1a.	"For the" handwritten		5,000.00	12,000.00	Rare
2.	Philadelphia		1,500.00	2,500.00	4,750.00
2a.	"For the" handwritten		Unknown	—	—
3.	Boston		1,500.00	2,500.00	4,750.00
3a.	"For the" handwritten		Unique	—	—
4.	Cincinnati		Rare	—	—
4a.	"For the" handwritten		Unknown	—	—
5.	St. Louis		Very Rare	—	—
5a.	"For the" handwritten		Unique	—	—

Legal Tender Notes

Face of Notes 61–63b.
Statue of Freedom *from atop Capitol building in Washington, DC*
At right, bust of Alexander Hamilton in oval frame.

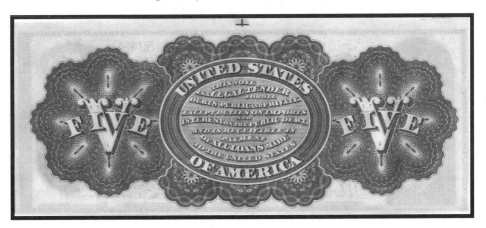

Back of Notes 61–63b.

No.	Act	Signatures		Seal	VG-8	F-12	VF-20	EF-40	Unc-63
61.	1862	Chittenden	Spinner	Small Red, no "Series"	$3,500.00	$8,000.00	—	—	—
		American Bank Note Co. on upper border							
61a.	1862	Chittenden	Spinner	Small Red, "Series" on face					
		American Bank Note Co. on upper border			275.00	425.00	$625.00	$800.00	$1,700.00
(The above two notes have the First Obligation on back.)									
62.	1862	Chittenden	Spinner	Small Red	300.00	475.00	675.00	875.00	3,200.00
63.	1863	Chittenden	Spinner	Small Red					
		American Bank Note Co. and National Bank Note Co. on lower border			275.00	425.00	625.00	800.00	1,700.00
63a.	1863	Chittenden	Spinner	Small Red, One Serial No.					
		American Bank Note Co. twice on lower border			275.00	425.00	625.00	800.00	1,700.00
63b.	1863	Chittenden	Spinner	Small Red, Two Serial Nos.					
		American Bank Note Co. twice on lower border			275.00	425.00	625.00	800.00	2,000.00
(The above four notes have the Second Obligation on back.)									

Legal Tender Notes

Face of Note 64.
A pioneer family in center, with bust of Andrew Jackson in oval frame at left.

Back of Note 64.

No.	Series	Signatures	Seal	VG-8	F-12	VF-20	EF-40	Unc-63
64.	1869	Allison Spinner	Large Red	$250.00	$400.00	$550.00	$800.00	$1,850.00

Face of Notes 65-92 (similar to the preceding with changes in color and seals).

Legal Tender Notes

Back of Notes 65-92.

Large red floral ornament around "Washington, D.C." at right; seal at left

No.	Series	Signatures		Seal	VG-8	F-12	VF-20	EF-40	Unc-63
65.	1875	Allison	New	Small Red, Rays ...	$160.00	$300.00	$400.00	$600.00	$1,400.00
66.		As above but Series A		....	300.00	500.00	700.00	1,100.00	8,000.00
67.		As above but Series B		....	200.00	350.00	450.00	750.00	1,750.00
68.	1875	Allison	Wyman	Small Red, Rays ...	160.00	250.00	340.00	475.00	1,300.00
69.	1878	Allison	Gilfillan	Small Red, Rays ...	160.00	275.00	380.00	525.00	1,350.00

Large seal replaces floral ornament, red serial numbers

No.	Series	Signatures		Seal	VG-8	F-12	VF-20	EF-40	Unc-63
70.	1880	Scofield	Gilfillan	Large Brown	$140.00	$500.00	$900.00	$1,500.00	$2,500.00
71.	1880	Bruce	Gilfillan	Large Brown	140.00	200.00	340.00	600.00	1,250.00
72.	1880	Bruce	Wyman	Large Brown	140.00	200.00	340.00	600.00	1,250.00

Same as above, blue serial numbers

No.	Series	Signatures		Seal	VG-8	F-12	VF-20	EF-40	Unc-63
73.	1880	Bruce	Wyman	Large Red, Plain ...	$140.00	$200.00	$340.00	$600.00	$1,000.00
74.	1880	Rosecrans	Jordan	Large Red, Plain ...	140.00	200.00	340.00	600.00	950.00
75.	1880	Rosecrans	Hyatt	Large Red, Plain ...	650.00	1,000.00	1,500.00	3,750.00	6,000.00
76.	1880	Rosecrans	Huston	Large Red, Spike ...	275.00	450.00	850.00	1,500.00	4,200.00
77.	1880	Rosecrans	Huston	Large Brown	275.00	475.00	800.00	1,600.00	8,000.00
78.	1880	Rosecrans	Nebeker	Large Brown	400.00	700.00	1,250.00	1,750.00	3,750.00
79.	1880	Rosecrans	Nebeker	Small Red, Scalloped	100.00	180.00	225.00	315.00	775.00
80.	1880	Tillman	Morgan	Small Red, Scalloped	100.00	180.00	225.00	315.00	775.00
81.	1880	Bruce	Roberts	Small Red, Scalloped	100.00	180.00	225.00	315.00	775.00
82.	1880	Lyons	Roberts	Small Red, Scalloped	100.00	180.00	225.00	315.00	1,500.00

Red "V" and "Dollars" added to left of design, red serial numbers

No.	Series	Signatures		Seal	VG-8	F-12	VF-20	EF-40	Unc-63
83.	1907	Vernon	Treat	Small Red, Scalloped	$120.00	$150.00	$195.00	$285.00	$525.00
84.	1907	Vernon	McClung	Small Red, Scalloped	120.00	150.00	195.00	285.00	750.00
85.	1907	Napier	McClung	Small Red, Scalloped	120.00	150.00	195.00	285.00	525.00
86.	1907	Napier	Thompson	Small Red, Scalloped	125.00	150.00	200.00	250.00	550.00
87.	1907	Parker	Burke	Small Red, Scalloped	120.00	150.00	195.00	285.00	525.00
88.	1907	Teehee	Burke	Small Red, Scalloped	120.00	150.00	195.00	285.00	525.00
89.	1907	Elliott	Burke	Small Red, Scalloped	120.00	150.00	215.00	330.00	1,000.00
90.	1907	Elliott	White	Small Red, Scalloped	120.00	150.00	195.00	285.00	625.00
91.	1907	Speelman	White	Small Red, Scalloped	115.00	140.00	185.00	265.00	480.00
92.	1907	Woods	White	Small Red, Scalloped	120.00	150.00	185.00	285.00	625.00

National Bank Notes
"First Charter Period" (Original Series and Series of 1875)

Face of Notes 394-408a.
Columbus Sighting Land *at left; at right, Columbus presenting a Native American princess, symbolic of America, to representatives of the Old World.*

Back of Notes 394-408a. The Landing of Columbus.

No.	Series	Signatures		Seal	VG-8	F-12	VF-20	EF-40	Unc-63
394.	Original	Chittenden	Spinner ...	Red, Rays	$950.00	$1,350.00	$1,750.00	$2,450.00	$5,250.00
397.	Original	Colby	Spinner ...	Red, Rays	950.00	1,350.00	1,750.00	2,450.00	5,250.00
398.	Original	Jeffries	Spinner ...	Red, Rays	5,500.00	7,500.00	8,750.00	10,000.00	17,500.00
399.	Original	Allison	Spinner ...	Red, Rays	950.00	1,350.00	1,750.00	2,450.00	5,250.00
401.	1875	Allison	New	Red, Scalloped	950.00	1,350.00	1,750.00	2,450.00	5,250.00
402.	1875	Allison	Wyman	Red, Scalloped	950.00	1,350.00	1,750.00	2,450.00	5,250.00
403.	1875	Allison	Gilfillan	Red, Scalloped	950.00	1,350.00	1,750.00	2,450.00	5,250.00
404.	1875	Scofield	Gilfillan	Red, Scalloped	950.00	1,350.00	1,750.00	2,450.00	5,250.00
405.	1875	Bruce	Gilfillan	Red, Scalloped	950.00	1,350.00	1,750.00	2,450.00	5,250.00
406.	1875	Bruce	Wyman	Red, Scalloped	950.00	1,350.00	1,750.00	2,450.00	5,250.00
406a.	1875	Bruce	Jordan	Red, Scalloped	Rare	—	—	—	—
407.	1875	Rosecrans	Huston	Red, Scalloped	950.00	1,350.00	1,750.00	2,450.00	5,250.00
408.	1875	Rosecrans	Jordan	Red, Scalloped	950.00	1,350.00	1,750.00	2,450.00	5,250.00
408a.	1875	Rosecrans	Nebeker ...	Red, Scalloped	Unique	—	—	—	—

"Second Charter Period" (Series of 1882)

First Issue: Series of 1882 with brown seal and brown back

Face of Notes 466-478.
Large bust of President James A. Garfield at left.

Back of Notes 466-478. Green bank charter numbers against an ornate background of brown lathe-work.

No.	Signatures		VG-8	F-12	VF-20	EF-40	Unc-63
466.	Bruce	Gilfillan	$550.00	$700.00	$950.00	$1,250.00	$2,200.00
467.	Bruce	Wyman	550.00	700.00	950.00	1,250.00	2,200.00
468.	Bruce	Jordan	550.00	700.00	950.00	1,250.00	2,200.00
469.	Rosecrans	Jordan	550.00	700.00	950.00	1,250.00	2,200.00
470.	Rosecrans	Hyatt	550.00	700.00	950.00	1,250.00	2,200.00
471.	Rosecrans	Huston	550.00	700.00	950.00	1,250.00	2,200.00
472.	Rosecrans	Nebeker	550.00	700.00	950.00	1,250.00	2,200.00
473.	Rosecrans	Morgan	625.00	950.00	1,750.00	2,500.00	3,700.00
474.	Tillman	Morgan	550.00	700.00	950.00	1,250.00	2,200.00
475.	Tillman	Roberts	550.00	700.00	950.00	1,250.00	2,200.00
476.	Bruce	Roberts	550.00	700.00	950.00	1,250.00	2,200.00
477.	Lyons	Roberts	550.00	700.00	950.00	1,250.00	2,200.00
477a.	Lyons	Treat	Unknown	—	—	—	—
478.	Vernon	Treat	550.00	950.00	1,500.00	2,700.00	—

LARGE-SIZE FIVE DOLLAR NOTES

"Second Charter Period" (Series of 1882)
Second Issue: Series of 1882 with blue seal and with "1882-1908" on green back

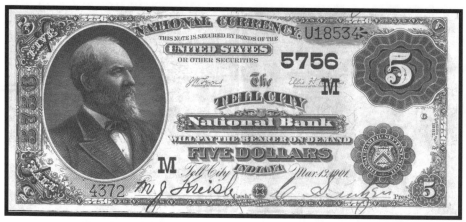

Face of Notes 532-538b. Large bust of President James A. Garfield at left.

Back of Notes 532-538b.

No.	Signatures		VG-8	F-12	VF-20	EF-40	Unc-63
532.	Rosecrans	Huston	$550.00	$700.00	$800.00	$950.00	$2,000.00
533.	Rosecrans	Nebeker	550.00	700.00	800.00	950.00	2,000.00
533a.	Rosecrans	Morgan	3 Known	—	—	—	—
534.	Tillman	Morgan	550.00	700.00	800.00	950.00	2,000.00
535.	Tillman	Roberts	550.00	700.00	800.00	950.00	2,000.00
536.	Bruce	Roberts	550.00	700.00	800.00	950.00	2,000.00
537.	Lyons	Roberts	550.00	700.00	800.00	950.00	2,000.00
538.	Vernon	Treat	550.00	700.00	800.00	950.00	2,000.00
538a.	Vernon	McClung	Unknown	—	—	—	—
538b.	Napier	McClung	1,750.00	2,750.00	3,000.00	3,750.00	5,500.00

"Second Charter Period" (Series of 1882)

Series of 1882 with blue seal and with "FIVE DOLLARS" on green back

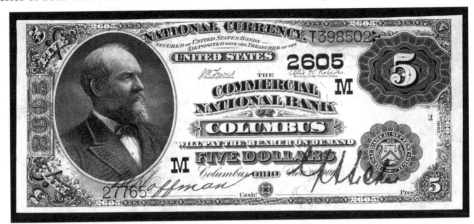

Face of Notes 573-575b. Large bust of President James A. Garfield at left.

Back of Notes 573-575b.

No.	Signatures		VG-8	F-12	VF-20	EF-40	Unc-63
573.	Tillman	Morgan	$575.00	$700.00	$850.00	$1,050.00	$2,700.00
573a.	Tillman	Roberts	800.00	1,000.00	1,250.00	1,500.00	3,000.00
574.	Lyons	Roberts	525.00	650.00	800.00	1,000.00	2,500.00
574a.	Bruce	Roberts	525.00	700.00	850.00	1,050.00	2,700.00
574b.	Lyons	Treat	Unknown	—	—	—	—
575.	Vernon	Treat	525.00	650.00	800.00	1,000.00	2,500.00
575a.	Napier	McClung	525.00	650.00	800.00	1,000.00	2,500.00
575b.	Teehee	Burke	Rare	—	—	—	—

These notes were issued from 1916 to 1922 in sheets of 5-5-5-5.

LARGE-SIZE FIVE DOLLAR NOTES

"Third Charter Period" (Series of 1902)
First Issues: Series of 1902 with red seal

Face of Notes 587-589. Bust of President Benjamin Harrison in oval frame at left.

Back of Notes 587-589. The Landing of the Pilgrims *in center.*

No.	Signatures			VG-8	F-12	VF-20	EF-40	Unc-63
587.	Lyons	Roberts	....	$525.00	$650.00	$875.00	$1,250.00	$2,750.00
588.	Lyons	Treat	....	525.00	650.00	875.00	1,250.00	2,750.00
589.	Vernon	Treat	....	525.00	650.00	875.00	1,250.00	2,750.00

Face of Notes 590-597a. (not shown) similiar to 587-589. Bust of President Benjamin Harrison in oval frame at left.

Back of Notes 590-597a similiar to 587-589 (not shown). The Landing of the Pilgrims *depicted.*

No.	Signatures			VG-8	F-12	VF-20	EF-40	Unc-63
590.	Lyons	Roberts	....	$190.00	$230.00	$275.00	$350.00	$725.00
591.	Lyons	Treat	....	190.00	230.00	275.00	350.00	725.00
592.	Vernon	Treat	....	190.00	230.00	275.00	350.00	725.00
593.	Vernon	McClung	....	190.00	230.00	275.00	350.00	725.00
594.	Napier	McClung	....	190.00	230.00	275.00	350.00	725.00
595.	Napier	Thompson	....	190.00	350.00	450.00	700.00	1,200.00
596.	Napier	Burke	....	190.00	230.00	275.00	350.00	725.00
597.	Parker	Burke	....	190.00	230.00	275.00	350.00	725.00
597a.	Teehee	Burke	....	Very Rare	—	—	—	—

LARGE-SIZE FIVE DOLLAR NOTES

"Third Charter Period" (Series of 1902)
Third Issue: Series of 1902 with blue seal and without "1902-1908" on back

Face of Notes 598-612 (not shown) similiar to 587-589. Bust of President Benjamin Harrison in oval frame at left. Back of Notes 598-612 (not shown) similiar to 587-589. The Landing of the Pilgrims *depicted.*

No.	Signatures		VG-8	F-12	VF-20	EF-40	Unc-63
598.	Lyons	Roberts	$175.00	$200.00	$235.00	$300.00	$625.00
599.	Lyons	Treat	175.00	200.00	235.00	300.00	625.00
600.	Vernon	Treat	175.00	200.00	235.00	300.00	625.00
601.	Vernon	McClung	175.00	200.00	235.00	300.00	625.00
602.	Napier	McClung	175.00	200.00	235.00	300.00	625.00
603.	Napier	Thompson	175.00	200.00	235.00	300.00	625.00
604.	Napier	Burke	175.00	200.00	235.00	300.00	625.00
605.	Parker	Burke	175.00	200.00	235.00	300.00	625.00
606.	Teehee	Burke	175.00	200.00	235.00	300.00	625.00
607.	Elliott	Burke	175.00	200.00	235.00	300.00	625.00
608.	Elliott	White	175.00	200.00	235.00	300.00	625.00
609.	Speelman	White	175.00	200.00	235.00	300.00	625.00
610.	Woods	White	175.00	200.00	235.00	300.00	625.00
611.	Woods	Tate	175.00	200.00	235.00	300.00	625.00
612.	Jones	Woods	250.00	400.00	550.00	750.00	2,850.00

National Gold Bank Notes

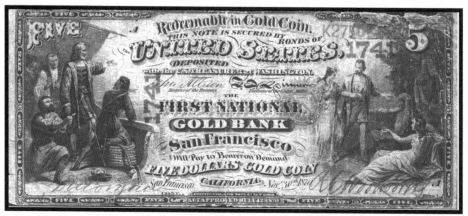

Face of Notes 1136-1141. Columbus Sighting Land *at left; at right, Columbus presenting a Native American princess, symbolic of America to allegorical representatives of the Old World.*

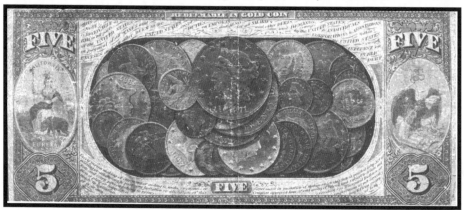

Back of Notes 1136-1141. An array of contemporary United States gold coins.

National Gold Bank Notes

No.	Date	Name of Bank	City	Fair	VG-8	F-12	VF-20	EF-40
1136.	1870	First National Gold Bank	San Francisco	$1,150.00	$2,500.00	$3,500.00	$6,000.00	$17,500.00
1137.	1872	National Gold Bank and Trust Company ..	San Francisco	1,500.00	5,000.00	15,000.00	Rare	Rare
1138.	1872	National Gold Bank of D.O. Mills and Co. .	Sacramento	1,500.00	5,000.00	15,000.00	35,000.00	Rare
1139.	1873	First National Gold Bank	Santa Barbara	1,500.00	5,000.00	Rare	—	—
1140.	1873	First National Gold Bank	Stockton	3,000.00	12,000.00	Rare	—	—
1141.	1874	Farmer's National Gold Bank	San Jose	1,200.00	2,500.00	7,000.00	25,000.00	—

Silver Certificates

Face of Notes 259-265. Bust of President Ulysses S. Grant.

Back of Notes 259-265. Five contemporary silver dollars, with the obverse of the coin in the center showing the date of the series, 1886.

No.	Series	Signatures		Seal	VG-8	F-12	VF-20	EF-40	Unc-63
259.	1886	Rosecrans	Jordan	Small Red, Plain	$425.00	$750.00	$1,650.00	$2,500.00	$5,500.00
260.	1886	Rosecrans	Hyatt	Small Red, Plain	425.00	750.00	1,650.00	2,500.00	4,500.00
261.	1886	Rosecrans	Hyatt	Large Red	425.00	750.00	1,650.00	2,500.00	5,000.00
262.	1886	Rosecrans	Huston	Large Red	425.00	750.00	1,650.00	2,500.00	5,000.00
263.	1886	Rosecrans	Huston	Large Brown	425.00	750.00	1,650.00	2,500.00	4,500.00
264.	1886	Rosecrans	Nebeker	Large Brown	425.00	750.00	1,650.00	2,500.00	5,500.00
265.	1886	Rosecrans	Nebeker	Small Red, Scalloped ...	425.00	750.00	1,650.00	2,500.00	6,000.00

Silver Certificates

Face of Notes 266-267. Bust of President Ulysses S. Grant

Back of Notes 266-267.

No.	Series	Signatures		Seal	VG-8	F-12	VF-20	EF-40	Unc-63
266.	1891	Rosecrans	Nebeker	Small Red, Scalloped ...	$250.00	$500.00	$900.00	$1,450.00	$4,500.00
267.	1891	Tillman	Morgan	Small Red	250.00	500.00	900.00	1,450.00	3,500.00

Face of Notes 268-270. Winged goddess representing Electricity as the controlling force in the world.

Silver Certificates

Back of Notes 268-270. Busts of generals Ulysses S. Grant and Philip Sheridan in ten-sided frames. The last of the three notes issued in the Educational Series.

No.	Series	Signatures	Seal	VG-8	F-12	VF-20	EF-40	Unc-63
268.	1896	Tillman Morgan	Small Red	$575.00	$1,100.00	$2,000.00	$2,800.00	$7,500.00
269.	1896	Bruce Roberts	Small Red	575.00	1,100.00	2,000.00	2,800.00	7,500.00
270.	1896	Lyons Roberts	Small Red	575.00	1,100.00	2,250.00	3,000.00	8,000.00

Face of Notes 271-281. Bust of the Oncpapa Sioux Indian chief most commonly known as Running Antelope or Chief Onepapa.

Back of Notes 271-281.

LARGE-SIZE FIVE DOLLAR NOTES

Silver Certificates

No.	Series	Signatures		Seal		VG-8	F-12	VF-20	EF-40	Unc-63
271.	1899	Lyons	Roberts	Blue	....	$450.00	$485.00	$700.00	$1,000.00	$2,400.00
272.	1899	Lyons	Treat	Blue	....	450.00	485.00	700.00	1,000.00	2,400.00
273.	1899	Vernon	Treat	Blue	....	450.00	485.00	700.00	1,000.00	2,400.00
274.	1899	Vernon	McClung	Blue	....	450.00	485.00	700.00	1,000.00	2,400.00
275.	1899	Napier	McClung	Blue	....	450.00	485.00	700.00	1,000.00	2,400.00
276.	1899	Napier	Thompson	Blue	....	575.00	750.00	1,400.00	2,000.00	7,000.00
277.	1899	Parker	Burke	Blue	....	450.00	485.00	700.00	1,000.00	2,400.00
278.	1899	Teehee	Burke	Blue	....	450.00	485.00	700.00	1,000.00	2,400.00
279.	1899	Elliott	Burke	Blue	....	450.00	485.00	700.00	1,000.00	2,400.00
280.	1899	Elliott	White	Blue	....	450.00	485.00	700.00	1,000.00	2,400.00
281.	1899	Speelman	White	Blue	....	450.00	485.00	700.00	1,000.00	2,400.00

Face of Note 282. Bust of Abraham Lincoln in a round frame,
giving rise to the characterization of this issue as the "Porthole Note."

Back of Note 282.

No.	Series	Signatures		Seal		VG-8	F-12	VF-20	EF-40	Unc-63
282.	1923 ...	Speelman	White	Blue	......	$460.00	$550.00	$825.00	$1,200.00	$2,150.00

Treasury or Coin Notes

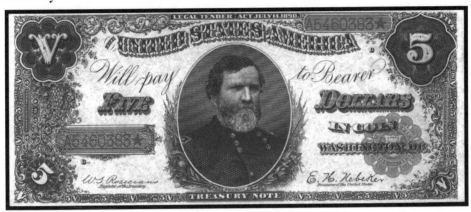

Face of Notes 359-361. Bust of Civil War General George H. Thomas.

Back of Notes 359-361.

No.	Series	Signatures		Seal	VG-8	F-12	VF-20	EF-40	Unc-63
359.	1890	Rosecrans	Huston	Large Brown	$300.00	$600.00	$1,100.00	$1,800.00	$4,200.00
360.	1890	Rosecrans	Nebeker	Large Brown	300.00	600.00	1,100.00	1,800.00	Rare
361.	1890	Rosecrans	Nebeker	Small Red	300.00	600.00	1,100.00	1,800.00	4,500.00

Treasury or Coin Notes

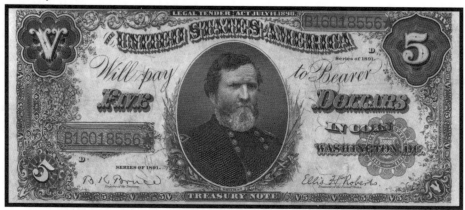

Face of Notes 362-365. Bust of Civil War General George H. Thomas.

Back of Notes 362-365.

No.	Series	Signatures		Seal	VG-8	F-12	VF-20	EF-40	Unc-63
362.	1891	Rosecrans	Nebeker	Small Red	$250.00	$350.00	$600.00	$800.00	$1,900.00
363.	1891	Tillman	Morgan	Small Red	250.00	350.00	600.00	800.00	1,900.00
364.	1891	Bruce	Roberts	Small Red	250.00	350.00	600.00	800.00	1,900.00
365.	1891	Lyons	Roberts	Small Red	300.00	450.00	750.00	1,000.00	10,000.00

Federal Reserve Bank Notes

Face of Notes 781-809a. Bust of Abraham Lincoln at left.

Treasury or Coin Notes

Back of Notes 781-809a. Columbus in sight of land at left. To right, Landing of the Pilgrims.

No.	Issuing Bank	Series	Government Signatures		Bank Signatures		VG-8	F-12	VF-20	EF-40	Unc-63
781.	Boston	1918	Teehee	Burke	Bullen	Morss	$300.00	$450.00	$650.00	$1,100.00	$2,800.00
782.	New York	1918	Teehee	Burke	Hendricks	Strong	175.00	260.00	475.00	675.00	1,100.00
783.	Philadelphia	1918	Teehee	Burke	Hardt	Passmore	225.00	320.00	550.00	800.00	1,450.00
784.	Philadelphia	1918	Teehee	Burke	Dyer	Passmore	225.00	320.00	550.00	800.00	2,000.00
785.	Cleveland	1918	Teehee	Burke	Baxter	Fancher	175.00	260.00	475.00	675.00	1,100.00
786.	Cleveland	1918	Teehee	Burke	Davis	Fancher	260.00	375.00	650.00	900.00	2,800.00
787.	Cleveland	1918	Elliott	Burke	Davis	Fancher	225.00	320.00	550.00	800.00	2,000.00
788.	Atlanta	1915	Teehee	Burke	Bell	Wellborn	260.00	375.00	650.00	900.00	—
789.	Atlanta	1915	Teehee	Burke	Pike	McCord	175.00	260.00	475.00	675.00	3,000.00
790.	Atlanta	1918	Teehee	Burke	Pike	McCord	175.00	260.00	475.00	675.00	1,100.00
791.	Atlanta	1918	Teehee	Burke	Bell	Wellborn	260.00	375.00	650.00	900.00	2,500.00
792.	Atlanta	1918	Elliott	Burke	Bell	Wellborn	280.00	400.00	700.00	1,000.00	3,000.00
793.	Chicago	1915	Teehee	Burke	McLallen	McDougal	225.00	320.00	550.00	800.00	2,000.00
794.	Chicago	1918	Teehee	Burke	McCloud	McDougal	175.00	260.00	475.00	675.00	1,100.00
795.	Chicago	1918	Teehee	Burke	Cramer	McDougal	300.00	400.00	725.00	1,100.00	—
796.	St. Louis	1918	Teehee	Burke	Attebery	Wells	175.00	260.00	475.00	675.00	1,700.00
797.	St. Louis	1918	Teehee	Burke	Attebery	Biggs	225.00	320.00	550.00	800.00	2,500.00
798.	St. Louis	1918	Elliott	Burke	White	Biggs	225.00	320.00	550.00	800.00	1,450.00
799.	Minneapolis	1918	Teehee	Burke	Cook	Wold	175.00	260.00	475.00	675.00	7,000.00
800.	Kansas City	1915	Teehee	Burke	Anderson	Miller	175.00	260.00	475.00	675.00	1,100.00
801.	Kansas City	1915	Teehee	Burke	Cross	Miller	280.00	400.00	700.00	1,000.00	—
802.	Kansas City	1915	Teehee	Burke	Helm	Miller	450.00	700.00	1,000.00	1,750.00	3,350.00
803.	Kansas City	1918	Teehee	Burke	Anderson	Miller	175.00	260.00	475.00	675.00	2,800.00
804.	Kansas City	1918	Elliott	Burke	Helm	Miller	175.00	260.00	475.00	675.00	2,800.00
805.	Dallas	1915	Teehee	Burke	Hoopes	Van Zandt	225.00	320.00	550.00	800.00	2,500.00
806.	Dallas	1915	Teehee	Burke	Talley	Van Zandt	280.00	400.00	700.00	1,000.00	—
807.	Dallas	1918	Teehee	Burke	Talley	Van Zandt	225.00	320.00	550.00	800.00	3,000.00
808.	San Francisco	1915	Teehee	Burke	Clerk	Lynch	225.00	320.00	550.00	800.00	1,450.00
809.	San Francisco	1918	Teehee	Burke	Clerk	Lynch	225.00	320.00	550.00	800.00	3,000.00
809a.	San Francisco	Similar, but with date May 18, 1914.					400.00	600.00	800.00	1,000.00	2,800.00

All other San Francisco notes are with date May 20, 1914. No notes were issued by the Richmond Bank.

LARGE-SIZE FIVE DOLLAR NOTES

Federal Reserve Notes

Face of Notes 832-891. Bust of Abraham Lincoln in center.

Back of Notes 832A-891C. Columbus in sight of land at left. To right, Landing of the Pilgrims.

Red Seals: **A.** Large district letter and numeral at top right and bottom left. Small letter at top left and bottom right. **B.** As above, with a small district letter and numeral added above letter at top left.

Blue Seals: **A.** Large letter and numeral at top left and bottom right. **B.** Large letter and numeral at top right with small district letters and numerals in the other three corners. **C.** Again, a large pair of letters and numerals, but positioned both vertically, more toward the center of the note and closer to the outside edge. Also, the seals to the sides of the portrait are closer to the note's center than the A issue.

A. Series of 1914 with red seal and signatures of Burke and McAdoo

No.	Issuing Bank	VG-8	F-12	VF-20	EF-40	Unc-63
832A.	Boston	$250.00	$400.00	$600.00	$900.00	$2,600.00
832B.	Boston	250.00	400.00	600.00	900.00	2,600.00
833A.	New York	200.00	350.00	525.00	750.00	2,100.00
833B.	New York	200.00	350.00	525.00	750.00	2,100.00
834A.	Philadelphia	250.00	400.00	600.00	900.00	2,600.00
834B.	Philadelphia	200.00	350.00	525.00	750.00	2,100.00
835A.	Cleveland	250.00	400.00	600.00	900.00	2,600.00
835B.	Cleveland	200.00	350.00	525.00	750.00	2,100.00
836A.	Richmond	350.00	550.00	775.00	1,200.00	3,500.00
836B.	Richmond	250.00	400.00	600.00	900.00	2,600.00
837A.	Atlanta	250.00	400.00	600.00	900.00	2,600.00
837B.	Atlanta	200.00	350.00	525.00	750.00	2,100.00
838A.	Chicago	200.00	350.00	525.00	750.00	2,100.00
838B.	Chicago	200.00	350.00	525.00	750.00	2,100.00
839A.	St. Louis	200.00	350.00	525.00	750.00	2,100.00
839B.	St. Louis	200.00	350.00	525.00	750.00	2,100.00

Federal Reserve Notes
A. Series of 1914 with red seal and signatures of Burke and McAdoo

No.	Issuing Bank	VG-8	F-12	VF-20	EF-40	Unc-63
840A.	Minneapolis	$250.00	$400.00	$600.00	$900.00	$2,600.00
840B.	Minneapolis	200.00	350.00	525.00	750.00	2,800.00
841A.	Kansas City	250.00	400.00	600.00	900.00	4,200.00
841B.	Kansas City	250.00	400.00	600.00	900.00	—
842A.	Dallas	350.00	550.00	725.00	1,200.00	3,500.00
842B.	Dallas	250.00	400.00	600.00	900.00	2,600.00
843A.	San Francisco	350.00	550.00	775.00	1,200.00	—
843B.	San Francisco	250.00	400.00	600.00	900.00	4,200.00

B. Series of 1914 with blue seal

No.	Issuing Bank	Signatures		VG	F-12	VF-20	EF-40	Unc-63
844.	Boston	Burke	McAdoo	$55.00	$65.00	$80.00	$100.00	$325.00
845.	Boston	Burke	Glass	65.00	80.00	125.00	225.00	750.00
846.	Boston	Burke	Houston	55.00	65.00	80.00	100.00	275.00
847A.	Boston	White	Mellon	55.00	65.00	80.00	100.00	350.00
847B.	Boston	White	Mellon	65.00	80.00	125.00	225.00	750.00
848.	New York	Burke	McAdoo	55.00	65.00	80.00	100.00	325.00
849.	New York	Burke	Glass	60.00	70.00	100.00	150.00	500.00
850.	New York	Burke	Houston	55.00	65.00	80.00	100.00	275.00
851A.	New York	White	Mellon	55.00	65.00	80.00	100.00	250.00
851B.	New York	White	Mellon	60.00	70.00	100.00	150.00	500.00
851C.	New York	White	Mellon	55.00	65.00	80.00	100.00	295.00
852.	Philadelphia	Burke	McAdoo	60.00	70.00	100.00	150.00	400.00
853.	Philadelphia	Burke	Glass	60.00	70.00	100.00	150.00	400.00
854.	Philadelphia	Burke	Houston	55.00	65.00	80.00	100.00	275.00
855A.	Philadelphia	White	Mellon	55.00	65.00	80.00	100.00	250.00
855B.	Philadelphia	White	Mellon	60.00	70.00	100.00	150.00	500.00
855C.	Philadelphia	White	Mellon	55.00	65.00	80.00	100.00	350.00
856.	Cleveland	Burke	McAdoo	60.00	70.00	100.00	150.00	500.00
857.	Cleveland	Burke	Glass	75.00	100.00	175.00	250.00	650.00
858A.	Cleveland	Burke	Houston	60.00	70.00	100.00	150.00	500.00
859A.	Cleveland	White	Mellon	55.00	65.00	80.00	100.00	250.00
859B.	Cleveland	White	Mellon	60.00	70.00	100.00	150.00	500.00
859C.	Cleveland	White	Mellon	55.00	65.00	80.00	150.00	295.00
860.	Richmond	Burke	McAdoo	60.00	70.00	100.00	150.00	500.00
861.	Richmond	Burke	Glass	65.00	80.00	125.00	225.00	750.00
862.	Richmond	Burke	Houston	55.00	65.00	80.00	100.00	275.00
863A.	Richmond	White	Mellon	55.00	65.00	80.00	100.00	350.00
863B.	Richmond	White	Mellon	100.00	250.00	450.00	750.00	—
864.	Atlanta	Burke	McAdoo	65.00	80.00	100.00	170.00	500.00
865.	Atlanta	Burke	Glass	65.00	80.00	125.00	225.00	750.00
866.	Atlanta	Burke	Houston	65.00	80.00	100.00	175.00	400.00
867A.	Atlanta	White	Mellon	55.00	65.00	80.00	100.00	250.00
867B.	Atlanta	White	Mellon	100.00	250.00	450.00	750.00	—
868.	Chicago	Burke	McAdoo	55.00	65.00	80.00	100.00	275.00
869.	Chicago	Burke	Glass	55.00	65.00	80.00	100.00	275.00
870.	Chicago	Burke	Houston	55.00	65.00	80.00	100.00	275.00
871A.	Chicago	White	Mellon	55.00	65.00	80.00	100.00	250.00
871B.	Chicago	White	Mellon	60.00	70.00	100.00	150.00	400.00
871C.	Chicago	White	Mellon	55.00	65.00	80.00	100.00	295.00
872.	St. Louis	Burke	McAdoo	55.00	65.00	80.00	100.00	275.00
873.	St. Louis	Burke	Glass	60.00	70.00	100.00	150.00	500.00
874.	St. Louis	Burke	Houston	55.00	65.00	80.00	100.00	275.00
875A.	St. Louis	White	Mellon	55.00	65.00	80.00	100.00	250.00
875B.	St. Louis	White	Mellon	60.00	70.00	100.00	150.00	400.00
876.	Minneapolis	Burke	McAdoo	55.00	65.00	80.00	100.00	350.00
877.	Minneapolis	Burke	Glass	55.00	65.00	80.00	100.00	275.00
878.	Minneapolis	Burke	Houston	55.00	65.00	80.00	100.00	500.00

LARGE-SIZE FIVE DOLLAR NOTES

Federal Reserve Notes

No.	Issuing Bank	Signatures		VG-8	F-12	VF-20	EF-40	Unc-63
879A.	Minneapolis	White	Mellon	$55.00	$65.00	$80.00	$100.00	$275.00
880.	Kansas City	Burke	McAdoo	55.00	65.00	80.00	100.00	275.00
881.	Kansas City	Burke	Glass	60.00	70.00	100.00	150.00	400.00
882.	Kansas City	Burke	Houston	55.00	65.00	80.00	100.00	275.00
883A.	Kansas City	White	Mellon	55.00	65.00	80.00	100.00	250.00
883B.	Kansas City	White	Mellon	75.00	100.00	175.00	250.00	650.00
884.	Dallas	Burke	McAdoo	55.00	65.00	80.00	100.00	275.00
885.	Dallas	Burke	Glass	75.00	100.00	175.00	250.00	500.00
886.	Dallas	Burke	Houston	55.00	65.00	80.00	100.00	275.00
887A.	Dallas	White	Mellon	55.00	65.00	80.00	100.00	250.00
887B.	Dallas	White	Mellon	70.00	90.00	140.00	200.00	500.00
888.	San Francisco	Burke	McAdoo	55.00	65.00	80.00	100.00	275.00
889.	San Francisco	Burke	Glass	75.00	100.00	175.00	250.00	650.00
890.	San Francisco	Burke	Houston	55.00	65.00	80.00	100.00	300.00
891A.	San Francisco	White	Mellon	55.00	65.00	80.00	100.00	250.00
891B.	San Francisco	White	Mellon	60.00	70.00	100.00	150.00	400.00
891C.	San Francisco	White	Mellon	75.00	100.00	175.00	250.00	650.00

Legal Tender Notes

Face of Notes 1525-1531.

Back of Notes 1525-1531.

No.	Series	Signatures		Quantity Printed	VF-20	Unc-63
1525.	1928	Woods	Mellon	267,209,616	$15.00	$85.00
1525*.	1928	Woods	Mellon		225.00	2,000.00
1526.	1928-A	Woods	Mills	58,194,600	20.00	125.00
1526*.	1928-A	Woods	Mills		1,700.00	5,000.00
1527.	1928-B	Julian	Morgenthau	147,827,340	15.00	50.00
1527*.	1928-B	Julian	Morgenthau		150.00	1,000.00
1528.	1928-C	Julian	Morgenthau	214,735,765	15.00	45.00
1528*.	1928-C	Julian	Morgenthau		100.00	700.00
1529.	1928-D	Julian	Vinson	9,297,120	45.00	250.00
1529*.	1928-D	Julian	Vinson		900.00	4,000.00
1530.	1928-E	Julian	Snyder	109,952,760	15.00	65.00
1530*.	1928-E	Julian	Snyder		125.00	700.00
1531.	1928-F	Clark	Snyder	104,194,704	12.00	45.00
1531*.	1928-F	Clark	Snyder		100.00	500.00

Legal Tender Notes

Face of Notes 1532-1535 (not shown). Similar to face of Notes 1525-1531.

Back of Notes 1532-1535 (not shown). Similar to back of Notes 1525-1531

No.	Series	Signatures		Quantity Printed	VF-20	Unc-63
1532.	1953	Priest	Humphrey	120,880,000	$10.00	$50.00
1532*.	1953	Priest	Humphrey	5,760,000	60.00	300.00
1533.	1953-A	Priest	Anderson	90,280,000	10.00	25.00
1533*.	1953-A	Priest	Anderson	5,400,000	50.00	175.00
1534.	1953-B	Smith	Dillon	44,640,000	10.00	25.00
1534*.	1953-B	Smith	Dillon	2,160,000	50.00	150.00
1535.	1953-C	Granahan	Dillon	8,640,000	15.00	55.00
1535*.	1953-C	Granahan	Dillon	320,000	60.00	300.00
1536.	1963	Granahan	Dillon	63,360,000	9.00	25.00
1536*	1963	Granahan	Dillon	3,840,000	15.00	85.00

National Bank Notes

Face of Note 1800.

Back of Note 1800.

No.		VF-20	Unc-63
1800-1.	Type 1	$100.00	$250.00
1800-2.	Type 2	100.00	250.00

These were issued from 1929 to 1935 in sheets of six notes.

SMALL-SIZE FIVE DOLLAR NOTES

Silver Certificates

Face of Notes 1650-1654.

Back of Notes 1650-1654.

No.	Series	Signatures		Quantity Printed	VF-20	Unc-63
1650.	1934	Julian	Morgenthau	393,088,368	$9.00	$55.00
1650*.	1934	Julian	Morgenthau	. . . .	70.00	400.00
1651.	1934-A . .	Julian	Morgenthau	656,265,948	8.50	25.00
1651*.	1934-A . .	Julian	Morgenthau	. . . .	45.00	350.00

Notes Issued for Use with the Armed Forces in Europe and North Africa

Face of Note 2307. Blue serial numbers with yellow seal.

Back of Note 2307.

No.	Denomination	Series	Quantity Printed	VF-20	Unc-63
2307.	Five Dollars	1934-A	. . . .	16,710,000	$75.00	$300.00
2307*.	Five Dollars	1934-A	. . . .	. . . .	175.00	1,200.00

Silver Certificates

Regular Issue Silver Certificates (continued from note 1651)

No.	Series	Signatures		Quantity Printed	VF-20	Unc-63
1652.	1934-B	Julian	Vinson	59,128,500	$10.00	$65.00
1652*.	1934-B	Julian	Vinson	. . . .	125.00	1,000.00
1653.	1934-C	Julian	Snyder	403,146,148	8.00	40.00
1653*.	1934-C	Julian	Snyder	. . . .	55.00	200.00
1654.	1934-D	Clark	Snyder	486,146,148	8.50	35.00
1654*.	1934-D	Clark	Snyder	. . . .	45.00	200.00

Face and Back of Notes 1655-1658 (not shown). Similar to face and back of Note 2307.

No.	Series	Signatures		Quantity Printed	VF-20	Unc-63
1655.	1953	Priest	Humphrey	339,600,000	$8.50	$35.00
1655*.	1953	Priest	Humphrey	15,120,000	25.00	90.00
1656.	1953-A	Priest	Anderson	232,400,000	8.50	35.00
1656*.	1953-A	Priest	Anderson	12,960,000	25.00	75.00
1657.	1953-B	Smith	Dillon	73,000,000†	8.50	30.00
1657*.	1953-B	Smith	Dillon	3,240,000	2,500.00	8,000.00
1658.	1953-C	Granahan	Dillon	. . . .	Not released	—

†Only 14,196,000 notes were released.

Federal Reserve Bank Notes

Face of Note 1850.

Back of Note 1850.

No.	Issuing Bank		Quantity Printed	VF-20	Unc-63
1850-A.	Boston	. . . .	3,180,000	$40.00	$150.00
1850-B.	New York	. . . .	2,100,000	40.00	200.00
1850-C.	Philadelphia	. . . .	3,096,000	40.00	150.00
1850-D.	Cleveland	. . . .	4,236,000	40.00	150.00
1850-F	Atlanta	. . . .	1,884,000	40.00	200.00
1850-G.	Chicago	. . . .	5,988,000	40.00	150.00
1850-H.	St. Louis	. . . .	276,000	600.00	6,000.00
1850-I.	Minneapolis	. . . .	684,000	125.00	1,000.00
1850-J.	Kansas City	. . . .	2,460,000	50.00	300.00
1850-K.	Dallas	. . . .	996,000	45.00	200.00
1850-L.	San Francisco	. . . .	360,000	1,750.00	10,000.00
1850*.	Most Common Districts	. . . .	. . . .	700.00	4,500.00

SMALL-SIZE FIVE DOLLAR NOTES

Federal Reserve Notes

Face of Notes 1950-1951 (not shown). Similar to face of Note 1850.
Back of Notes 1950-1951(not shown). Similar to back of Note 1850.

Series of 1928
Signatures of Tate and Mellon

No.	Issuing Bank	Quantity Printed		VF-20	Unc-63
1950-A.	Boston	8,025,300		$55.00	$375.00
1950-A*.	Boston			275.00	1,500.00
1950-B.	New York	14,701,884		35.00	200.00
1950-B*.	New York			200.00	1,000.00
1950-C.	Philadelphia	11,819,712		35.00	200.00
1950-C*.	Philadelphia			200.00	1,000.00
1950-D.	Cleveland	9,049,500		35.00	200.00
1950-D*.	Cleveland			200.00	800.00
1950-E.	Richmond	6,027,600		35.00	200.00
1950-E*.	Richmond			250.00	1,300.00
1950-F.	Atlanta	10,964,400		35.00	200.00
1950-F*.	Atlanta			250.00	1,100.00
1950-G.	Chicago	12,320,052		35.00	200.00
1950-G*.	Chicago			200.00	900.00
1950-H.	St. Louis	4,675,200		55.00	275.00
1950-A.	Boston	8,025,300		55.00	375.00
1950-A*.	Boston			275.00	1,500.00
1950-B.	New York	14,701,884		35.00	200.00
1950-B*.	New York			200.00	1,000.00
1950-C.	Philadelphia	11,819,712		35.00	200.00
1950-C*.	Philadelphia			200.00	1,000.00
1950-D.	Cleveland	9,049,500		35.00	200.00
1950-D*.	Cleveland			200.00	800.00
1950-E.	Richmond	6,027,600		35.00	200.00
1950-E*.	Richmond			250.00	1,300.00
1950-F.	Atlanta	10,964,400		35.00	200.00
1950-F*.	Atlanta			250.00	1,100.00
1950-G.	Chicago	12,320,052		35.00	200.00
1950-G*.	Chicago			200.00	900.00
1950-H.	St. Louis	4,675,200		55.00	275.00
1950-H*.	St. Louis			250.00	1,100.00
1950-I.	Minneapolis	4,284,300		225.00	1,100.00
1950-I*.	Minneapolis			550.00	2,250.00
1950-J.	Kansas City	4,480,800		35.00	275.00
1950-J*.	Kansas City			300.00	1,250.00
1950-K.	Dallas	8,137,824		35.00	175.00
1950-K*.	Dallas			250.00	950.00
1950-L.	San Francisco	9,792,000		30.00	275.00
1950-L*.	San Francisco			300.00	1,500.00

Series of 1928-A
Signatures of Woods and Mellon

No.	Issuing Bank	Quantity Printed		VF-20	Unc-63
1951-A.	Boston	9,404,352		$50.00	$250.00
1951-A*.	Boston			500.00	1,250.00
1951-B.	New York	42,878,196		40.00	200.00
1951-B*.	New York			500.00	1,250.00
1951-C.	Philadelphia	10,806,012		45.00	225.00
1951-C*.	Philadelphia			300.00	1,000.00
1951-D.	Cleveland	6,822,000		40.00	175.00
1951-D*.	Cleveland			200.00	1,000.00
1951-E.	Richmond	2,409,900		50.00	225.00
1951-E*.	Richmond			200.00	1,000.00
1951-F.	Atlanta	3,537,600		50.00	300.00
1951-F*.	Atlanta			550.00	1,750.00
1951-G.	Chicago	37,882,176		40.00	175.00
1951-G*.	Chicago			200.00	1,000.00
1951-H.	St. Louis	2,731,824		50.00	225.00
1951-H*.	St. Louis			550.00	1,750.00
1951-I.	Minneapolis	652,800		550.00	1,750.00
1951-J.	Kansas City	3,572,400		55.00	300.00
1951-K	Dallas	2,564,400		65.00	300.00
1951-K*	Dallas			500.00	1,750.00
1951-L	San Francisco	6,565,500		50.00	250.00
1951-L*.	San Francisco			200.00	1,000.00

Federal Reserve Notes

Face of Notes 1952-1960.

Back of Notes 1952-1960.

Series of 1928-B
Signatures of Woods and Mellon

No.	Issuing Bank	Quantity Printed	VF-20	Unc-63
1952-A.	Boston	28,430,724	$20.00	$65.00
1952-A*.	Boston		200.00	900.00
1952-B.	New York	51,157,536	20.00	65.00
1952-B*.	New York		200.00	800.00
1952-C.	Philadelphia	25,698,396	20.00	65.00
1952-C*.	Philadelphia		200.00	900.00
1952-D.	Cleveland	24,874,272	20.00	65.00
1952-D*.	Cleveland		200.00	900.00
1952-E.	Richmond	15,151,932	25.00	100.00
1952-E*.	Richmond		250.00	1,000.00
1952-F.	Atlanta	13,386,420	25.00	100.00
1952-F*.	Atlanta		200.00	900.00
1952-G.	Chicago	17,157,036	20.00	65.00
1952-G*.	Chicago		250.00	1,000.00
1952-H.	St. Louis	20,251,716	20.00	65.00
1952-H*.	St. Louis		200.00	800.00
1952-I.	Minneapolis	6,954,060	40.00	175.00
1952-I*.	Minneapolis		250.00	1,000.00
1952-J.	Kansas City	10,677,636	20.00	65.00
1952-J*.	Kansas City		250.00	900.00
1952-K.	Dallas	4,334,400	25.00	100.00
1952-K*.	Dallas		250.00	1,000.00
1952-L.	San Francisco	28,840,000	20.00	65.00
1952-L*.	San Francisco		250.00	900.00

Series of 1928-C
Signatures of Woods and Mills

No.	Issuing Bank	Quantity Printed	VF-20	Unc-63
1953-D.	Cleveland	3,293,640	Unknown	—
1953-F.	Atlanta	2,056,200	$1,000.00	$3,500.00
1953-L.	San Francisco	266,304	Unknown	—

SMALL-SIZE FIVE DOLLAR NOTES

Federal Reserve Notes

Series of 1928-D
Signatures of Woods and Woodin

No.	Issuing Bank	Quantity Printed	VF-20	Unc-63
1954-F.	Atlanta	1,281,600	.... $1,500.00	$6,000.00

Series of 1934
Signatures of Julian and Morgenthau
The quantity printed is the combined total for both light and dark seal notes

A. Notes with a vivid light green seal

No.	Issuing Bank	Quantity Printed	VF-20	Unc-63
1955-A.	Boston	30,510,036	$15.00	$85.00
1955-A*.	Boston		400.00	1,500.00
1955-B.	New York	47,888,760	15.00	80.00
1955-B*.	New York		400.00	1,000.00
1955-C.	Philadelphia	47,327,760	15.00	85.00
1955-C*.	Philadelphia		400.00	1,500.00
1955-D.	Cleveland	62,273,508	15.00	85.00
1955-D*.	Cleveland		400.00	1,500.00
1955-E.	Richmond	62,128,452	15.00	85.00
1955-E*.	Richmond		400.00	1,500.00
1955-F.	Atlanta	50,548,608	20.00	80.00
1955-F*.	Atlanta		400.00	1,500.00
1955-G.	Chicago	31,299,156	15.00	85.00
1955-G*.	Chicago		400.00	1,000.00
1955-H.	St. Louis	48,737,280	15.00	90.00
1955-H*.	St. Louis		400.00	1,500.00
1955-I.	Minneapolis	16,795,392	$30.00	$100.00
1955-I*.	Minneapolis		400.00	2,000.00
1955-J.	Kansas City	31,854,432	35.00	95.00
1955-J*.	Kansas City		400.00	1,500.00
1955-K.	Dallas	33,332,208	15.00	85.00
1955-K*.	Dallas		400.00	2,000.00
1955-L.	San Francisco	39,324,168	15.00	85.00
1955-L*.	San Francisco		400.00	1,750.00

B. Notes with a darker and duller blue-green seal

No.	Issuing Bank	VF-20	Unc-63
1956-A.	Boston	$20.00	$60.00
1956-A*.	Boston	100.00	350.00
1956-B.	New York	17.50	55.00
1956-B*.	New York	100.00	350.00
1956-C.	Philadelphia	17.50	55.00
1956-C*.	Philadelphia	100.00	350.00
1956-D.	Cleveland	15.00	50.00
1956-D*.	Cleveland	100.00	350.00
1956-E.	Richmond	15.00	50.00
1956-E*.	Richmond	100.00	350.00
1956-F.	Atlanta	17.50	55.00
1956-F*.	Atlanta	125.00	400.00
1956-G.	Chicago	20.00	60.00
1956-G*.	Chicago	100.00	350.00
1956-H.	St. Louis	17.50	55.00
1956-H*.	St. Louis	100.00	350.00

Federal Reserve Notes

No.	Issuing Bank	VF-20	Unc-63
1956-I.	Minneapolis	$25.00	$65.00
1956-I*.	Minneapolis	225.00	900.00
1956-J.	Kansas City	20.00	60.00
1956-J*.	Kansas City	125.00	400.00
1956-K.	Dallas	25.00	65.00
1956-K*.	Dallas	125.00	400.00
1956-L.	San Francisco	20.00	60.00
1956-L*.	San Francisco	125.00	400.00

Notes issued for Hawaii after the attack on Pearl Harbor

Face of Note 2301. Brown seal.

Back of Note 2301.

No.	Denomination	Series	Quantity Printed	VF-20	Unc-63
2301.	Five Dollars	1934	9,416,000	$125.00	$650.00
2301*.	Five Dollars	1934		3,500.00	10,000.00
2302.	Five Dollars	1934-A	incl. above	125.00	625.00
2302*.	Five Dollars	1934-A		7,500 .00	Rare

Regular Issue Federal Reserve Notes (continued from note 1956)
Series of 1934-A
Signatures of Julian and Morgenthau

No.	Issuing Bank	Quantity Printed	VF-20	Unc-63
1957-A.	Boston	23,231,568	$12.50	$30.00
1957-A*.	Boston		50.00	350.00
1957-B.	New York	143,199,336	12.50	30.00
1957-B*.	New York		50.00	350.00
1957-C.	Philadelphia	30,691,632	12.50	30.00
1957-C*.	Philadelphia		50.00	350.00
1957-D.	Cleveland	1,610,676	15.00	35.00
1957-D*.	Cleveland		75.00	650.00
1957-E.	Richmond	6,555,168	15.00	35.00
1957-E*.	Richmond		60.00	600.00
1957-F.	Atlanta	22,811,916	30.00	85.00
1957-F*.	Atlanta		100.00	700.00
1957-G.	Chicago	88,376,376	12.50	30.00
1957-G*.	Chicago		50.00	350.00
1957-H.	St. Louis	7,843,452	30.00	85.00
1957-H*.	St. Louis		50.00	500.00
1957-L.	San Francisco	72,118,452	15.00	40.00
1957-L*.	San Francisco		50.00	350.00

SMALL-SIZE FIVE DOLLAR NOTES

Federal Reserve Notes

Series of 1934-B
Signatures of Julian and Vinson

No.	Issuing Bank	Quantity Printed	VF-20	Unc-63
1958-A.	Boston	3,457,800	$20.00	$90.00
1958-A*.	Boston		125.00	1,500.00
1958-B.	New York	14,099,580	15.00	80.00
1958-B*.	New York		100.00	800.00
1958-C.	Philadelphia	8,306,820	15.00	85.00
1958-C*.	Philadelphia		125.00	1,000.00
1958-D.	Cleveland	11,348,184	15.00	85.00
1958-D*.	Cleveland		125.00	1,000.00
1958-E.	Richmond	5,902,848	25.00	95.00
1958-E*.	Richmond		125.00	1,500.00
1958-F.	Atlanta	4,314,048	25.00	95.00
1958-F*.	Atlanta		225.00	1,500.00
1958-G.	Chicago	9,070,932	15.00	75.00
1958-G*.	Chicago		125.00	1,000.00
1958-H.	St. Louis	4,307,712	20.00	85.00
1958-H*.	St. Louis		125.00	1,000.00
1958-I.	Minneapolis	2,482,500	50.00	150.00
1958-I*.	Minneapolis		150.00	1,500.00
1958-J.	Kansas City	73,800	1,500.00	3,500.00
1958-L.	San Francisco	9,910,296	15.00	75.00
1958-L*.	San Francisco		125.00	2,000.00

Series of 1934-C
Signatures of Julian and Snyder

No.	Issuing Bank	Quantity Printed	VF-20	Unc-63
1959-A.	Boston	14,463,600	$20.00	$70.00
1959-A*.	Boston		125.00	1,000.00
1959-B.	New York	74,383,248	15.00	60.00
1959-B*.	New York		125.00	800.00
1959-C.	Philadelphia	22,879,212	15.00	60.00
1959-C*.	Philadelphia		150.00	1,000.00
1959-D.	Cleveland	19,898,256	15.00	60.00
1959-D*.	Cleveland		100.00	1,000.00
1959-E.	Richmond	23,800,524	15.00	60.00
1959-E*.	Richmond		150.00	1,100.00
1959-F.	Atlanta	23,572,968	15.00	60.00
1959-F*.	Atlanta		150.00	1,500.00
1959-G.	Chicago	60,598,812	15.00	60.00
1959-G*.	Chicago		125.00	800.00
1959-H.	St. Louis	20,393,340	25.00	80.00
1959-H*.	St. Louis		125.00	1,000.00
1959-I.	Minneapolis	5,089,200	30.00	175.00
1959-I*.	Minneapolis		225.00	2,000.00
1959-J.	Kansas City	8,313,504	25.00	80.00
1959-J*.	Kansas City		300.00	1,000.00
1959-K.	Dallas	5,107,800	30.00	90.00
1959-K*.	Dallas		225.00	1,500.00
1959-L.	San Francisco	9,451,944	25.00	80.00
1959-L*.	San Francisco		150.00	1,000.00

Federal Reserve Notes

Series of 1934-D
Signatures of Clark and Snyder

No.	Issuing Bank	Quantity Printed	VF-20	Unc-63
1960-A	Boston	12,660,552	$20.00	$75.00
1960-A*.	Boston		150.00	1,000.00
1960-B	New York	50,976,576	15.00	65.00
1960-B*.	New York		100.00	700.00
1960-C	Philadelphia	12,106,740	15.00	65.00
1960-C*.	Philadelphia		100.00	800.00
1960-D	Cleveland	8,969,052	15.00	75.00
1960-D*.	Cleveland		200.00	1,500.00
1960-E	Richmond	13,333,032	25.00	80.00
1960-E*.	Richmond		400.00	2,000.00
1960-F.	Atlanta	9,599,352	300.00	1,500.00
1960-F*.	Atlanta		600.00	5,000.00
1960-G	Chicago	36,601,680	15.00	80.00
1960-G*.	Chicago		100.00	800.00
1960-H	St. Louis	8,093,412	25.00	80.00
1960-H*.	St. Louis		150.00	1,000.00
1960-I.	Minneapolis	3,594,900	50.00	400.00
1960-I*	Minneapolis		500.00	2,000.00
1960-J.	Kansas City	6,538,740	30.00	90.00
1960-J*.	Kansas City		250.00	1,200.00
1960-K	Dallas	4,139,016	45.00	175.00
1960-K*.	Dallas		150.00	1,000.00
1960-L	San Francisco	11,704,200	30.00	90.00
1960-L*.	San Francisco		150.00	1,000.00

Face of Notes 1961-1966 (not shown).

Face of Notes 1961-1966 (not shown).

Series of 1950
Signatures of Clark and Snyder

No.	Issuing Bank	Quantity Printed	VF-20	Unc-63
1961-A.	Boston	30,672,000	$12.50	$65.00
1961-A*.	Boston	408,000	40.00	300.00
1961-B.	New York	106,768,000	12.50	65.00
1961-B*.	New York	1,464,000	30.00	250.00
1961-C.	Philadelphia	44,784,000	12.50	65.00
1961-C*.	Philadelphia	600,000	40.00	300.00
1961-D.	Cleveland	54,000,000	12.50	65.00
1961-D*.	Cleveland	744,000	40.00	300.00
1961-E.	Richmond	47,088,000	12.50	65.00
1961-E*.	Richmond	684,000	50.00	500.00
1961-F.	Atlanta	52,416,000	12.50	65.00
1961-F*.	Atlanta	696,000	40.00	300.00
1961-G.	Chicago	85,104,000	12.50	65.00
1961-G*.	Chicago	1,176,000	30.00	250.00
1961-H.	St. Louis	36,864,000	15.00	70.00
1961-H*.	St. Louis	552,000	30.00	250.00
1961-I.	Minneapolis	11,796,000	12.50	65.00
1961-I*.	Minneapolis	144,000	100.00	750.00
1961-J.	Kansas City	25,428,000	12.50	65.00
1961-J*.	Kansas City	360,000	30.00	250.00
1961-K.	Dallas	22,848,000	12.50	65.00
1961.K*.	Dallas	372,000	85.00	650.00
1961-L.	San Francisco	55,008,000	12.50	65.00
1961-L*.	San Francisco	744,000	40.00	300.00

SMALL-SIZE FIVE DOLLAR NOTES

Federal Reserve Notes

Series of 1950-A
Signatures of Priest and Humphrey

No.	Issuing Bank	Quantity Printed	VF-20	Unc-63
1962-A.	Boston	53,568,000	$10.00	$25.00
1962-A*.	Boston	2,808,000	25.00	85.00
1962-B.	New York	186,472,000	10.00	25.00
1962-B*.	New York	9,216,000	22.50	70.00
1962-C.	Philadelphia	69,616,000	10.00	25.00
1962-C*.	Philadelphia	4,320,000	25.00	85.00
1962-D.	Cleveland	45,360,000	10.00	25.00
1962-D*.	Cleveland	2,376,000	25.00	85.00
1962-E.	Richmond	76,672,000	10.00	25.00
1962-E*.	Richmond	5,400,000	50.00	150.00
1962-F.	Atlanta	86,464,000	10.00	25.00
1962-F*.	Atlanta	5,040,000	25.00	85.00
1962-G.	Chicago	129,296,000	10.00	25.00
1962-G*.	Chicago	6,264,000	20.00	65.00
1962-H.	St. Louis	54,936,000	10.00	25.00
1962-H*.	St. Louis	3,384,000	35.00	100.00
1962-I.	Minneapolis	11,232,000	15.00	35.00
1962-I *.	Minneapolis	864,000	65.00	350.00
1962-J.	Kansas City	29,952,000	12.50	30.00
1962-J*.	Kansas City	1,088,000	35.00	100.00
1962-K.	Dallas	24,984,000	15.00	35.00
1962-K*.	Dallas	1,368,000	50.00	150.00
1962-L.	San Francisco	90,712,000	10.00	25.00
1962-L*.	San Francisco	744,000	25.00	85.00

Series of 1950-B
Signatures of Priest and Anderson

No.	Issuing Bank	Quantity Printed	VF-20	Unc-63
1963-A.	Boston	30,880,000	$8.00	$25.00
1963-A*.	Boston	2,520,000	15.00	60.00
1963-B.	New York	85,960,000	8.00	25.00
1963-B*.	New York	4,680,060	15.00	60.00
1963-C.	Philadelphia	43,560,000	8.00	25.00
1963-C*.	Philadelphia	2,880,000	15.00	60.00
1963-D.	Cleveland	38,800,000	8.00	25.00
1963-D*.	Cleveland	2,880,000	15.00	60.00
1963-E.	Richmond	52,920,000	8.00	25.00
1963-E*.	Richmond	2,080,000	15.00	60.00
1963-F.	Atlanta	80,560,000	8.00	25.00
1963-F*.	Atlanta	3,960,000	20.00	70.00
1963-G.	Chicago	104,320,000	8.00	25.00
1963-G*.	Chicago	6,120,000	15.00	60.00
1963-H.	St. Louis	25,840,000	8.00	25.00
1963-H*.	St. Louis	1,440,000	20.00	70.00
1963-I.	Minneapolis	20,880,000	10.00	30.00
1963-I*.	Minneapolis	792,000	40.00	150.00
1963-J.	Kansas City	32,400,000	8.00	25.00
1963-J*.	Kansas City	2,520,000	20.00	70.00
1963-K.	Dallas	52,120,000	8.00	25.00
1963-K*.	Dallas	3,240,000	20.00	70.00
1963-L.	San Francisco	56,080,000	8.00	25.00
1963-L*.	San Francisco	3,600,000	25.00	75.00

Federal Reserve Notes
Series of 1950-C
Signatures of Smith and Dillon

No.	Issuing Bank	Quantity Printed	VF-20	Unc-63
1964-A.	Boston	20,880,000	$8.00	$25.00
1964-A*.	Boston	720,000	30.00	150.00
1964-B.	New York	47,440,000	8.00	25.00
1964-B*.	New York	2,880,000	15.00	70.00
1964-C.	Philadelphia	29,520,000	8.00	25.00
1964-C*.	Philadelphia	1,800,000	25.00	75.00
1964-D.	Cleveland	33,840,000	8.00	25.00
1964-D*.	Cleveland	1,800,000	30.00	100.00
1964-E.	Richmond	33,480,000	8.00	25.00
1964-E*.	Richmond	2,160,000	30.00	100.00
1964-F.	Atlanta	54,360,000	8.00	25.00
1964-F*.	Atlanta	3,240,000	15.00	60.00
1964-G.	Chicago	56,880,000	8.00	25.00
1964-G*.	Chicago	3,240,000	15.00	60.00
1964-H.	St. Louis	22,680,000	10.00	30.00
1964-H*.	St. Louis	720,000	35.00	125.00
1964-I.	Minneapolis	12,960,000	15.00	50.00
1964-I*.	Minneapolis	720,000	40.00	150.00
1964-J.	Kansas City	24,760,000	8.00	25.00
1964-J*.	Kansas City	1,800,000	30.00	120.00
1964-K.	Dallas	3,960,000	25.00	75.00
1964-K*.	Dallas	360,000	50.00	200.00
1964-L.	San Francisco	25,920,000	8.00	25.00
1964-L*.	San Francisco	1,440,000	40.00	150.00

Series of 1950-D
Signatures of Granahan and Dillon

No.	Issuing Bank	Quantity Printed	VF-20	Unc-63
1965-A.	Boston	25,200,000	$8.00	$25.00
1965-A*.	Boston	1,080,000	30.00	120.00
1965-B.	New York	102,160,000	8.00	25.00
1965-B*.	New York	5,040,000	15.00	60.00
1965-C.	Philadelphia	21,520,000	8.00	25.00
1966-C*.	Philadelphia	1,080,000	25.00	75.00
1965-D.	Cleveland	23,400,000	8.00	25.00
1965-D*.	Cleveland	1,080,000	25.00	75.00
1965-E.	Richmond	42,490,000	8.00	25.00
1965-E*.	Richmond	1,080,000	40.00	150.00
1965-F.	Atlanta	35,200,000	8.00	25.00
1965-F*.	Atlanta	1,800,000	25.00	75.00
1965-G.	Chicago	67,240,000	8.00	25.00
1965-G*.	Chicago	3,600,000	15.00	60.00
1965-H.	St. Louis	20,160,000	8.00	25.00
1965-H*.	St. Louis	720,000	35.00	100.00
1965-I.	Minneapolis	7,920,000	10.00	30.00
1965-I*.	Minneapolis	360,000	40.00	150.00
1966-J.	Kansas City	11,160,000	8.00	25.00
1965-J*.	Kansas City	720,000	35.00	100.00
1965-K.	Dallas	7,200,000	10.00	30.00
1965-K*.	Dallas	360,000	40.00	150.00
1965-L.	San Francisco	53,280,000	8.00	25.00
1965-L*.	San Francisco	3,600,000	15.00	60.00

SMALL-SIZE FIVE DOLLAR NOTES

Federal Reserve Notes
Series of 1950-E
Signatures of Granahan and Fowler

No.	Issuing Bank	Quantity Printed	VF-20	Unc-63
1966-B.	New York	82,000,000	$10.00	$40.00
1966-B*.	New York	6,678,000	25.00	75.00
1966-G.	Chicago	14,760,000	20.00	80.00
1966-G*.	Chicago	1,080,000	50.00	200.00
1966-L.	San Francisco	24,400,000	15.00	60.00
1966-L*.	San Francisco	1,800,000	50.00	200.00

Face of Notes 1967-1985 (not shown).
Back of Notes 1967-1985 (not shown).

Series of 1963
Signatures of Granahan and Dillon

No.	Issuing Bank	Quantity Printed	VF-20	Unc-63
1967-A.	Boston	4,480,000	$7.00	$20.00
1967-A*.	Boston	640,000	12.50	50.00
1967-B.	New York	12,160,000	7.00	20.00
1967-B*.	New York	1,280,000	10.00	40.00
1997-C.	Philadelphia	8,320,000	7.00	20.00
1967-C*.	Philadelphia	1,920,000	10.00	40.00
1967-D.	Cleveland	10,240,000	7.00	20.00
1967-D*.	Cleveland	1,920,000	10.00	40.00
1967-F.	Atlanta	17,920,000	7.00	20.00
1967-F*.	Atlanta	2,560,000	12.50	50.00
1967-G.	Chicago	22,400,000	7.00	20.00
1997-G*.	Chicago	3,200,000	10.00	40.00
1967-H.	St. Louis	14,080,000	7.00	20.00
1967-H*.	St. Louis	1,920,000	10.00	40.00
1967-J.	Kansas City	1,920,000	7.00	20.00
1967-J*.	Kansas City	640,000	12.50	50.00
1967-K.	Dallas	5,760,000	7.00	20.00
1967-K*.	Dallas	1,920,000	12.50	50.00
1967-L.	San Francisco	18,560,000	7.00	20.00
1967-L*.	San Francisco	1,920,000	10.00	40.00

Series of 1963
Signatures of Granahan and Fowler

No.	Issuing Bank	Quantity Printed	VF-20	Unc-63
1968-A.	Boston	77,440,000	$6.00	$15.00
1968-A*.	Boston	5,760,000	9.00	30.00
1968-B.	New York	98,080,000	6.00	15.00
1968-B*.	New York	7,680,000	9.00	25.00
1968-C.	Philadelphia	106,400,000	6.00	15.00
1968-C*.	Philadelphia	10,240,000	9.00	25.00
1968-D.	Cleveland	83,840,000	6.00	15.00
1968-D*.	Cleveland	7,040,000	9.00	25.00
1968-E.	Richmond	118,560,000	6.00	15.00
1967-F.	Atlanta	17,920,000	7.00	20.00
1967-F*.	Atlanta	2,560,000	12.50	50.00
1967-G.	Chicago	22,400,000	7.00	20.00
1997-G*.	Chicago	3,200,000	10.00	40.00
1967-H.	St. Louis	14,080,000	7.00	20.00
1967-H*.	St. Louis	1,920,000	10.00	40.00
1967-J.	Kansas City	1,920,000	7.00	20.00
1967-J*.	Kansas City	640,000	12.50	50.00
1967-K.	Dallas	5,760,000	7.00	20.00
1967-K*.	Dallas	1,920,000	12.50	50.00
1967-L.	San Francisco	18,560,000	7.00	20.00
1967-L*.	San Francisco	1,920,000	10.00	40.00

Federal Reserve Notes

Series of 1963-A
Signatures of Granahan and Fowler

No.	Issuing Bank	Quantity Printed	VF-20	Unc-63
1968-A.	Boston	77,440,000	$6.00	$15.00
1968-A*.	Boston	5,760,000	9.00	30.00
1968-B.	New York	98,080,000	6.00	15.00
1968-B*.	New York	7,680,000	9.00	25.00
1968-C.	Philadelphia	106,400,000	6.00	15.00
1968-C*.	Philadelphia	10,240,000	9.00	25.00
1968-D.	Cleveland	83,840,000	6.00	15.00
1968-D*.	Cleveland	7,040,000	9.00	25.00
1968-E.	Richmond	118,560,000	6.00	15.00
1968-E*.	Richmond	10,880,000	10.00	30.00
1968-F.	Atlanta	117,920,000	6.00	15.00
1968-F*.	Atlanta	9,600,000	9.00	25.00
1968-G.	Chicago	213,440,000	6.00	15.00
1968-G*.	Chicago	16,640,000	9.00	25.00
1968-H.	St. Louis	56,960,000	6.00	15.00
1968-H*.	St. Louis	5,120,000	9.00	25.00
1968-I.	Minneapolis	32,640,000	6.00	15.00
1968-I*.	Minneapolis	3,200,000	20.00	55.00
1968-J.	Kansas City	55,040,000	6.00	15.00
1968-J*.	Kansas City	5,760,000	15.00	35.00
1968-K.	Dallas	64,000,000	6.00	15.00
1968-K*.	Dallas	3,840,000	10.00	35.00
1968-L.	San Francisco	128,900,000	6.00	15.00
1968-L*.	San Francisco	12,153,000	10.00	35.00

Series of 1969
Signatures of Elston and Kennedy with new Treasury seal

No.	Issuing Bank	Quantity Printed	VF-20	Unc-63
1969-A.	Boston	51,200,000	$6.00	$15.00
1969-A*.	Boston	1,920,000	9.00	40.00
1969-B.	New York	198,560,000	6.00	15.00
1969-B*.	New York	8,960,000	9.00	30.00
1969-C.	Philadelphia	69,120,000	6.00	15.00
1969-C*.	Philadelphia	2,560,000	9.00	30.00

Series of 1969
Signatures of Elston and Kennedy with new Treasury seal

No.	Issuing Bank	Quantity Printed	VF-20	Unc-63
1969-D.	Cleveland	56,320,000	$6.00	$15.00
1969-D*.	Cleveland	2,560,000	10.00	30.00
1969-E.	Richmond	84,480,000	6.00	15.00
1969-E*.	Richmond	3,200,000	10.00	30.00
1969-F.	Atlanta	84,480,000	6.00	15.00
1969-F*.	Atlanta	3,840,000	10.00	30.00
1969-G.	Chicago	125,600,000	6.00	15.00
1969-G*.	Chicago	5,120,000	10.00	30.00
1969-H.	St. Louis	27,520,000	6.00	15.00
1969-H*.	St. Louis	1,280,000	10.00	40.00
1969-I.	Minneapolis	16,640,000	6.00	15.00
1969-I*.	Minneapolis	640,000	15.00	60.00
1969-J.	Kansas City	48,640,000	6.00	15.00
1969-J*.	Kansas City	3,192,000	10.00	30.00
1969-K.	Dallas	39,680,000	6.00	15.00
1969-K*.	Dallas	1,920,000	10.00	30.00
1969-L.	San Francisco	103,840,000	6.00	15.00
1969-L*.	San Francisco	4,480,000	10.00	30.00

SMALL-SIZE FIVE DOLLAR NOTES

Federal Reserve Notes
Series of 1969-A
Signatures of Kabis and Connally

No.	Issuing Bank	Quantity Printed	VF-20	Unc-63
1970-A.	Boston	23,040,000	$8.00	$20.00
1970-A*.	Boston	1,280,000	12.50	55.00
1970-B.	New York	62,240,000	8.00	20.00
1970-B*.	New York	1,760,000	12.50	40.00
1970-C.	Philadelphia	41,160,000	8.00	20.00
1970-C*.	Philadelphia	1,920,000	12.50	40.00
1970-D.	Cleveland	21,120,000	8.00	20.00
1970-D*.	Cleveland	640,000	15.00	60.00
1970-E.	Richmond	37,920,000	8.00	20.00
1970-E*.	Richmond	1,120,000	12.50	45.00
1970-F.	Atlanta	25,120,000	8.00	20.00
1970-F*.	Atlanta	480,000	17.50	75.00
1970-G.	Chicago	60,800,000	8.00	20.00
1970-G*.	Chicago	1,920,000	12.50	45.00
1970-H.	St. Louis	15,360,000	8.00	20.00
1970-H*.	St. Louis	640,000	15.00	45.00
1970-I.	Minneapolis	8,960,000	8.00	20.00
1970-I*.	Minneapolis	640,000	20.00	80.00
1970-J.	Kansas City	17,920,000	8.00	20.00
1970-J*.	Kansas City	640,000	15.00	60.00
1970-K.	Dallas	21,120,000	8.00	20.00
1970-K*.	Dallas	640,000	17.50	60.00
1970-L.	San Francisco	44,800,000	8.00	20.00
1970-L*.	San Francisco	1,920,000	15.00	50.00

Series of 1969-B
Signatures of Banuelos and Connally

No.	Issuing Bank	Quantity Printed	VF-20	Unc-63
1971-A.	Boston	5,760,000	$17.50	$85.00
1971-B.	New York	34,560,000	15.00	50.00
1971-B*.	New York	634,000	30.00	150.00
1971-C.	Philadelphia	5,120,000	15.00	50.00
1971-D.	Cleveland	12,160,000	15.00	50.00
1971-E.	Richmond	15,360,000	15.00	50.00
1971-E*.	Richmond	640,000	30.00	150.00
1971-F.	Atlanta	18,560,000	15.00	50.00
1971-F*.	Atlanta	640,000	30.00	125.00
1971-G.	Chicago	27,040,000	15.00	50.00
1971-G*.	Chicago	480,000	40.00	150.00
1971-H.	St. Louis	5,120,000	17.50	75.00
1971-I.	Minneapolis	8,320,000	17.50	75.00
1971-J.	Kansas City	8,320,000	17.50	75.00
1971-J*.	Kansas City	640,000	50.00	250.00
1971-K.	Dallas	12,160,000	15.00	75.00
1971-L.	San Francisco	23,160,000	15.00	50.00
1971-L*.	San Francisco	640,000	30.00	150.00

Series of 1969-C
Signatures of Banuelos and Shultz

No.	Issuing Bank	Quantity Printed	VF-20	Unc-63
1972-A.	Boston	50,720,000	$7.00	$17.50
1972-A*.	Boston	1,920,000	10.00	55.00
1972-B.	New York	120,000,000	7.00	17.50
1972-B*.	New York	2,400,000	9.00	40.00
1972-C.	Philadelphia	53,760,000	7.00	17.50
1972-C*.	Philadelphia	1,280,000	9.00	40.00
1972-D.	Cleveland	43,680,000	7.00	17.50
1972-D*.	Cleveland	1,120,000	9.00	40.00
1972-E.	Richmond	73,760,000	7.00	17.50
1972-E*.	Richmond	640,000	10.00	55.00
1972-F.	Atlanta	81,440,000	7.00	17.50
1972-F*.	Atlanta	3,200,000	9.00	40.00
1972-G.	Chicago	54,400,000	7.00	17.50

Federal Reserve Notes

No.	Issuing Bank	Quantity Printed	VF-20	Unc-63
1972-H.	St. Louis	37,760,000	$7.00	$17.50
1972-H*.	St. Louis	1,280,000	10.00	50.00
1972-I.	Minneapolis	14,080,000	9.00	40.00
1972-J.	Kansas City	41,120,000	7.00	17.50
1972-J*.	Kansas City	1,920,000	9.00	40.00
1972-K.	Dallas	41,120,000	7.00	17.50
1972-K*.	Dallas	1,920,000	10.00	50.00
1972-L.	San Francisco	80,800,000	7.00	17.50
1972-L*.	San Francisco	3,680,000	9.00	40.00
1972-E*.	Richmond	640,000	10.00	55.00
1972-F.	Atlanta	81,440,000	7.00	17.50
1972-F*.	Atlanta	3,200,000	9.00	40.00
1972-G.	Chicago	54,400,000	7.00	17.50
1972-H.	St. Louis	37,760,000	7.00	17.50
1972-H*.	St. Louis	1,280,000	10.00	50.00
1972-I.	Minneapolis	14,080,000	9.00	40.00
1972-J.	Kansas City	41,120,000	7.00	17.50
1972-J*.	Kansas City	1,920,000	9.00	40.00
1972-K.	Dallas	41,120,000	7.00	17.50
1972-K*.	Dallas	1,920,000	10.00	50.00
1972-L.	San Francisco	80,800,000	7.00	17.50
1972-L*.	San Francisco	3,680,000	9.00	40.00

Series of 1974
Signatures of Neff and Simon

No.	Issuing Bank	Quantity Printed	VF-20	Unc-63
1973-A.	Boston	58,240,000	$7.00	$12.50
1973-A*.	Boston	1,408,000	10.00	40.00
1973-B.	New York	153,120,000	7.00	12.50
1973-B*.	New York	2,656,000	10.00	35.00
1973-C.	Philadelphia	53,920,000	7.00	12.50
1973-C*.	Philadelphia	3,040,000	10.00	35.00
1973-D.	Cleveland	78,080,000	7.00	12.50
1973-D*.	Cleveland	1,920,000	10.00	35.00
1973-E.	Richmond	135,200,000	7.00	12.50
1973-E*.	Richmond	1,760,000	10.00	40.00
1973-F.	Atlanta	127,520,000	7.00	12.50
1973-F*.	Atlanta	3,040,000	10.00	35.00
1973-G.	Chicago	95,520,000	7.00	12.50
1973-G*.	Chicago	1,760,000	10.00	35.00
1973-H.	St. Louis	64,800,000	7.00	12.50
1973-H*.	St. Louis	640,000	20.00	65.00
1973-I.	Minneapolis	41,600,000	7.00	12.50
1973-I*.	Minneapolis	2,560,000	10.00	35.00

Series of 1974
Signatures of Neff and Simon

No.	Issuing Bank	Quantity Printed	VF-20	Unc-63
1973-J.	Kansas City	42,240,000	$7.00	$12.50
1973-J*.	Kansas City	2,176,000	10.00	35.00
1973-K.	Dallas	57,600,000	7.00	12.50
1973-K*.	Dallas	1,408,000	12.50	40.00
1973-L.	San Francisco	139,680,000	7.00	12.50
1973-L*.	San Francisco	5,088,000	10.00	35.00

Series of 1977
Signatures of Morton and Blumenthal

No.	Issuing Bank	Quantity Printed	VF-20	Unc-63
1974-A.	Boston	60,800,000	$7.00	$12.50
1974-A*.	Boston	256,000	35.00	80.00
1974-B.	New York	183,040,000	7.00	12.50
1974-B*.	New York	3,072,000	10.00	35.00
1974-C.	Philadelphia	78,720,000	7.00	12.50
1974-C*.	Philadelphia	1,280,000	10.00	40.00
1974-D.	Cleveland	72,960,000	7.00	12.50
1974-D*.	Cleveland	1,152,000	10.00	40.00

SMALL-SIZE FIVE DOLLAR NOTES

Federal Reserve Notes

No.	Issuing Bank	Quantity Printed	VF-20	Unc-63
1974-E.	Richmond	110,720,000	$7.00	$12.50
1974-E*.	Richmond	2,816,000	10.00	40.00
1974-F.	Atlanta	127,360,000	7.00	12.50
1974-F*.	Atlanta	1,920,000	10.00	40.00
1974-G.	Chicago	177,920,000	7.00	12.50
1974-G*.	Chicago	2,816,000	10.00	40.00
1974-H.	St. Louis	46,080,000	7.00	12.50
1974-H*.	St. Louis	128,000	55.00	125.00
1974-I.	Minneapolis	21,760,000	7.00	12.50
1974-J.	Kansas City	78,080,000	7.00	12.50
1974-J*.	Kansas City	1,408,000	10.00	40.00
1974-K.	Dallas	60,800,000	7.00	12.50
1974-K*.	Dallas	2,408,000	25.00	60.00
1974-L.	San Francisco	135,040,000	7.00	12.50
1974-L*.	San Francisco	2,432,000	15.00	35.00

Series of 1977-A
Signatures of Morton and Miller

No.	Issuing Bank	Quantity Printed	VF-20	Unc-63
1975-A.	Boston	48,000,000	$6.00	$12.50
1975-A*.	Boston	512,000	20.00	60.00
1975-B.	New York	113,920,000	6.00	12.50
1975-B*.	New York	2,304,000	15.00	35.00
1975-C.	Philadelphia	55,680,000	6.00	12.50
1975-C*.	Philadelphia	640,000	15.00	35.00
1975-D.	Cleveland	58,880,000	6.00	12.50
1975-D*.	Cleveland	1,280,000	15.00	35.00
1975-E.	Richmond	77,440,000	6.00	12.50
1975-E*.	Richmond	768,000	35.00	85.00
1975-F.	Atlanta	76,160,000	6.00	12.50
1975-F*.	Atlanta	1,152,000	15.00	35.00
1975-G.	Chicago	80,640,000	6.00	12.50
1975-G*.	Chicago	1,408,000	15.00	35.00
1975-H.	St. Louis	42,240,000	6.00	12.50
1975-H*.	St. Louis	640,000	20.00	50.00
1975-I.	Minneapolis	10,240,000	6.00	12.50
1975-I*.	Minneapolis	256,000	35.00	85.00
1975-J.	Kansas City	52,480,000	6.00	12.50
1975-J*.	Kansas City	1,024,000	20.00	50.00
1975-K.	Dallas	76,160,000	6.00	12.50
1975-K*.	Dallas	1,408,000	20.00	40.00
1975-L.	San Francisco	106,880,000	6.00	12.50
1975-L*.	San Francisco	1,152,000	15.00	35.00

Series of 1981
Signatures of Buchanan and Regan

No.	Issuing Bank	Quantity Printed	VF-20	Unc-63
1976-A.	Boston	109,000,000	$10.00	$25.00
1976-B.	New York	250,880,000	10.00	25.00
1976-B*.	New York	4,464,000	20.00	45.00
1976-C.	Philadelphia	112,640,000	10.00	25.00
1976-C*.	Philadelphia	640,000	25.00	50.00
1976-D.	Cleveland	122,240,000	10.00	25.00
1976-D*.	Cleveland	1,268,000	25.00	60.00
1976-E.	Richmond	234,880,000	10.00	25.00
1976-E*.	Richmond	640,000	20.00	45.00
1976-F.	Atlanta	234,880,000	10.00	25.00
1976-F*.	Atlanta	1,644,000	22.50	50.00
1976-G.	Chicago	241,280,000	10.00	25.00
1976-G*.	Chicago	768,000	20.00	45.00
1976-H.	St. Louis	199,680,000	10.00	25.00
1976-H*.	St. Louis	628,000	30.00	70.00
1976-I.	Minneapolis	109,440,000	10.00	25.00
1976-I*.	Minneapolis	640,000	45.00	90.00
1976-J.	Kansas City	125,440,000	10.00	25.00
1976-J*.	Kansas City	960,000	30.00	70.00

Federal Reserve Notes

No.	Issuing Bank	Quantity Printed	VF-20	Unc-63
1976-K.	Dallas	138,240,000	$10.00	$25.00
1976-K*.	Dallas	640,000	22.50	50.00
1976-L	San Francisco	263,680,000	10.00	25.00
1976-L*.	San Francisco	2,560,000	20.00	45.00

Series of 1981-A
Signatures of Ortega and Regan

No.	Issuing Bank	Quantity Printed	VF-20	Unc-63
1977-A.	Boston	192,000,000	$15.00	$40.00
1977-B.	New York	448,000,000	15.00	40.00
1977-B*.	New York	3,200,000	30.00	75.00
1977-C.	Philadelphia	169,600,000	15.00	40.00
1977-D.	Cleveland	214,400,000	15.00	40.00
1977-E.	Richmond	332,800,000	15.00	40.00
1977-E*.	Richmond	3,200,000	30.00	75.00
1977-F.	Atlanta	352,000,000	15.00	40.00
1977-G.	Chicago	345,600,000	15.00	40.00
1977-H.	St. Louis	128,000,000	15.00	40.00
1977-I.	Minneapolis	73,800,000	15.00	40.00
1977-J.	Kansas City	134,400,000	15.00	40.00
1977-K.	Dallas	176,000,000	15.00	40.00
1977-L	San Francisco	438,400,000	15.00	40.00
1977-L*.	San Francisco	3,200,000	30.00	75.00

Series of 1985
Signatures of Ortega and Baker

No.	Issuing Bank	Quantity Printed	VF-20	Unc-63
1978-A.	Boston	192,000,000	$7.50	$17.50
1978-B.	New York	451,200,000	7.50	17.50
1978-B*.	New York	3,200,000	30.00	80.00
1978-C.	Philadelphia	170,400,000	7.50	17.00
1978-C*.	Philadelphia	6,400,000	20.00	50.00
1978-D.	Cleveland	216,000,000	7.50	17.50
1978-E.	Richmond	335,200,000	7.50	17.50
1978-E*.	Richmond	3,200,000	25.00	60.00
1978-F.	Atlanta	354,400,000	7.50	17.50
1978-F*.	Atlanta	6,400,000	20.00	50.00
1978-G.	Chicago	348,000,000	7.50	17.50
1978-G*.	Chicago	6,400,000	20.00	50.00
1978-H.	St. Louis	128,000,000	7.50	17.50
1978-I.	Minneapolis	173,600,000	7.50	17.50
1978-J.	Kansas City	135,200,000	7.50	17.50

Series of 1985
Signatures of Ortega and Baker

No.	Issuing Bank	Quantity Printed	VF-20	Unc-63
1978-K.	Dallas	176,800,000	$7.50	$17.50
1978-K*.	Dallas	3,200,000	20.00	50.00
1978-L.	San Francisco	460,800,000	7.50	17.50
1978-L*.	San Francisco	3,200,000	25.00	60.00

Series of 1988
Signatures of Ortega and Brady

No.	Issuing Bank	Quantity Printed	VF-20	Unc-63
1979-A.	Boston	86,400,000	$7.50	$17.50
1979-A*.	Boston	768,000	35.00	85.00
1979-B.	New York	185,600,000	7.50	17.50
1979-B*.	New York	3,200,000	20.00	50.00
1979-C.	Philadelphia	54,400,000	7.50	17.50
1979-D.	Cleveland	111,200,000	7.50	30.00
1979-E.	Richmond	131,200,000	7.50	17.50
1979-F.	Atlanta	137,200,000	7.50	17.50
1979-F*.	Atlanta	6,400,000	15.00	40.00

SMALL-SIZE FIVE DOLLAR NOTES

Federal Reserve Notes

No.	Issuing Bank	Quantity Printed	VF-20	Unc-63
1979-G.	Chicago	134,400,000	$7.50	$17.50
1979-H.	St. Louis	51,200,000	7.50	17.50
1979-I.	Minneapolis	9,600,000	15.00	40.00
1979-J.	Kansas City	44,800,000	7.50	17.50
1979-K.	Dallas	54,500,000	7.50	17.50
1979-L.	San Francisco	70,400,000	7.50	17.50

Series of 1988-A
Signatures of Villalpando and Brady
Printed in Washington, DC

No.	Issuing Bank	Quantity Printed	VF-20	Unc-63
1980-A.	Boston	140,800,000	$7.50	$17.50
1980-A*.	Boston	3,200,000	15.00	50.00
1980-B.	New York	640,000,000	7.50	17.50
1980-B*.	New York	4,608,000	10.00	30.00
1980-C.	Philadelphia	70,400,000	7.50	17.50
1980-D.	Cleveland	166,000,000	7.50	17.50
1980-D*.	Cleveland	4,864,000	10.00	30.00
1980-E.	Richmond	486,400,000	7.50	17.50
1980-E*.	Richmond	3,020,000	10.00	30.00
1980-F.	Atlanta	192,000,000	7.50	17.50
1980-F*.	Atlanta	2,640,000	15.00	40.00
1980-G.	Chicago	633,600,000	7.50	17.50
1980-H*.	St. Louis	1,280,000	10.00	30.00
1980-I.	Minneapolis	73,600,000	7.50	17.50
1980-I*.	Minneapolis	3,200,000	20.00	50.00
1980-J.	Kansas City	115,200,000	7.50	17.50
1980-J*.	Kansas City	44,800,000	10.00	30.00
1980-K.	Dallas	128,000,000	7.50	17.50
1980-L.	San Francisco	492,800,000	7.50	17.50

Series of 1988-A
Signatures of Villalpando and Brady. Printed at the Western Facility (Fort Worth, Texas).
Notes printed in Fort Worth may be identified by a small "FW" on the right front side next to the plate. Check letter-number.

No.	Issuing Bank	Quantity Printed	VF-20	Unc-63
1981-C.	Philadelphia	25,600,000	$6.00	$15.00
1981-F.	Atlanta	282,400,000	6.00	15.00
1981-F*.	Atlanta	640,000	15.00	35.00
1981-G.	Chicago	76,800,000	6.00	15.00
1981-G*.	Chicago	1,280,000	15.00	35.00
1981-J.	Kansas City	25,600,000	6.00	15.00
1981-K.	Dallas	44,800,000	6.00	15.00
1981-L.	San Francisco	179,200,000	6.00	15.00
1981-L*.	San Francisco	3,200,000	15.00	35.00
1982-A.	Boston	38,400,000	6.00	15.00
1982-B.	New York	102,400,000	6.00	15.00
1982-B*.	New York	2,816,000	15.00	35.00
1982-C.	Philadelphia	38,400,000	6.00	15.00
1982-E.	Richmond	76,800,000	6.00	15.00
1982-E*.	Richmond	1,920,000	15.00	35.00
1982-F.	Atlanta	70,400,000	6.00	15.00

Federal Reserve Notes

Series of 1993
Signatures of Withrow and Bentsen
Printed at the Western Facility (Fort Worth, Texas)

No.	Issuing Bank	Quantity Printed	VF-20	Unc-63
1983-G.	Chicago	64,000,000	$6.00	$15.00
1983-G*.	Chicago	1,280,000	35.00	95.00
1983-H.	St. Louis	64,000,000	6.00	15.00
1983-H*.	St. Louis	2,560,000	15.00	35.00
1983-I.	Minneapolis	6,400,000	75.00	250.00
1983-J.	Kansas City	32,000,000	6.00	15.00
1983-K.	Dallas	57,600,000	6.00	15.00
1983-L.	San Francisco	185,600,000	6.00	15.00
1983-L*.	San Francisco	2,560,000	10.00	30.00

Series of 1995
Signatures of Withrow and Rubin
Printed in Washington, DC

No.	Issuing Bank	Quantity Printed	VF-20	Unc-63
1984-A.	Boston	160,000,000	$6.00	$10.00
1984-A*.	Boston	640,000	25.00	75.00
1984-B.	New York	390,040,444	6.00	10.00
1984-B*.	New York	3,840,000	10.00	30.00
1984-C.	Philadelphia	128,000,000	6.00	10.00
1984-D.	Cleveland	89,600,000	6.00	10.00
1984-E.	Richmond	300,800,000	6.00	10.00
1984-F.	Atlanta	179,200,000	6.00	10.00

Series of 1995
Signatures of Withrow and Rubin
Printed at the Western Facility (Fort Worth, Texas)

No.	Issuing Bank	Quantity Printed	VF-20	Unc-63
1985-A.	Boston	57,600,000	$6.00	$10.00
1985-B.	New York	76,800,000	6.00	10.00
1985-C.	Philadelphia	38,000,000	6.00	10.00
1985-D.	Cleveland	64,000,000	6.00	10.00
1985-D*.	Cleveland	3,200,000	10.00	30.00
1985-E.	Richmond	108,000,000	6.00	10.00
1985-F.	Atlanta	448,000,000	6.00	10.00
1985-F*.	Atlanta	70,400,000	15.00	40.00
1985-G.	Chicago	524,800,000	6.00	10.00
1985-G*.	Chicago	9,600,000	15.00	25.00
1985-H.	St. Louis	204,800,000	6.00	10.00
1985-I.	Minneapolis	64,000,000	6.00	10.00
1985-J.	Kansas City	160,000,000	6.00	10.00
1985-K.	Dallas	204,800,000	6.00	10.00
1985-L.	San Francisco	706,800,000	6.00	10.00

SMALL-SIZE FIVE DOLLAR NOTES

Federal Reserve Notes

Face of Notes 1986-

Back of Notes 1986-

Series of 1999
Signatures of Withrow and Summers
Printed in Washington, DC

No.	Issuing Bank	Quantity Printed	Unc-63
1986-A .	Boston	19,200,000	$10.00
1986-B.	New York	76,800,000	10.00
1986-C.	Philadelphia	57,600,000	10.00
1986-D.	Cleveland	25,600,000	10.00
1986-E.	Richmond	96,000,000	10.00
1986-E*.	Richmond	739,200	75.00

Series of 1999
Signatures of Withrow and Summers
Printed at the Western Facility (Fort Worth, Texas)

No.	Issuing Bank	Quantity Printed	Unc-63
1987-A.	Boston	70,400,000	$10.00
1987-A*.	Boston	3,200,000	25.00
1987-B.	New York	256,000,000	10.00
1987-B*.	New York	3,840,00	25.00
1987-C.	Philadelphia	89,600,000	10.00
1987-D.	Cleveland	12,800,000	10.00
1987-E.	Richmond	185,600,000	10.00
1987-E*.	Richmond	3,200,000	25.00
1987-F.	Atlanta	211,200,000	10.00
1987-F*.	Atlanta	10,915,200	25.00
1987-G.	Chicago	140,800,000	10.00
1987-H.	St. Louis	44,800,000	10.00
1987-I.	Minneapolis	12,800,000	10.00
1987-J.	Kansas City	32,000,000	10.00
1987-J*.	Kansas City	3,200,000	25.00
1987-K.	Dallas	121,600,000	10.00
1987-K*.	Dallas	3,200,000	25.00
1987-L.	San Francisco	243,200,000	10.00

Federal Reserve Notes

Series of 2001
Signatures of of Marin and O'Neill
None printed

Series of 2001
Signatures of Marin and O'Neill
Printed at the Western Facility (Fort Worth, Texas)

No.	Issuing Bank	Quantity Printed	Unc-63
1989-A.	Boston	128,000,000	Current
1989-B.	New York	121,600,000	Current
1989-C.	Philadelphia	64,000,000	Current
1989-D.	Cleveland	83,200,000	Current
1989-E.	Richmond	51,200,000	Current
1989-F.	Atlanta	224,000,000	Current
1989-F*.	Atlanta	3,200,000	Current
1989-G.	Chicago	185,600,000	Current
1989-H.	St. Louis	102,400,000	Current
1989-I.	Minneapolis	32,000,000	Current
1989-J.	Kansas City	76,800,000	Current
1989-K.	Dallas	211,200,000	Current
1989-K*.	Dallas	3,200,000	Current
1989-L.	San Francisco	281,600,000	Current

Series of 2003
Signatures of Marin and Snow
None printed

Series of 2003
Signatures of Marin and Snow
Printed at the Western Facility (Fort Worth, Texas)

No.	Issuing Bank	Unc-63
1990-A.	Boston	Current
1990-B.	New York	Current
1990-C.	Philadelphia	Current
1990-D.	Cleveland	Current
1990-E.	Richmond	Current
1990-F.	Atlanta	Current
1990-F.	Atlanta	Current
1990-G.	Chicago	Current
1990-H.	St. Louis	Current
1990-I.	Minneapolis	Current
1990-J.	Kansas City	Current
1990-K.	Dallas	Current
1990-K*.	Dallas	Current
1990-L.	San Francisco	Current

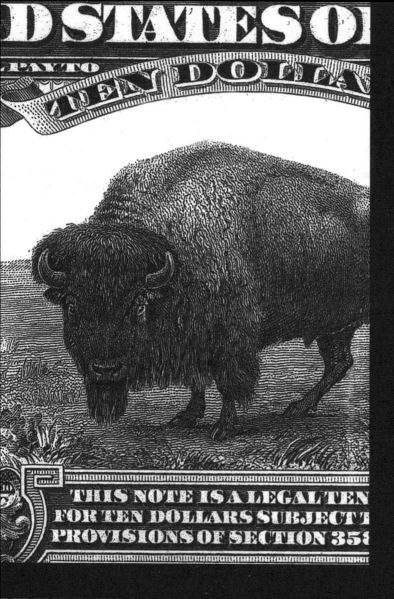

"Eye-pleasing and unique designs await the collector of $10 notes, not to mention the occasional rarity and some of the most popular motifs in American numismatics..."

$10

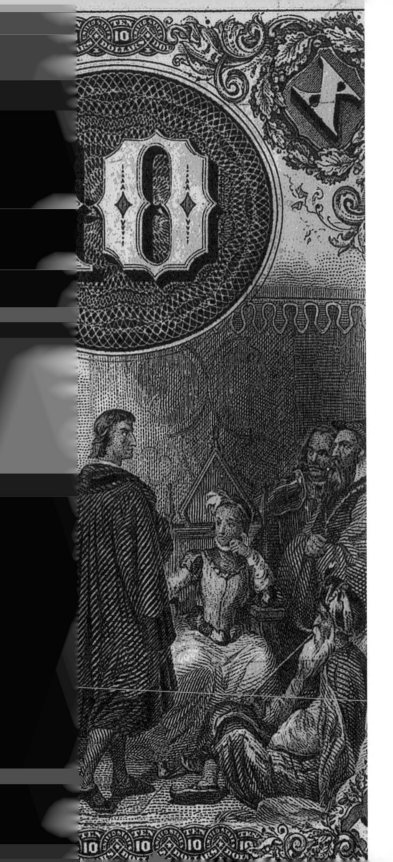

TEN DOLLAR NOTES

COLLECTING TEN DOLLAR NOTES

Large-size $10 bills enter a rarefied atmosphere, not to the extent of the much larger denominations, but still introducing general elements of scarcity beyond the $1, $2, and $5, especially in higher grades. In addition to the generally collectable series, certain currently rare issues were produced in the Civil War era (including Demand Notes, Interest Bearing Notes, and Compound Interest Treasury Notes).

Large-Size $10 Notes

$10 Interest Bearing Notes, Large-Size: The first $10 Interest Bearing Notes were produced under the Act of March 3, 1863. From the 620,000 issued, only slightly more than 500 are outstanding today on Treasury records. These are rarities and are seldom seen in the marketplace. Fewer than three dozen are believed to exist.

$10 Demand Notes of 1861, Large-Size: Depicting President Abraham Lincoln on the face, these notes were issued during the first year of the Civil War. They were redeemable in coins, including gold. All examples are rare today, and in high grades they are virtually unknown. These were payable at Treasury offices in Boston, Cincinnati, New York, Philadelphia, and St. Louis. Early bills bear the inked signatures (by Treasury clerks) of minor officers in the Treasury Department. Printing was by the American Bank Note Co., New York.

$10 Compound Interest Treasury Notes, Large-Size: Notes issued under the acts of March 3, 1863, and June 20, 1864, were intended to raise money to fight the Civil War. They were made in denominations up to $1,000, with $10 being the lowest. Those of the $10 value depict Salmon Chase, a perched eagle (similar to that used later on the "Black Eagle" $1 Silver Certificate of 1899), and a standing goddess designated as Peace. The reverse, in green, has an interest table that gives the value of the note for six-month periods up to three years after issue. Produced in small quantities, and mostly redeemed, these are rarities today.

$10 Legal Tender Notes, Large-Size: The Series of 1862 $10 Legal Tender Notes, also called United States Notes, were made in substantial quantities. Today examples are easily collected in circulated grades. Various differences exist, including First Obligation and Second Obligation backs.

The Series of 1869 Legal Tender Notes illustrate Daniel Webster at the lower left of the face, and at the lower right, the illustration of *Pocahontas Presented at Court*, a motif similar to that on the $5 National Bank notes. This is one of the "Rainbow Note" issues, on blue-tinted paper (to the left, viewed from the face). At the center bottom of the face is an eagle which, turned upside down, looks like a donkey—hence the nickname "Jackass Note." This same eagle was used on Fractional Currency shields issued by the Treasury Department in the late 1860s.

The eye-pleasing back of the Series of 1869 notes consists of three sections in rich green. At the center is much technical wording. Such inscriptions, common to other notes as well, generally tell what such bills can and cannot be used for—not all were legal tender for everything. The backs of the Legal Tender Notes were changed in the Series of 1880, with ornate vignettes, grouped together in clusters, and wording.

The Series of 1901 "Bison Note," as it is known, is sometimes humorously called the "Buffalo Bill." The bison depicted, Black Diamond of the Central Park Zoo, found its way to the reverse of the five cent piece of 1913, and was so popular that generations later it was revived for certain commemoratives and other coins. Lewis and Clark appear on the face, styled differently from the same two men used on the 1903 Louisiana Purchase Exposition gold dollars.

The Series of 1923 Legal Tender Notes, with a red seal, depict Andrew Jackson on the face. These were made in only one signature combination, Speelman-White.

$10 National Bank Notes, Large-Size: These commence with the Original Series, continuing to the Series of 1875. Some numismatists combine these two series and call them "First Charter." The face of these notes depicts, on the left side, Benjamin Franklin flying a kite (officially, *Franklin and Electricity*). On the right side is the patriotic arrangement *America Seizing the Lightning*, with a goddess and an eagle. The back shows *DeSoto Discovering the Mississippi*, a vignette later used on a small-size $500 Federal Reserve Note.

The Series of 1882 (called "Second Charter" by some) continues the same face design as used earlier, but with some revisions done at the Treasury Department. Reverses occur in three styles. The Brown Back bills are primarily in brown, with a blue-green ornament at the center with the charter number. The Date Back (1882-1908) and Value Back (TEN DOLLARS) notes are also part of the suite. The Brown Back notes are by far the most available, although they are considerably scarcer than the $5 version. In the National Bank note series the availability decreases as the denomination increases.

The Series of 1902 notes (nicknamed "Third Charter" by some) exist in varieties similar to those described for $5, with red seal notes, then two issues: the 1902-1908 Date Back and the plentiful 1902 Plain Back. Both of these latter varieties have blue seals. Many Series of 1902 Plain Back bills have rubber-stamped signatures of bank officials, often faded.

Generally, large-size National Bank notes of all types were issued in four-subject sheets ($10-$10-$10-$20), with plate letters A-B-C-A. There were some infrequent variations, including sheets with four $10 bills using plate letters A-B-C-D. By studying such things the specialist will know at a glance that a $10 bill with a D plate letter is quite unusual (but not with added value, as few are aware of such).

Large-size $10 National Bank notes are collected in several ways—by design type, by state, city, or bank, etc. The Series of 1902 Plain Back bills are quite plentiful, but the earlier varieties can be elusive. Availability depends upon the issuer, and there are rare states and territories. Generally, those of large banks in eastern cities are more common.

$10 National Gold Bank Notes, Large-Size: The National Gold Bank Notes of the early 1870s continue the same face as used on the Original Series. The back features a montage of gold coins. Although thousands of these bills were produced, most were redeemed, and today all range from scarce to rare. Most numismatists desire a single example to illustrate the type. As is the case with National Gold Bank notes of all denominations, most show extensive wear.

$10 Silver Certificates, Large-Size: These commence with the Series of 1878, depicting early financier Robert Morris on the face, and on the reverse the word SILVER in immense letters (obviously pleasing to "Silverites," who were quite prominent in politics at the time, and who exerted great pressure on the government to support the market price of that metal). The thought was to issue bills specifically payable in silver dollars, backed by coins held in storage. On the face the inscription SILVER DOLLARS is done in a series of interesting vignettes, one for each letter, connected together in a straight row. This was the "theater marquee" style, also used elsewhere for different denominations (including in a few bank title blocks in the Series of 1882 $5 National Bank Notes).

The Series of 1886 Silver Certificates illustrate Vice President Thomas A. Hendricks, who died in office in late 1885. He is surrounded by a frame that earned this bill the nickname "Tombstone Note." Numismatists enjoy collecting things with nicknames, and this particular issue is widely sought for this reason alone, as few people have heard of Hendricks. Such notes were printed for a long time, including seven different signature combinations and Treasury seal variations. They are far scarcer than $10 Legal Tender Notes of the same era.

$10 Refunding Certificates, Large-Size: The $10 Refunding Certificates of 1879, actually "baby bonds" rather than currency notes, are usually collected with the $10 bill series. Two varieties were issued: Friedberg-213 (extremely rare) and the usually seen F-214.

$10 Treasury or Coin Notes, Large-Size: A popular and highly desired entry in the $10 denomination are the Series of 1890 notes depicting Civil War general Philip Sheridan on the obverse, and on the reverse the word TEN in ornamented letters. Three signature combinations were made, but usually this style is collected only as a type. Then came the Series of 1891 with the same face but a simpler reverse back. All are scarce and usually display evidence of circulation.

$10 Federal Reserve Notes, Large-Size: Notes of the Series of 1914, some with red seals, others with blue, depict Jackson on the face and, on the reverse, separate illustrations of a farming scene and factories. Red seal notes have Treasury signatures of Burke and McAdoo. Blue seal notes exist with several different signature combinations. For both colors of seals, varieties can be collected by Federal Reserve district.

$10 Federal Reserve Bank Notes, Large-Size: Federal Reserve Bank Notes of 1915 and 1918 are similar to the Federal Reserve Notes of 1914, but with the city and bank name more prominent on the face. While signature varieties exist, these are usually collected as singles for type, or as one from each of the different districts. Only seven of the 12 districts issued notes of this type.

$10 Gold Certificates, Large-Size: Gold Certificates of the $10 denomination, with the reverse printed in bright yellow-orange, commence with the Series of 1907. They were made in different signature combinations through the Series of 1922, the last being particularly numerous.

Small-Size $10 Notes

Small-size $10 notes are often collected by types, although signature varieties exist, as do star notes, the last including some exceptional rarities. All depict Alexander Hamilton on the face and the Treasury Building on the back.

$10 National Bank Notes, Small-Size: Series of 1929 National Bank Notes remained in use through early 1935. There are two styles, Type 1 (generally more plentiful) and Type 2, each printed in six-subject sheets, the arrangement being the same for other denominations in these series. Each has a brown Treasury seal and brown serial numbers. Sheets of Type 1 bills each had the same serial number on a given sheet, prefixed by a letter, A through F (such as A000001A to F000001A). Sheets of Type 2 bills were numbered continuously, with a sheet starting with A000001 and ending with A000006. These $10 bills are widely collected today, usually by geographical location.

$10 Silver Certificates, Small-Size: These notes commence with the Series of 1933. The text of their obligation mentions "coin"—a rarity. Many of these were destroyed, to be replaced with the differently worded Series of 1934. Later Silver Certificates were continued through the Series 1953-B signature combination.

$10 Gold Certificates, Small-Size: These Gold Certificates bear a gold seal and a reverse design showing the Treasury Building. They were made in the Series of 1928 and 1928-A, the latter never released. Examples of the Series of 1928 are readily available today.

$10 Federal Reserve Bank Notes, Small-Size: These notes of the Series of 1929, brown seal, are collectable from each of the Federal Reserve districts. They were produced for just a short time. Their printing quantities varied widely, as do their availability today.

$10 Federal Reserve Notes, Small-Size: The small-size $10 Federal Reserve Notes begin with the Series of 1928. Since that time, such bills have been issued by the 12 different Federal Reserve Banks. Each bears identification by bank letter and number, such as 1-A for Boston. Each has a green Treasury seal. Certain early varieties are very scarce in higher grades, but the demand for them is limited. Some variations in seal tint (light or dark green) exist.

Certain of the Series of 1934 Federal Reserve Notes were made with brown seals and HAWAII overprints, and Series 1934 and 1934-A notes were issued with yellow seals for use in the North African and related campaigns.

Commencing with Series 1999 the face and back designs were modified, with Hamilton given a larger and different portrait. Other improvements to the design and paper were largely intended to deter counterfeiting. The Treasury Building, earlier shown in a corner view, was redone to a less artistic front view.

Although the $10 denomination is not as widely collected as $1, $2, and $5 bills, many numismatists seek the different bank and signature combinations as they are issued. Star or replacement notes form a specialty and are highly prized.

Interest Bearing Notes

Face of Note 196. Eagle holding flag. Bust of Salmon P. Chase at left and Peace standing at right.

Back of Note 196.

No.	Denomination			VG-8	F-12	VF-20
196.	Ten Dollars.	Very Rare (about 9 known)	ABNCo	Rare	Rare	—
196a.	Ten Dollars.	Rare (about 25 known)	BEP	$2,500.00	$6,000.00	—

Demand Notes

Face of Notes 6-10a. Eagle perched on olive branch before American shield.
Bust of Abraham Lincoln at left; representation of Art standing at right.

Back of Notes 6-10a.

No.	Payable at	VG-8	F-12	VF-20
6.	New York	$2,000.00	$4,000.00	$8,000.00
6a.	"For the" handwritten	Rare	—	—
7.	Philadelphia	2,000.00	4,000.00	8,000.00
7a.	"For the" handwritten	Extremely Rare (3 Known)	—	—
8.	Boston	2,000.00	4,000.00	8,000.00
8a.	"For the" handwritten	Two known	—	—
9.	Cincinnati	Extremely Rare	—	—
9a.	"For the" handwritten	Unique	—	—
10.	St. Louis	Extremely Rare	—	—
10a.	"For the" handwritten	Unknown	—	—

Legal Tender Notes

Face of Note 93. Eagle perched on olive branch before American shield. Bust of Abraham Lincoln at left; representation of Art standing at right behind Treasury seal.

Back of Note 93.

No.	Act	Signatures	Seal	VG-8	F-12	VF-20	EF-40	Unc-63
93.	1862	Chittenden Spinner	Small Red	$550.00	$900.00	$1,400.00	$2,300.00	$5,500.00

Legal Tender Notes

Face of Notes 94–95b. Eagle perched on olive branch before American shield. Bust of Abraham Lincoln at left; representation of Art standing at right behind Treasury seal.

Back of Notes 94–95b.

No.	Act	Signatures		Seal	VG-8	F-12	VF-20	EF-40	Unc-63
94.	1862	Chittenden	Spinner	Small Red	$600.00	$1,000.00	$1,700.00	$2,750.00	$7,000.00
95.	1863	Chittenden	Spinner	Small Red					
		National Bank Note Co. on lower border			550.00	950.00	1,500.00	2,500.00	6,000.00
95a.	1863	Chittenden .....Spinner		Small Red, One Serial No.					
		American Bank Note Co. on lower border			600.00	1,000.00	1,700.00	2,750.00	7,000.00
95b.	1863	Chittenden	Spinner	Small Red, Two Serial Nos.					
		American Bank Note Co. on lower border			550.00	900.00	1,400.00	2,300.00	5,500.00

Legal Tender Notes

Face of Note 96. Bust of Daniel Webster in lower left; at right, the presentation of the Indian Princess Pocahontas to the court in England. At bottom center is a small eagle which, when held upside down, resembles the head of a donkey, giving rise to the appellation "Jackass Note."

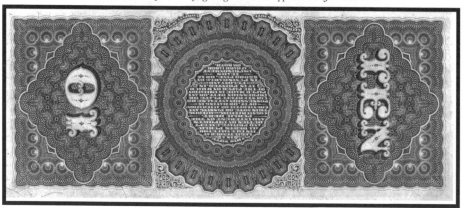

Back of Note 96.

No.	Act	Signatures	Seal	VG-8	F-12	VF-20	EF-40	Unc-63
96.	1869	Allison Spinner	.... Large Red	$350.00	$700.00	$900.00	$1,450.00	$5,200.00

Face of Notes 97-113. Bust of Daniel Webster in lower left; at right, the presentation of the Indian Princess Pocahontas to the court in England. At bottom center is a small eagle which, when held upside down, resembles the head of a donkey, giving rise to the appellation "Jackass Note."

Legal Tender Notes

Back of Notes 97-113.

Red "TEN" in red ornamental design at right center; seal at left

No.	Series	Signatures		Seal	VG-8	F-12	VF-20	EF-40	Unc-63
97.	1875	Allison	New	Small Red, Rays	$800.00	$1,500.00	$2,250.00	$4,500.00	—
98.	....	Same as above but Series A ..			450.00	700.00	950.00	1,350.00	6,750.00
99.	1878	Allison	Gilfillan	Small Red, Rays	425.00	675.00	875.00	1,100.00	1,400.00

Large seal replaces "TEN"; red serial numbers

No.	Series	Signatures		Seal	VG-8	F-12	VF-20	EF-40	Unc-63
100.	1880	Scofield	Gilfillan	Large Brown	$250.00	$500.00	$725.00	$1,075.00	$2,400.00
101.	1880	Bruce	Gilfillan	Large Brown	275.00	550.00	800.00	1,200.00	2,750.00
102.	1880	Bruce	Wyman	Large Brown	275.00	500.00	700.00	1,000.00	2,200.00

Same, but with blue serial numbers

No.	Series	Signatures		Seal	VG-8	F-12	VF-20	EF-40	Unc-63
103.	1880	Bruce	Wyman	Large Red, Plain	$250.00	$475.00	$750.00	$1,075.00	$2,400.00
104.	1880	Rosecrans	Jordan	Large Red, Plain	250.00	500.00	800.00	1,200.00	—
105.	1880	Rosecrans	Hyatt	Large Red, Plain	250.00	500.00	800.00	1,200.00	2,400.00
106.	1880	Rosecrans	Hyatt	Large Red, Spike	250.00	475.00	750.00	1,075.00	2,400.00
107.	1880	Rosecrans	Huston	Large Red, Spike	250.00	475.00	750.00	1,075.00	2,300.00
108.	1880	Rosecrans	Huston	Large Brown	250.00	475.00	750.00	1,075.00	2,300.00
109.	1880	Rosecrans	Nebeker	Large Brown	Extremely Rare	(2 Known)	—	—	—
110.	1880	Rosecrans	Nebeker	Small Red, Scalloped	225.00	425.00	600.00	950.00	2,100.00
111.	1880	Tillman	Morgan	Small Red, Scalloped	225.00	425.00	600.00	825.00	1,850.00
112.	1880	Bruce	Roberts	Small Red, Scalloped	300.00	500.00	750.00	1,150.00	4,000.00
113.	1880	Lyons	Roberts	Small Red, Scalloped	225.00	425.00	600.00	825.00	1,850.00

Legal Tender Notes

Face of Notes 114-122. Bison flanked by portraits of the explorers Meriwether Lewis and William Clark.

Back of Notes 114-122. Columbia standing.

No.	Series	Signatures		Seal	VG-8	F-12	VF-20	EF-40	Unc-63
114.	1901	Lyons	Roberts	Small Red, Scalloped	$450.00	$550.00	$775.00	$1,350.00	$3,000.00
115.	1901	Lyons	Treat	Small Red, Scalloped	450.00	550.00	775.00	1,350.00	3,000.00
116.	1901	Vernon	Treat	Small Red, Scalloped	450.00	550.00	775.00	1,350.00	3,000.00
117.	1901	Vernon	McClung	Small Red, Scalloped	450.00	550.00	775.00	1,350.00	3,000.00
118.	1901	Napier	McClung	Small Red, Scalloped	450.00	550.00	775.00	1,350.00	3,000.00
119.	1901	Parker	Burke	Small Red, Scalloped	450.00	550.00	775.00	1,350.00	3,000.00
120.	1901	Teehee	Burke	Small Red, Scalloped	450.00	550.00	775.00	1,350.00	3,000.00
121.	1901	Elliott	White	Small Red, Scalloped	450.00	550.00	775.00	1,350.00	3,000.00
122.	1901	Speelman	White	Small Red, Scalloped	450.00	550.00	775.00	1,350.00	3,000.00

Legal Tender Notes

Face of Note 123. Bust of Andrew Jackson.

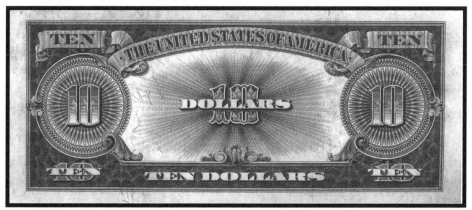

Back of Note 123.

No.	Series	Signatures	Seal	VG-8	F-12	VF-20	EF-40	Unc-63
123.	1923	Speelman White	Small Red, Scalloped	$400.00	$900.00	$1,450.00	$2,300.00	$4,500.00

Compound Interest Treasury Notes

Face of Notes 190-190b. At center, eagle perched on flag. Bust of Salmon P. Chase at left; female representing Peace at right. "COMPOUND INTEREST TREASURY NOTE" stamped in bronze ink.

Back of Notes 190-190b.

No.	Act	Overprint Date	Signatures		VG-8	F-12	VF-20	EF-40
190.	1863	June 10, 1864	Chittenden	Spinner	$3,000.00	$6,500.00	$8,500.00	—
190a.	1864	July 15, 1864	Chittenden	Spinner	2,400.00	5,000.00	7,500.00	—
190b.	1864	Aug. 15 - Dec. 15, 1864	Colby	Spinner	1,800.00	3,750.00	6,000.00	12,500.00

National Bank Notes
"First Charter Period" (Original Series and Series of 1875)

Face of Notes 409-423a. Historical vignette of Franklin and the Lightning at left. At right, Liberty grasping lightning in her left hand, being carried aloft by an eagle.

Back of Notes 409-423a. DeSoto Discovering the Mississippi, 1541.

No.	Series	Signatures		Seal	VG-8	F-12	VF-20	EF-40	Unc-63
409.	Original	Chittenden	Spinner	Red, Rays	$1,250.00	$1,650.00	$2,250.00	$2,750.00	$5,250.00
412.	Original	Colby	Spinner	Red, Rays	1,250.00	1,650.00	2,250.00	2,750.00	5,250.00
413.	Original	Jeffries	Spinner	Red, Rays	Rare	—	—	—	—
414.	Original	Allison	Spinner	Red, Rays	1,250.00	1,650.00	2,250.00	2,750.00	5,250.00
416.	1875	Allison	New	Red, Scalloped	1,250.00	1,650.00	2,250.00	2,750.00	5,250.00
417.	1875	Allison	Wyman	Red, Scalloped	1,250.00	1,650.00	2,250.00	2,750.00	5,250.00
418.	1875	Allison	Gilfillan	Red, Scalloped	1,250.00	1,650.00	2,250.00	2,750.00	5,250.00
419.	1875	Scofield	Gilfillan	Red, Scalloped	1,250.00	1,650.00	2,250.00	2,750.00	5,250.00
420.	1875	Bruce	Gilfillan	Red, Scalloped	1,250.00	1,650.00	2,250.00	2,750.00	5,250.00
421.	1875	Bruce	Wyman	Red, Scalloped	1,250.00	1,650.00	2,250.00	2,750.00	5,250.00
422.	1875	Rosecrans	Huston	Red, Scalloped	1,250.00	1,650.00	2,250.00	2,750.00	5,250.00
423.	1875	Rosecrans	Nebeker	Red, Scalloped	1,250.00	1,650.00	2,250.00	2,750.00	5,250.00
423a.	1875	Tillman	Morgan	Red, Scalloped	1 Reported	—	—	—	—

"Second Charter Period" (Series of 1882)
Brown Backs

Face of Notes 479-492. Historical vignette of Franklin and the Lightning at left. At right, Liberty grasping lightning in her left hand, being carried aloft by an eagle.

Back of Notes 479-492. Green bank charter numbers against and ornate background of brown lathe-work.

No.	Signatures		VG-8	F-12	VF-20	EF-40	Unc-63
479.	Bruce	Gilfillan	$750.00	$900.00	$1,250.00	$1,650.00	$3,500.00
480.	Bruce	Wyman	750.00	900.00	1,250.00	1,650.00	3,500.00
481.	Bruce	Jordan	750.00	900.00	1,250.00	1,650.00	3,500.00
482.	Rosecrans	Jordan	750.00	900.00	1,250.00	1,650.00	3,500.00
483.	Rosecrans	Hyatt	750.00	900.00	1,250.00	1,650.00	3,500.00
484.	Rosecrans	Huston	750.00	900.00	1,250.00	1,650.00	3,500.00
485.	Rosecrans	Nebeker	750.00	900.00	1,250.00	1,650.00	3,500.00
486.	Rosecrans	Morgan	1,750.00	2,250.00	3,250.00	4,250.00	7,500.00
487.	Tillman	Morgan	750.00	900.00	1,250.00	1,650.00	3,500.00
488.	Tillman	Roberts	750.00	900.00	1,250.00	1,650.00	3,500.00
489.	Bruce	Roberts	750.00	900.00	1,250.00	1,650.00	3,500.00
490.	Lyons	Roberts	750.00	900.00	1,250.00	1,650.00	3,500.00
491.	Lyon	Treat	750.00	900.00	1,250.00	1,650.00	3,500.00
492.	Vernon	Treat	750.00	900.00	1,250.00	1,650.00	3,500.00

"Second Charter Period" (Series of 1882)
Date Backs

Face of Notes 539-548. Historical vignette of Franklin and the Lightning at left. At right, Liberty grasping lightning in her left hand, being carried aloft by an eagle.

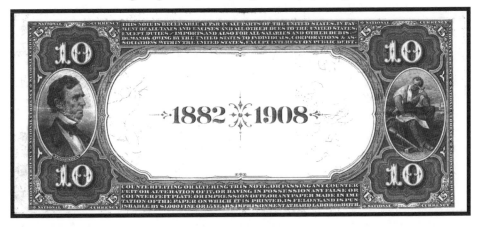

Back of Notes 539-548.

No.	Signatures		VG-8	F-12	VF-20	EF-40	Unc-63
539.	Rosecrans	Huston	$700.00	$850.00	$1,200.00	$1,900.00	$3,000.00
540.	Rosecrans	Nebeker	700.00	850.00	1,200.00	1,900.00	3,000.00
541.	Rosecrans	Morgan	1,250.00	1,750.00	3,000.00	3,750.00	7,000.00
542.	Tillman	Morgan	700.00	850.00	1,200.00	1,900.00	3,000.00
543.	Tillman	Roberts	700.00	850.00	1,200.00	1,900.00	3,000.00
544.	Bruce	Roberts	700.00	850.00	1,200.00	1,900.00	3,000.00
545.	Lyons	Roberts	700.00	850.00	1,200.00	1,900.00	3,000.00
546.	Vernon	Treat	700.00	850.00	1,200.00	1,900.00	3,000.00
547.	Vernon	McClung	700.00	850.00	1,200.00	1,900.00	3,000.00
548.	Napier	McClung	700.00	850.00	1,200.00	1,900.00	3,000.00

"Second Charter Period" (Series of 1882)
Value Backs

Face of Notes 576-579b.
Historical vignette of Franklin and the Lightning *at left.*
At right, Liberty grasping lightning in her left hand, being carried aloft by an eagle.

Back of Notes 576-579b.

No.	Signatures		VG-8	F-12	VF-20	EF-40	Unc-63
576.	Tillman	Morgan	$800.00	$1,000.00	$1,400.00	$2,500.00	$3,800.00
576a.	Tillman	Roberts	800.00	1,000.00	1,400.00	2,500.00	3,800.00
576b.	Bruce	Roberts	800.00	1,000.00	1,400.00	2,500.00	3,800.00
577.	Lyons	Roberts	725.00	900.00	1,250.00	2,100.00	3,250.00
577a.	Lyons	Treat	Unknown	—	—	—	—
578.	Vernon	Treat	740.00	925.00	1,275.00	2,175.00	3,400.00
579.	Napier	McClung	740.00	925.00	1,275.00	2,175.00	3,400.00
579a.	Parker	Burke	Unknown	—	—	—	—
579b.	Teehee	Burke	800.00	1,000.00	1,400.00	2,500.00	3,800.00

"Third Charter Period" (Series of 1902)
First Issue: Series of 1902 with red seal

Face of Notes 613-615. Bust of President William McKinley in round frame.

Back of Notes 613-615. Female figure standing before steamships of the period.

No.	Signatures		VG-8	F-12	VF-20	EF-40	Unc-63
613.	Lyons	Roberts	$725.00	$875.00	$1,250.00	$1,650.00	$3,250.00
614.	Lyons	Treat	725.00	875.00	1,250.00	1,650.00	3,250.00
615.	Vernon	Treat	725.00	875.00	1,250.00	1,650.00	3,250.00

LARGE-SIZE TEN DOLLAR NOTES

"Third Charter Period" (Series of 1902)
Second Issue: Series of 1902 with blue seal and with "1902-1908" on back

Face of Notes 616-623a. Bust of President William McKinley in round frame.

Back of Notes 616-623a. Female figure standing before steamships of the period.

No.	Signatures		VG-8	F-12	VF-20	EF-40	Unc-63
616.	Lyons	Roberts	$200.00	$250.00	$290.00	$350.00	$750.00
617.	Lyons	Treat	200.00	250.00	290.00	350.00	750.00
618.	Vernon	Treat	200.00	250.00	290.00	350.00	750.00
619.	Vernon	McClung	200.00	250.00	290.00	350.00	750.00
620.	Napier	McClung	200.00	250.00	290.00	350.00	750.00
621.	Napier	Thompson	325.00	375.00	425.00	500.00	1,100.00
622.	Napier	Burke	200.00	250.00	290.00	350.00	750.00
623.	Parker	Burke	200.00	250.00	290.00	350.00	750.00
623a.	Teehee	Burke	200.00	250.00	290.00	350.00	750.00

"Third Charter Period" (Series of 1902)

Third Issue: Series of 1902 with blue seal and without "1902-1908" on back

Face of Notes 6246-638. Bust of President William McKinley in round frame.

Back of Notes 624-638. Female figure standing before steamships of the period.

No.	Signatures		VG-8	F-12	VF-20	EF-40	Unc-63
624.	Lyons	Roberts	$175.00	$225.00	$260.00	$370.00	$650.00
625.	Lyons	Treat	175.00	225.00	260.00	370.00	650.00
626.	Vernon	Treat	175.00	225.00	260.00	370.00	650.00
627.	Vernon	McClung	175.00	225.00	260.00	370.00	650.00
628.	Napier	McClung	175.00	225.00	260.00	370.00	650.00
629.	Napier	Thompson	325.00	375.00	425.00	500.00	1,100.00
630.	Napier	Burke	175.00	225.00	260.00	370.00	650.00
631.	Parker	Burke	175.00	225.00	260.00	370.00	650.00
632.	Teehee	Burke	175.00	225.00	260.00	370.00	650.00
633.	Elliott	Burke	175.00	225.00	260.00	370.00	650.00
634.	Elliott	White	175.00	225.00	260.00	370.00	650.00
635.	Speelman	White	175.00	225.00	260.00	370.00	650.00
636.	Woods	White	175.00	225.00	260.00	370.00	650.00
637.	Woods	Tate	200.00	225.00	300.00	450.00	750.00
638.	Jones	Woods	600.00	725.00	800.00	1,000.00	2,500.00

National Gold Bank Notes

Face of Notes 1142-1151a. Historical vignette of Franklin and the Lightning *at left. At right, Liberty grasping lightning in her left hand, being carried aloft by an eagle.*

Back of Notes 1142-1151a. An array of contemporary United States gold coins.

No.	Date	Name of Bank	City	Fair	VG-8	F-12	VF-20
1142.	1870 ...	First National Gold Bank	San Francisco	$2,750.00	$7,500.00	$11,500.00	$20,000.00
1143.	1872 ...	National Gold Bank and Trust Company	San Francisco	4,000.00	10,000.00	16,500.00	—
1144.	1872 ...	National Gold Bank of D.O. Mills and Co.	Sacramento	4,000.00	10,000.00	16,500.00	Rare
1145.	1873 ...	First National Gold Bank	Santa Barbara	7,500.00	20,000.00	—	—
1146.	1873 ...	First National Gold Bank	Stockton	4,000.00	10,000.00	16,500.00	—
1147.	1875 ...	First National Gold Bank	Stockton	4,000.00	10,000.00	16,500.00	—
1148.	1874 ...	Farmer's National Gold Bank	San Jose	4,000.00	10,000.00	16,500.00	—
1149.	1874 ...	First National Gold Bank	Petaluma	4,000.00	10,000.00	16,500.00	—
1150.	1875 ...	First National Gold Bank	Petaluma	4,000.00	10,000.00	16,500.00	—
1151.	1875 ...	First National Gold Bank	Oakland	4,000.00	10,000.00	16,500.00	—
1151a.	1875 ...	Union National Gold Bank	Oakland	15,000.00	—	—	—

Silver Certificates

Design similar to notes of the Series of 1880, which follows.
Bust of Superintendent of Finance Robert Morris. (1781-1784): seal at top; large "Ten" underneath.

All notes below are countersigned; all have the signatures of Scofield and Gilfillan and a large red seal; and are without the legend "Series of 1878." All have engraved countersignatures except for the notes 284a, 284c, and 285, upon which the signatures are written.

No.	Series	Countersigned By	Payable At	Deposited With		
283.	1878	W.G. White	New York	Assistant Treasurer of the U.S.	....	Unique
					2005 Heritage Auction, sold for $253,000	
284.	1878	J.C Hopper	New York	Assistant Treasurer of the U.S.	....	Extremely Rare
284a*.	1878	T. Hillhouse	New York	Assistant Treasurer of the U.S.	....	Unknown
284b.	1878	T. Hillhouse	New York	Assistant Treasurer of the U.S.	....	Rare
284c*	1878	R.M. Anthony	San Francisco	Assistant Treasurer of the U.S.	....	Unknown
285*.	1878	A.U. Wyman	Washington, DC	Treasurer of the U.S.	....	Extremely Rare
285a.	1878	A.U. Wyman	Washington, DC	Treasurer of the U.S.	....	Rare

Face of Notes 286-286a. Bust of Superintendent of Finance (1781-1784) Robert Morris. Seal at top; large "X" below.

Back of Notes 286-290.

Silver Certificates

All notes are countersigned with signatures of Scofield and Gilfillan, a large brown seal at the top and a large "X" below

No.	Series	Countersigned By	Payable At	Deposited With	VG-8	F-12	VF-20
286.	1880	T. Hillhouse	New York	Assistant Treasurer of the U.S.	$6,500.00	$13,000.00	$22,000.00
286a.	1880	A.U. Wyman	Washington, DC	Treasurer of the U.S.		Unknown	

Similar to above; seal at top; large brown "X" below, but without a countersigned signature

No.	Series	Signatures		Seal	VG-8	F-12	VF-20	EF-40	Unc-63
287.	1880	Scofield	Gilfillan	Large Brown	$900.00	$1,500.00	$2,750.00	$4,000.00	$10,000.00
288.	1880	Bruce	Gilfillan	Large Brown	900.00	1,500.00	2,750.00	4,000.00	7,500.00
289.	1880	Bruce	Wyman	Large Brown	900.00	1,500.00	2,750.00	4,000.00	7,500.00

Similar to above but with seal in center and no large "X"

No.	Series	Signatures		Seal	VG-8	F-12	VF-20	EF-40	Unc-63
290.	1880	Bruce	Wyman	Large Red	$1,050.00	$1,650.00	$3,500.00	$5,000.00	$15,000.00

Face of Notes 291-297. Bust of Vice President (March 4–November 25, 1885) Thomas A. Hendricks. The style of the frame has caused this to be called the "Tombstone Note."

Back of Notes 291-297.

Silver Certificates

No.	Series	Signatures		Seal	VG-8	F-12	VF-20	EF-40	Unc-63
291.	1886	Rosecrans	Jordan	Small Red, Plain	$575.00	$950.00	$2,000.00	$3,250.00	$8,000.00
292.	1886	Rosecrans	Hyatt	Small Red, Plain	475.00	800.00	1,750.00	2,750.00	8,250.00
293.	1886	Rosecrans	Hyatt	Large Red	475.00	800.00	1,750.00	2,750.00	6,750.00
294.	1886	Rosecrans	Huston	Large Red	475.00	800.00	1,750.00	2,750.00	6,750.00
295.	1886	Rosecrans	Huston	Large Brown	475.00	800.00	1,750.00	2,750.00	8,750.00
296.	1886	Rosecrans	Nebeker	Large Brown	475.00	800.00	1,750.00	2,750.00	6,750.00
297.	1886	Rosecrans	Nebeker	Small Red, Scalloped	575.00	950.00	2,000.00	3,250.00	8,000.00

Face of Notes 298-301. A small plate letter alone at left center of face.

Back of Notes 298-301.

No.	Series	Signatures		Seal	VG-8	F-12	VF-20	EF-40	Unc-63
298.	1891	Rosecrans	Nebeker	Small Red	$240.00	$475.00	$850.00	$1,300.00	$3,900.00
299.	1891	Tillman	Morgan	Small Red	240.00	475.00	850.00	1,300.00	3,300.00
300.	1891	Bruce	Roberts	Small Red	240.00	475.00	850.00	1,300.00	3,900.00
301.	1891	Lyons	Roberts	Small Red	240.00	475.00	850.00	1,300.00	3,300.00

Similar to above with a large blue "X" at left center of face

No.	Series	Signatures		Seal	VG-8	F-12	VF-20	EF-40	Unc-63
302.	1908	Vernon	Treat	Blue	$300.00	$475.00	$900.00	$1,375.00	$3,300.00
303.	1908	Vernon	McClung	Blue	300.00	475.00	900.00	1,375.00	3,300.00
304.	1908	Parker	Burke	Blue	300.00	475.00	900.00	1,375.00	3,300.00

Refunding Certificates

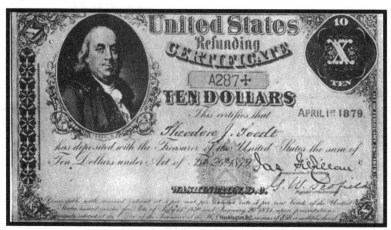

Face of Note 213. Bust of Benjamin Franklin.

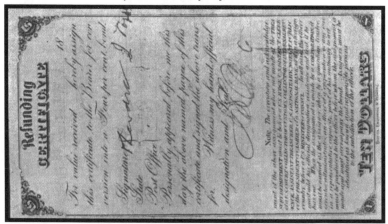

Back of Note 213.

No.	Denomination		
213.	Ten Dollars.	Payable to order	Extremely Rare

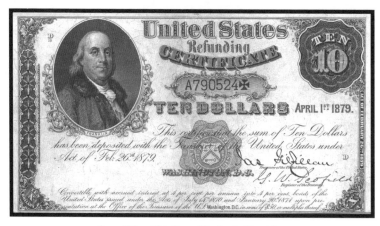

Face of Note 214. Bust of Benjamin Franklin.

Refunding Certificates

Back of Note 214.

No.	Denomination		VG-8	F-12	VF-20	EF-40	Unc-63
214.	Ten Dollars .... Payable to bearer		$1,400.00	$1,950.00	$2,750.00	$5,500.00	$9,000.00

Treasury or Coin Notes

Face of Notes 366-368. Bust of General Philip H. Sheridan.

Back of Notes 366-368.

LARGE-SIZE TEN DOLLAR NOTES

Treasury or Coin Notes

No.	Series	Signatures		Seal	VG-8	F-12	VF-20	EF-40	Unc-63
366.	1890	Rosecrans	Huston	Large Brown	$600.00	$925.00	$1,650.00	$2,550.00	$5,250.00
367.	1890	Rosecrans	Nebeker	Large Brown	675.00	1,050.00	1,775.00	2,800.00	5,600.00
368.	1890	Rosecrans	Nebeker	Small Red	600.00	925.00	1,650.00	2,550.00	4,250.00

Face of Notes 369-371. Bust of General Philip H. Sheridan.

Back of Notes 369-371.

No.	Series	Signatures		Seal	VG-8	F-12	VF-20	EF-40	Unc-63
369.	1891	Rosecrans	Nebeker	Small Red	$350.00	$725.00	$1,200.00	$1,600.00	$3,600.00
370.	1891	Tillman	Morgan	Small Red	350.00	725.00	1,200.00	1,600.00	3,800.00
371.	1891	Bruce	Roberts	Small Red	350.00	725.00	1,200.00	1,600.00	10,000.00

Gold Certificates

Face of Notes 1167-1173a. Treasurer of the U.S. (1775-1789) Michael Hillegas.

Back of Notes 1167-1173a.

No.	Series	Signatures		Seal	VG-8	F-12	VF-20	EF-40	Unc-63
1167.	1907	Vernon	Treat	Gold	$145.00	$175.00	$250.00	$400.00	$1,000.00
1168.	1907	Vernon	McClung	Gold	145.00	175.00	250.00	400.00	1,000.00
1169.	1907	Napier	McClung	Gold Act of 1882	145.00	175.00	250.00	400.00	1,000.00
1169a.	1907	Napier	McClung	Gold Act of 1907	145.00	175.00	250.00	400.00	1,000.00
1170.	1907	Napier	Thompson	Gold Act of 1882	225.00	275.00	400.00	600.00	1,500.00
1170a.	1907	Napier	Thompson	Gold Act of 1907	200.00	250.00	350.00	500.00	1,250.00
1171.	1907	Parker	Burke	Gold	145.00	175.00	250.00	400.00	1,000.00
1172.	1907	Teehee	Burke	Gold	145.00	175.00	250.00	400.00	1,000.00
1173.	1922	Speelman	White	Gold	135.00	165.00	225.00	350.00	850.00
1173a.	1922	Speelman	White	Gold, Small Serial Numbers	155.00	190.00	260.00	420.00	1,200.00

Federal Reserve Bank Notes

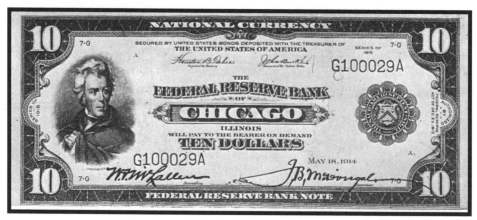

Face of Notes 810-821. Bust of Andrew Jackson at left.

Back of Notes 810-821. Scenes depicting agriculture and commerce.

No.	Issuing Bank	Series	Government Signatures		Bank Signatures		VG-8	F-12	VF-20	EF-40	Unc-63
810.	New York	1918	Teehee	Burke	Hendricks	Strong	1,050.00	$1,350.00	$1,800.00	$2,600.00	$3,750.00
811.	Atlanta	1915	Teehee	Burke	Bell	Wellborn	4,000.00	6,000.00	—	—	—
812.	Atlanta	1918	Elliott	Burke	Bell	Wellborn	1,050.00	1,350.00	1,800.00	2,600.00	4,500.00
813.	Chicago	1915	Teehee	Burke	McLallen	McDougal	1,050.00	1,350.00	1,800.00	2,600.00	3,750.00
814.	Chicago	1918	Teehee	Burke	McCloud	McDougal	1,050.00	1,350.00	1,800.00	2,600.00	—
815.	St. Louis	1918	Teehee	Burke	Attebery	Wells	1,050.00	1,350.00	1,800.00	2,600.00	4,500.00
816.	Kansas City	1915	Teehee	Burke	Anderson	Miller	1,050.00	1,350.00	1,800.00	2,600.00	4,500.00
817.	Kansas City	1915	Teehee	Burke	Cross	Miller	1,050.00	1,350.00	1,800.00	2,600.00	3,750.00

Bank signatures plate engraved.

No.	Issuing Bank	Series	Government Signatures		Bank Signatures		VG-8	F-12	VF-20	EF-40	Unc-63
817a.	Kansas City	1915	Teehee	Burke	Cross	Miller	Rare	—	—	—	—

Bank signatures hand-stamped in red with Cross as "Acting" Secretary.

No.	Issuing Bank	Series	Government Signatures		Bank Signatures		VG-8	F-12	VF-20	EF-40	Unc-63
818.	Kansas City	1915	Teehee	Burke	Helm	Miller	$4,000.00	$6,000.00	$12,000.00	$18,000.00	—
819.	Dallas	1915	Teehee	Burke	Hoopes	Van Zandt	1,050.00	1,350.00	1,800.00	2,600.00	$3,750.00
820.	Dallas	1915	Teehee	Burke	Gilbert	Van Zandt	1,750.00	2,750.00	4,000.00	6,000.00	—
821.	Dallas	1915	Teehee	Burke	Talley	Van Zandt	1,750.00	2,750.00	4,000.00	6,000.00	—

No $10 Federal Reserve Bank Notes were issued by the banks at Boston, Philadelphia, Cleveland, Richmond, Minneapolis, and San Francisco.

Federal Reserve Notes

Face of Notes 892A-903B (blue seal, type A pictured). Bust of Andrew Jackson in center.

Back of Notes 892A-903B. Scenes depicting agriculture and commerce.

Series of 1914 with red seal and signatures of Burke and McAdoo

A. Large district letter and numeral at top right and bottom left. Small letter at top left and bottom right.
B. As above, with a small district letter and numeral added above letter at top left.

No.	Issuing Bank	VG-8	F-12	VF-20	EF-40	Unc-63
892A.	Boston	$360.00	$650.00	$875.00	$1,325.00	$2,950.00
892B.	Boston	650.00	1,250.00	2,750.00	—	—
893A.	New York	360.00	650.00	875.00	1,325.00	2,950.00
893B.	New York	325.00	550.00	750.00	1,150.00	2,300.00
894A.	Philadelphia	500.00	1,000.00	1,800.00	3,000.00	4,000.00
894B.	Philadelphia	360.00	650.00	875.00	1,325.00	2,300.00
895A.	Cleveland	500.00	1,000.00	1,800.00	3,000.00	6,500.00
895B.	Cleveland	360.00	650.00	875.00	1,325.00	—
896A.	Richmond	500.00	1,000.00	1,800.00	3,000.00	8,000.00
896B.	Richmond	500.00	1,000.00	1,800.00	3,500.00	—
897A.	Atlanta	500.00	1,000.00	1,800.00	3,500.00	6,500.00
897B.	Atlanta	500.00	1,000.00	1,800.00	3,500.00	6,500.00
898A.	Chicago	325.00	550.00	750.00	1,150.00	2,300.00
898B.	Chicago	325.00	550.00	750.00	1,150.00	2,500.00
899A.	St. Louis	325.00	550.00	750.00	1,150.00	2,300.00
899B.	St. Louis	500.00	1,000.00	1,800.00	3,500.00	5,000.00
900A.	Minneapolis	360.00	650.00	875.00	1,325.00	5,000.00
900B.	Minneapolis	500.00	1,000.00	1,800.00	3,500.00	6,500.00
901A.	Kansas City	360.00	650.00	875.00	1,325.00	—
901B.	Kansas City	500.00	1,000.00	1,800.00	3,500.00	6,500.00
902A.	Dallas	360.00	650.00	875.00	1,325.00	—
902B.	Dallas	500.00	1,000.00	1,800.00	3,500.00	—
903A.	San Francisco	500.00	1,000.00	1,800.00	2,750.00	—
903B.	San Francisco	500.00	1,000.00	1,800.00	3,750.00	6,500.00

LARGE-SIZE TEN DOLLAR NOTES

Federal Reserve Notes

B. Series of 1914 with blue seal

A. Large letter and numeral at top left and bottom right. **B.** Large letter and numeral at top right with small district letters and numerals in the other three corners. **C.** Again, a large pair of letters and numerals, but positioned both vertically, more toward the center of the note and closer to the outside edge. Also, the seals to the sides of the portrait are closer to the note's center than the A issue.

No.	Issuing Bank	Signatures		VG-8	F-12	VF-20	EF-40	Unc-63
904.	Boston	Burke	McAdoo	$65.00	$75.00	$85.00	$125.00	$500.00
905.	Boston	Burke	Glass	70.00	85.00	100.00	150.00	—
906.	Boston	Burke	Houston	65.00	75.00	85.00	125.00	325.00
907A.	Boston	White	Mellon	65.00	75.00	85.00	125.00	325.00
907B.	Boston	White	Mellon	70.00	85.00	100.00	150.00	400.00
908.	New York	Burke	McAdoo	65.00	75.00	85.00	125.00	—
909.	New York	Burke	Glass	65.00	75.00	85.00	125.00	325.00
910.	New York	Burke	Houston	65.00	75.00	85.00	125.00	325.00
911A.	New York	White	Mellon	65.00	75.00	85.00	125.00	325.00
911B.	New York	White	Mellon	70.00	85.00	100.00	150.00	400.00
911C.	New York	White	Mellon	70.00	85.00	100.00	150.00	400.00
912.	Philadelphia	Burke	McAdoo	70.00	85.00	100.00	150.00	500.00
913.	Philadelphia	Burke	Glass	70.00	85.00	100.00	150.00	400.00
914.	Philadelphia	Burke	Houston	65.00	75.00	85.00	125.00	325.00
915A.	Philadelphia	White	Mellon	65.00	75.00	85.00	125.00	325.00
915C.	Philadelphia	White	Mellon	70.00	85.00	100.00	150.00	400.00
916.	Cleveland	Burke	McAdoo	70.00	85.00	100.00	150.00	400.00
917.	Cleveland	Burke	Glass	70.00	85.00	100.00	150.00	400.00
918.	Cleveland	Burke	Houston	70.00	85.00	100.00	150.00	400.00
919A.	Cleveland	White	Mellon	65.00	75.00	85.00	125.00	325.00
919B.	Cleveland	White	Mellon	70.00	85.00	100.00	150.00	400.00
919C.	Cleveland	White	Mellon	70.00	85.00	100.00	150.00	450.00
920.	Richmond	Burke	McAdoo	70.00	85.00	100.00	150.00	400.00
921.	Richmond	Burke	Glass	100.00	175.00	350.00	500.00	950.00
922.	Richmond	Burke	Houston	65.00	75.00	85.00	125.00	325.00
923.	Richmond	White	Mellon	65.00	75.00	85.00	125.00	325.00
924.	Atlanta	Burke	McAdoo	70.00	85.00	100.00	150.00	500.00
925.	Atlanta	Burke	Glass	85.00	100.00	150.00	250.00	650.00
926.	Atlanta	Burke	Houston	70.00	85.00	100.00	150.00	400.00
927A.	Atlanta	White	Mellon	65.00	75.00	85.00	125.00	325.00
927B.	Atlanta	White	Mellon	70.00	85.00	100.00	150.00	—
928.	Chicago	Burke	McAdoo	65.00	75.00	85.00	125.00	325.00
929.	Chicago	Burke	Glass	65.00	75.00	85.00	125.00	325.00
930.	Chicago	Burke	Houston	65.00	75.00	85.00	125.00	325.00
931A.	Chicago	White	Mellon	65.00	75.00	85.00	125.00	325.00
931B.	Chicago	White	Mellon	70.00	85.00	100.00	150.00	400.00
931C.	Chicago	White	Mellon	70.00	85.00	100.00	150.00	400.00
932.	St. Louis	Burke	McAdoo	65.00	75.00	85.00	125.00	325.00
933.	St. Louis	Burke	Glass	70.00	85.00	100.00	150.00	500.00
934.	St. Louis	Burke	Houston	65.00	75.00	85.00	125.00	325.00
935.	St. Louis	White	Mellon	70.00	85.00	100.00	150.00	500.00
936.	Minneapolis	Burke	McAdoo	65.00	75.00	85.00	125.00	325.00
937.	Minneapolis	Burke	Glass	70.00	85.00	100.00	150.00	650.00
938.	Minneapolis	Burke	Houston	65.00	75.00	85.00	125.00	500.00
939.	Minneapolis	White	Mellon	65.00	75.00	85.00	125.00	325.00
940.	Kansas City	Burke	McAdoo	65.00	75.00	85.00	125.00	325.00
941.	Kansas City	Burke	Glass	125.00	200.00	350.00	570.00	900.00
942.	Kansas City	Burke	Houston	70.00	85.00	100.00	150.00	400.00
943A.	Kansas City	White	Mellon	70.00	85.00	100.00	150.00	400.00
944.	Dallas	Burke	McAdoo	70.00	85.00	100.00	150.00	400.00
945.	Dallas	Burke	Glass	300.00	500.00	1,000.00	1,500.00	—
946.	Dallas	Burke	Houston	85.00	100.00	150.00	250.00	—
947.	Dallas	White	Mellon	70.00	85.00	100.00	150.00	500.00
948.	San Francisco	Burke	McAdoo	100.00	150.00	250.00	500.00	—
949.	San Francisco	Burke	Glass	100.00	150.00	250.00	500.00	—
950.	San Francisco	Burke	Houston	100.00	150.00	250.00	500.00	950.00
951A.	San Francisco	White	Mellon	65.00	75.00	85.00	125.00	325.00
951B.	San Francisco	White	Mellon	75.00	100.00	125.00	200.00	650.00
951C.	San Francisco	White	Mellon	75.00	90.00	115.00	175.00	500.00

National Bank Notes (Brown Seal)

Face of Note 1801.

Back of Note 1801.

No.		VF-20	Unc-63
1801-1.	Type 1	$100.00	$250.00
1801-2.	Type 2	100.00	250.00

Silver Certificates (Blue Seal)

Face of Note 1700.

Back of Note 1700.

Silver Certificates (Blue Seal)

No.	Series	Signatures		Quantity Printed	VF-20	Unc-63
1700.	1933	Julian	Woodin	216,000	$6,500.00	$12,000.00
1700*.	1933	Julian	Woodin		Unique	—
1700a.	1933-A	Julian	Morgenthau	336,000	Unknown	(not released)

Face of Notes 1701-1705.

Back of Notes 1701-1705.

No.	Series	Signatures	Quantity Printed	VF-20	Unc-63
1701.	1934	Julian Morgenthau 88,692,864		$40.00	$150.00
1701*.	1934	Julian Morgenthau		225.00	1,000.00

Notes issued for use with the Armed Forces in Europe and North Africa

Face of Notes 2308-2309. Blue serial numbers and yellow seal.

Back of Notes 2308-2309.

Silver Certificates (Blue Seal)

No.	Denomination	Series	Quantity Printed	VF-20	Unc-63
2308.	Ten Dollars	1934		$4,000.00	Rare
2308*.	Ten Dollars	1934		Unique	—
2309.	Ten Dollars	1934-A	21,860,000†	70.00	$250.00
2309*.	Ten Dollars	1934-A		225.00	1,500.00

* This is the combined amount printed for 50th series 1934 and 1934-A.

Regular Issues (continued from Note 1701)

No.	Series	Signatures		Quantity Printed	VF-20	Unc-63
1702.	1934-A	Julian	Morgenthau	42,346,428	$45.00	$175.00
1702*.	1934-A	Julian	Morgenthau		200.00	1,500.00
1703.	1934-B	Julian	Vinson	337,740	225.00	2,250.00
1703*.	1934-B	Julian	Vinson		2,750.00	Rare
1704.	1934-C	Julian	Snyder	20,032,632	35.00	150.00
1704*.	1934-C	Julian	Snyder		90.00	500.00
1705.	1934-D	Clark	Snyder	11,801,112	45.00	225.00
1705*.	1934-D	Clark	Snyder		275.00	2,500.00

Face of Notes 1706-1708.

Back of Notes 1706-1708.

No.	Series	Signatures		Quantity Printed	VF-20	Unc-63
1706.	1953	Priest	Humphrey	10,440,000	$50.00	$175.00
1706*.	1953	Priest	Humphrey	576,000	150.00	750.00
1707.	1953-A	Priest	Anderson	1,080,000	65.00	225.00
1707*.	1953-A	Priest	Anderson	144,000	200.00	1,200.00
1708.	1953-B	Smith	Dillon	720,000	50.00	150.00

Gold Certificates (Gold Seal)

Face of Note 2400.

Back of Note 2400.

No.	Series	Signatures			Quantity Printed		VG-8	F-12	VF-20	EF-40	Unc-63
2400.	1928	Wood	Mellon	....	130,812,000	.... $70.00	$80.00	$120.00	$175.00	$600.00
2400*.	1928	Woods	Mellon	....		.... 175.00	300.00	600.00	1,500.00	5,000.00
2401.	1928-A	Woods	Mellon	....	2,544,000	...... Not Issued	—	—	—	—

Federal Reserve Bank Notes (Brown Seal)

Face of Note 1860.

Back of Note 1860.

Gold Certificates (Gold Seal)

No.	Issuing Bank	Quantity Printed	VF-20	Unc-63
1860-A.	Boston	1,680,000	$50.00	$225.00
1860-B.	New York	5,556,000	45.00	150.00
1860-C.	Philadelphia	1,416,000	45.00	200.00
1860-D.	Cleveland	2,412,000	45.00	175.00
1860-E.	Richmond	1,356,000	45.00	400.00
1860-F.	Atlanta	1,056,000	45.00	250.00
1860-G.	Chicago	3,156,000	45.00	150.00
1860-H.	St. Louis	1,584,000	45.00	175.00
1860-I.	Minneapolis	58,000	65.00	350.00
1860-J.	Kansas City	1,284,000	45.00	225.00
1860-K.	Dallas	504,000	500.00	2,000.00
1860-L.	San Francisco	1,080,000	75.00	1,200.00
1860*.	Most Common Districts		400.00	2,000.00

Federal Reserve Notes (Green Seal)

Face of Notes 2000-2001.

Back of Notes 2000-2001.

Series of 1928
Signatures of Tate and Mellon

No.	Issuing Bank	Quantity Printed	VF-20	Unc-63
2000-A.	Boston	9,804,552	$60.00	$400.00
2000-A*.	Boston		400.00	1,750.00
2000-B.	New York	11,295,796	30.00	200.00
2000-B*.	New York		350.00	1,500.00
2000-C.	Philadelphia	8,114,412	35.00	250.00
2000-C*.	Philadelphia		350.00	1,500.00
2000-D.	Cleveland	75,708,120	30.00	180.00
2000-D*.	Cleveland		350.00	1,500.00
2000-E.	Richmond	4,534,800	50.00	300.00
2000-E*.	Richmond		500.00	1,800.00
2000-F.	Atlanta	6,807,720	35.00	250.00
2000-F*.	Atlanta		450.00	1,750.00
2000-G.	Chicago	8,130,000	30.00	180.00
2000-G*.	Chicago		400.00	1,750.00
2000-H.	St. Louis	4,124,100	35.00	200.00
2000-H*.	St. Louis		250.00	1,000.00
2000-I.	Minneapolis	3,874,440	50.00	400.00

SMALL-SIZE TEN DOLLAR NOTES

Federal Reserve Notes (Green Seal)

No.	Issuing Bank	Quantity Printed	VF-20	Unc-63
2000-I*.	Minneapolis		$450.00	$1,800.00
2000-J.	Kansas City	3,620,400	40.00	275.00
2000-J*.	Kansas City		250.00	1,100.00
2000-K.	Dallas	4,855,500	50.00	375.00
2000-K*.	Dallas		1,000.00	4,000.00
2000-L.	San Francisco	7,086,900	35.00	200.00
2000-L*.	San Francisco		1,500.00	5,000.00

Series of 1928-A
Signatures of Woods and Mellon

No.	Issuing Bank	Quantity Printed	VF-20	Unc-63
2001-A.	Boston	2,893,440	$50.00	$450.00
2001-A*.	Boston		300.00	1,500.00
2001-B.	New York	18,631,056	40.00	250.00
2001-B*.	New York		250.00	1,000.00
2001-C.	Philadelphia	2,710,680	50.00	275.00
2001-C*.	Philadelphia		300.00	1,500.00
2001-D.	Cleveland	5,610,000	45.00	250.00
2001-D*.	Cleveland		225.00	1,200.00
2001-E.	Richmond	552,300	100.00	700.00
2001-E*.	Richmond		400.00	1,750.00
2001-F.	Atlanta	3,033,480	50.00	450.00
2001-F*.	Atlanta		350.00	1,750.00
2001-G.	Chicago	8,715,000	40.00	250.00
2001-G*.	Chicago		200.00	900.00
2001-H.	St. Louis	531,600	50.00	250.00
2001-H*.	St. Louis		250.00	1,000.00
2001-I.	Minneapolis	102,600	550.00	2,250.00
2001-J.	Kansas City	410,400	350.00	1,200.00
2001-K.	Dallas	961,800	350.00	1,350.00
2001-L.	San Francisco	2,547,900	75.00	350.00
2001-L*.	San Francisco		350.00	1,500.00

Face of Notes 2002-2009.

Back of Notes 2002-2009.

Federal Reserve Notes (Green Seal)

Series of 1928-B
Signatures of Woods and Mellon
Exists with both light and dark green seals

No.	Issuing Bank	Quantity Printed	VF-20	Unc-63
2002-A.	Boston	33,218,088	$20.00	$85.00
2002-A*.	Boston		150.00	1,000.00
2002-B.	New York	44,808,308	20.00	75.00
2002-B*.	New York		200.00	1,000.00
2002-C.	Philadelphia	22,689,216	20.00	85.00
2002-C*.	Philadelphia		125.00	1,000.00
2002-D.	Cleveland	17,418,024	20.00	75.00
2002-D*.	Cleveland		125.00	750.00
2002-E.	Richmond	12,714,504	25.00	100.00
2002-E*.	Richmond		150.00	1,000.00
2002-F.	Atlanta	5,246,700	27.50	110.00
2002-F*.	Atlanta		200.00	1,200.00
2002-G.	Chicago	38,035,000	20.00	75.00
2002-G*.	Chicago		125.00	650.00
2002-H.	St. Louis	10,814,664	25.00	85.00
2002-H*.	St. Louis		150.00	1,200.00
2002-I.	Minneapolis	5,294,460	25.00	100.00
2002-I*.	Minneapolis		150.00	1,200.00
2002-J.	Kansas City	7,748,040	25.00	85.00
2002-J*.	Kansas City		400.00	2,000.00
2002-K.	Dallas	3,396,096	25.00	100.00
2002-L.	San Francisco	22,695,300	20.00	75.00
2002-I*	San Francisco		125.00	1,000.00

Series of 1928-C
Signatures of Woods and Mills

No.	Issuing Bank	Quantity Printed	VF-20	Unc-63
2003-B.	New York	2,902,678	$75.00	$450.00
2003-D.	Cleveland	4,230,428	450.00	5,000.00
2003-D*.	Cleveland		Very	Rare
2003-E.	Richmond	304,800	Rare	—
2003-F.	Atlanta	688,380	Unknown	
2003-G.	Chicago	2,423,400	75.00	550.00

Series of 1934-A
Signatures of Julian and Morgenthau
Notes with a vivid, light green seal

The number of notes printed is the combined total for both light and dark seal notes

No.	Issuing Bank	Quantity Printed	VF-20	Unc-63
2004-A.	Boston	46,276,152	$20.00	$100.00
2004-A*.	Boston		50.00	700.00
2004-B.	New York	117,298,008	20.00	65.00
2004-B*.	New York		50.00	500.00
2004-C.	Philadelphia	34,770,768	20.00	70.00
2004-C*.	Philadelphia		50.00	500.00
2004-D.	Cleveland	28,764,108	20.00	80.00
2004-D*.	Cleveland		90.00	600.00
2004-E.	Richmond	16,437,252	20.00	80.00
2004-E*.	Richmond		200.00	1,200.00
2004-F.	Atlanta	20,656,872	20.00	80.00
2004-F*.	Atlanta		50.00	750.00
2004-G.	Chicago	69,962,064	20.00	65.00
2004-G*.	Chicago		50.00	500.00
2004-H.	St. Louis	22,593,204	20.00	80.00
2004-H*.	St. Louis		60.00	600.00
2004-I.	Minneapolis	16,840,980	25.00	125.00

SMALL-SIZE TEN DOLLAR NOTES

Federal Reserve Notes (Green Seal)

No.	Issuing Bank	Quantity Printed	VF-20	Unc-63
2004-I*.	Minneapolis		$125.00	$900.00
2004-J.	Kansas City	22,627,824	20.00	80.00
2004-J*.	Kansas City		100.00	900.00
2004-K.	Dallas	21,403,488	20.00	250.00
2004-K*.	Dallas		125.00	1,400.00
2004-L.	San Francisco	37,402,308	20.00	85.00
2004-L*.	San Francisco		90.00	900.00

B. Notes with a darker and duller blue-green seal

No.	Issuing Bank	VF-20	Unc-63
2005-A.	Boston	$20.00	$80.00
2005-A*.	Boston	40.00	400.00
2005-B.	New York	20.00	60.00
2005-B*.	New York	40.00	400.00
2005-C.	Philadelphia	20.00	60.00
2005-C*.	Philadelphia	40.00	400.00
2005-D.	Cleveland	20.00	60.00
2005-D*.	Cleveland	80.00	600.00
2005-E.	Richmond	20.00	80.00
2005-E*.	Richmond	125.00	700.00
2005-F.	Atlanta	20.00	60.00
2005-F*.	Atlanta	125.00	700.00
2005-G.	Chicago	20.00	60.00
2005-G*.	Chicago	40.00	400.00
2005-H.	St. Louis	20.00	80.00
2005-H*.	St. Louis	40.00	400.00
2005-I.	Minneapolis	20.00	100.00
2005-I*.	Minneapolis	125.00	650.00
2005-J.	Kansas City	20.00	60.00
2005-J*.	Kansas City	40.00	400.00
2005-K.	Dallas	20.00	80.00
2005-K*.	Dallas	40.00	400.00
2005-L.	San Francisco	20.00	60.00
2005-L*.	San Francisco	40.00	400.00

Series of 1934-A
Signatures of Julian and Morgenthau

No.	Issuing Bank	Quantity Printed	VF-20	Unc-63
2006-A.	Boston	104,540,088	$15.00	$50.00
2006-A*.	Boston		50.00	250.00
2006-B.	New York	281,940,996	15.00	50.00
2006-B*.	New York		50.00	200.00
2006-C.	Philadelphia	95,338,032	15.00	50.00
2006-C*.	Philadelphia		50.00	250.00
2006-D.	Cleveland	93,332,004	15.00	60.00
2006-D*.	Cleveland		50.00	250.00
2006-E.	Richmond	101,037,912	15.00	50.00
2006-E*.	Richmond		50.00	250.00
2006-F.	Atlanta	85,478,160	15.00	50.00
2006-F*.	Atlanta		75.00	300.00
2006-G.	Chicago	177,285,960	15.00	50.00
2006-G*.	Chicago		50.00	200.00
2006-H.	St. Louis	50,694,312	15.00	60.00
2006-H*.	St. Louis		50.00	250.00
2006-I.	Minneapolis	16,340,016	15.00	50.00
2006-I*.	Minneapolis		100.00	350.00
2006-J.	Kansas City	31,069,978	15.00	55.00
2006-J*.	Kansas City		50.00	250.00
2006-K.	Dallas	28,263,156	15.00	55.00
2006-K*.	Dallas		75.00	300.00
2006-L.	San Francisco	125,537,592	15.00	50.00
2006-L*.	San Francisco		50.00	250.00

Federal Reserve Notes (Green Seal)

Notes issued for Hawaii after the attack on Pearl Harbor

Face of Note 2303. Brown seal.

Back of Note 2303.

No.	Denomination	Series	Quantity Printed	VF-20	Unc-63
2303.	Ten Dollars	1934-A	10,424,000	$100.00	$800.00
2303*.	Ten Dollars	1934-A		1,250.00	7,500.00

Regular Issues (continued from Note 2006)
Series of 1934–B
Signatures of Julian and Vinson

No.	Issuing Bank	Quantity Printed	EF-40	Unc-63
2007-A.	Boston	3,999,600	$40.00	$125.00
2007-A*.	Boston		175.00	600.00
2007-B.	New York	34,815,948	20.00	65.00
2007-B*.	New York		150.00	400.00
2007-C.	Philadelphia	10,339,020	25.00	75.00
2007-C*.	Philadelphia		150.00	600.00
2007-D.	Cleveland	1,394,700	30.00	115.00
2007-D*.	Cleveland		150.00	1,000.00
2007-E.	Richmond	4,018,272	35.00	115.00
2007-E*.	Richmond		150.00	1,000.00
2007-F.	Atlanta	6,746,076	25.00	85.00
2007-F*.	Atlanta		150.00	1,400.00
2007-G.	Chicago	18,130,836	25.00	60.00
2007-G*.	Chicago		150.00	400.00
2007-H.	St. Louis	6,849,348	25.00	85.00
2007-H*.	St. Louis		150.00	600.00
2007-I.	Minneapolis	2,254,800	40.00	125.00
2007-I*.	Minneapolis		250.00	1,400.00
2007-J.	Kansas City	3,835,764	35.00	115.00
2007-J*.	Kansas City		250.00	800.00
2007-K.	Dallas	3,085,200	40.00	125.00
2007-K*.	Dallas		250.00	1,400.00
2007-L.	San Francisco	9,076,800	25.00	85.00
2007-L*.	San Francisco		150.00	600.00

SMALL-SIZE TEN DOLLAR NOTES

Federal Reserve Notes (Green Seal)

Series of 1934-C
Signatures of Julian and Snyder

No.	Issuing Bank	Quantity Printed	EF-40	Unc-63
2008-A.	Boston	42,431,404	$20.00	$50.00
2008-A*.	Boston		100.00	400.00
2008-B.	New York	115,675,644	20.00	45.00
2008-B*.	New York		100.00	300.00
2008-C.	Philadelphia	46,874,760	20.00	50.00
2008-C*.	Philadelphia		100.00	400.00
2008-D.	Cleveland	332,400	20.00	45.00
2008-D*.	Cleveland		100.00	400.00
2008-E.	Richmond	37,422,600	20.00	50.00
2008-E*.	Richmond		100.00	400.00
2008-F.	Atlanta	44,838,264	20.00	55.00
2008-F*.	Atlanta		100.00	400.00
2008-G.	Chicago	105,875,412	20.00	45.00
2008-G*.	Chicago		75.00	300.00
2008-H	St. Louis	36,541,404	20.00	55.00
2008-H*.	St. Louis		100.00	400.00
2008-I.	Minneapolis	11,944,848	20.00	80.00
2008-I*.	Minneapolis		250.00	800.00
2008-J.	Kansas City	20,874,072	20.00	55.00
2008-J*.	Kansas City		100.00	400.00
2008-K.	Dallas	25,642,620	20.00	55.00
2008-K*.	Dallas		150.00	550.00
2008-L.	San Francisco	49,164,480	25.00	50.00
2008-L*.	San Francisco		100.00	400.00

Series of 1934-D
Signatures of Clark and Snyder

No.	Issuing Bank	Quantity Printed	EF-40	Unc-63
2009-A.	Boston	19,917,900	$25.00	$55.00
2009-A*.	Boston		175.00	500.00
2009-B.	New York	64,067,904	25.00	55.00
2009-B*.	New York		150.00	400.00
2009-C.	Philadelphia	18,432,000	25.00	55.00
2009-C*.	Philadelphia		150.00	400.00
2009-D.	Cleveland	20,291,316	25.00	55.00
2009-D*.	Cleveland		150.00	400.00
2009-E.	Richmond	18,090,312	25.00	55.00
2009-E*.	Richmond		250.00	1,200.00
2009-F.	Atlanta	17,064,816	25.00	55.00
2009-F*.	Atlanta		175.00	450.00
2009-G.	Chicago	55,943,844	15.00	55.00
2009-G*.	Chicago		150.00	400.00
2009-H.	St. Louis	15,828,048	35.00	75.00
2009-H*.	St. Louis		175.00	500.00
2009-I.	Minneapolis	5,237,220	45.00	100.00
2009-I*.	Minneapolis		200.00	750.00
2009-J.	Kansas City	7,992,000	30.00	70.00
2009-J*.	Kansas City		250.00	750.00
2009-K.	Dallas	7,178,196	30.00	70.00
2009-K*.	Dallas		300.00	1,250.00
2009-L.	San Francisco	23,956,584	30.00	70.00
2009-L*.	San Francisco		300.00	1,250.00

Federal Reserve Notes (Green Seal)

Face of Notes 2010-2015.

Back of Notes 2010-2015.

Series of 1950
Signatures of Clark and Snyder

No.	Issuing Bank	Quantity Printed	EF-40	Unc-63
2010-A.	Boston	70,992,000	$25.00	$70.00
2010-A*.	Boston	1,008,000	150.00	525.00
2010-B.	New York	218,576,000	25.00	55.00
2010-B*.	New York	2,586,000	100.00	400.00
2010-C.	Philadelphia	76,320,000	25.00	60.00
2010-C*.	Philadelphia	1,008,000	150.00	525.00
2010-D.	Cleveland	76,032,000	25.00	60.00
2010-D*.	Cleveland	1,008,000	150.00	525.00
2010-E.	Richmond	61,776,000	25.00	65.00
2010-E*.	Richmond	876,000	150.00	525.00
2010-F.	Atlanta	63,792,000	25.00	60.00
2010-F*.	Atlanta	864,000	150.00	525.00
2010-G.	Chicago	161,056,000	25.00	55.00
2010-G*.	Chicago	2,088,000	100.00	400.00
2010-H.	St. Louis	47,808,000	30.00	70.00
2010-H*.	St. Louis	648,000	150.00	525.00
2010-I.	Minneapolis	18,864,000	35.00	75.00
2010-I*.	Minneapolis	552,000	150.00	800.00
2010-J.	Kansas City	36,332,000	30.00	70.00
2010-J*.	Kansas City	456,000	150.00	600.00
2010-K.	Dallas	33,264,000	30.00	70.00
2010-K*.	Dallas	480,000	150.00	600.00
2010-L.	San Francisco	76,896,000	25.00	60.00
2010-L*.	San Francisco	1,152,000	150.00	525.00

SMALL-SIZE TEN DOLLAR NOTES

Federal Reserve Notes (Green Seal)

Series of 1950-A
Signatures of Priest and Humphrey

No.	Issuing Bank	Quantity Printed	EF-40	Unc-63
2011-A.	Boston	104,248,000	$25.00	$55.00
2011-A*.	Boston	5,112,000	100.00	225.00
2011-B.	New York	356,664,000	25.00	45.00
2011-B*.	New York	16,992,000	75.00	200.00
2011-C.	Philadelphia	71,920,000	25.00	55.00
2011-C*.	Philadelphia	3,672,000	100.00	225.00
2011-D.	Cleveland	75,088,000	25.00	55.00
2011-D*.	Cleveland	3,672,000	100.00	225.00
2011-E.	Richmond	82,144,000	25.00	55.00
2011-E*.	Richmond	4,392,000	100.00	225.00
2011-F.	Atlanta	73,288,000	25.00	55.00
2011-F*.	Atlanta	3,816,000	100.00	225.00
2011-G.	Chicago	235,064,000	25.00	45.00
2011-G*.	Chicago	11,160,000	75.00	200.00
2011-H.	St. Louis	46,512,000	20.00	60.00
2011-H*.	St. Louis	2,880,000	100.00	225.00
2011-I.	Minneapolis	8,136,000	35.00	75.00
2011-I*.	Minneapolis	432,000	150.00	350.00
2011-J.	Kansas City	25,488,000	30.00	60.00
2011-J*.	Kansas City	2,304,000	100.00	225.00
2011-K.	Dallas	21,816,000	30.00	60.00
2011-K*.	Dallas	1,584,000	100.00	300.00
2011-L.	San Francisco	101,584,000	25.00	55.00
2011-L*.	San Francisco	6,408,000	100.00	225.00

Series of 1950-B
Signatures of Priest and Anderson

No.	Issuing Bank	Quantity Printed	EF-40	Unc-63
2012-A.	Boston	49,240,000	$15.00	$35.00
2012-A*.	Boston	2,880,000	60.00	150.00
2012-B.	New York	170,840,000	15.00	32.50
2012-B*.	New York	8,280,000	50.00	150.00
2012-C.	Philadelphia	66,880,000	15.00	35.00
2012-C*.	Philadelphia	3,240,000	50.00	145.00
2012-D.	Cleveland	55,360,000	15.00	35.00
2012-D*.	Cleveland	2,880,000	50.00	150.00
2012-E.	Richmond	51,120,000	15.00	35.00
2012-E*.	Richmond	2,880,000	100.00	300.00
2012-F.	Atlanta	66,520,000	15.00	35.00
2012-F*.	Atlanta	2,880,000	60.00	150.00
2012-G.	Chicago	165,080,000	15.00	32.50
2012-G*.	Chicago	6,480,000	50.00	140.00
2012-H.	St. Louis	33,040,000	15.00	35.00
2012-H*.	St. Louis	1,800,000	60.00	200.00
2012-I.	Minneapolis	13,320,000	20.00	47.50
2012-I*.	Minneapolis	720,000	90.00	400.00
2012-J.	Kansas City	33,480,000	20.00	55.00
2012-J*.	Kansas City	2,520,000	60.00	150.00
2012-K.	Dallas	26,280,000	15.00	35.00
2012-K*.	Dallas	1,440,000	60.00	200.00
2012-L.	San Francisco	55,000,000	15.00	35.00
2012-L*.	San Francisco	2,880,000	60.00	200.00

Federal Reserve Notes (Green Seal)

Series of 1950-C
Signatures of Smith and Dillon

No.	Issuing Bank	Quantity Printed	EF-40	Unc-63
2013-A.	Boston	51,120,000	$15.00	$40.00
2013-A*.	Boston	2,160,000	100.00	225.00
2013-B.	New York	126,520,000	15.00	37.50
2013-B*.	New York	6,840,000	50.00	150.00
2013-C.	Philadelphia	25,200,000	15.00	40.00
2013-C*.	Philadelphia	720,000	75.00	300.00
2013-D.	Cleveland	33,120,000	15.00	40.00
2013-D*.	Cleveland	1,800,000	50.00	275.00
2013-E.	Richmond	45,640,000	15.00	40.00
2013-E*.	Richmond	1,800,000	75.00	350.00
2013-F.	Atlanta	38,880,000	15.00	40.00
2013-F*.	Atlanta	2,880,000	75.00	275.00
2013-G.	Chicago	69,400,000	15.00	40.00
2013-G*.	Chicago	3,600,000	50.00	150.00
2013-H.	St. Louis	23,040,000	15.00	40.00
2013-H*.	St. Louis	1,080,000	90.00	175.00
2013-I.	Minneapolis	9,000,000	20.00	65.00
2013-I*.	Minneapolis	720,000	95.00	250.00
2013-J.	Kansas City	23,320,000	15.00	40.00
2013-J*.	Kansas City	800,000	75.00	225.00
2013-K.	Dallas	17,640,000	15.00	40.00
2013-K*.	Dallas	720,000	75.00	250.00
2013-L.	San Francisco	35,640,000	15.00	40.00
2013-L*.	San Francisco	1,800,000	60.00	175.00

Series of 1950-D
Signatures of Granahan and Dillon

No.	Issuing Bank	Quantity Printed	EF-40	Unc-63
2014-A.	Boston	38,800,000	$15.00	$40.00
2014-A*.	Boston	1,800,000	50.00	225.00
2014-B.	New York	150,320,000	15.00	37.50
2014-B*.	New York	6,840,000	50.00	225.00
2014-C.	Philadelphia	19,080,000	15.00	40.00
2014-C*.	Philadelphia	1,080,000	50.00	225.00
2014-D.	Cleveland	24,120,000	15.00	40.00
2014-D*.	Cleveland	360,000	50.00	225.00
2014-E.	Richmond	33,840,000	15.00	40.00
2014-E*.	Richmond	720,000	50.00	225.00
2014-F.	Atlanta	36,000,000	15.00	40.00
2014-F*.	Atlanta	1,440,000	55.00	250.00
2014-G.	Chicago	115,480,000	15.00	37.50
2014-G*.	Chicago	5,040,000	40.00	200.00
2014-H.	St. Louis	10,440,000	15.00	42.50
2014-H*.	St. Louis	720,000	55.00	250.00
2014-J.	Kansas City	15,480,000	15.00	40.00
2014-J*.	Kansas City	1,080,000	50.00	225.00
2014-K.	Dallas	18,280,000	15.00	40.00
2014-K*.	Dallas	800,000	50.00	300.00
2014-L.	San Francisco	62,560,000	15.00	40.00
2014-L*.	San Francisco	3,600,000	40.00	235.00

Series of 1950-E
Signatures of Granahan and Fowler

No.	Issuing Bank	Quantity Printed	EF-40	Unc-63
2015-B.	New York	12,600,000	$35.00	$100.00
2015-B*.	New York	2,621,000	125.00	325.00
2015-G.	Chicago	65,080,000	35.00	100.00
2015-G*.	Chicago	4,320,000	125.00	325.00
2015-L.	San Francisco	17,280,000	40.00	120.00
2015-L*.	San Francisco	720,000	150.00	375.00

Federal Reserve Notes (Green Seal)

Face of Notes 2016-2032.

Back of Notes 2016-2032.

Series of 1963
Signatures of Granahan and Dillon

No.	Issuing Bank	Quantity Printed	EF-40	Unc-63
2016-A.	Boston	5,760,000	$15.00	$60.00
2016-A*.	Boston	640,000	50.00	150.00
2016-B.	New York	24,960,000	15.00	45.00
2016-B*.	New York	1,920,000	50.00	150.00
2016-C.	Philadelphia	6,400,000	15.00	60.00
2016-C*.	Philadelphia	1,280,000	50.00	175.00
2016-D.	Cleveland	7,040,000	15.00	60.00
2016-D*.	Cleveland	640,000	50.00	150.00
2016-E.	Richmond	4,480,000	15.00	60.00
2016-E*.	Richmond	640,000	50.00	150.00
2016-F.	Atlanta	10,880,000	15.00	60.00
2016-F*.	Atlanta	1,280,000	50.00	150.00
2016-G.	Chicago	35,200,000	15.00	45.00
2016-G*.	Chicago	2,560,000	50.00	150.00
2016-H.	St. Louis	13,440,000	15.00	60.00
2016-H*.	St. Louis	1,280,000	50.00	150.00
2016-J.	Kansas City	3,840,000	15.00	60.00
2016-J*.	Kansas City	640,000	65.00	175.00
2016-K.	Dallas	5,120,000	15.00	60.00
2016-K*.	Dallas	640,000	65.00	175.00
2016-L.	San Francisco	14,080,000	15.00	60.00
2016-L*.	San Francisco	1,280,000	60.00	150.00

Federal Reserve Notes (Green Seal)

Series of 1963-A
Signatures of Granahan and Fowler

No.	Issuing Bank	Quantity Printed	EF-40	Unc-63
2017-A.	Boston	131,360,000	$15.00	$35.00
2017-A*.	Boston	6,400,000	20.00	70.00
2017-B.	New York	199,360,000	15.00	35.00
2017-B*.	New York	9,600,000	20.00	50.00
2017-C.	Philadelphia	100,000,000	15.00	35.00
2017-C*.	Philadelphia	4,480,000	20.00	70.00
2017-D.	Cleveland	72,960,000	15.00	35.00
2017-D*.	Cleveland	3,840,000	20.00	70.00
2017-E.	Richmond	114,720,000	15.00	35.00
2017-E*.	Richmond	5,120,000	20.00	70.00
2017-F.	Atlanta	80,000,000	15.00	35.00
2017-F*.	Atlanta	3,840,000	20.00	75.00
2017-G.	Chicago	195,520,000	15.00	35.00
2017-G*.	Chicago	9,600,000	20.00	50.00
2017-H.	St. Louis	43,520,000	15.00	35.00
2017-H*.	St. Louis	1,920,000	30.00	75.00
2017-I.	Minneapolis	16,640,000	15.00	50.00
2017-I*.	Minneapolis	640,000	30.00	85.00
2017-J.	Kansas City	31,360,000	15.00	35.00
2017-J*.	Kansas City	1,920,000	30.00	75.00
2017-K.	Dallas	51,200,000	15.00	35.00
2017-K*.	Dallas	1,920,000	30.00	75.00
2017-L.	San Francisco	87,200,000	15.00	35.00
2017-L*.	San Francisco	5,120,000	20.00	70.00

Series of 1969
Signatures of Elston and Kennedy. With new Treasury seal

No.	Issuing Bank	Quantity Printed	EF-40	Unc-63
2018-A.	Boston	71,880,000	$15.00	$35.00
2018-A*.	Boston	2,560,000	20.00	65.00
2018-B.	New York	247,360,000	15.00	35.00
2018-B*.	New York	10,240,000	20.00	65.00
2018-C.	Philadelphia	56,960,000	15.00	35.00
2018-C*.	Philadelphia	2,560,000	20.00	65.00
2018-D.	Cleveland	57,600,000	15.00	35.00
2018-D*.	Cleveland	2,560,000	20.00	65.00
2018-E.	Richmond	56,960,000	15.00	35.00
2018-E*.	Richmond	2,560,000	20.00	65.00
2018-F.	Atlanta	53,760,000	15.00	35.00
2018-F*.	Atlanta	2,560,000	20.00	65.00
2018-G.	Chicago	142,240,000	15.00	35.00
2018-G*.	Chicago	6,400,000	20.00	65.00
2018-H.	St. Louis	22,400,000	15.00	35.00
2018-H*.	St. Louis	640,000	65.00	175.00
2018-I.	Minneapolis	12,800,000	15.00	35.00
2018-I*.	Minneapolis	1,280,000	30.00	75.00
2018-J.	Kansas City	31,360,000	15.00	35.00
2018-J*.	Kansas City	1,280,000	20.00	65.00
2018-K.	Dallas	30,080,000	15.00	35.00
2018-K*.	Dallas	1,280,000	20.00	65.00
2018-L.	San Francisco	56,320,000	15.00	35.00
2018-L*.	San Francisco	3,185,000	20.00	65.00

SMALL-SIZE TEN DOLLAR NOTES

Federal Reserve Notes (Green Seal)

Series of 1969-A
Signatures of Kabis and Connally

No.	Issuing Bank	Quantity Printed	EF-40	Unc-63
2019-A.	Boston	41,120,000	$15.00	$35.00
2019-A*.	Boston	1,920,000	20.00	65.00
2019-B.	New York	111,840,000	15.00	35.00
2019-B*.	New York	3,840,000	20.00	65.00
2019-C.	Philadelphia	24,320,000	15.00	35.00
2019-C*.	Philadelphia	1,920,000	20.00	65.00
2019-D.	Cleveland	23,680,000	15.00	35.00
2019-D*.	Cleveland	1,276,000	20.00	65.00
2019-E.	Richmond	25,600,000	15.00	35.00
2019-E*.	Richmond	640,000	30.00	100.00
2019-F.	Atlanta	13,440,000	15.00	35.00
2019-F*.	Atlanta	640,000	30.00	100.00
2019-G.	Chicago	80,160,000	15.00	35.00
2019-G*.	Chicago	3,560,000	20.00	65.00
2019-H.	St. Louis	15,360,000	15.00	35.00
2019-H*.	St. Louis	640,000	30.00	100.00
2019-I.	Minneapolis	8,320,000	15.00	35.00
2019-J.	Kansas City	10,880,000	15.00	35.00
2019-K.	Dallas	20,480,000	15.00	35.00
2019-K*.	Dallas	640,000	30.00	100.00
2019-L.	San Francisco	23,840,000	15.00	35.00
2019-L*.	San Francisco	640,000	20.00	100.00

Series of 1969-B
Signatures of Banuelos and Connally

No.	Issuing Bank	Quantity Printed	EF-40	Unc-63
2020-A.	Boston	16,640,000	$60.00	$125.00
2020-B.	New York	60,320,000	60.00	125.00
2020-B*.	New York	1,920,000	85.00	175.00
2020-C.	Philadelphia	16,000,000	60.00	125.00
2020-D.	Cleveland	12,800,000	60.00	125.00
2020-E.	Richmond	12,160,000	60.00	125.00
2020-E*.	Richmond	640,000	125.00	250.00
2020-F.	Atlanta	13,440,000	60.00	125.00
2020-F*.	Atlanta	640,000	125.00	250.00
2020-G.	Chicago	32,640,000	60.00	125.00
2020-G*.	Chicago	1,268,000	40.00	120.00
2020-H.	St. Louis	8,960,000	60.00	125.00
2020-H*.	St. Louis	1,280,000	150.00	350.00
2020-I.	Minneapolis	3,200,000	60.00	125.00
2020-J.	Kansas City	5,120,000	60.00	125.00
2020-J*.	Kansas City	640,000	125.00	250.00
2020-K.	Dallas	5,760,000	60.00	125.00
2020-L.	San Francisco	23,840,000	75.00	175.00
2020-L*.	San Francisco	640,000	125.00	250.00

Federal Reserve Notes (Green Seal)

Series of 1969-C
Signatures of Banuelos and Shultz

No.	Issuing Bank	Quantity Printed	EF-40	Unc-63
2021-A.	Boston	44,800,000	$15.00	$35.00
2021-A*.	Boston	640,000	45.00	100.00
2021-B.	New York	203,200,000	12.00	30.00
2021-B*.	New York	7,040,000	30.00	70.00
2021-C.	Philadelphia	69,920,000	15.00	35.00
2021-C*.	Philadelphia	1,280,000	35.00	80.00
2021-D.	Cleveland	46,880,000	15.00	35.00
2021-D*.	Cleveland	2,400,000	35.00	80.00
2021-E.	Richmond	45,600,000	15.00	35.00
2021-E*.	Richmond	1,120,000	35.00	80.00
2021-F.	Atlanta	46,240,000	15.00	35.00
2021-F*.	Atlanta	1,920,000	35.00	80.00
2021-G.	Chicago	55,200,000	12.00	30.00
2021-G*.	Chicago	880,000	35.00	80.00
2021-H.	St. Louis	29,800,000	15.00	35.00
2021-H*.	St. Louis	1,280,000	35.00	80.00
2021-I.	Minneapolis	11,520,000	15.00	35.00
2021-I*.	Minneapolis	640,000	55.00	120.00
2021-J.	Kansas City	23,040,000	15.00	35.00
2021-J*.	Kansas City	640,000	55.00	120.00
2021-K.	Dallas	24,960,000	15.00	35.00
2021-K*.	Dallas	640,000	50.00	100.00
2021-L.	San Francisco	56,960,000	15.00	35.00
2021-L*.	San Francisco	640,000	50.00	100.00

Series of 1974
Signatures of Neff and Simon

No.	Issuing Bank	Quantity Printed	EF-40	Unc-63
2022-A.	Boston	104,480,000	$15.00	$35.00
2022-A*.	Boston	1,888,000	20.00	50.00
2022-B.	New York	239,040,000	12.00	30.00
2022-B*.	New York	4,192,000	20.00	50.00
2022-C.	Philadelphia	69,280,000	15.00	35.00
2022-C*.	Philadelphia	2,400,000	20.00	50.00
2022-D.	Cleveland	82,080,000	15.00	35.00
2022-D*.	Cleveland	1,760,000	20.00	50.00
2022-E.	Richmond	105,760,000	15.00	35.00
2022-E*.	Richmond	3,040,000	20.00	50.00
2022-F.	Atlanta	75,520,000	15.00	35.00
2022-F*.	Atlanta	3,200,000	20.00	50.00
2022-G.	Chicago	104,320,000	12.00	30.00
2022-G*.	Chicago	4,352,000	20.00	50.00
2022-H.	St. Louis	46,240,000	15.00	35.00
2022-H*.	St. Louis	1,120,000	20.00	50.00
2022-I.	Minneapolis	27,520,000	15.00	35.00
2022-I*.	Minneapolis	1,024,000	40.00	90.00
2022-J.	Kansas City	24,320,000	15.00	35.00
2022-J*.	Kansas City	640,000	20.00	75.00
2022-K.	Dallas	39,840,000	15.00	35.00
2022-K*.	Dallas	1,760,000	20.00	50.00
2022-L.	San Francisco	70,560,000	15.00	35.00
2022-L*.	San Francisco	1,760,000	20.00	50.00

SMALL-SIZE TEN DOLLAR NOTES

Federal Reserve Notes (Green Seal)

Series of 1977
Signatures of Morton and Blumenthal

No.	Issuing Bank	Quantity Printed	EF-40	Unc-63
2023-A.	Boston	96,640,000	$17.50	$35.00
2023-A*.	Boston	2,688,000	30.00	70.00
2023-B.	New York	277,120,000	17.50	35.00
2023-B*.	New York	7,168,000	30.00	70.00
2023-C.	Philadelphia	83,200,000	17.50	35.00
2023-C*.	Philadelphia	896,000	40.00	85.00
2023-D.	Cleveland	83,200,000	17.50	35.00
2023-D*.	Cleveland	768,000	40.00	85.00
2023-E.	Richmond	71,040,000	17.50	35.00
2023-E*.	Richmond	1,920,000	35.00	80.00
2023-F.	Atlanta	88,960,000	17.50	35.00
2023-F*.	Atlanta	1,536,000	35.00	80.00
2023-G.	Chicago	174,720,000	17.50	35.00
2023-G*.	Chicago	3,968,000	35.00	80.00
2023-H.	St. Louis	46,720,000	17.50	35.00
2023-H*.	St. Louis	896,000	40.00	85.00
2023-I.	Minneapolis	10,240,000	20.00	45.00
2023-I*.	Minneapolis	256,000	55.00	125.00
2023-J.	Kansas City	50,560,000	17.50	35.00
2023-J*.	Kansas City	896,000	40.00	85.00
2023-K.	Dallas	53,760,000	17.50	35.00
2023-K*.	Dallas	640,000	40.00	85.00
2023-L.	San Francisco	73,600,000	17.50	35.00
2023-L*.	San Francisco	1,792,000	35.00	80.00

Series of 1977-A
Signatures of Morton and Miller

No.	Issuing Bank	Quantity Printed	EF-40	Unc-63
2024-A.	Boston	83,840,000	$12.50	$35.00
2024-A*.	Boston	1,664,000	50.00	95.00
2024-B.	New York	259,280,000	12.00	25.00
2024-B*.	New York	5,248,000	20.00	55.00
2024-C.	Philadelphia	96,000,000	12.50	35.00
2024-C*.	Philadelphia	2,048,000	20.00	55.00
2024-D.	Cleveland	44,800,000	17.50	50.00
2024-D*.	Cleveland	2,048,000	20.00	55.00
2024-E.	Richmond	104,320,000	12.50	35.00
2024-E*.	Richmond	3,072,000	20.00	55.00
2024-F.	Atlanta	33,920,000	12.50	35.00
2024-F*.	Atlanta	640,000	20.00	55.00
2024-G.	Chicago	108,160,000	12.50	35.00
2024-G*.	Chicago	3,200,000	20.00	55.00
2024-H.	St. Louis	27,520,000	12.50	35.00
2024-H*.	St. Louis	640,000	20.00	55.00
2024-I.	Minneapolis	7,680,000	12.50	50.00
2024-I*.	Minneapolis	128,000	50.00	100.00
2024-J.	Kansas City	40,320,000	12.50	35.00
2024-J*.	Kansas City	2,136,000	20.00	55.00
2024-K.	Dallas	60,160,000	12.50	35.00
2024-K*.	Dallas	4,224,000	20.00	55.00
2024-L.	San Francisco	59,520,000	12.50	35.00
2024-L*.	San Francisco	2,048,000	20.00	55.00

Federal Reserve Notes (Green Seal)

Series of 1981
Signatures of Buchanan and Regan

No.	Issuing Bank	Quantity Printed	EF-40	Unc-63
2025-A.	Boston	172,160,000	$17.50	$37.50
2025-A*.	Boston	1,280,000	25.00	90.00
2025-B.	New York	434,560,000	12.00	25.00
2025-B*.	New York	1,920,000	20.00	70.00
2025-C.	Philadelphia	131,840,000	17.50	37.50
2025-C*.	Philadelphia	632,000	30.00	125.00
2025-D.	Cleveland	122,240,000	17.50	37.50
2025-D*.	Cleveland	1,268,000	25.00	90.00
2025-E.	Richmond	131,840,000	17.50	37.50
2025-E*.	Richmond	2,576,000	25.00	90.00
2025-F.	Atlanta	131,840,000	17.50	37.50
2025-F*.	Atlanta	1,908,000	25.00	90.00
2025-G.	Chicago	254,080,000	12.00	25.00
2025-G*.	Chicago	1,280,000	20.00	70.00
2025-H.	St. Louis	55,280,000	20.00	40.00
2025-I.	Minneapolis	23,680,000	25.00	50.00
2025-I*.	Minneapolis	256,000	50.00	150.00
2025-J.	Kansas City	53,120,000	20.00	40.00
2025-K.	Dallas	50,560,000	20.00	40.00
2025-L.	San Francisco	144,000,000	17.50	37.50
2025-L*.	San Francisco	1,280,000	25.00	90.00

Series of 1981-A
Signatures of Ortega and Regan

No.	Issuing Bank	Quantity Printed	EF-40	Unc-63
2026-A.	Boston	112,000,000	$15.00	$30.00
2026-B.	New York	259,000,000	15.00	30.00
2026-B*.	New York	3,200,000	20.00	70.00
2026-C.	Philadelphia	48,000,000	15.00	30.00
2026-D.	Cleveland	80,000,000	15.00	30.00
2026-E.	Richmond	92,800,000	15.00	30.00
2026-E*.	Richmond	3,200,000	25.00	80.00
2026-F.	Atlanta	83,200,000	15.00	30.00
2026-F*.	Atlanta	4,736,000	25.00	80.00
2026-G.	Chicago	183,600,000	15.00	30.00
2026-H.	St. Louis	25,600,000	15.00	30.00
2026-I.	Minneapolis	19,200,000	15.00	30.00
2026-J.	Kansas City	48,000,000	15.00	30.00
2026-K.	Dallas	48,000,000	15.00	30.00
2026-L.	San Francisco	115,200,000	15.00	30.00

Series of 1985
Signatures of Ortega and Baker

No.	Issuing Bank	Quantity Printed	EF-40	Unc-63
2027-A.	Boston	380,800,000	$15.00	$30.00
2027-A*.	Boston	7,296,000	20.00	50.00
2027-B.	New York	1,027,200,000	15.00	25.00
2027-B*.	New York	3,200,000	20.00	50.00
2027-C.	Philadelphia	163,200,000	15.00	30.00
2027-D.	Cleveland	304,000,000	15.00	30.00
2027-D*.	Cleveland	3,200,000	25.00	75.00
2027-E.	Richmond	211,200,000	15.00	30.00
2027-F.	Atlanta	297,600,000	15.00	30.00
2027-F*.	Atlanta	3,200,000	30.00	85.00
2027-G.	Chicago	358,400,000	15.00	25.00
2027-H.	St. Louis	131,200,000	15.00	30.00
2027-H*.	St. Louis	3,200,000	25.00	75.00
2027-I.	Minneapolis	64,000,000	15.00	30.00
2027-J.	Kansas City	86,400,000	15.00	30.00
2027-K.	Dallas	115,200,000	15.00	30.00
2027-K*.	Dallas	3,136,000	20.00	50.00
2027-L.	San Francisco	300,800,000	15.00	30.00
2027-L*.	San Francisco	3,200,000	20.00	50.00

SMALL-SIZE TEN DOLLAR NOTES

Federal Reserve Notes (Green Seal)

Series of 1988
None printed

Series of 1988-A
Signatures of Villalpando and Brady

No.	Issuing Bank	Quantity Printed	EF-40	Unc-63
2028-A.	Boston	198,400,000	$15.00	$30.00
2028-A*.	Boston	6,400,000	30.00	90.00
2028-B.	New York	339,200,000	15.00	30.00
2028-B*.	New York	3,200,000	20.00	70.00
2028-C.	Philadelphia	57,600,000	15.00	30.00
2028-D.	Cleveland	128,000,000	15.00	30.00
2028-D*.	Cleveland	3,200,000	30.00	90.00
2028-E.	Richmond	105,600,000	15.00	30.00
2028-F.	Atlanta	236,800,000	15.00	30.00
2028-G.	Chicago	236,800,000	15.00	30.00
2028-H.	St. Louis	70,400,000	15.00	30.00
2028-I.	Minneapolis	19,200,000	15.00	30.00
2028-J.	Kansas City	51,200,000	15.00	30.00
2028-K.	Dallas	115,200,000	15.00	30.00
2028-L.	San Francisco	217,600,000	15.00	30.00
2028-L*.	San Francisco	3,200,000	30.00	90.00

Series of 1990
Signatures of Villalpando and Brady
Printed in Washington, DC
Security thread and micro-size printing introduced

No.	Issuing Bank	Quantity Printed	EF-40	Unc-63
2029-A.	Boston	128,000,000	$12.50	$20.00
2029-B.	New York	742,400,000	12.50	20.00
2029-B*.	New York	16,874,000	17.50	30.00
2029-C.	Philadelphia	19,200,000	12.50	20.00
2029-C*.	Philadelphia	2,560,000	17.50	35.00
2029-D.	Cleveland	89,600,000	12.50	20.00
2029-E.	Richmond	105,600,000	12.50	20.00
2029-F.	Atlanta	160,000,000	12.50	20.00
2029-G.	Chicago	307,200,000	12.50	20.00
2029-G*.	Chicago	2,560,000	17.50	35.00
2029-H.	St. Louis	70,400,000	12.50	20.00
2029-H*.	St. Louis	1,920,000	15.00	35.00
2029-I.	Minneapolis	12,800,000	12.50	20.00
2029-J.	Kansas City	70,400,000	12.50	20.00
2029-K.	Dallas	57,600,000	12.50	20.00
2029-L	San Francisco	83,200,000	12.50	20.00

Series of 1993
Signatures of Withrow and Bentsen
Printed in Washington, DC

No.	Issuing Bank	Quantity Printed	EF-40	Unc-63
2030-A.	Boston	147,200,000	$12.50	$20.00
2030-B.	New York	480,000,000	12.50	20.00
2030-B*.	New York	5,120,000	15.00	30.00
2030-C.	Philadelphia	83,200,000	12.50	20.00
2030-C*.	Philadelphia	1,920,000	20.00	40.00
2030-D.	Cleveland	115,200,000	12.50	20.00
2030-F.	Atlanta	121,600,000	12.50	20.00
2030-G.	Chicago	128,000,000	12.50	20.00
2030-G*.	Chicago	2,176,000	15.00	30.00
2030-H.	St. Louis	89,600,000	12.50	20.00
2030-J.	Kansas City	19,200,000	12.50	20.00
2030-L.	San Francisco	192,000,000	12.50	20.00

Federal Reserve Notes (Green Seal)
Series of 1995
Signatures of Withrow and Rubin
Printed in Washington, DC

No.	Issuing Bank	Quantity Printed	EF-40	Unc-63
2031-A.	Boston	192,000,000	$12.50	$25.00
2031-B.	New York	358,400,000	12.50	25.00
2031-C.	Philadelphia	57,600,000	12.50	25.00
2031-D.	Cleveland	108,000,000	12.50	25.00
2031-E.	Richmond	153,600,000	12.50	25.00
2031-E*.	Richmond	1,280,000	25.00	50.00
2031-F.	Atlanta	70,400,000	12.50	25.00
2031-F*.	Atlanta	640,000	70.00	135.00

Series of 1995
Signature of Withrow and Rubin
Printed at the Western Facility (Fort Worth, Texas)

No.	Issuing Bank	Quantity Printed	EF-40	Unc-63
2032-B.	New York	76,800,000	$12.50	$25.00
2032-C.	Philadelphia	89,600,000	12.50	25.00
2032-D.	Cleveland	70,400,000	12.50	25.00
2032-D*.	Cleveland	1,920,00	15.00	40.00
2032-E.	Richmond	134,400,000	12.50	25.00
2032-E*.	Richmond	1,280,000	15.00	45.00
2032-F.	Atlanta	377,600,000	12.50	25.00
2032-F*.	Atlanta	320,000	20.00	60.00
2032-G.	Chicago	448,000,000	12.50	25.00
2032-G*.	Chicago	3,200,000	15.00	40.00
2032-H.	St. Louis	153,600,000	12.50	25.00
2032-H*.	St. Louis	6,400,000	15.00	40.00
2032-I.	Minneapolis	70,400,000	12.50	25.00
2032-J.	Kansas City	147,200,000	12.50	25.00
2032-K.	Dallas	166,400,000	12.50	25.00
2032-L.	San Francisco	275,200,000	12.50	25.00
2032-L*.	San Francisco	3,200,000	15.00	40.00

Face of Notes 2033-

Back of Notes 2033-

SMALL-SIZE TEN DOLLAR NOTES

Federal Reserve Notes (Green Seal)
Series of 1999
Signatures of Withrow and Summers
Printed in Washington, DC

No.	Issuing Bank	Quantity Printed	Unc-63
2033-A.	Boston	83,200,000	$20.00
2033-B.	New York	300,800,000	20.00
2033-B*.	New York	3,200,000	30.00
2033-C.	Philadelphia	64,000,000	20.00
2033-C*	Philadelphia	3,520,000	40.00
2033-D.	Cleveland	51,520,000	20.00
2033-D*.	Cleveland	2,240,000	35.00
2033-E.	Richmond	112,800,000	20.00
2033-E*.	Richmond	675,200	100.00
2033-F.	Atlanta	96,000,000	20.00
2033-G.	Chicago	83,200,000	20.00
2033-H.	St. Louis	38,400,000	20.00
2033-I.	Minneapolis	6,400,000	20.00
2033-J.	Kansas City	12,800,000	20.00
2033-K.	Dallas	44,800,000	20.00
2033-L.	San Francisco	32,000,000	20.00

Series of 1999
Signature of Withrow and Summers
Printed at the Western Facility (Fort Worth, Texas)

No.	Issuing Bank	Quantity Printed	Unc-63
2034-A*.	Boston	3,200,000	$35.00
2034-B*.	New York	3,200,000	35.00
2034-F.	Atlanta	83,200,000	20.00
2034-F*.	Atlanta	7,715,200	35.00
2034-G.	Chicago	44,800,000	20.00
2034-J.	Kansas City	51,200,000	20.00
2034-K.	Dallas	128,000,000	20.00
2034-L.	San Francisco	44,800,000	20.00

Series of 2001
Signatures of Marin and O'Neill
Printed in Washington, DC

No.	Issuing Bank	Quantity Printed	Unc-63
2035-B.	New York	121,600,000	Current
2035-B*.	New York	320,000	$110.00
2035-C.	Philadelphia	108,800,000	Current
2035-D.	Cleveland	57,600,000	Current
2035-D*.	Cleveland	1,280,000	40.00
2035-E.	Richmond	117,760,000	Current
2035-F.	Atlanta	38,400,000	Current
2035-G.	Chicago	51,200,000	Current
2035-G*.	Chicago	640,000	40.00
2035-H.	St. Louis	12,800,000	Current

Federal Reserve Notes (Green Seal)

Series of 2001
Signatures of Marin and O'Neill
Printed at the Western Facility (Fort Worth, Texas)

No.	Issuing Bank	Quantity Printed	Unc-63
2036-A.	Boston	147,200,000	Current
2036-B.	New York	121,600,000	Current
2036-C.	Philadelphia	32,000,000	Current
2036-E.	Richmond	44,800,000	Current
2036-F.	Atlanta	76,800,000	Current
2036-G.	Chicago	153,600,000	Current
2036-H.	St. Louis	64,000,000	Current
2036-I.	Minneapolis	32,000,000	Current
2036-K	Dallas	38,400,000	Current
2036-K*	Dallas	3,200,000	$40.00
2036-L.	San Francisco	44,800,000	Current
2036-L*.	San Francisco	3,200,000	40.00

Series of 2003
Signatures of Marin and Snow
Printed in Washington, DC

No.	Issuing Bank	Unc-63
2037-A.	Boston	Current
2037-A*.	Boston	Current
2037-B.	New York	Current
2037-C.	Philadelphia	Current
2037-D.	Cleveland	Current
2037-D*.	Cleveland	Current
2037-E.	Richmond	Current
2037-F.	Atlanta	Current
2037-G.	Chicago	Current
2037-H.	St. Louis	Current
2037-H*.	St. Louis	Current
2037-I.	Minneapolis	Current
2037-J.	Kansas City	Current
2037-K.	Dallas	Current
2037-L.	San Francisco	Current

Series of 2003
Signatures of Marin and Snow
None printed

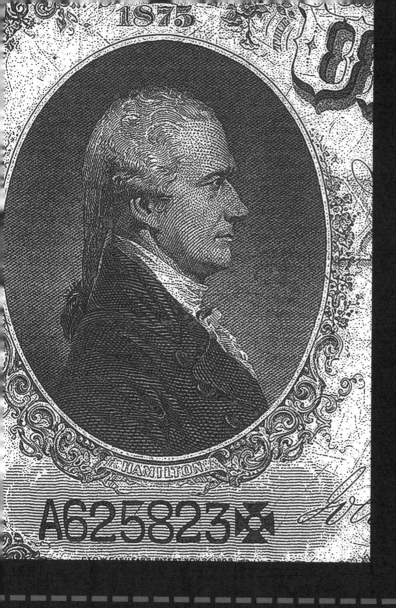

"With more than 140 years of history, the $20 denomination offers a wealth of color and artistry, and many collecting possibilities…"

A541543

llau
d.States.

TWENTY DOLLAR NOTES

COLLECTING TWENTY DOLLAR NOTES

The $20 denomination reaches farther into the elite area of collecting. Large-size $20 notes, while available for some types, can be rare in higher grades and extremely rare for certain varieties. Their high face value resulted in few being saved. Over the years most numismatists have sought examples for type, not for signature combinations, although there have been some impressive exceptions.

Large-Size $20 Notes

$20 Interest Bearing Notes, Large-Size: Interest Bearing Notes for certain high denominations, $50 to $5,000, were issued in 1861. However, it was not until the passage of the Act of March 3, 1863, that the $20 value was made. Some 822,000 were issued, of which over 500 are recorded as being outstanding on the Treasury Department books. However, likely most of these were lost in bank fires, shipwrecks, thefts, and other mishaps. Today, the number known is fewer than two dozen.

$20 Demand Notes of 1861, Large-Size: The Demand Notes of 1861 were issued to be payable at Treasury Department offices in Boston, Cincinnati, New York, Philadelphia, and St. Louis. The plates were by the American Bank Note Company and the National Bank Note Company (both of New York City). Likely the engraving was done at National, judging from the style (overlapping petals with inscriptions on them, similar to their designs on state-chartered bank bills). The exact delineation between American and National and their overlapping of designs has never been explained clearly in the literature. Availability ranges from extremely rare to unknown. Accordingly, most numismatists will experience these issues only through illustrations, as in this book.

$20 Legal Tender Notes, Large-Size: Next in the $20 lineup is the Legal Tender Series of 1862 and 1863, essentially incorporating the preceding design, varieties with one or the other of the National or American imprints. These come on the market with some regularity but are usually seen in circulated grades. Choice examples are elusive.

The Series of 1869 $20 Legal Tender Note design features the profile bust of Alexander Hamilton at the left, and a standing figure of Liberty at the right. During this era there were many different representations of a goddess representing America, sometimes called Liberty (often with a liberty pole), sometimes called Columbia, or with other designations. In this particular version she wears a metal helmet with an eagle on the top. The Series of 1869 bills, part of the "Rainbow Notes" of this year, with colorful faces, have a rich geometric design printed in green on the reverse, somewhat Egyptianesque in aspect. This was soon changed with the Series of 1875, continuing through the Series of 1880, with the back restyled, showing detailed inscriptions at the left and an open space at the right. $20 issues of the various series 1869 through 1880 are available as types, although Uncirculated examples can be rare. Signature combinations are not often collected, but for the specialist the Series of 1880 with brown Treasury seal and the Rosecrans-Nebeker signature combination represents a well-known rarity.

$20 Compound Interest Treasury Notes, Large-Size: The $20 denomination in this series was authorized under the Act of June 30, 1864. The back includes a schedule of interest as it compounded over a period of time. Such bills are extremely rare today, although they are collectable. Two signature combinations exist: Chittenden-Spinner, on the list of great rarities seldom seen on the market; and the sometimes (but not often) encountered Colby-Spinner.

$20 National Bank Notes, Large-Size: National Bank Notes of the $20 denomination are divided into the same categories as the earlier-discussed $10 bills, but with different designs. The Original Series notes come first, and depict on the face a scene, *Battle of Lexington*, 1775, on the left, and, on the right, the goddess Loyalty. On the back is the vignette, *Baptism of Pocahontas*, this being another "scenic" feature per the wishes of Spencer M. Clark, head of the Currency Bureau, who sought to present a panorama of motifs from American history.

Then follow $20 issues of the Series of 1882 (sometimes called "Second Charter"), incorporating the same face layout as used for the Original Series and Series of 1875, created by the American Bank Note Company, but from plates now with the imprint of the Bureau of Engraving and Printing. Three different back designs by the BEP are similar in concept to those used on other denominations in the Series of 1882. Most often seen is the so-called Brown Back type, with that color used for the text and frame, with blue-green ornaments at the center enclosing the charter number of the bank. Also issued were the Date Back bills inscribed 1882-1908 and the Value Back notes inscribed TWENTY DOLLARS.

Then followed the Series of 1902 ("Third Charter"), made in the largest quantities and the most available today. These commence with the red seal version, somewhat scarce and very popular today, followed by two with blue seals, one having the Date Back (1902-1908) and the other having a Plain Back. The latter are by far the most plentiful. Large-size National Bank bills of the $20 denomination are scarcer than the $5 and $10 issues, but enough exist that it is possible to obtain examples to illustrate the types. Regarding states, towns, and individual banks, the quest for these is much more daunting, and there are quite a few banks for which lower values are known, but none of the $20 or higher denominations.

$20 National Gold Bank Notes, Large-Size: The National Gold Bank Notes of the early 1870s continue the same face as used on the Original Series. The back has the montage of gold coins dominated by an 1871 $20. Although thousands of these bills were produced, most were redeemed, and today all are rare. Most numismatists desire to have a single example to illustrate the type. As is the case with National Gold Bank notes of all denominations, most show extensive wear.

$20 Silver Certificates, Large-Size: These begin with the Series of 1878, with SILVER DOLLARS in individual letter elements joined together in the "theater marquee" style on the face, and the very large imprint SILVER on the back, quite interesting from a typographical viewpoint. Depicted on the face is Captain Stephen Decatur, a figure from American naval history.

The Series of 1880 $20 notes followed, then the Series of 1886, the last with new designs with ornate engravings, the back being particularly distinctive and sometimes referred to as the "Diamond Back Note." This style lasted for a relatively short time, and was replaced by the Series of 1891 back, with more white space. Silver Certificates of the large size are fairly scarce today, but for type purposes, come on the market regularly. Most often seen are those of the Series of 1891.

$20 Treasury or Coin Notes, Large-Size: Treasury Notes of the Series of 1890, with TWENTY in ornate letters on the back, join the other much-appreciated bills in this elegant series. Depicted on the $20 is the portrait of John Marshall, chief justice of the Supreme Court. Marshall also appeared on the Series of 1891 bills, with the reverse simplified to show open spaces—a numismatic shame.

$20 Gold Certificates, Large-Size: Gold Certificates of the $20 denomination were first issued under the Act of March 3, 1863. Of the earliest issue, with an eagle perched on a shield at the left of the face, 100,000 were printed, of which only 48,000 were passed into the channels of commerce. By 1895 just nine bills were reported as outstanding, and today, the existing pieces can be counted on the fingers of one hand. The distribution versus the availability of currency is interesting to contemplate, with few rules in effect. These and other large-denomination bills that were mainly held by banks and financial institutions, rather than by the general public, were mostly redeemed, and fewer examples survive today.

Next among the $20 designs is the Series of 1882 with the martyred James Garfield pictured on the right. On the back is an allegorical representation, *Ocean Telegraph*, memorializing the connection of the Atlantic cable, engineered by Cyrus W. Field and which for a brief time in August 1858 excited America (until the signal failed, after which true success awaited another cable-laying after the Civil War). Never mind: in 1858, there were great celebrations, including the issuance of large and impressive gold medals.

Then follow Gold Certificates of the Series of 1905, depicting George Washington on the face and the Great Seal of the United States on the back, popularly known as "Technicolor Notes" today, from the multiple colors used on the face. These were produced with series dates 1905 through 1922. Later varieties are fairly easily acquired.

$20 Federal Reserve Notes, Large-Size: Federal Reserve Notes of the 1914 Series (first with red seals, later with blue) illustrate on the face President Grover Cleveland, and on the back two disconnected motifs featuring a railroad locomotive and automobile, and an oceangoing passenger liner. Red seal notes all have Treasury signatures of Burke and McAdoo. Blue seal notes exist with several different signature combinations. For both colors, varieties can be collected by Federal Reserve Bank district.

$20 Federal Reserve Bank Notes, Large-Size: The Series of 1915 and Series of 1918 notes are next, with Cleveland's portrait repositioned to the far left, to allow room for the imprint of the Federal Reserve Bank and city. The reverse remains the same. Eleven varieties exist of banks and signatures. Only six of the 12 banks issued $20 notes of this series.

Small-Size $20 Notes

Small-size $20 notes are often collected by types, although signature varieties exist, as do star notes, the last including some remarkable rarities. All depict Andrew Jackson on the face and the White House on the back. Modern issues are produced for the various Federal Reserve Banks and across multiple signature combinations, but are not widely collected due to their high face value. However, without question the modern issues have their own element of history and interest.

$20 National Bank Notes, Small-Size: Series of 1929 National Bank notes were issued through early 1935. There are two styles, Type 1 (generally more plentiful) and Type 2, each printed in six-subject sheets, the arrangement being the same for other denominations in these series. Each has a brown Treasury seal and brown serial numbers.

These $20 bills are widely collected today, usually by geographical location, but are somewhat scarce.

$20 Gold Certificates, Small-Size: Small-size Gold Certificates, gold seal, were made in the Series of 1928 and 1928-A, the latter never released. Examples of the Series of 1928 are readily available today.

$20 Federal Reserve Bank Notes, Small-Size: Federal Reserve Bank Notes of the Series of 1929, brown seal, are collectable from each of the Federal Reserve districts. These were produced for just a short time.

$20 Federal Reserve Notes, Small-Size: Small-size Federal Reserve Notes, with a green seal, have been produced continually since the Series of 1928. Many different varieties exist with combinations of banks and signatures. Certain of the Series of 1934 $20 bills were made with brown seals and HAWAII overprints. Most seen today are in circulated grades.

Commencing with Series of 2004 the face and back designs were modified, with Hamilton given a larger and different portrait. Improvements to the design and paper were largely intended to deter counterfeiting. Another face of the White House, the north portico, appears on the restyled notes.

Small-size $20 bills can be collected today as modern issues, but the high face value precludes widespread popularity. Certain individual listings range from scarce to rare in Uncirculated grade, this being particularly true of the earlier varieties.

Interest Bearing Notes

Face of Notes 197-197a. Mortar firing; bust of Abraham Lincoln at right; female representing Victory at left.

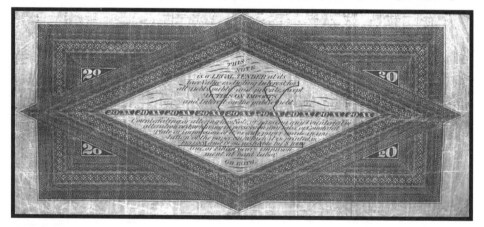

Back of Notes 197-197a.

No.	Denomination			VG-8	F-12	VF-20
197.	Twenty Dollars. .... Rare (about 10 known).	ABN Co.		$6,500.00	$17,500.00	—
197a.	Twenty Dollars. .... Scarce (less than 30 known).	BEP		4,600.00	13,500.00	—

Paper money historians are presently undecided about the possible existence of a third variety of $20 Interest Bearing Note, with other imprints.

Demand Notes

Face of Notes 11-15. Liberty standing with sword and shield.

Back of Notes 11-15.

No.	Payable at	VG-8	F-12	VF-20	EF-40
11.	New York	$17,000.00	$25,000.00	$45,000.00	$65,000.00
11a.	"For the" handwritten	Unique	—	—	—
12.	Philadelphia	17,000.00	25,000.00	45,000.00	65,000.00
12a.	"For the" handwritten	Unknown	—	—	—
13.	Boston	20,000.00	—	—	—
13a.	"For the" handwritten	Unknown	—	—	—
14.	Cincinnati	Unique	—	—	—
14a.	"For the" handwritten	Unknown	—	—	—
15.	St. Louis	Unknown	—	—	—

Legal Tender Notes

Face of Notes 124-126b. Liberty standing with sword and shield with Treasury seal at lower right.

Back of Notes 124-126b.

First Obligation on back

No.	Act	Signatures		Seal		VG-8	F-12	VF-20	EF-40	Unc-63
124.	1862	Chittenden	Spinner	Red	. . . .	$1,200.00	$2,000.00	$2,500.00	$4,500.00	—

Second Obligation on back

No.	Act	Signatures		Seal		VG-8	F-12	VF-20	EF-40	Unc-63
125.	1862	Chittenden	Spinner	Red	. . . .	$1,350.00	$2,300.00	$3,500.00	$4,500.00	—
126.	1863	Chittenden	Spinner	Red	. . . .	1,350.00	2,300.00	3,500.00	4,500.00	$9,000.00

Above with National Bank Note Co. and American Bank Note Co. on lower border

No.	Act	Signatures		Seal	VG-8	F-12	VF-20	EF-40	Unc-63
126a.	1863	Chittenden	Spinner	Red, One Serial No. . .	$1,700.00	$2,900.00	$4,000.00	$6,000.00	—

Above with American Bank Note Co. on lower border

No.	Act	Signatures	Seal	VG-8	F-12	VF-20	EF-40	Unc-63
126b.	1863	Chittenden	Spinner . . . . .Red, Two Serial Nos. . . .	$1,350.00	$2,300.00	$3,500.00	$4,500.00	$9,000.00

Above with American Bank Note Co. on lower border

Legal Tender Notes

Face of Note 127. Profile bust of Alexander Hamilton in oval frame at left. Helmeted Victory with shield and sword.

Back of Note 127.

No.	Act	Signatures	Seal	VG-8	F-12	VF-20	EF-40	Unc-63
127.	1869	Allison Spinner	Large Red	$1,100.00	$2,000.00	$2,750.00	$4,000.00	$10,000.00

Legal Tender Notes

*Face of Notes 128-145 (variations exist). Profile bust of Alexander Hamilton in oval frame at left.
Helmeted Victory with shield and sword.*

Back of Notes 128-147.

Face as shown above with red mark of value "XX" at right and left center of note

No.	Act	Signatures	Seal	VG-8	F-12	VF-20	EF-40	Unc-63
128.	1875	Allison New	Small Red, Rays	$675.00	$925.00	$1,450.00	$1,950.00	$4,200.00
129.	1878	Allison Gilfillan	Small Red, Rays	625.00	850.00	1100.00	1500.00	3,000.00

No red "XX"; blue serial numbers

No.	Act	Signatures	Seal	VG-8	F-12	VF-20	EF-40	Unc-63
130.	1880	Scofield Gilfillan	Large Brown	$700.00	$1,150.00	$1,500.00	$2,500.00	$8,000.00
131.	1880	Bruce Gilfillan	Large Brown	450.00	750.00	1,050.00	2,100.00	5,000.00
132.	1880	Bruce Wyman	Large Brown	300.00	600.00	860.00	1,600.00	4,250.00
133.	1880	Bruce Wyman	Large Red, Plain	450.00	750.00	1,050.00	2,900.00	8,000.00
134.	1880	Rosecrans Jordan	Large Red, Plain	300.00	600.00	860.00	1,600.00	4,250.00
135.	1880	Rosecrans Hyatt	Large Red, Plain	300.00	600.00	860.00	1,600.00	4,250.00
136.	1880.	Rosecrans Hyatt	Large Red, Spiked	275.00	560.00	800.00	1,400.00	2,900.00
137.	1880.	Rosecrans Huston	Large Red, Spiked	275.00	560.00	800.00	1,400.00	2,900.00
138.	1880	Rosecrans Huston	Large Brown	275.00	560.00	800.00	1,400.00	2,900.00
139.	1880	Rosecrans Nebeker	Large Brown	750.00	1,500.00	2,500.00	4,500.00	—
140.	1880	Rosecrans Nebeker	Small Red, Scalloped	250.00	450.00	650.00	1,200.00	1,800.00
141.	1880	Tillman Morgan	Small Red, Scalloped	250.00	450.00	650.00	1,200.00	1,800.00

Legal Tender Notes

No.	Act	Signatures	Seal	VG-8	F-12	VF-20	EF-40	Unc-63
142.	1880	Bruce Roberts	Small Red, Scalloped	$250.00	$450.00	$650.00	$1,200.00	$1,800.00
143.	1880	Lyons Roberts	Small Red, Scalloped	250.00	450.00	650.00	1,200.00	2,600.00
144.	1880	Vernon Treat	Small Red, Scalloped	250.00	450.00	650.00	1,200.00	1,800.00
145.	1880	Vernon McClung	Small Red, Scalloped	250.00	450.00	650.00	1,200.00	4,000.00

Same as above, but red serial numbers

No.	Act	Signatures	Seal	VG-8	F-12	VF-20	EF-40	Unc-63
146.	1880	Teehee Burke ......Small Red, Scalloped ...		$250.00	$375.00	$625.00	$1,050.00	$1,550.00
147.	1880	Elliott White ......Small Red, Scalloped ...		225.00	320.00	575.00	925.00	1,300.00

Compound Interest Treasury Notes

Face of Notes 191-191a. Mortar firing; bust of Abraham Lincoln at right; female representing Victory at left.
"COMPOUND INTEREST TREASURY NOTE" stamped in bronze ink.

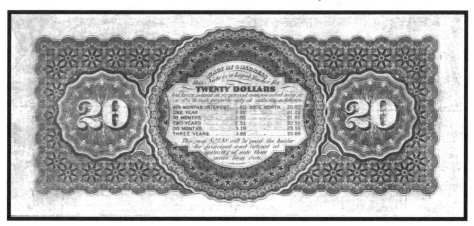

Back of Notes 191-191a.

No.	Act	Overprint Date	Signatures		VG-8	F-12	VF-20	EF-40
191.	1864	July 15, 1864	Chittenden	Spinner	Extremely Rare	—	—	—
191a.	1864	Aug. 15, 1864 - Oct. 16, 1865	Colby	Spinner	$2,100.00	$3,250.00	$10,000.00	$15,000.00

National Bank Notes

"First Charter Period" (Original Series and Series of 1895)

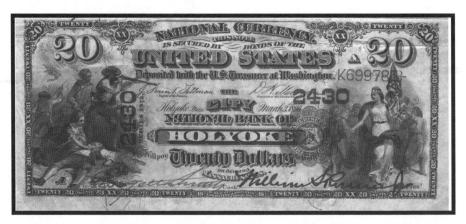

Face of Notes 424-439. Battle of Lexington 1775 *at left;*
at right, Columbia holding flag and leading patriotic procession.

Back of Notes 424-439. The Baptism of Pocahontas.

No.	Act	Signatures		Seal	VG-8	F-12	VF-20	EF-40	Unc-63
424.	Original	Chittenden	Spinner	Red, Rays	$2,100.00	$2,450.00	$3,350.00	$4,000.00	$8,000.00
427.	Original	Colby	Spinner	Red, Rays	2,100.00	2,450.00	3,350.00	4,000.00	8,000.00
428.	Original	Jeffries	Spinner	Red, Rays	Very Rare	—	—	—	—
429.	Original	Allison	Spinner	Red, Rays	2,100.00	2,450.00	3,350.00	4,000.00	8,000.00
431.	1875	Allison	New	Red, Scalloped ...	2,100.00	2,450.00	3,350.00	4,000.00	8,000.00
432.	1875	Allison	Wyman	Red, Scalloped ...	2,100.00	2,450.00	3,350.00	4,000.00	8,000.00
433.	1875	Allison	Gilfillan	Red, Scalloped ...	2,100.00	2,450.00	3,350.00	4,000.00	8,000.00
434.	1875	Scofield	Gilfillan	Red, Scalloped ...	2,100.00	2,450.00	3,350.00	4,000.00	8,000.00
435.	1875	Bruce	Gilfillan	Red, Scalloped ...	2,100.00	2,450.00	3,350.00	4,000.00	8,000.00
436.	1875	Bruce	Wyman	Red, Scalloped ...	Very Rare	—	—	—	—
437.	1875	Rosecrans	Huston	Red, Scalloped ...	Rare	—	—	—	—
438.	1875	Rosecrans	Nebeker ...	Red, Scalloped ...	Rare	—	—	—	—
439.	1875	Tillman	Morgan	Red, Scalloped ...	Unique	—	—	—	—

"Second Charter Period" (Series of 1882)
Brown Backs

Face of Notes 493-506. Battle of Lexington 1775 *at left;*
at right, Columbia holding flag and leading patriotic procession.

Back of Notes 493-506. Green bank charter numbers against ornate background of brown lathe-work.

No.	Signatures		VG-8	F-12	VF-20	EF-40	Unc-63
493.	Bruce	Gilfillan	$1,000.00	$1,250.00	$1,600.00	$2,000.00	$3,400.00
494.	Bruce	Wyman	1,000.00	1,250.00	1,600.00	2,000.00	3,400.00
495.	Bruce	Jordan	1,000.00	1,250.00	1,600.00	2,000.00	3,400.00
496.	Rosecrans	Jordan	1,000.00	1,250.00	1,600.00	2,000.00	3,400.00
497.	Rosecrans	Hyatt	1,000.00	1,250.00	1,600.00	2,000.00	3,400.00
498.	Rosecrans	Huston	1,000.00	1,250.00	1,600.00	2,000.00	3,400.00
499.	Rosecrans	Nebeker	1,000.00	1,250.00	1,600.00	2,000.00	3,400.00
500.	Rosecrans	Morgan	1,750.00	2,500.00	4,500.00	7,500.00	—
501.	Tillman	Morgan	1,000.00	1,250.00	1,600.00	2,000.00	3,400.00
502.	Tillman	Roberts	1,000.00	1,250.00	1,600.00	2,000.00	3,400.00
503.	Bruce	Roberts	1,000.00	1,250.00	1,600.00	2,000.00	3,400.00
504.	Lyons	Roberts	1,000.00	1,250.00	1,600.00	2,000.00	3,400.00
505.	Lyons	Treat	1,400.00	1,650.00	2,500.00	3,700.00	—
506.	Vernon	Treat	1,400.00	1,650.00	2,500.00	3,700.00	—

"Second Charter Period" (Series of 1882)
Date Backs

Face of Notes 549-557. Battle of Lexington 1775 at left;
at right, Columbia holding flag and leading patriotic procession.

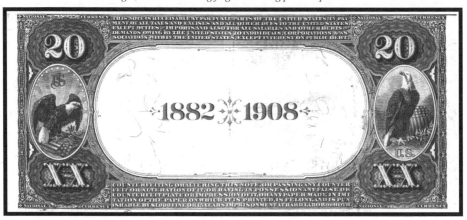

Back of Notes 549-557.

No.	Signatures		VG-8	F-12	VF-20	EF-40	Unc-63
549.	Rosecrans	Huston	$1,150.00	$1,450.00	$1,900.00	$2,500.00	$4,500.00
550.	Rosecrans	Nebeker	950.00	1,200.00	1,600.00	2,100.00	3,600.00
551.	Rosecrans	Morgan	2 Known	—	—	—	—
552.	Tillman	Morgan	950.00	1,200.00	1,600.00	2,100.00	3,600.00
553.	Tillman	Roberts	1,050.00	1,300.00	1,750.00	2,300.00	3,900.00
554.	Bruce	Roberts	1,050.00	1,300.00	1,750.00	2,300.00	3,900.00
555.	Lyons	Roberts	950.00	1,200.00	1,600.00	2,100.00	3,600.00
556.	Vernon	Treat	950.00	1,200.00	1,600.00	2,100.00	3,600.00
556a.	Vernon	McClung	Unique	—	—	—	—
557.	Napier	McClung	1,150.00	1,450.00	1,900.00	2,500.00	4,500.00

"Second Charter Period" (Series of 1882)
Value Backs

Face of Notes 580-585. Battle of Lexington 1775 at left;
at right, Columbia holding flag and leading patriotic procession.

Back of Notes 580-585.

No.	Signatures		VG-8	F-12	VF-20	EF-40	Unc-63
580.	Tillman	Morgan	$1,200.00	$1,500.00	$2,100.00	$2,750.00	$4,500.00
580a.	Tillman	Roberts	Rare (4 Known)	—	—	—	—
580b.	Bruce	Roberts	Rare (3 Known)	—	—	—	—
581.	Lyons	Roberts	950.00	1,250.00	1,700.00	2,250.00	3,750.00
582.	Lyons	Treat	—	—	Unique	—	—
583.	Vernon	Treat	950.00	1,250.00	1,700.00	2,250.00	3,750.00
584.	Napier	McClung	950.00	1,250.00	1,700.00	2,250.00	3,750.00
584a.	Parker	Burke	Rare (2 Known)	—	—	—	—
585.	Teehee	Burke	Rare (4 Known)	—	—	—	—

"Third Charter Period" (Series of 1902)
First Issue: Series of 1902 with red seal

Face of Notes 639-641. Bust of Treasury Secretary (1865-1869, 1884-1885) Hugh McCulloch.

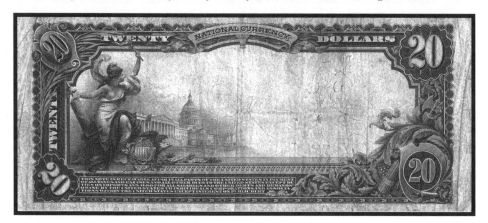

Back of Notes 639-641. Columbia and the Capitol building.

No.	Signatures		VG-8	F-12	VF-20	EF-40	Unc-63
639.	Lyons	Roberts	$900.00	$1,050.00	$1,500.00	$2,000.00	$4,500.00
640.	Lyons	Treat	900.00	1,050.00	1,500.00	2,000.00	4,500.00
641.	Vernon	Treat	900.00	1,050.00	1,500.00	2,000.00	4,500.00

"Third Charter Period" (Series of 1902)
Second Issue: Series of 1902 with blue seal and with "1902-1908" on back

Face of Notes 642-649a. Bust of Treasury Secretary (1865-1869, 1884-1885) Hugh McCulloch.

Back of Note 642-649. Columbia and the Capitol building.

No.	Signatures		VG-8	F-12	VF-20	EF-40	Unc-63
642.	Lyons	Roberts	$210.00	$265.00	$320.00	$385.00	$800.00
643.	Lyons	Treat	210.00	265.00	320.00	385.00	800.00
644.	Vernon	Treat	210.00	265.00	320.00	385.00	800.00
645.	Vernon	McClung	210.00	265.00	320.00	385.00	800.00
646.	Napier	McClung	210.00	265.00	320.00	385.00	800.00
647.	Napier	Thompson	250.00	300.00	360.00	450.00	1,000.00
648.	Napier	Burke	210.00	265.00	320.00	385.00	800.00
649.	Parker	Burke	210.00	265.00	320.00	385.00	800.00
649a.	Teehee	Burke	Rare (2 Known)	—	—	—	—

"Third Charter Period" (Series of 1902)
Third Issue: Series of 1902 with blue seal and without "1902-1908" on back

Face of Notes 650-663a. Bust of Treasury Secretary (1865-1869, 1884-1885) Hugh McCulloch.

Back of Notes 650-663a. Columbia and the Capitol building.

No.	Signatures		VG-8	F-12	VF-20	EF-40	Unc-63
650.	Lyons	Roberts	$210.00	$265.00	$320.00	$385.00	$800.00
651.	Lyons	Treat	210.00	265.00	320.00	385.00	800.00
652.	Vernon	Treat	210.00	265.00	320.00	385.00	800.00
653.	Vernon	McClung	210.00	265.00	320.00	385.00	800.00
654.	Napier	McClung	210.00	265.00	320.00	385.00	800.00
655.	Napier	Thompson	210.00	265.00	320.00	385.00	800.00
656.	Napier	Burke	210.00	265.00	320.00	385.00	800.00
657.	Parker	Burke	210.00	265.00	320.00	385.00	800.00
658.	Teehee	Burke	210.00	265.00	320.00	385.00	800.00
659.	Elliott	Burke	210.00	265.00	320.00	385.00	800.00
660.	Elliott	White	210.00	265.00	320.00	385.00	800.00
661.	Speelman	White	210.00	265.00	320.00	385.00	800.00
662.	Woods	White	260.00	325.00	400.00	500.00	1,100.00
663.	Woods	Tate	260.00	325.00	400.00	500.00	2,500.00
663a.	Jones	Woods	Rare (2 Known)	—	—	—	—

National Gold Bank Notes

Face of Notes 1152-1159b. Battle of Lexington 1775 *at left;*
at right Columbia holding flag and leading patriotic procession.

Back of Notes 1152-1159b. An array of contemporary United States gold coins.

No.	Date	Name of Bank	City	Fair	VG-8	F-12	VF-20
1152.	1870 ...	First National Gold Bank	San Francisco ..	$2,750.00	$7,500.00	$17,500.00	$30,000.00
1153.	1875 ...	Series. First National Gold Bank	San Francisco ..	2,750.00	7,500.00	17,500.00	30,000.00
1154.	1872....	National Gold Bank of D.O. Mills and Co. ...	Sacramento	2,750.00	7,500.00	17,500.00	30,000.00
1155.	1873....	First National Gold Bank	Stockton	2,750.00	7,000.00	17,500.00	30,000.00
1155a.	1875 ...	First National Gold Bank	Stockton	Unique	—	—	—
1156.	1874 ...	Farmer's National Gold Bank	San Jose	2,750.00	7,500.00	17,500.00	30,000.00
1157.	1875 ...	Series. First National Gold Bank	Petaluma	2 Known	–	—	—
1158.	1875 ...	First National Gold Bank	Oakland	3,250.00	12,500.00	24,000.00	40,000.00
1159.	1875 ...	Union National Gold Bank	Oakland	2 Known	—	—	—
1159a.	1873 ...	First National Gold Bank	Santa Barbara ..	Unique	—	—	—
1159b.	1872 ...	National Gold Bank and Trust Company ...	San Francisco ..	Unknown	—	—	—

Silver Certificates

Face of Notes 305-308. Bust of War of 1812 naval hero Stephen Decatur.

Back of Notes 305-308.

All notes are countersigned and with signatures of Scofield and Gilfillan and a large red seal except the 1880 series (large brown seal). The 1878 notes lack the legend "Series of 1878."
All have engraved countersignatures except 306b, which is autographed.

Face as above with large seal at top and large "Twenty" below

No.	Series	Countersigned By	Payable At	Deposited With	VG-8	F-12	VF-20
305.	1878 ...	J.C. Hopper	New York	Assistant Treasurer of the U.S. ..		Extremely Rare	—
306.	1878 ...	T. Hillhouse	New York	Assistant Treasurer of the U.S ..		Extremely Rare	—
306a.	1878 ...	R.M. Anthony ...	San Francisco	Assistant Treasurer of the U.S. ..		Unknown	—
306b.	1878 ...	A.U. Wyman	Washington	Treasurer of the U.S.		Extremely Rare	—
307.	1878. ...	A.U. Wyman	Washington	Treasurer of the U.S.	$10,000.00	$15,000.00	—

Face as above with large "XX" below

No.	Series	Countersigned By	Payable At	Deposited With	VG-8	F-12	VF-20
308.	1880 ...	T. Hillhouse	New York	Assistant Treasurer of the U.S. ...	$11,000.00	$17,500.00	—

Silver Certificates

Face of Notes 309-312. As preceding, with large seal at top of note, large "XX" below. No countersigned signature.

Back of Notes 309-312.

No.	Series	Signatures		Seal	VG-8	F-12	VF-20	EF-40	Unc-63
309.	1880	Scofield	Gilfillan	Large Brown	$1,750.00	$3,300.00	$5,500.00	$10,000.00	—
310.	1880	Bruce	Gilfillan	Large Brown	1,750.00	3,300.00	5,500.00	10,000.00	—
311.	1880	Bruce	Wyman	Large Brown	1,750.00	3,300.00	5,500.00	10,000.00	$30,000.00

As above, but with small seal at bottom, no "XX"

No.	Series	Signatures		Seal	VG-8	F-12	VF-20	EF-40	Unc-63
312.	1880.	Bruce	Wyman	Small Red	$2,400.00	$4,000.00	$6,000.00	$12,000.00	—

Silver Certificates

Face of Notes 313-316. Bust of Treasury Secretary (1885-1887) Daniel Manning in oval frame between figures symbolizing Agriculture and Industry. Large seal at upper left.

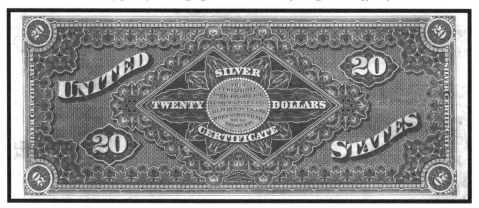

Back of Notes 313-316.

No.	Series	Signatures	Seal	VG-8	F-12	VF-20	EF-40	Unc-63
313.	1886	Rosecrans Hyatt	Large Red	$1,850.00	$3,100.00	$5,250.00	$14,000.00	—
314.	1886	Rosecrans Huston	Large Brown	1,850.00	3,100.00	5,250.00	9,500.00	40,000.00
315.	1886	Rosecrans Nebeker	Large Brown	1,850.00	3,100.00	5,250.00	13,000.00	40,000.00

As above, with small seal at lower right

No.	Series	Signatures	Seal	VG-8	F-12	VF-20	EF-40	Unc-63
316.	1886	Rosecrans Nebeker	Small Red	$1,800.00	$3,100.00	$5,250.00	$11,500.00	$40,000.00

Silver Certificates

Face of Notes 317-322. Bust of Treasury Secretary (1885-1887) Daniel Manning in oval frame between figures symbolizing Agriculture and Industry.

Back of Notes 317-322.

No.	Series	Signatures		Seal	VG-8	F-12	VF-20	EF-40	Unc-63
317.	1891	Rosecrans	Nebeker	Small Red	$400.00	$1,175.00	$1,850.00	$2,500.00	$7,500.00
318.	1891	Tillman	Morgan	Small Red	400.00	1,175.00	1,850.00	2,500.00	7,500.00
319.	1891	Bruce	Roberts	Small Red	400.00	1,175.00	1,850.00	2,500.00	7,500.00
320.	1891	Lyons	Roberts ...	Small Red	400.00	1,175.00	1,850.00	2,500.00	7,500.00

As preceding but with large blue "XX" added at left center

No.	Series	Signatures		Seal	VG-8	F-12	VF-20	EF-40	Unc-63
321.	1891	Parker	Burke	Blue	$400.00	$1,100.00	$1,750.00	$2,350.00	$5,250.00
322.	1891	Teehee	Burke	Blue	400.00	1,100.00	1,750.00	2,350.00	7,250.00

Treasury or Coin Notes

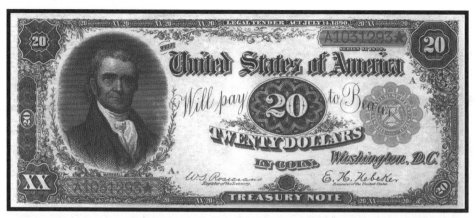

Face of Notes 372-374. Bust of Secretary of State (1800-1801) and Chief Justice (1801-1835) John Marshall.

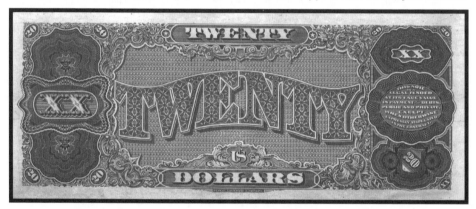

Back of Notes 372-374.

No.	Series	Signatures		Seal	VG-8	F-12	VF-20	EF-40	Unc-63
372.	1890	Rosecrans	Huston	Large Brown	$2,000.00	$3,400.00	$5,750.00	$8,500.00	$20,000.00
373.	1890	Rosecrans	Nebeker	Large Brown	4,000.00	8,000.00	17,500.00	—	—
374.	1890	Rosecrans	Nebeker	Small Red	2,000.00	3,400.00	5,750.00	8,500.00	17,000.00

Treasury or Coin Notes

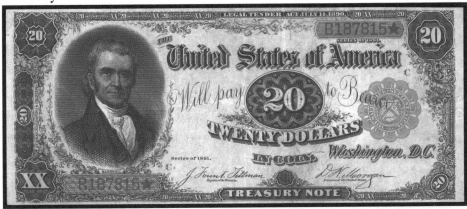

Face of Notes 375-375a. Bust of Secretary of State (1800-1801) and Chief Justice (1801-1835) John Marshall.

Back of Notes 375-375a.

No.	Series	Signatures		Seal	VG-8	F-12	VF-20	EF-40	Unc-63
375	1891	Tillman	Morgan	Small Red	2,500.00	$3,250.00	$5,000.00	$8,500.00	$14,000.00
375a.	1891	Bruce	Roberts	Small Red	Rare (2 Known) —	—	—	—	—

Gold Certificates

Face of Note 1166b (not shown). Eagle perched on flag-draped shield.

Back of Note 1166b (not shown). Elaborate design.

No.	Denomination	
1166b.	Twenty Dollar Note.	.... Extremely Rare

Gold Certificates

Face of Notes 1174-1178. Bust of President James A. Garfield in oval frame at right.

Back of Notes 1174-1178.

No.	Series	Signatures		Seal	VG-8	F-12	VF-20	EF-40	Unc-63
1174.	1882	Bruce	Gilfillan	Brown	$6,000.00	$10,000.00	$14,000.00	Rare	—
1175.	1882	Bruce	Gilfillan	Brown	2 Known	—	—	—	—

With autographed countersignature by Thomas C. Acton, Assistant Treasurer, payable at New York

No.	Series	Signatures		Seal	VG-8	F-12	VF-20	EF-40	Unc-63
1175a.	1882	Bruce	Gilfillan	Brown	$5,000.00	$8,250.00	$12,000.00	Rare	—

As No. 1175 but with engraved countersignature

No.	Series	Signatures		Seal	VG-8	F-12	VF-20	EF-40	Unc-63
1176.	1882	Bruce	Wyman	Brown	$2,750.00	$5,000.00	$7,250.00	$12,000.00	—
1177.	1882	Rosecrans	Huston	Large Brown	2,750.00	5,000.00	7,250.00	12,000.00	—
1178.	1882	Lyons	Roberts	Small Red	380.00	675.00	1,300.00	2,500.00	6,750.00

Gold Certificates

Face of Notes 1179-1187. Bust of George Washington.

Back of Notes 1179-1187.

No.	Series	Signatures		Seal	VG-8	F-12	VF-20	EF-40	Unc-63
1179.	1905	Lyons	Roberts	Small Red	$700.00	$1,450.00	$2,600.00	$3,900.00	$11,000.00
1180.	1905	Lyons	Treat	Small Red	700.00	1,450.00	2,600.00	3,900.00	10,000.00
1181.	1906	Vernon	Treat	Gold	245.00	300.00	375.00	575.00	1,500.00
1182.	1906	Vernon	McClung	Gold	245.00	300.00	375.00	575.00	1,500.00
1183.	1906	Napier	McClung	Gold	245.00	300.00	375.00	575.00	1,500.00
1184.	1906	Napier	Thompson ...	Gold	300.00	375.00	500.00	750.00	2,000.00
1185.	1906	Parker	Burke	Gold	245.00	300.00	375.00	575.00	1,500.00
1186.	1906	Teehee	Burke	Gold	245.00	300.00	375.00	575.00	1,500.00
1187.	1922	Speelman	White	Gold	225.00	275.00	320.00	510.00	1,250.00

Federal Reserve Notes

Face of Notes 952-1011 (varieties exist; see below). Bust of President Grover Cleveland in center.

Back of Notes 952A-1011C. Transportation scenes feature an automobile, a train, a plane, and ships of the era.

Red Seals: A. Large district letter and numeral at top right and bottom left. Small letter at top left and bottom right. **B.** As above, with a small district letter and numeral added above letter at top left.

Blue Seals: A. Large letter and numeral at top left and bottom right. **B.** Large letter and numeral at top right with small district letters and numerals in the other three corners. **C.** Again, a large pair of letters and numerals, but positioned both vertically, more toward the center of the note and closer to the outside edge. Also, the seals to the sides of the portrait are closer to the note's center than the A issue.

A. Series of 1914 with red seal and signatures of Burke and McAdoo

No.	Issuing Bank	VG-8	F-12	VF-20	EF-40	Unc-63
952A.	Boston	$475.00	$950.00	$1,250.00	$2,500.00	$5,000.00
952B.	Boston	—	—	—	$2,100.00	—
953A.	New York	275.00	575.00	950.00	1,400.00	4,200.00
953B.	New York	275.00	575.00	950.00	1,400.00	3,400.00
954A.	Philadelphia	475.00	950.00	1,500.00	3,200.00	6,000.00
954B.	Philadelphia	475.00	950.00	1,500.00	3,200.00	—
955A.	Cleveland	750.00	1,350.00	2,250.00	4,500.00	7,000.00
955B.	Cleveland	475.00	950.00	1,500.00	2,750.00	—
956A.	Richmond	550.00	1,200.00	2,000.00	4,000.00	—
956B.	Richmond	550.00	1,200.00	2,200.00	—	—
957A.	Atlanta	550.00	1,200.00	2,000.00	4,000.00	—
958A.	Chicago	275.00	575.00	950.00	1,400.00	3,400.00
958B.	Chicago	475.00	950.00	1,500.00	3,200.00	4,100.00
959A.	St. Louis	275.00	575.00	950.00	1,400.00	4,400.00
959B.	St. Louis	474.00	950.00	1,500.00	3,200.00	3,500.00

Federal Reserve Notes

No.	Issuing Bank	VG-8	F-12	VF-20	EF-40	Unc-63
960A.	Minneapolis	$475.00	$950.00	$1,500.00	$3,200.00	$6,000.00
960B.	Minneapolis	550.00	1,200.00	2,000.00	4,000.00	—
961A.	Kansas City	475.00	950.00	1,500.00	3,200.00	6,000.00
961B.	Kansas City	750.00	1,350.00	2,250.00	—	—
962A.	Dallas	475.00	950.00	1,500.00	3,200.00	6,000.00
963A.	San Francisco	550.00	1,200.00	2,000.00	4,000.00	—
963B.	San Francisco	550.00	1,200.00	2,000.00	4,000.00	—

B. Series of 1914 with blue seal

No.	Issuing Bank	Signatures		VG-8	F-12	VF-20	EF-40	Unc-63
964.	Boston	Burke	McAdoo	$115.00	$150.00	$225.00	$450.00	$700.00
965.	Boston	Burke	Glass	90.00	200.00	140.00	175.00	700.00
966.	Boston	Burke	Houston	115.00	150.00	225.00	450.00	700.00
967.	Boston	White	Mellon	85.00	105.00	140.00	195.00	375.00
968.	New York	Burke	McAdoo	85.00	105.00	140.00	195.00	375.00
969.	New York	Burke	Glass	115.00	150.00	225.00	450.00	700.00
970.	New York	Burke	Houston	95.00	120.00	160.00	225.00	450.00
971A.	New York	White	Mellon	85.00	105.00	140.00	195.00	375.00
971B.	New York	White	Mellon	120.00	160.00	275.00	450.00	800.00
972.	Philadelphia	Burke	McAdoo	95.00	120.00	160.00	225.00	450.00
973.	Philadelphia	Burke	Glass	115.00	150.00	225.00	450.00	650.00
974.	Philadelphia	Burke	Houston	95.00	120.00	160.00	225.00	700.00
975.	Philadelphia	White	Mellon	85.00	105.00	140.00	195.00	450.00
976.	Cleveland	Burke	McAdoo	85.00	105.00	140.00	195.00	420.00
977.	Cleveland	Burke	Glass	115.00	150.00	225.00	325.00	420.00
978.	Cleveland	Burke	Houston	95.00	120.00	160.00	225.00	420.00
979A.	Cleveland	White	Mellon	85.00	120.00	160.00	225.00	375.00
979B.	Cleveland	White	Mellon	115.00	150.00	225.00	500.00	1,400.00
980.	Richmond	Burke	McAdoo	115.00	150.00	225.00	500.00	700.00
981.	Richmond	Burke	Glass	115.00	150.00	225.00	500.00	700.00
982.	Richmond	Burke	Houston	100.00	140.00	200.00	450.00	700.00
983A.	Richmond	White	Mellon	95.00	120.00	160.00	225.00	550.00
984.	Atlanta	Burke	McAdoo	85.00	105.00	140.00	195.00	400.00
985.	Atlanta	Burke	Glass	None Printed	—	—	—	—
986.	Atlanta	Burke	Houston	85.00	105.00	140.00	195.00	400.00
987A.	Atlanta	White	Mellon	85.00	105.00	140.00	195.00	375.00
988.	Chicago	Burke	McAdoo	85.00	105.00	140.00	195.00	375.00
989.	Chicago	Burke	Glass	85.00	105.00	140.00	195.00	400.00
990.	Chicago	Burke	Houston	85.00	105.00	140.00	195.00	450.00
991A.	Chicago	White	Mellon	85.00	105.00	140.00	195.00	380.00
991B.	Chicago	White	Mellon	115.00	150.00	225.00	500.00	700.00
991C.	Chicago	White	Mellon	300.00	450.00	650.00	900.00	—
992.	St. Louis	Burke	McAdoo	85.00	105.00	140.00	195.00	380.00
993.	St. Louis	Burke	Glass	170.00	325.00	470.00	750.00	—
994.	St. Louis	Burke	Houston	85.00	105.00	140.00	195.00	—
995.	St. Louis	White	Mellon	85.00	105.00	140.00	195.00	450.00
996.	Minneapolis	Burke	McAdoo	100.00	125.00	170.00	275.00	700.00
997.	Minneapolis	Burke	Glass	170.00	325.00	470.00	750.00	1,100.00
998.	Minneapolis	Burke	Houston	100.00	125.00	170.00	275.00	500.00
999.	Minneapolis	White	Mellon	100.00	125.00	170.00	275.00	750.00
1000.	Kansas City	Burke	McAdoo	95.00	120.00	160.00	225.00	500.00
1001.	Kansas City	Burke	Glass	None Reported	—	—	—	—
1002.	Kansas City	Burke	Houston	95.00	120.00	160.00	225.00	500.00
1003.	Kansas City	White	Mellon	95.00	120.00	160.00	225.00	600.00
1004.	Dallas	Burke	McAdoo	95.00	120.00	160.00	225.00	700.00
1005.	Dallas	Burke	Glass	200.00	350.00	500.00	850.00	1,100.00
1006.	Dallas	Burke	Houston	100.00	125.00	170.00	275.00	600.00
1007.	Dallas	White	Mellon	95.00	120.00	160.00	225.00	450.00
1008.	San Francisco	Burke	McAdoo	95.00	120.00	160.00	225.00	650.00
1009.	San Francisco	Burke	Glass	110.00	150.00	190.00	325.00	700.00
1010.	San Francisco	Burke	Houston	100.00	125.00	170.00	275.00	700.00
1011A.	San Francisco	White	Mellon	85.00	105.00	140.00	195.00	450.00
1011B.	San Francisco	White	Mellon	115.00	150.00	225.00	500.00	1,100.00
1011C.	San Francisco	White	Mellon	300.00	450.00	650.00	900.00	—

Federal Reserve Bank Notes

Face of Notes 822-830. Bust of President Grover Cleveland at left.

Back of Notes 822-830. Transportation scenes feature an automobile, a train, a plane, and ships of the era.

No.	Issuing Bank	Series	Signature		VG-8	F-12	VF-20	EF-40	Unc-63
822.	Atlanta	1915	Teehee	Burke					
			Bell-Cashier	Wellborn	$1,600.00	$2,500.00	$3,250.00	$4,750.00	—
822-1	Atlanta			Same but with Bell-Secretary. ...	1,600.00	2,500.00	3,250.00	4,750.00	—
822a.	Atlanta	1915	Teehee	Burke					
			Pike	McCord	Unique - CAA 2002 EF @ $43,700 —	—	—	—	—
823.	Atlanta	1918	Elliott	Burke					
			Bell	Wellborn	1,000.00	1,350.00	1,750.00	2,200.00	$5,000.00
824.	Chicago	1915	Teehee	Burke					
			McLallen	McDougal	1,000.00	1,350.00	1,750.00	2,200.00	5,000.00
825.	St. Louis	1918	Teehee	Burke					
			Attebery	Wells	1,000.00	1,350.00	1,750.00	2,200.00	—
826.	Kansas City	1915	Teehee	Burke					
			Anderson	Miller	1,200.00	1,500.00	1,900.00	2,600.00	—
827.	Kansas City	1915	Teehee	Burke					
			Cross	Miller	1,000.00	1,350.00	1,750.00	2,200.00	—
828.	Dallas	1915	Teehee	Burke					
			Hoopes	Van Zandt	1,200.00	1,500.00	1,900.00	2,600.00	6,000.00
829.	Dallas	1915	Teehee	Burke					
			Gilbert	Van Zandt	1,600.00	2,500.00	3,250.00	4,750.00	—
830.	Dallas	1915	Teehee	Burke					
			Talley	Van Zandt	2,000.00	3,500.00	5,000.00	8,000.00	—

No notes were issued by the banks in Boston, New York, Philadelphia, Cleveland, Richmond, Minneapolis, and San Francisco.

National Bank Notes (Brown Seal)

Face of Note 1802.

Back of Note 1802.

No.		VF-20	Unc-63
1802-1.	Type 1	$100.00	$250.00
1802-2.	Type 2	100.00	300.00

SMALL-SIZE TWENTY DOLLAR NOTES

Gold Certificates (Gold Seal)

Face of Notes 2402-2403.
Back of Notes 2402-2403 (not shown) similar to back of Note 1802.

No.	Series	Signatures	Quantity Printed	VG-8	F-12	VF-20	EF-40	Unc-63
2402.	1928	....Woods Mellon	66,204,000	$80.00	$90.00	$115.00	$175.00	$600.00
2402.*	1928	....Woods Mellon		200.00	500.00	700.00	2,500.00	5,000.00
2403.	1928-A	..Woods Mills	1,500,000		Not Issued			

SMALL-SIZE TWENTY DOLLAR NOTES

Federal Reserve Bank Notes (Brown Seal)

Face of Notes 1870A.-1870L.

Back of Notes 1870A.-1870L.

No.	Issuing Bank	Quantity Printed	VG-8	F-12	VF-20	EF-40	Unc-63
1870-A.	Boston	972,000	$35.00	$40.00	$45.00	$50.00	$225.00
1870-B.	New York	2,568,000	35.00	40.00	45.00	50.00	90.00
1870-C.	Philadelphia	1,008,000	35.00	40.00	45.00	50.00	90.00
1870-D.	Cleveland	1,020,000	35.00	40.00	45.00	50.00	90.00
1870-E.	Richmond	1,632,000	35.00	40.00	45.00	50.00	100.00
1870-F.	Atlanta	960,000	35.00	40.00	45.00	50.00	200.00
1870-G.	Chicago	2,028,000	35.00	40.00	45.00	50.00	90.00
1870-H.	St. Louis	444,000	35.00	40.00	45.00	50.00	225.00
1870-I.	Minneapolis	864,000	55.00	80.00	100.00	125.00	200.00
1870-J.	Kansas City	612,000	35.00	40.00	125.00	150.00	225.00
1870-K.	Dallas	468,000	60.00	80.00	100.00	250.00	700.00
1870-L.	San Francisco	888,000	55.00	75.00	100.00	250.00	2,000.00
1870*.	Most Common Districts		100.00	150.00	200.00	250.00	400.00

Federal Reserve Notes (Green Seal)

Face of Notes 2050-2051.

Back of Notes 2050-2051.

Federal Reserve Notes (Green Seal)

Series of 1928
Signatures of Tate and Mellon

No.	Issuing Bank	Quantity Printed	VF-20	EF-40	Unc-63
2050-A.	Boston	3,790,880	$50.00	$125.00	$350.00
2050-A*.	Boston		300.00	800.00	2,000.00
2050-B.	New York	12,797,200	50.00	75.00	225.00
2050-B*.	New York		150.00	400.00	1,200.00
2050-C.	Philadelphia	3,797,200	50.00	95.00	225.00
2050-C*.	Philadelphia		300.00	500.00	1,500.00
2050-D.	Cleveland	10,626,900	50.00	75.00	175.00
2050-D*.	Cleveland		150.00	350.00	1,300.00
2050-E.	Richmond	4,119,600	50.00	100.00	225.00
2050-E*.	Richmond		425.00	900.00	2,500.00
2050-F.	Atlanta	3,842,388	50.00	95.00	225.00
2050-F*.	Atlanta		425.00	750.00	2,500.00
2050-G.	Chicago	10,891,740	45.00	75.00	175.00
2050-G*.	Chicago		150.00	500.00	1,500.00
2050-H.	St. Louis	2,523,300	40.00	80.00	200.00
2050-H*.	St. Louis		300.00	650.00	2,000.00
2050-I.	Minneapolis	2,633,100	40.00	100.00	300.00
2050-I*.	Minneapolis		425.00	850.00	3,000.00
2050-J.	Kansas City	2,584,500	40.00	75.00	200.00
2050-J*.	Kansas City		300.00	600.00	1,750.00
2050-K.	Dallas	1,568,500	50.00	150.00	350.00
2050-K*.	Dallas		1,500.00	2,500.00	5,000.00
2050-L.	San Francisco	8,404,800	40.00	95.00	225.00
2050-L*.	San Francisco		300.00	650.00	1,750.00

Series of 1928-A
Signatures of Woods and Mellon

No.	Issuing Bank	Quantity Printed	VF-20	EF-40	Unc-63
2051-A.	Boston	1,293,900	$85.00	$150.00	$450.00
2051-A*.	Boston		850.00	1,100.00	4,500.00
2051-B.	New York	1,055,800	50.00	125.00	400.00
2051-B*.	New York		700.00	900.00	3,500.00
2051-C.	Philadelphia	1,717,200	85.00	125.00	425.00
2051-C*.	Philadelphia		850.00	1,100.00	4,000.00
2051-D.	Cleveland	625,200	50.00	125.00	400.00
2051-D*.	Cleveland		850.00	1,100.00	3,500.00
2051-E.	Richmond	1,534,500	50.00	125.00	450.00
2051-E*.	Richmond		850.00	1,100.00	3,500.00
2051-F.	Atlanta	1,442,400	50.00	125.00	450.00
2051-F*.	Atlanta		850.00	1,100.00	3,500.00
2051-G.	Chicago	822,000	60.00	100.00	400.00
2051-G*.	Chicago		700.00	900.00	3,000.00
2061-H.	St. Louis	573,300	65.00	125.00	450.00
2051-H*.	St. Louis		700.00	900.00	3,500.00
2051-J.	Kansas City	113,900	120.00	175.00	700.00
2051-J*.	Kansas City		1,200.00	2,000.00	5,000.00
2051-K.	Dallas	1,032,000	50.00	100.00	350.00
2051-K*.	Dallas		750.00	1,000.00	3,500.00

Federal Reserve Notes (Green Seal)

Face of Notes 2052-2056.

Back of Notes 2052-2056.

Series of 1928-B
Signatures of Woods and Mellon
This series comes with both light and dark green seals

No.	Issuing Bank	Quantity Printed	VF-20	EF-40	Unc-63
2052-A.	Boston	7,749,636	$35.00	$55.00	$100.00
2052-A*.	Boston		175.00	800.00	1500.00
2052-B.	New York	19,448,436	30.00	55.00	85.00
2052-B*.	New York		175.00	400.00	800.00
2052-C.	Philadelphia	8,095,548	35.00	55.00	100.00
2052-C*.	Philadelphia		175.00	800.00	1750.00
2052-D.	Cleveland	11,684,196	30.00	55.00	100.00
2052-D*.	Cleveland		175.00	800.00	1750.00
2052-E.	Richmond	4,413,900	35.00	55.00	120.00
2052-E*.	Richmond		400.00	1000.00	2000.00
2052-F.	Atlanta 2,390,240		100.00	250.00	450.00
2052-F*.	Atlanta		400.00	1000.00	2000.00
2052-G.	Chicago 17,220,276		30.00	55.00	85.00
2052-G*.	Chicago		175.00	400.00	800.00
2052-H.	St. Louis	3,834,600	30.00	55.00	100.00
2052-H*.	St. Louis		250.00	750.00	1500.00
2052-I.	Minneapolis	3,298,920	30.00	55.00	110.00
2052-I*.	Minneapolis		300.00	1000.00	2500.00
2052-J.	Kansas City	4,941,252	35.00	55.00	100.00
2052-J*.	Kansas City		175.00	800.00	1750.00
2052-K.	Dallas 2,406,060		30.00	55.00	150.00
2052-K*.	Dallas		200.00	800.00	2000.00
2052-L.	San Francisco	9,689,124	35.00	55.00	100.00
2052-L*.	San Francisco		175.00	600.00	1750.00

Series of 1928-C
Signatures of Woods and Mills

No.	Issuing Bank	Quantity Printed	VF-20	EF-40	Unc-63
2053-G.	Chicago	3,363,300	$550.00	$900.00	$2,250.00
2053-L.	San Francisco	1,420,200	800.00	1,500.00	5,000.00
2053*.		Unknown	—	—	—

Federal Reserve Notes (Green Seal)

Series of 1934
Signatures of Julian and Morgenthau

As on the $5 and $10 notes, there are two distinct shades of green seals in this series: the light, vivid green and the darker, duller blue green. On the $20 notes, however, the values are about the same.

No.	Issuing Bank	Quantity Printed	VF-20	EF-40	Unc-63
2054-A.	Boston	37,673,068	$30.00	$50.00	$80.00
2054-A*.	Boston		100.00	200.00	600.00
2054-B.	New York	27,573,264	30.00	50.00	80.00
2054-B*.	New York		100.00	200.00	600.00
2054-C.	Philadelphia	53,209,968	30.00	50.00	80.00
2054-C*.	Philadelphia		100.00	200.00	600.00
2054-D.	Cleveland	48,301,416	30.00	50.00	80.00
2054-D*.	Cleveland		100.00	200.00	600.00
2054-E.	Richmond	36,259,224	30.00	50.00	80.00
2054-E*.	Richmond		100.00	200.00	600.00
2054-F.	Atlanta	41,547,660	30.00	50.00	80.00
2054-F*.	Atlanta		100.00	200.00	600.00
2054-G.	Chicago	20,777,832	30.00	50.00	80.00
2054-G*.	Chicago		100.00	200.00	600.00
2054-H.	St. Louis	27,174,552	30.00	50.00	80.00
2054-H*.	St. Louis		100.00	200.00	600.00
2054-I.	Minneapolis	16,795,116	30.00	50.00	80.00
2054-I*.	Minneapolis		100.00	200.00	600.00
2054-J.	Kansas City	28,865,304	30.00	50.00	80.00
2054-J*.	Kansas City		100.00	200.00	600.00
2054-K.	Dallas	20,852,160	30.00	50.00	80.00
2054-K*.	Dallas		100.00	200.00	600.00
2054-L.	San Francisco	32,203,956	30.00	50.00	80.00
2054-L*.	San Francisco		100.00	200.00	600.00

Notes issued for Hawaii after the attack on Pearl Harbor

Face of Notes 2304-2305. Brown Seal.

Back of Notes 2304-2305.

SMALL-SIZE TWENTY DOLLAR NOTES

Federal Reserve Notes (Green Seal)

No.	Series	Quantity Printed	VF-20	EF-40	Unc-63
2304.	1934	11,246,000	$100.00	$400.00	$3,000.00
2304*.	1934	52,000	3,000.00	5,000.00	15,000.00
2305.	1934-A	incl. above	85.00	200.00	950.00
2305*.	1934-A	2,500	1,500.00	2,000.00	10,000.00

Regular Issues (continued from Note 2054)
Series of 1934-A
Signatures of Julian and Morganthau

No.	Issuing Bank	Quantity Printed	VF-20	EF-40	Unc-63
2055-A.	Boston	3,302,416	$35.00	$45.00	$75.00
2055-A*.	Boston		100.00	200.00	500.00
2055-B.	New York	102,555,538		30.00	65.00
2055-B*.	New York		75.00	100.00	400.00
2055-C.	Philadelphia	3,371,316	35.00	45.00	75.00
2055-C*.	Philadelphia		100.00	200.00	500.00
2055-D.	Cleveland	23,475,108	30.00	40.00	65.00
2055-D*.	Cleveland		100.00	200.00	500.00
2055-E.	Richmond	46,816,224	30.00	40.00	65.00
2055-E*.	Richmond		100.00	200.00	500.00
2055-F.	Atlanta	6,756,816	30.00	40.00	65.00
2055-F*.	Atlanta		100.00	200.00	500.00
2055-G.	Chicago	91,141,452		30.00	60.00
2055-G*.	Chicago		75.00	100.00	400.00
2055-H.	St. Louis	3,701,568	30.00	40.00	65.00
2055-H*.	St. Louis		100.00	200.00	500.00
2055-I.	Minneapolis	1,162,500	35.00	45.00	75.00
2055-I*.	Minneapolis		100.00	200.00	600.00
2055-J.	Kansas City	3,221,184	30.00	40.00	65.00
2055-J*.	Kansas City		100.00	200.00	500.00
2055-K.	Dallas	2,531,700	35.00	45.00	70.00
2055-K*.	Dallas		100.00	200.00	500.00
2055-L.	San Francisco	94,454,112	30.00	40.00	65.00
2055-L*.	San Francisco		100.00	200.00	500.00

Series of 1934-B
Signatures of Julian and Vinson

No.	Issuing Bank	Quantity Printed	VF-20	EF-40	Unc-63
2056-A.	Boston	3,904,800	$30.00	$40.00	$80.00
2056-A*.	Boston		125.00	150.00	650.00
2056-B.	New York	14,876,436	30.00	40.00	65.00
2056-B*.	New York		125.00	150.00	600.00
2056-C.	Philadelphia	3,271,452	30.00	40.00	80.00
2056-C*.	Philadelphia		125.00	150.00	600.00
2056-D.	Cleveland	2,814,600	30.00	40.00	80.00
2056-D*.	Cleveland		125.00	150.00	600.00
2056-E.	Richmond	9,451,632	30.00	40.00	100.00
2056-E*.	Richmond		125.00	150.00	600.00
2056-F.	Atlanta	6,887,640	30.00	40.00	100.00
2056-F*.	Atlanta		125.00	150.00	600.00
2056-G.	Chicago	9,084,600	30.00	40.00	65.00
2056-G*.	Chicago		125.00	150.00	600.00
2056-H.	St. Louis	5,817,300	30.00	40.00	80.00
2056-H*.	St. Louis		125.00	150.00	600.00
2056-I.	Minneapolis	2,304,800	30.00	40.00	125.00
2056-I*.	Minneapolis		150.00	175.00	750.00
2056-J.	Kansas City	3,524,244	30.00	40.00	95.00
2056-J*.	Kansas City		150.00	175.00	700.00
2056-K.	Dallas	2,807,388	30.00	40.00	95.00
2056-K*.	Dallas		150.00	175.00	600.00
2056-L.	San Francisco	5,289,540	30.00	40.00	85.00
2056-L*.	San Francisco		150.00	175.00	600.00

Federal Reserve Notes (Green Seal)

Series of 1934-C
Signatures of Julian and Snyder

This series exists with two different backs, the latter one with significantly more arboreal embellishment. The first, slightly older type is a little scarcer.

Back found on Note 2057.

Back of Notes 2057-2058.

No.	Issuing Bank	Quantity Printed	VF-20	EF-40	Unc-63
2057-A.	Boston	7,397,352	$65.00	$30.00	$40.00
2057-A*.	Boston		110.00	125.00	450.00
2057-B.	New York	18,668,148	30.00	40.00	50.00
2057-B*.	New York		110.00	125.00	400.00
2057-C.	Philadelphia	11,590,752	30.00	45.00	50.00
2057-C*.	Philadelphia		110.00	125.00	450.00
2057-D.	Cleveland	17,912,424	30.00	40.00	50.00
2057-D*.	Cleveland		110.00	125.00	450.00
2057-E.	Richmond	22,526,568	30.00	40.00	50.00
2057-E*.	Richmond		110.00	125.00	450.00
2057-F.	Atlanta	18,858,876	30.00	40.00	50.00
2057-F*.	Atlanta		110.00	150.00	750.00
2057-G.	Chicago	26,031,660	30.00	40.00	50.00
2057-G*.	Chicago		110.00	125.00	450.00
2057-H.	St. Louis	13,276,984	30.00	40.00	50.00
2057-H*.	St. Louis		110.00	125.00	450.00
2057-I.	Minneapolis	3,490,200	40.00	50.00	70.00
2057-I*.	Minneapolis		125.00	150.00	450.00
2057-J.	Kansas City	9,675,468	30.00	40.00	55.00
2057-J*.	Kansas City		110.00	125.00	450.00
2057-K.	Dallas	10,205,364	30.00	40.00	55.00
2057-K*.	Dallas		110.00	125.00	450.00
2057-L.	San Francisco	20,580,000	30.00	40.00	50.00
2057-L*.	San Francisco		110.00	125.00	450.00

Federal Reserve Notes (Green Seal)

Series of 1934-D
Signatures of Clark and Snyder

No.	Issuing Bank	Quantity Printed	VF-20	EF-40	Unc-63
2058-A.	Boston	4,520,000	$30.00	$50.00	$60.00
2058-A*.	Boston		150.00	250.00	500.00
2058-B.	New York	27,894,260	30.00	40.00	50.00
2058-B*.	New York		110.00	125.00	300.00
2058-C.	Philadelphia	6,022,428	30.00	40.00	50.00
2058-C*.	Philadelphia		150.00	175.00	450.00
2058-D.	Cleveland	8,981,688	30.00	40.00	50.00
2058-D*.	Cleveland		110.00	125.00	300.00
2058-E.	Richmond	14,055,984	30.00	40.00	50.00
2058-E*.	Richmond		110.00	125.00	300.00
2058-F.	Atlanta	7,495,440	30.00	40.00	50.00
2058-F*.	Atlanta		150.00	175.00	450.00
2058-G.	Chicago	15,187,596	30.00	40.00	50.00
2058-G*.	Chicago		150.00	175.00	450.00
2058-H.	St. Louis	5,923,248	30.00	40.00	50.00
2058-H*.	St. Louis		150.00	175.00	450.00
2058-I.	Minneapolis	2,422,416	30.00	40.00	55.00
2058-I*.	Minneapolis		150.00	175.00	450.00
2058-J.	Kansas City	4,211,904	30.00	40.00	50.00
2058-J*.	Kansas City		150.00	175.00	450.00
2058-K.	Dallas	3,707,364	30.00	40.00	50.00
2058-K*.	Dallas		150.00	175.00	450.00
2058-L.	San Francisco	12,015,228	30.00	40.00	50.00
2058-L*.	San Francisco		110.00	125.00	300.00

Face of Notes 2059-2064.

Back of Notes 2059-2064.

Federal Reserve Notes (Green Seal)

Series of 1950
Signatures of Clark and Snyder

No.	Issuing Bank	Quantity Printed	VF-20	EF-40	Unc-63
2059-A.	Boston	23,184,000	$25.00	$30.00	$60.00
2059-I*.	Boston		70.00	80.00	400.00
2059-B.	New York	80,064,000	25.00	30.00	60.00
2059-I*.	New York		70.00	80.00	400.00
2059-C.	Philadelphia	29,520,000	25.00	30.00	60.00
2059-C*.	Philadelphia		70.00	80.00	400.00
2059-D.	Cleveland	51,120,000	25.00	30.00	60.00
2059-D*.	Cleveland		70.00	80.00	400.00
2059-E.	Richmond	67,536,000	25.00	30.00	60.00
2059-E*.	Richmond		70.00	80.00	400.00
2059-F.	Atlanta	39,312,000	25.00	30.00	60.00
2059-F*.	Atlanta		70.00	80.00	400.00
2059-G.	Chicago	70,464,000	35.00	40.00	60.00
2059-G*.	Chicago		70.00	80.00	400.00
2059-H.	St. Louis	27,352,000	25.00	30.00	60.00
2059-H*.	St. Louis		70.00	80.00	400.00
2059-I.	Minneapolis	9,216,000	30.00	40.00	70.00
2059-I*.	Minneapolis		70.00	80.00	400.00
2059-J.	Kansas City	22,752,000	30.00	40.00	70.00
2059-J*.	Kansas City		70.00	80.00	400.00
2059-K.	Dallas	22,656,000	25.00	30.00	70.00
2059-K*.	Dallas		70.00	80.00	400.00
2059-L.	San Francisco	70,272,000	25.00	30.00	70.00
2059-L*.	San Francisco		70.00	80.00	400.00

Series of 1950-A
Signatures of Priest and Humphrey

No.	Issuing Bank	Quantity Printed	VF-20	EF-40	Unc-63
2060-A.	Boston	19,656,000			$45.00
2060-A*.	Boston		$85.00	$100.00	200.00
2060-B.	New York	82,568,000			45.00
2060-B*.	New York		85.00	100.00	200.00
2060-C.	Philadelphia	16,560,000			45.00
2060-C*.	Philadelphia		85.00	100.00	200.00
2060-D.	Cleveland	50,320,000			45.00
2060-D*.	Cleveland		85.00	100.00	200.00
2060-E.	Richmond	69,544,000			45.00
2060-E*.	Richmond		85.00	100.00	200.00
2060-F.	Atlanta	27,648,000			45.00
2060-F*.	Atlanta		85.00	100.00	200.00
2060-G.	Chicago	73,720,000			45.00
2060-G*.	Chicago		85.00	100.00	200.00
2060-H.	St. Louis	22,680,000			45.00
2060-H*.	St. Louis		85.00	100.00	200.00
2060-I.	Minneapolis	5,544,000			45.00
2060-I*.	Minneapolis		85.00	100.00	200.00
2060-J.	Kansas City	22,968,000			45.00
2060-J*.	Kansas City		85.00	100.00	200.00
2060-K.	Dallas	10,728,000			45.00
2060-K*.	Dallas		85.00	100.00	200.00
2060-L.	San Francisco	85,528,000			45.00
2060-L*.	San Francisco		85.00	100.00	200.00

SMALL-SIZE TWENTY DOLLAR NOTES

Federal Reserve Notes (Green Seal)

Series of 1950-B
Signatures of Priest and Anderson

No.	Issuing Bank	Quantity Printed	VF-20	EF-40	Unc-63
2061-A.	Boston	5,040,000			$45.00
2061-A*.	Boston		$60.00	$75.00	200.00
2061-B.	New York	49,960,000			45.00
2061-B*.	New York		60.00	75.00	200.00
2061-C.	Philadelphia	7,920,000			45.00
2061-C*.	Philadelphia		60.00	75.00	200.00
2061-D.	Cleveland	38,160,000			45.00
2061-D*.	Cleveland		60.00	75.00	200.00
2061-E.	Richmond	42,120,000			45.00
2061-E*.	Richmond		60.00	75.00	200.00
2061-F.	Atlanta	40,240,000			45.00
2061-F*.	Atlanta		60.00	75.00	200.00
2061-G.	Chicago	80,560,000			40.00
2061-G*.	Chicago		60.00	75.00	200.00
2061-H.	St. Louis	19,440,000			45.00
2061-H*.	St. Louis		60.00	75.00	200.00
2061-I.	Minneapolis	12,240,000			40.00
2061-I*.	Minneapolis		60.00	75.00	200.00
2061-J.	Kansas City	28,440,000			40.00
2061-J*.	Kansas City		60.00	75.00	200.00
2061-K.	Dallas	11,880,000			40.00
2061-K*.	Dallas		60.00	75.00	200.00
2061-L.	San Francisco	51,040,000			40.00
2061-L*.	San Francisco		60.00	75.00	200.00

Series of 1950-C
Signatures of Smith and Dillon

No.	Issuing Bank	Quantity Printed	VF-20	EF-40	Unc-63
2062-A.	Boston	7,200,000			$45.00
2062-A*.	Boston		$75.00	$100.00	225.00
2062-B.	New York	43,200,000			45.00
2062-B*.	New York		75.00	100.00	225.00
2062-C.	Philadelphia	7,560,000			45.00
2062-C*.	Philadelphia		75.00	100.00	225.00
2062-D.	Cleveland	28,440,000			45.00
2062-D*.	Cleveland		75.00	100.00	225.00
2062-E.	Richmond	37,000,000			45.00
2062-E*.	Richmond		75.00	100.00	225.00
2062-F.	Atlanta	19,080,000			45.00
2062-F*.	Atlanta		75.00	100.00	225.00
2062-G.	Chicago	29,160,000			45.00
2062-G*.	Chicago		75.00	100.00	225.00
2062-H.	St. Louis	12,960,000			45.00
2062-H*.	St. Louis		75.00	100.00	225.00
2062-I.	Minneapolis	6,480,000	30.00	40.00	60.00
2062-I*.	Minneapolis		75.00	100.00	225.00
2062-J.	Kansas City	18,360,000			45.00
2062-J*.	Kansas City		75.00	100.00	225.00
2062-K.	Dallas	9,000,000			45.00
2062-K*.	Dallas		75.00	100.00	225.00
2062-L.	San Francisco	45,360,000			45.00
2062-L*.	San Francisco		75.00	100.00	225.00

Federal Reserve Notes (Green Seal)

Series of 1950-D
Signatures of Granahan and Dillon

No.	Issuing Bank	Quantity Printed	VF-20	EF-40	Unc-63
2063-A.	Boston	9,320,000			$45.00
2062-A*.	Boston		$100.00	$125.00	175.00
2063-B.	New York	64,280,000			45.00
2062-B*.	New York		100.00	125.00	175.00
2063-C.	Philadelphia	5,400,000			45.00
2062-C*.	Philadelphia		100.00	125.00	175.00
2063-D.	Cleveland	23,760,000			45.00
2062-D*.	Cleveland		100.00	125.00	175.00
2063-E.	Richmond	30,240,000			45.00
2062-E*.	Richmond		100.00	125.00	175.00
2063-F.	Atlanta	22,680,000			45.00
2062-F*.	Atlanta		100.00	125.00	175.00
2063-G.	Chicago	67,960,000			45.00
2062-G*.	Chicago		100.00	125.00	175.00
2063-H.	St. Louis	6,120,000			50.00
2062-H*.	St. Louis		100.00	125.00	175.00
2063-I.	Minneapolis	3,240,000	30.00	50.00	65.00
2062-I*.	Minneapolis		100.00	125.00	200.00
2063-J.	Kansas City	8,200,000			45.00
2062-J*.	Kansas City		100.00	125.00	175.00
2063-K.	Dallas	6,480,000			45.00
2062-K*.	Dallas		100.00	125.00	175.00
2063-L.	San Francisco	69,400,000			45.00
2063-L*.	San Francisco		100.00	125.00	175.00

Series of 1950-E
Signatures of Granahan and Fowler

No.	Issuing Bank	Quantity Printed	VF-20	EF-40	Unc-63
2064-B.	New York	8,640,000	$50.00	$60.00	$150.00
2064-B*.	New York		150.00	200.00	500.00
2064-G.	Chicago	9,360,000	50.00	75.00	200.00
2064-G*.	Chicago		200.00	300.00	600.00
2064-L.	San Francisco	8,640,000	50.00	75.00	200.00
2064-L*.	San Francisco		200.00	300.00	800.00

Face of Notes 2065-2082.

Back of Notes 2065-2082.

Federal Reserve Notes (Green Seal)

Series of 1963
Signatures of Granahan and Dillon

No.	Issuing Bank	Quantity Printed	VF-20	EF-40	Unc-63
2065-A.	Boston	2,560,000			$100.00
2065-A*.	Boston		$40.00	$60.00	200.00
2065-B.	New York	1,6640,000			75.00
2065-B*.	New York		40.00	60.00	150.00
2065-D.	Cleveland	7,680,000			100.00
2065-D*.	Cleveland		40.00	60.00	200.00
2065-E.	Richmond	4,480,000			100.00
2065-E*.	Richmond		40.00	60.00	200.00
2065-F.	Atlanta	10,240,000			100.00
2065-F*.	Atlanta		40.00	60.00	200.00
2065-G.	Chicago	2,560,000			75.00
2065-G*.	Chicago		40.00	60.00	150.00
2065-H.	St. Louis	3,200,000			100.00
2065-H*.	St. Louis		40.00	50.00	200.00
2065-J.	Kansas City	3,840,000			100.00
2065-J*.	Kansas City		40.00	60.00	200.00
2065-K.	Dallas	2,560,000			100.00
2065-K*.	Dallas		40.00	60.00	200.00
2065-L.	San Francisco	7,040,000			100.00
2065-L*.	San Francisco		45.00	60.00	200.00

Series of 1963-A
Signatures of Granahan and Fowler

No.	Issuing Bank	Quantity Printed	VF-20	EF-40	Unc-63
2066-A.	Boston	23,680,000			$45.00
2066-A*.	Boston	1,280,000	$45.00	$60.00	100.00
2066-B.	New York	93,600,000		30.00	40.00
2066-B*.	New York	3,840,000	35.00	50.00	75.00
2066-C.	Philadelphia	17,920,000			45.00
2066-C*.	Philadelphia	640,000	65.00	90.00	125.00
2066-D.	Cleveland	68,480,000			45.00
2066-D*.	Cleveland	2,560,000	45.00	60.00	100.00
2066-E.	Richmond	128,800,000			45.00
2066-E*.	Richmond	5,760,000	45.00	60.00	100.00
2066-F.	Atlanta	42,880,000			45.00
2066-F*.	Atlanta	1,920,000	45.00	60.00	100.00
2066-G.	Chicago	156,320,000		30.00	40.00
2066-G*.	Chicago	7,040,000	35.00	50.00	75.00
2066-H.	St. Louis	34,560,000			45.00
2066-H*.	St. Louis	1,920,000	45.00	60.00	100.00
2066-I.	Minneapolis	10,240,000			45.00
2066-I*.	Minneapolis	640,000	65.00	90.00	120.00
2066-J.	Kansas City	37,120,000			45.00
2066-J*.	Kansas City	1,920,000	45.00	60.00	100.00
2066-K.	Dallas	38,400,000			45.00
2066-K*.	Dallas	1,280,000	45.00	60.00	100.00
2066-L.	San Francisco	169,120,000			45.00
2066-L*.	San Francisco	8,320,000	45.00	60.00	100.00

Series of 1969
Signatures of Elston and Kennedy with new Treasury seal

No.	Issuing Bank	Quantity Printed	VF-20	EF-40	Unc-63
2067-A.	Boston	19,200,000			$50.00
2067-A*.	Boston	1,280,000	$45.00	$55.00	90.00
2067-B.	New York	106,400,000			40.00
2067-B*.	New York	5,106,000	30.00	45.00	75.00
2067-C.	Philadelphia	10,880,000			50.00
2067-C*.	Philadelphia	1,280,000	45.00	55.00	90.00
2067-D.	Cleveland	60,160,000			50.00

Federal Reserve Notes (Green Seal)

Series of 1969
Signatures of Elston and Kennedy with new Treasury seal

No.	Issuing Bank	Quantity Printed	VF-20	EF-40	Unc-63
2067-D*.	Cleveland	2,560,000	$45.00	$55.00	$90.00
2067-E.	Richmond	66,560,000			50.00
2067-E*.	Richmond	2,560,000	45.00	55.00	75.00
2067-F.	Atlanta	36,480,000			150.00
2067-F*.	Atlanta	1,280,000	45.00	55.00	75.00
2067-G.	Chicago	107,680,000			40.00
2067-G*.	Chicago	3,200,000	45.00	55.00	75.00
2067-H.	St. Louis	19,200,000			50.00
2067-H*.	St. Louis	640,000	45.00	55.00	85.00
2067-I.	Minneapolis	12,160,000			50.00
2067-I*.	Minneapolis	640,000	45.00	55.00	85.00
2067-J.	Kansas City	39,040,000			50.00
2067-J*.	Kansas City	1,280,000	45.00	55.00	75.00
2067-K.	Dallas	25,600,000			50.00
2067-K*.	Dallas	640,000	50.00	60.00	80.00
2067-L.	San Francisco	103,840,000			50.00
2067-L*.	San Francisco	5,120,000	45.00	55.00	75.00

Series of 1969-A
Signatures of Kabis and Connally

No.	Issuing Bank	Quantity Printed	VF-20	EF-40	Unc-63
2068-A.	Boston	13,440,000	$25.00	$35.00	$50.00
2068-B.	New York	69,760,000			45.00
2068-B*.	New York	2,460,000	40.00	50.00	75.00
2068-C.	Philadelphia	13,440,000			50.00
2068-D.	Cleveland	29,440,000			50.00
2068-D*.	Cleveland	640,000	45.00	55.00	125.00
2068-E.	Richmond	42,400,000			50.00
2068-E*.	Richmond	1,920,000	40.00	50.00	90.00
2068-F.	Atlanta	13,440,000			50.00
2068-G.	Chicago	81,640,000			45.00
2068-G*.	Chicago	1,920,000	40.00	50.00	70.00
2068-H.	St. Louis	14,080,000			50.00
2068-H*.	St. Louis	640,000	45.00	55.00	125.00
2068-I.	Minneapolis	7,040,000			50.00
2068-J.	Kansas City	16,040,000			50.00
2068-K.	Dallas	14,720,000			50.00
2068-K*.	Dallas	640,000	45.00	55.00	125.00
2068-L.	San Francisco	50,560,000			50.00
2068-L*.	San Francisco	1,280,000	55.00	65.00	100.00

Series of 1969-B
Signatures of Banuelos and Connally

No.	Issuing Bank	Quantity Printed	VF-20	EF-40	Unc-63
2069-B.	New York	39,200,000	$40.00	$50.00	$100.00
2069-B*.	New York	480,000	100.00	125.00	400.00
2069-D.	Cleveland	6,400,000	40.00	50.00	100.00
2069-E.	Richmond	27,520,000	40.00	50.00	100.00
2069-F.	Atlanta	14,080,000	40.00	50.00	100.00
2069-F*.	Atlanta	640,000	150.00	200.00	700.00
2069-G.	Chicago	14,240,000	40.00	50.00	100.00
2069-G*.	Chicago	1,112,000	100.00	125.00	400.00
2069-H.	St. Louis	5,120,000	45.00	50.00	125.00
2069-I.	Minneapolis	2,560,000	50.00	55.00	125.00
2069-J.	Kansas City	3,840,000	50.00	55.00	125.00
2069-J*.	Kansas City	640,000	125.00	150.00	500.00
2069-K.	Dallas	12,160,000	45.00	50.00	125.00
2069-L.	San Francisco	26,000,000	40.00	50.00	125.00
2069-L*.	San Francisco	640,000	110.00	150.00	500.00

SMALL-SIZE TWENTY DOLLAR NOTES

Federal Reserve Notes (Green Seal)

Series of 1969-C
Signatures of Banuelos and Shultz

No.	Issuing Bank	Quantity Printed	VF-20	EF-40	Unc-63
2070-A.	Boston	17,280,000			$50.00
2070-A*.	Boston	640,000	$50.00	$60.00	125.00
2070-B.	New York	135,200,000		25.00	45.00
2070-B*.	New York	1,640,000			85.00
2070-C.	Philadelphia	40,960,000			50.00
2070-C*.	Philadelphia	640,000	50.00	60.00	100.00
2070-D.	Cleveland	57,760,000	35.00	50.00	65.00
2070-D*.	Cleveland	480,000	50.00	60.00	150.00
2070-E.	Richmond	80,160,000	25.00	35.00	50.00
2070-E*.	Richmond	1,920,000	40.00	50.00	100.00
2070-F.	Atlanta	35,840,000			50.00
2070-F*.	Atlanta	640,000	50.00	60.00	125.00
2070-G.	Chicago	78,720,000		25.00	45.00
2070-G*.	Chicago	640,000			85.00
2070-H.	St. Louis	33,920,000			50.00
2070-H*.	St. Louis	640,000	50.00	60.00	125.00
2070-I.	Minneapolis	14,080,000			50.00
2070-I*.	Minneapolis	640,000	50.00	60.00	125.00
2070-J.	Kansas City	32,000,000			50.00
2070-J*.	Kansas City	640,000	50.00	60.00	125.00
2070-K.	Dallas	31,360,000			50.00
2070-K*.	Dallas	1,920,000	45.00	55.00	100.00
2070-L.	San Francisco	82,080,000			50.00
2070-L*.	San Francisco	1,120,000	45.00	55.00	100.00

Series of 1974
Signatures of Neff and Simon

No.	Issuing Bank	Quantity Printed	VF-20	EF-40	Unc-63
2071-A.	Boston	56,960,000			$50.00
2071-A*.	Boston	768,000	$50.00	$60.00	100.00
2071-B.	New York	296,640,000		25.00	40.00
2071-B*.	New York	7,616,000	35.00	40.00	70.00
2071-C.	Philadelphia	59,680,000			50.00
2071-C*.	Philadelphia	1,760,000	35.00	45.00	90.00
2071-D.	Cleveland	148,000,000			80.00
2071-D*.	Cleveland	3,296,000	40.00	50.00	90.00
2071-E.	Richmond	149,920,000			50.00
2071-E*.	Richmond	3,040,000	40.00	50.00	90.00
2071-F.	Atlanta	53,280,000			50.00
2071-F*.	Atlanta	480,000	50.00	60.00	100.00
2071-G.	Chicago	249,920,000		25.00	40.00
2071-G*.	Chicago	4,608,000	35.00	40.00	70.00
2071-H.	St. Louis	73,120,000			50.00
2071-H*.	St. Louis	1,120,000	40.00	50.00	90.00
2071-I.	Minneapolis	39,040,000			50.00
2071-I*.	Minneapolis	1,280,000	50.00	60.00	100.00
2071-J.	Kansas City	74,400,000			50.00
2071-J*.	Kansas City	736,000	50.00	60.00	100.00
2071-K.	Dallas	68,640,000			50.00
2071-K*.	Dallas	608,000	50.00	60.00	100.00
2071-L.	San Francisco	128,800,000			50.00
2071-L*.	San Francisco	4,320,000	45.00	55.00	90.00

Series of 1977
Signatures of Morton and Blumenthal

No.	Issuing Bank	Quantity Printed	VF-20	EF-40	Unc-63
2072-A.	Boston	94,720,000			$45.00
2072-A*.	Boston	2,688,000	$35.00	$45.00	60.00
2072-B.	New York	569,600,000			40.00
2072-B*.	New York	12,416,000	25.00	35.00	55.00
2072-C.	Philadelphia	117,760,000			45.00
2072-C*.	Philadelphia	2,176,000	25.00	35.00	45.00

Federal Reserve Notes (Green Seal)
Series of 1977
Signatures of Morton and Blumenthal

No.	Issuing Bank	Quantity Printed	VF-20	EF-40	Unc-63
2072-D.	Cleveland	189,440,000			$45.00
2072-D*.	Cleveland	5,632,000	$35.00	$45.00	70.00
2072-E.	Richmond	257,280,000			45.00
2072-E*.	Richmond	6,272,000	35.00	45.00	70.00
2072-F.	Atlanta	70,400,000			45.00
2072-F*.	Atlanta	2,698,000	35.00	45.00	70.00
2072-G.	Chicago	358,400,000			40.00
2072-G*.	Chicago	7,552,000	25.00	35.00	55.00
2072-H.	St. Louis	98,560,000			45.00
2072-H*.	St. Louis	1,792,000	35.00	45.00	70.00
2072-I.	Minneapolis	15,360,000			45.00
2072-I*.	Minneapolis	512,000	50.00	60.00	125.00
2072-J.	Kansas City	148,480,000			45.00
2072-J*.	Kansas City	4,864,000	35.00	45.00	70.00
2072-K.	Dallas	163,840,000			45.00
2072-K*.	Dallas	6,656,000	25.00	35.00	45.00
2072-L.	San Francisco	263,680,000			45.00
2072-L*.	San Francisco	6,528,000	35.00	45.00	70.00

Series of 1981
Signatures of Buchanan and Regan

No.	Issuing Bank	Quantity Printed	VF-20	EF-40	Unc-63
2073-A.	Boston	191,360,000			$60.00
2073-A*.	Boston	1,024,000	$25.00	$55.00	75.00
2073-B.	New York	559,360,000			50.00
2073-B*.	New York	5,312,000	25.00	35.00	60.00
2073-C.	Philadelphia	146,560,000			60.00
2073-C*.	Philadelphia	1,280,000	45.00	55.00	75.00
2073-D.	Cleveland	146,560,000			60.00
2073-D*.	Cleveland	1,280,000	45.00	55.00	75.00
2073-E.	Richmond	296,320,000			60.00
2073-E*.	Richmond	1,280,000	45.00	55.00	75.00
2073-F.	Atlanta	93,440,000			60.00
2073-F*.	Atlanta	3,200,000	45.00	55.00	75.00
2073-G.	Chicago	361,600,000			60.00
2073-G*.	Chicago	2,688,000	25.00	35.00	50.00
2073-H.	St. Louis	76,160,000			60.00
2073-H*.	St. Louis	1,536,000	45.00	55.00	75.00
2073-I.	Minneapolis	23,040,000			60.00
2073-I*.	Minneapolis	256,000	55.00	65.00	150.00
2073-J.	Kansas City	147,840,000			60.00
2073-J*.	Kansas City	1,280,000	45.00	55.00	75.00
2073-K.	Dallas	95,360,000			60.00
2073-K*.	Dallas	896,000	50.00	60.00	100.00
2073-L.	San Francisco	404,480,000			60.00
2073-L*.	San Francisco	1,424,000	45.00	55.00	75.00

Series of 1981-A
Signatures of Ortega and Regan

No.	Issuing Bank	Quantity Printed	VF-20	EF-40	Unc-63
2074-A.	Boston	156,800,000			$45.00
2074-B.	New York	352,000,000			40.00
2074-C.	Philadelphia	57,600,000			45.00
2074-C*.	Philadelphia	3,840,000	$35.00	$40.00	75.00
2074-D.	Cleveland	160,000,000			45.00
2074-D*.	Cleveland	3,840,000	35.00	40.00	75.00
2074-E.	Richmond	214,400,000			45.00
2074-F.	Atlanta	140,800,000			45.00
2074-F*.	Atlanta	3,200,000	35.00	40.00	75.00
2074-G.	Chicago	211,200,000			45.00
2074-H.	St. Louis	73,600,000			45.00
2074-I.	Minneapolis	19,200,000			55.00
2074-J.	Kansas City	86,400,000			45.00
2074-K.	Dallas	99,200,000			45.00
2074-L.	San Francisco	457,600,000			45.00
2074-L*.	San Francisco	6,400,000	35.00	40.00	75.00

SMALL-SIZE TWENTY DOLLAR NOTES

Federal Reserve Notes (Green Seal)
Series of 1985
Signatures of Ortega and Baker

No.	Issuing Bank	Quantity Printed	Unc-63
2075-A.	Boston	416,000,000	$45.00
2075-A*.	Boston	3,200,000	85.00
2075-B.	New York	1,728,000,000	45.00
2075-B*.	New York	5,760,000	85.00
2075-C.	Philadephia	224,000,000	45.00
2075-C*.	Philadelphia	6,400,000	85.00
2075-D.	Cleveland	585,600,000	45.00
2075-D*.	Cleveland	6,400,000	85.00
2075-E.	Richmond	864,000,000	45.00
2075-E*.	Richmond	6,400,000	85.00
2073-F.	Atlanta	313,600,000	45.00
2075-G.	Chicago	729,600,000	45.00
2075-G*.	Chicago	5,760,000	85.00
2073-H.	St. Louis	203,400,000	45.00
2075-I.	Minneapolis	112,000,000	45.00
2075-J.	Kansas City	204,800,000	45.00
2075-J*.	Kansas City	3,200,000	85.00
2075-K.	Dallas	192,000,000	45.00
2075-K*.	Dallas	3,200,000	85.00
2075-L.	San Francisco	1,129,600,000	45.00
2075-L*.	San Francisco	3,200,000	85.00

Series of 1988
None printed.

Series of 1988-A
Signatures of Villalpando and Brady

No.	Issuing Bank	Quantity Printed	Unc-63
2076-A.	Boston	313,600,000	$45.00
2076-B.	New York	979,200,000	45.00
2076-B*.	New York	6,560,000	85.00
2076-C.	Philadelphia	96,000,000	45.00
2076-C*.	Philadelphia	3,200,000	85.00
2076-D.	Cleveland	307,200,000	45.00
2076-E.	Richmond	281,600,000	45.00
2076-F.	Atlanta	288,000,000	45.00
2076-F*.	Atlanta	3,200,000	85.00
2076-G.	Chicago	563,200,000	45.00
2076-G*.	Chicago	3,200,000	85.00
2076-H.	St. Louis	108,800,000	45.00
2076-I.	Minneapolis	25,600,000	45.00
2076-J.	Kansas City	137,200,000	45.00
2076-K.	Dallas	51,200,000	45.00
2076-K*.	Dallas	3,200,000	85.00
2076-L.	San Francisco	729,600,000	45.00

Series of 1990
Signatures of Villalpando and Brady with security thread and micro-size printing
Printed in Washington, DC

No.	Issuing Bank	Quantity Printed	VF-20	Unc-63
2077-A.	Boston	345,600,000		$30.00
2077-A*.	Boston	3,200,000	$35.00	50.00
2077-B.	New York	1,446,400,000		30.00
2077-B*.	New York	16,640,000	35.00	50.00
2077-C.	Philadelphia	96,000,000		30.00
2077-D.	Cleveland	281,600,000		30.00
2077-D*.	Cleveland	3,200,000	35.00	50.00
2077-E.	Richmond	307,200,000		30.00
2077-E*.	Richmond	3,200,000	35.00	50.00
2077-F.	Atlanta	460,800,000		30.00
2077-I.	Minneapolis	70,400,000		32.50

Federal Reserve Notes (Green Seal)

Series of 1990
Signatures of Villalpando and Brady with security thread and micro-size printing
Printed in Washington, DC

No.	Issuing Bank	Quantity Printed	VF-20	EF-40	Unc-63
2077-G.	Chicago	652,800,000			$30.00
2077-H.	St. Louis	172,800,000			30.00
2077-H*.	St. Louis	3,200,000			50.00
2077-J.	Kansas City	83,200,000			32.50
2077-K.	Dallas	25,600,000			32.50
2077-L.	San Francisco	416,000,000			32.50

Series of 1990
Signatures of Villalpando and Brady. With security thread and micro-size printing
Printed at the Western Facility (Fort Worth, Texas)
Notes printed in Ft. Worth may be identified by a small "FW" on the right front side next to the plate. Check letter-number.

No.	Issuing Bank	Quantity Printed	VF-20	Unc-63
2078-F*.	Atlanta	1,280,000	$35.00	$65.00
2078-G*.	Chicago	13,400,000	35.00	65.00
2078-I*.	Minneapolis	5,120,000	35.00	65.00
2078-L.	San Francisco	(incl. above)		32.50

Series of 1993
Signatures of Withrow and Bentsen
Printed in Washington, DC

No.	Issuing Bank	Quantity Printed	VF-20	Unc-63
2079-A.	Boston	288,000,000	$25.00	$40.00
2079-A*.	Boston	2,560,000	30.00	50.00
2079-B.	New York	640,000,000	25.00	40.00
2079-B*.	New York	4,920,000	30.00	50.00
2079-C.	Philadelphia	147,200,000	25.00	40.00
2079-D.	Cleveland	329,600,000	25.00	40.00
2079-D*.	Cleveland	1,920,000	30.00	50.00
2079-E.	Richmond	656,000,000	25.00	40.00
2079-E*.	Richmond	8,960,000	30.00	50.00
2079-F.	Atlanta	300,800,000	25.00	40.00
2079-H.	St. Louis	19,200,000	25.00	40.00

Series of 1993
Signatures of Withrow and Bentsen
Printed at the Western Facility (Fort Worth, Texas)

No.	Issuing Bank	Quantity Printed	VF-20	Unc-63
2080-F.	Atlanta	51,200,000	$25.00	$45.00
2080-F*.	Atlanta	3,200,000	30.00	70.00
2080-G.	Chicago	390,400,000	25.00	45.00
2080-H.	St. Louis	166,400,000	25.00	45.00
2080-J.	Kansas City	102,400,000	25.00	45.00
2080-L.	San Francisco	806,400,000	25.00	45.00
2080-L*.	San Francisco	7,680,000	30.00	70.00

Series of 1995
Signatures of Withrow and Rubin
Printed in Washington, DC

No.	Issuing Bank	Quantity Printed	VF-20	Unc-63
2081-B.	New York	403,200,000		$35.00
2081-B*.	New York	5,760,000	$30.00	60.00
2081-C.	Philadelphia	70,400,000		35.00
2081-D.	Cleveland	140,800,000		35.00
2081-D*.	Cleveland	640,000	30.00	100.00
2081-E.	Richmond	166,400,000		35.00

Federal Reserve Notes (Green Seal)
Series of 1995
Signatures of Withrow and Rubin
Printed at the Western Facility (Fort Worth, Texas)

No.	Issuing Bank	Quantity Printed	VF-20	Unc-63
2082-F.	Atlanta	307,200,000		$35.00
2082-F*.	Atlanta	3,200,000	$30.00	75.00
2082-G.	Chicago	492,800,000		35.00
2082-H.	St. Louis	140,800,000		35.00
2082-I.	Minneapolis	44,800,000		35.00
2082-J.	Kansas City	230,400,000		35.00
2082-K.	Dallas	249,600,000		35.00
2082-L.	San Francisco	614,400,000		35.00

Face of Notes 2083-2088.

Back of Notes 2083-2088.

Series of 1996
Signatures of Withrow and Rubin
Printed in Washington, DC

No.	Issuing Bank	Quantity Printed	Unc-63
2083-A.	Boston	883,200,000	$27.50
2083-A*.	Boston	10,880,000	32.50
2083-B.	New York	896,000,000	27.50
2083-B*.	New York	3,200,000	32.50
2083-C.	Philadelphia	506,400,000	27.50
2083-C*.	Philadelphia	3,200,000	32.50
2083-D.	Cleveland	364,000,000	27.50
2083-D*.	Cleveland	6,400,000	32.50
2083-E.	Richmond		27.50

Series of 1996
Signatures of Withrow and Rubin
Printed at the Western Facility (Fort Worth, Texas)

No.	Issuing Bank	Quantity Printed	Unc-63
2084-E*.	Richmond	3,200,000	$32.50
2084-F.	Atlanta	925,600,000	27.50
2084-F*.	Atlanta	3,200,000	32.50
2084-G.	Chicago	1,151,200,000	27.50
2084-G*.	Chicago	12,800,000	32.50
2084-H.	St. Louis	257,600,000	27.50
2084-H*.	St. Louis	640,000	125.00
2084-I.	Minneapolis	112,800,000	27.50

Federal Reserve Notes (Green Seal)

Series of 1996
Signatures of Withrow and Rubin
Printed at the Western Facility (Fort Worth, Texas)

No.	Issuing Bank	Quantity Printed	Unc-63
2084-J.	Kansas City	276,800,000	$27.50
2084-K.	Dallas	276,800,000	27.50
2084-L.	San Francisco	457,600,000	27.50
2084-L*.	San Francisco	7,040,000	32.50

Series of 1999
Signatures of Withrow and Summers

No.	Issuing Bank	Quantity Printed	Unc-63
2085-E.	Richmond	492,800,000	Current
2085-E*.	Richmond	3,200,000	Current

Printed in Washington, DC

No.	Issuing Bank	Quantity Printed	Unc-63
2085-A.	Boston	57,600,000	Current
2085-A*.	Boston	1,920,000	Current
2085-B.	New York	608,000,000	Current
2085-B*.	New York	1,920,000	Current
2085-C.	Philadelphia	192,000,000	Current
2085-D.	Cleveland	268,800,000	Current
2085-D*.	Cleveland	5,760,000	Current

Series of 1999
Signatures of Withrow and Summers
Printed at the Western Facility (Fort Worth, Texas)

No.	Issuing Bank	Quantity Printed	Unc-63
2086-B*.	New York	3,200,000	Current
2086-D.	Cleveland	12,800,000	Current
2086-F.	Atlanta	409,600,000	Current
2086-F*.	Atlanta	12,800,000	Current
2086-G.	Chicago	704,000,000	Current
2086-G*.	Chicago	7,040,000	Current
2086-H.	St. Louis	102,400,000	Current
2086-I.	Minneapolis	25,600,000	Current
2086-J.	Kansas City	70,400,000	Current
2086-L.	San Francisco	32,000,000	Current
2086-L*.	San Francisco	3,200,000	Current

Series of 2001
Signatures of Marin and O'Neill. Printed in Washington, DC

No.	Issuing Bank	Quantity Printed	Unc-63
2087-B.	New York	403,200,000	Current
2087-B*.	New York	320,000	Current
2087-D.	Cleveland	83,200,000	Current
2087-E.	Richmond	140,800,000	Current

Series of 2001
Signatures of Marin and O'Neill. Printed at the Western Facility (Fort Worth, Texas)

No.	Issuing Bank	Quantity Printed	Unc-63
2088-B.	New York	249,600,000	Current
2088-E.	Richmond	153,600,000	Current
2088-F.	Atlanta	313,600,000	Current
2088-G.	Chicago	224,000,000	Current
2088-G*.	Chicago	3,200,000	Current
2088-H.	St. Louis	44,800,000	Current
2088-I.	Minneapolis	57,600,000	Current
2088-J.	Kansas City	112,000,000	Current
2088-K.	Dallas	166,400,000	Current
2088-L.	San Francisco	384,000,000	Current
2088-L*.	San Francisco	3,200,000	Current

Federal Reserve Notes (Green Seal)

Series of 2004
Signatures of Marin and Snow
Printed in Washington, DC

No.	Issuing Bank	Unc-63
2089-A.	Boston	Current
2089-A*.	Boston	Current
2089-B.	New York	Current
2089-B*.	New York	Current
2089-C.	Philadelphia	Current
2089-C*.	Philadelphia	Current
2089-D.	Cleveland	Current
2089-E.	Richmond	Current
2089-E*.	Richmond	Current

Face of Notes 2090 -

Back of Notes 2090 -

Series of 2004
Signatures of Marin and Snow
Printed at the Western Facility (Fort Worth, Texas)

No.	Issuing Bank	Unc-63
2090-D.	Cleveland	Current
2090-E.	Richmond	Current
2090-E*.	Richmond	Current
2090-F.	Atlanta	Current
2090-F*.	Atlanta	Current
2090-G.	Chicago	Current
2090-G*.	Chicago	Current
2090-H.	St. Louis	Current
2090-I.	Minneapolis	Current
2090-I*.	Minneapolis	Current
2090-J.	Kansas City	Current
2090-J*.	Kansas City	Current
2090-K.	Dallas	Current
2090-L.	San Francisco	Current
2090-L*.	San Francisco	Current

TS OF THE UNITED STATES IN
DUE TO THE UNITED STATES
LARIES AND OTHER DEBTS AND
DIVIDUALS CORPORATIONS AND
EPT INTEREST ON PUBLIC DEBT

50 · 50 · 50 · 50 · 50 · 50 · FIFTY · 50

"Climbing into the higher face values, the collector of
$50 notes meets a challenging—but not overwhelming
—and pleasurable pursuit…"

$50

FIFTY DOLLAR NOTES

COLLECTING FIFTY DOLLAR NOTES

Large-Size $50 Notes

$50 Interest Bearing Notes, Large-Size: Issued under various authorizations (from the Act of March 2, 1861, through the Act of March 3, 1865), these exist in different designs and signature combinations. All are extremely rare, with the very first issue, that of 1861, nonexistent, except for a proof impression. Even advanced numismatists who have generous budgets consider themselves fortunate to get one or two different pieces to illustrate the types. From this denomination upward, most numismatic interest is more of an academic than a collecting nature.

$50 Legal Tender Notes, Large-Size: Legal Tender or United States $50 notes were issued under dates of 1862 and 1863, from plates by the American Bank Note Company and/or the National Bank Note Company, some with the imprint of one firm, some with the imprint of the other, and still further varieties with both. The nature of the decorations suggests that most of the work was done by National. Issued in large quantities at the time, today surviving examples are scarce, as nearly all were redeemed. When seen the typical grade is well circulated.

Next are the Series of 1869 notes, of which 604,000 were printed, but of which only about five dozen are known today. As is true of many of the higher-denomination bills, when examples are encountered they are expensive, reflecting their rarity. Then follow the Legal Tender United States notes of the Series of 1874 through the Series 1880. These are scarce and are in strong demand. There are several design types and varieties among these issues.

$50 Compound Interest Treasury Notes, Large-Size: Next in the $50 series are the Compound Interest Treasury Notes authorized under the Acts of March 3, 1863, and June 30, 1864. Fortunate is the well-financed numismatist who can secure a single example to illustrate the type. When seen, such notes are apt to be well circulated. Fewer than 20 examples are known today across the different varieties.

$50 National Bank Notes, Large-Size: $50 Dollar Notes follow the arrangement of lower denominations, and can be divided into the Original Series and Series of 1875 (called "First Charter" by some), Series of 1882 ("Second Charter"), and Series of 1902 ("Third Charter").

The face of the Original Series notes, continued through the Series of 1882, depicts on the left *Washington Crossing the Delaware*, and on the right a soldier kneeling in prayer, the vignette titled *Victory*. On the reverse the *Embarkation of the Pilgrims* is shown, another panoramic scene.

Series of 1882 notes occur in the Brown Back style as well as the Date Back (1882-1908) and the ultra-rare Value Back (FIFTY DOLLARS), of which only about a half dozen exist.

Then come the Series of 1902 $50 notes, with red seal and two varieties of blue seal (one having 1902-1908 on the back and being scarcer, and the other having a plain back). These are usually capitalized in listings as Red Seal, Date Back, and Plain Back, or abbreviated as RS, DB, and PB, this nomenclature applying to other National Bank note denominations as well. The 1902 Plain Backs are scarce, while most other large-size $50 bills of this series range from rare to very rare. As is true of all National Bank Notes, there are rare states, towns, and banks.

$50 National Gold Bank Notes, Large-Size: National Gold Bank notes of the $50 denomination were issued by banks in California, in the cities of Oakland, Petaluma, Sacramento, San Francisco, San Jose, and Santa Barbara. All such bills are rare, with only six Original Series and just one Series of 1875 known to numismatists today. Issues of several banks are known to have been released, but none exist in numismatic collections—the ultimate degree of rarity.

$50 Silver Certificates, Large-Size: Silver Certificates in the $50 series commence with the Series of 1878 and continue among large-size designs through the Series of 1891, each being payable in silver dollars. Shown on the face is Edward Everett, best known as an orator from Massachusetts, although he held a number of political offices. It was Everett who, at the dedication of the Gettysburg National Battlefield in 1863, gave a two-hour oration, just before Abraham Lincoln spoke for a few minutes. In the 1850s and early 1860s Everett gave more than 200 speeches concerning George Washington and his Mount Vernon home, during the campaign to restore the structure. The early $50 issues of the Series of 1878 and 1880 have the word SILVER in large letters across the back—impressive, to say the least. Those of the Series of 1891 have an open design on the back. These later bills exist in moderate numbers, but are expensive when found, due to demand.

$50 Treasury or Coin Notes, Large-Size: In the $50 denomination these do not include the ornate Series of 1890, leaving just the Series of 1891 with open spaces on the back. Depicted on the obverse is William Henry Seward, secretary of state from 1861 through 1869—best remembered for arranging the purchase of Alaska for $7,200,000. These notes are very rare and infrequently traded.

$50 Gold Certificates, Large-Size: Gold Certificates in the $50 series begin with the Series of 1882. Depicted on the face is Silas Wright, a U.S. senator and later governor of New York, whose name may be best recognized by specialists in trivia. If Wright had anything particular to do with gold metal, he is not remembered in this context today. Indeed, he died on August 27, 1847, before the Gold Rush. Last in the large-size $50 Gold Certificates are the Series of 1913 and 1922, with U.S. Grant. These exist in fair numbers today, usually in lower grades, and are affordable.

$50 Federal Reserve Notes, Large-Size: Federal Reserve Notes of the large size were issued under the Series of 1914. Red seal notes all have Treasury signatures of Burke and McAdoo. Blue seal notes exist with several different signature combinations. For both colors of seals, varieties can be collected by Federal Reserve Bank districts. Their high face value precludes a widespread interest in acquiring them. Accordingly, prices are moderate for certain varieties that are truly scarce, particular for blue-seal issues.

$50 Federal Reserve Bank Notes, Large-Size: Next comes the Series of 1918, with the city and bank on the face, issued just in one location, St. Louis, and in one signature combination. This is a classic for type, with an original distribution of 4,000 pieces. Curiously, although only 33 are reported outstanding on Treasury Department books, over 50 are known to exist today!

Small-Size $50 Notes

All have the portrait of U.S. Grant on the face and a depiction of the United States Capitol on the back, the latter with a panorama of Washington, DC in the background (until the Series of 1996).

Among small-size $50 notes of the late 1920s and early 1930s, National Bank Notes are avidly collected, and are scarce. Most others are sought only as an example of the type. Federal Reserve Notes are still being printed for, and distributed by, the 12 different banks, but they are not widely collected by varieties.

$50 National Bank Notes, Small-Size: The Series of 1929 National Bank Notes were printed from that year through early 1935. There are two styles, Type 1 and Type 2, each printed in six-subject sheets, the arrangement being the same for other denominations in these series. Each has a brown Treasury seal and brown serial numbers. Typical with other denominations, there are rare states, towns, and banks. In general, $50 bills range from scarce to very rare across the board, with the Type 2 issues being particularly so.

$50 Gold Certificates, Small-Size: Small-size Gold Certificates were produced in the Series of 1928. Examples are seen with some frequency on the market today, usually in circulated grades.

$50 Federal Reserve Bank Notes, Small-Size: Federal Reserve Bank Notes of the Series of 1929, brown seal, are collectable from certain of the banks, but not all. None were printed for Boston, Philadelphia, Richmond, Atlanta, or St. Louis.

$50 Federal Reserve Notes, Small-Size: Small-size Federal Reserve Notes, still being made today, can be collected by Federal Reserve bank and series. Again, the high face value precludes widespread popularity.

In 2004 the face and back designs were modified. The portrait of Grant was enlarged. On the back the Capitol design was changed and the distant view of the city was eliminated. Subtle background colors of blue and red were added to both sides, and elements of the American flag (stars and stripes) were included. An official Treasury announcement told of these security features, some of which have been used on other new designs of other denominations: a security thread embedded in the paper; color-shifting ink; and a watermark portrait visible on both face and back. Quite a difference from the federal currency of the 1860s!

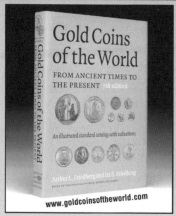

Interest Bearing Notes

Face of Note 198. Bust of Alexander Hamilton at lower right; at left, female representation of Loyalty.

Back of Note 198. This photo courtesy of Paul Kagin.

No.	Denomination	
198.	Fifty Dollars.	Extremely Rare (4 Known)

Interest Bearing Notes

Face of Note 202a. Female depicting Justice seated in center;
busts of Andrew Jackson at left and Salmon P. Chase at right.

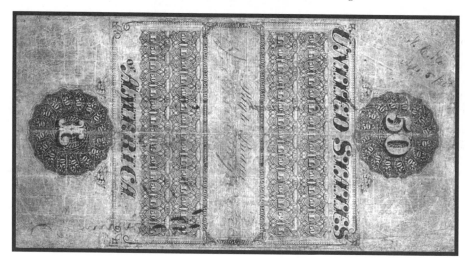

Back of Note 202a.

No.	Denomination		
202a.	Fifty Dollars. . . . .*2005 Heritage Auction, sold for $368,000* . . . . .2 Known

Interest Bearing Notes

Face of Note 203. From left to right, females representing Caduceus, Justice, and Loyalty.

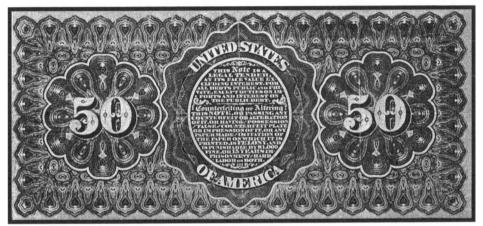

Back of Note 203.

No.	Denomination	
203.	Fifty Dollars.	Extremely Rare (7 Known)

Face of Note 207 (not shown). Large eagle standing on olive branch.

Back of Note 207 (not shown). Value, numerically in center and in words at edges, with ornate field.

No.	Denomination	
207.	Fifty Dollars.	Extremely Rare (Unique)

Interest Bearing Notes

Face of Note 212. Large eagle.

Back of Note 212.

No.	Denomination	
212.	Fifty Dollars.	Extremely Rare (7 Known)

Face similiar to the preceding.

No.	Denomination	
212d.	Fifty Dollars.	Extremely Rare (8 Known)

Interest Bearing Notes

Face of Notes 148-150a. Profile bust of Alexander Hamilton in oval frame.

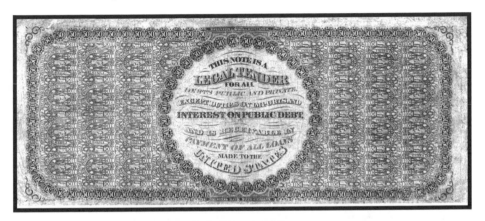

Back of Notes 148-150a.

No.	Act	Signatures		Seal	VG-8	F-12	VF-20	EF-40	Unc-63
148.	1862	Chittenden	Spinner	Red	$4,500.00	$12,000.00	$20,000.00	—	—

First Obligation on back

No.	Act	Signatures		Seal	VG-8	F-12	VF-20	EF-40	Unc-63
150.	1863	Chittenden	Spinner	Red	$4,750.00	$9,500.00	$15,000.00	—	—

Second Obligation on back
National Bank Note Co. printed on top border

No.	Act	Signatures		Seal	VG-8	F-12	VF-20	EF-40	Unc-63
150a.	1863.	Chittenden	Spinner	Red	$4,750.00	$9,500.00	$15,000.00	—	—

National Bank Note Co. and American Bank Note Co. printed on top border

Legal Tender Notes

Face of Note 151. Peace standing at left; at right, bust of Henry Clay.

Back of Note 151.

No.	Series	Signatures	Seal	VG-8	F-12	VF-20	EF-40	Unc-63
151.	1869	Allison Spinner	Large Red	$7,000.00	$17,500.00	$30,000.00	$45,000.00	$60,000.00

Face of Notes 152-164. Bust of Benjamin Franklin in oval frame at left; at right, half-length bust of Liberty, with large red "L" (for 50) at right and left center of note.

Legal Tender Notes

Back of Notes 152-164.

No.	Series	Signatures		Seal	VG-8	F-12	VF-20	EF-40	Unc-63
152.	1874 ...	Spinner	Allison	Small Red, Rays ...	$3,000.00	$6,000.00	$8,000.00	$12,000.00	$34,000.00
153.	1875 ...	Wyman	Allison	Small Red, Rays ...	Rare (3 Known)	—	—	—	—
154.	1878 ...	Gilfillan	Allison	Small Red, Rays ...	2,750.00	5,500.00	7,700.00	14,000.00	37,000.00

Face as above but without the "L's"

No.	Series	Signatures		Seal	VG-8	F-12	VF-20	EF-40	Unc-63
155.	1880 ...	Gilfillan	Bruce	Large Brown	$5,000.00	$6,500.00	$9,500.00	$12,000.00	—
156.	1880 ...	Wyman	Bruce	Large Brown	3,500.00	6,000.00	8,000.00	10,500.00	$32,500.00
157.	1880 ...	Jordan	Rosecrans ...	Large Red, Plain	4,250.00	6,250.00	9,000.00	12,000.00	—
158.	1880 ...	Hyatt	Rosecrans ...	Large Red, Plain	5,000.00	7,000.00	10,000.00	15,000.00	29,000.00
159.	1880 ...	Hyatt	Rosecrans ...	Large Red, Spiked	3,750.00	5,750.00	8,000.00	11,000.00	—
160.	1880 ...	Huston	Rosecrans ...	Large Red, Spiked	4,250.00	6,250.00	9,000.00	12,000.00	—
161.	1880 ...	Huston	Rosecrans ...	Large Brown	2,250.00	4,500.00	6,250.00	8,500.00	14,500.00
162.	1880 ...	Tillman	Morgan	Small Red, Scalloped ...	2,400.00	5,000.00	7,500.00	9,500.00	—
163.	1880 ...	Bruce	Roberts	Small Red, Scalloped ...	Rare (5 Known, one is Unc.)	—	—	—	—
164.	1880 ...	Lyons	Roberts	Small Red, Scalloped ...	1,800.00	3,750.00	5,200.00	7,200.00	11,000.00

Compound Interest Treasury Notes

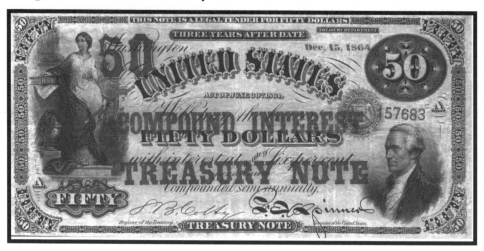

Face of Notes 192-192b. Female representing Loyalty at left; at right, bust of Alexander Hamilton.
"COMPOUND INTEREST TREASURY NOTE" stamped in bronze ink.

Back of Notes 192-192b.

No.	Series		Signatures			
192.	1863 ... June 10, 1864	Chittenden	Spinner	Unique	—
192a.	1864 ... July 15, 1864	Chittenden	Spinner	Unknown	—
192b.	1864 ... Aug. 15, 1864 - Sep. 1, 1865	Colby	Spinner	Rare	—

National Bank Notes
"First Charter Period" (Original Series and Series of 1875)

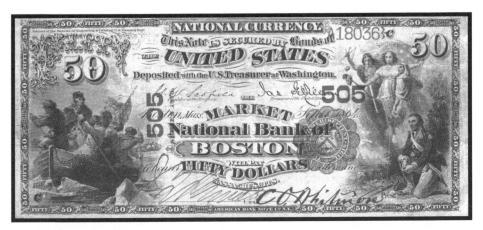

Face of Notes 440-451. Washington Crossing the Delaware *at left; at right,* Prayer for Victory.

Back of Notes 440-451. Embarkation of the Pilgrims.

National Bank Notes

"First Charter Period" (Original Series and Series of 1875)

No.	Series	Signatures		Seal	VG-8	F-12	VF-20	Unc-63
440.	Original	Chittenden	Spinner	Red, Rays	$10,000.00	$14,000.00	$18,000.00	$32,500.00
442.	Original	Colby	Spinner	Red, Rays	10,000.00	14,000.00	18,000.00	32,500.00
443.	Original	Allison	Spinner	Red, Rays	10,000.00	14,000.00	18,000.00	32,500.00
444.	1875	Allison	New	Red, Scalloped	10,000.00	14,000.00	18,000.00	32,500.00
444a.	1875	Allison	Wyman	Red, Scalloped	4 Known	—	—	—
445.	1875	Allison	Gilfillan	Red, Scalloped	4 Known	—	—	—
446.	1875	Scofield	Gilfillan	Red, Scalloped	10,000.00	14,000.00	18,000.00	32,500.00
447.	1875	Bruce	Gilfillan	Red, Scalloped	10,000.00	14,000.00	18,000.00	32,500.00
448.	1875	Bruce	Wyman	Red, Scalloped	10,000.00	14,000.00	18,000.00	32,500.00
449.	1875.	Rosecrans	Huston	Red, Scalloped	Unique	—	—	—
450.	1875.	Rosecrans	Nebeker	Red, Scalloped	Unique	—	—	—
451	1875	Tillman	Morgan	Red, Scalloped	2 Known	—	—	—

"Second Charter Period" (Series of 1882)
Brown Back

Face of Notes 507-518a. Washington Crossing the Delaware *at left; at right,* Prayer for Victory.

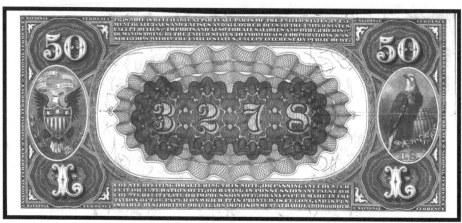

Back of Notes 507-518a. Green bank charter numbers against ornate background of brown lathe-work.

"Second Charter Period" (Series of 1882)

No.	Signatures		VG-8	F-12	VF-20	EF-40	Unc-63
507.	Bruce	Gilfillan	$4,000.00	$5,000.00	$6,000.00	$7,300.00	$11,750.00
508.	Bruce	Wyman	4,000.00	5,000.00	6,000.00	7,300.00	11,750.00
509.	Bruce	Jordan	4,000.00	5,000.00	6,000.00	7,300.00	11,750.00
510.	Rosecrans	Jordan	4,000.00	5,000.00	6,000.00	7,300.00	11,750.00
511.	Rosecrans	Hyatt	4,000.00	5,000.00	6,000.00	7,300.00	11,750.00
512.	Rosecrans	Huston	4,000.00	5,000.00	6,000.00	7,300.00	11,750.00
513.	Rosecrans	Nebeke	4,000.00	5,000.00	6,000.00	7,300.00	11,750.00
514.	Rosecrans	Morgan	4,000.00	5,000.00	6,000.00	7,300.00	11,750.00
515.	Tillman	Morgan	4,000.00	5,000.00	6,000.00	7,300.00	11,750.00
516.	Tillman	Roberts	4,000.00	5,000.00	6,000.00	7,300.00	11,750.00
517.	Bruce	Roberts	4,000.00	5,000.00	6,000.00	7,300.00	11,750.00
518.	Lyons	Roberts	4,000.00	5,000.00	6,000.00	7,300.00	11,750.00
518a.	Vernon	Treat	2 Known	—	—	—	—

Date Backs

Face of Notes 558-565. Washington Crossing the Delaware *at left; at right,* Prayer for Victory.

Back of Notes 558-565.

"Second Charter Period" (Series of 1882)

Date Backs

No.	Signatures		VG-8	F-12	VF-20	EF-40	Unc-63
558.	Rosecrans	Huston	$4,000.00	$5,000.00	$6,000.00	$7,500.00	$10,000.00
559.	Rosecrans	Nebeker	4,000.00	5,000.00	6,000.00	7,500.00	10,000.00
560	Tillman	Morgan	4,000.00	5,000.00	6,000.00	7,500.00	10,000.00
561	Tillman	Roberts	4,000.00	5,000.00	6,000.00	7,500.00	10,500.00
562	Bruce	Roberts	4,000.00	5,000.00	6,000.00	7,500.00	10,500.00
563.	Lyons	Roberts	4,000.00	5,000.00	6,000.00	7,500.00	10,000.00
564.	Vernon	Treat	4,000.00	5,000.00	6,000.00	7,500.00	11,000.00
565.	Napier	McClung	4,000.00	5,000.00	6,000.00	7,500.00	12,000.00

Value Backs

Face of Note 586. Washington Crossing the Delaware *at left; at right,* Prayer for Victory.

Back of Note 586.

"Second Charter Period" (Series of 1882)
Value Backs

No.	Signatures			
586.	Lyons Roberts	. . . .	Only two banks issued	Very Rare (7 Known)

"Third Charter Period" (Series of 1902)
First Issue: Series of 1902 with red seal

Face of Notes 664-666.
Facing bust of Secretary of the Treasury (1877-1881) and Secretary of State (1897-1898) John Sherman.

Back of Notes 664-666. Train and female af left; at right, man in ancient dress reclining, holding tools.

No.	Signatures		VG-8	F-12	VF-20	EF-40	Unc-63
664.	Lyons	Roberts	$4,000.00	$5,000.00	$5,600.00	$7,500.00	$12,500.00
665.	Lyons	Treat	4,000.00	5,000.00	5,600.00	7,500.00	12,500.00
666.	Vernon	Treat	4,000.00	5,000.00	5,600.00	7,500.00	12,500.00

"Third Charter Period" (Series of 1902)
Second Issue: Series of 1902 with blue seal and with "1902-1908" on back

Face of Notes 667-674a.
Bust of Secretary of the Treasury (1877-1881) and Secretary of State (1897-1898) John Sherman.

Back of Notes 667-674a.
Train and female af left; at right, man in ancient dress reclining, holding tools.

No.	Signatures		VG-8	F-12	VF-20	EF-40	Unc-63
667.	Lyons	Roberts	$1,100.00	$1,400.00	$1,750.00	$2,800.00	$5,000.00
668.	Lyons	Treat	1,100.00	1,400.00	1,750.00	2,800.00	5,000.00
669.	Vernon	Treat	1,100.00	1,400.00	1,750.00	2,800.00	5,000.00
670.	Vernon	McClung	1,100.00	1,400.00	1,750.00	2,800.00	5,000.00
671.	Napier	McClung	1,100.00	1,400.00	1,750.00	2,800.00	5,000.00
672.	Napier	Thompson	1,250.00	1,500.00	2,000.00	3,200.00	5,750.00
673.	Napier	Burke	1,100.00	1,400.00	1,750.00	2,800.00	5,000.00
674.	Parker	Burke	1,100.00	1,400.00	1,750.00	2,800.00	5,000.00
674a.	Teehee	Burke	1,200.00	1,500.00	1,750.00	2,800.00	5,000.00

"Third Charter Period" (Series of 1902)
Third Issue: Series of 1902 with blue seal and without "1902-1908" on back

Face of Notes 675-685a.
Facing bust of Secretary of the Treasury (1877-1881) and Secretary of State (1897-1898) John Sherman.

Back of Notes 675-685a. Train and female af left; at right, man in ancient dress reclining, holding tools.

No.	Signatures		VG-8	F-12	VF-20	EF-40	Unc-63
675.	Lyons	Roberts	$1,300.00	$1,450.00	$1,700.00	$2,300.00	$4,750.00
676.	Lyons	Treat	1,300.00	1,450.00	1,700.00	2,300.00	4,750.00
677.	Vernon	Treat	1,300.00	1,450.00	1,700.00	2,300.00	4,750.00
678.	Vernon	McClung	1,300.00	1,450.00	1,700.00	2,300.00	4,750.00
679.	Napier	McClung	1,300.00	1,450.00	1,700.00	2,300.00	4,750.00
679a.	Napier	Thompson	1,300.00	1,450.00	1,700.00	2,300.00	4,750.00
680.	Napier	Burke	1,300.00	1,450.00	1,700.00	2,300.00	4,750.00
681.	Parker	Burke	1,300.00	1,450.00	1,700.00	2,300.00	4,750.00
682.	Teehee	Burke	1,300.00	1,450.00	1,700.00	2,300.00	4,750.00
683.	Elliott	Burke	1,300.00	1,450.00	1,700.00	2,300.00	4,750.00
684.	Elhott	White	1,300.00	1,450.00	1,700.00	2,300.00	4,750.00
685.	Speelman	White	1,300.00	1,450.00	1,700.00	2,300.00	4,750.00
685a.	Woods	White	2,000.00	2,250.00	2,500.00	3,250.00	6,500.00

Gold Certificates
Face of 1188-1189a not shown, much like face of 1190-1197

Face of Notes 1188-1190. Bust of Senator and Governor (NY) Silas Wright.

Back of Notes 1188-1197. Eagle at right standing on shield.

Autographed countersignature by Thomas C. Acton, Assistant Treasurer, payable at New York.

No.	Series	Signatures		Seal	VG-8	F-12	VF-20	EF-40	Unc-63
1188.	1882	Bruce	Gilfillan	Brown	Rare	—	—	—	—
1189.	1882	Bruce	Gilfillan	Brown .... Extremely Rare	—	—	—	—	—

Engraved countersignature as above.

No.	Series	Signatures		Seal	VG-8	F-12	VF-20	EF-40	Unc-63
1189a.	1882 ...	Bruce	Gilfillan	Brown $10,000.00	$20,000.00	$35,000.00	Rare	—	

No.	Series	Signatures		Seal	VG-8	F-12	VF-20	EF-40	Unc-63
1190.	1882	Bruce	Wyman	Brown $14,000.00	$25,000	—	—	—	—
1191.	1882	Rosecrans	Hyatt	Large Red ....Extremely Rare	—	—	—	—	—
1192.	1882	Rosecrans	Huston	Large Brown 10,000.00	15,000.00	$25,000.00	$60,000.00	—	
1192a.	1882	Rosecrans	Huston	Small Red .... Unique	—	—	—	—	
1193.	1882	Lyons	Roberts	Small Red 750.00	1,300.00	2,500.00	$3,500.00	$6,000.00	
1194.	1882	Lyons	Treat	Small Red 850.00	1,500.00	3,500.00	4,000.00	6,500.00	
1195.	1882	Vernon	Treat	Small Red 950.00	1,600.00	3,000.00	4,500.00	7,000.00	
1196.	1882	Vernon	McClung	Small Red 850.00	1,500.00	2,500.00	4,000.00	6,500.00	
1197.	1882	Napier	McClung	Small Red 750.00	1,300.00	2,500.00	3,500.00	6,000.00	

*W*hen the time to sell comes, you want the highest price.
*P*eriod.

Len Glazer
Senior Numismatist
Ext. 390
Len@HeritageCurrency.com

Whether you are selling a few extra notes from your holdings, or a comprehensive collection built over decades, Heritage Currency Auctions of America has an auction venue that will maximize your profits. And our printed catalogs and online Permanent Auction Archives will memorialize your collection forever.

Heritage Currency Auctions of America is part of America's largest numismatic auction house, offering you worldwide bidder demand through our exclusive Interactive Internet program on our award-winning websites. There you will find 140,000+ fellow numismatists registered as bidder-members at HeritageCurrency. com and HeritageCoins.com.

Allen Mincho
Senior Numismatist
Ext. 327
AllenM@HeritageCurrency.com

When you consign with Heritage Currency Auctions of America, you will benefit from our decades of experience, our award-winning catalogs & catalogers, the world's finest numismatic mailing list, and proven marketing expertise. Our state-of-the-art digital photography has won praises from around the world, with full-color, enlargeable images of every single-note lot posted on the Internet. Bidders trust our catalog descriptions and our full-color images, spending nearly $200 million at auction with Heritage last year.

Dustin Johnston
Senior Numismatist
Ext.302
Dustin@HeritageCurrency.com

We thank our devoted clients for their past, present, and future patronage. We invite your consignments and bidding participation in our upcoming Signature Auctions. Let us bring your currency to the buyers around the world. To include your currency collection in one of our other upcoming auctions, please contact a Consignment Director today: 1-800-872-6467 Ext. 222 • 24-hour voicemail or visit our website at HeritageCurrency.com

HERITAGE
CURRENCY AUCTIONS OF AMERICA

3500 Maple Avenue, 17th Floor • Dallas, Texas 75219-3941
1-(800-872-6467) • 214-528-3500 • FAX: 214-443-8425 • e-mail:
Consign@HeritageCurrency.com

David Lisot
Senior Numismatist
Ext. 303
DavidL@HeritageCurrency.com

2275

National Gold Bank Notes

Face of Notes 1160-1161f. Washington Crossing the Delaware *at left; at right,* Prayer for Victory. *Similar to the First Charter Period National Bank Note of the same denomination (not shown).*

Back of Notes 1160-1161f. An array of contemporary United States gold coins. Similar to the other National Gold Bank Notes (not shown).

No.	Date	Name of Bank	City	VG-8	F-12
1160.	1870	First National Gold Bank	San Francisco	Extremely Rare	—
1160a.	1875	Series. First National Gold Bank	San Francisco	Unique	—
1161.	1874	Farmer's National Gold Bank	San Jose	Unique	—
1161a.	1872	National Gold Bank and Trust Company	San Francisco	Unknown	—
1161b.	1872	National Gold Bank of D.O. Mills and Co. ...	Sacramento	Unknown	—
1161c.	1873	First National Gold Bank	Stockton	Unknown	—
1161d.	1873	First National Gold Bank	Santa Barbara	Unknown	—
1161e.	1874	Series. First National Gold Bank	Petaluma	Unknown	—
1161f.	1873	Union National Gold Bank	Oakland	Unknown	—

Silver Certificates

Face of Notes 323-329. Bust of Secretary of State (1852-1855) Edward Everett. Large seal at top, "FIFTY" underneath on Series of 1878 (shown above); "L" below on Series of 1880.

Back of Notes 323-329. Countersigned; all notes with signatures of Scofield and Gilfillan and large red seal. The 1878 notes are without the legend "Series of 1878." All have engraved countersignatures except Notes 323 and 324a, which are autographed.

Silver Certificates

No.	Series	Countersigned By	Payable At		
323*.	1878	W.G. White or J.C. Hopper	New York	....	Unknown
324.	1878	T. Hillhouse	New York	....	Extremely Rare
324-a.	1878	R.M. Anthony	San Francisco		Unique
324-b*.	1878	A.U. Wyman	Washington, DC	....	Unknown
324-c.	1878	A.U. Wyman	Washington, DC	....	Extremely Rare

As above, but no countersigned signature.

No.	Series	Signatures		Seal	VG-8	F-12	VF-20	EF-40	Unc-63
325.	1880	Scofield	Gilfillan	Large Brown, rays	Unique	—	—	—	—
326.	1880	Bruce	Gilfillan	Large Brown, rays	$17,500.00	$20,000.00	$35,000.00	$55,000.00	Rare
327.	1880	Bruce	Wyman	Large Brown, rays	20,000.00	25,000.00	40,000.00	60,000.00	Rare

As above, with large seal in center, no "L" or " Fifty."

No.	Series	Signatures		Seal	VG-8	F-12	VF-20	EF-40	Unc-63
328.	1880	Rosecrans	Huston	Large Brown, spikes	$7,500.00	$10,000.00	$20,000.00	$35,000.00	$65,000.00

As above, with small seal at right center.

No.	Series	Signatures		Seal	VG-8	F-12	VF-20	EF-40	Unc-63
329.	1880	Rosecrans	Nebeker	Small Red	$7,000.00	$10,000.00	$20,000.00	$35,000.00	$65,000.00

Face of Notes 330-335. Bust of Secretary of State (1852-1855) Edward Everett.

Back of Notes 330-335.

LARGE-SIZE FIFTY DOLLAR NOTES

Silver Certificates

No.	Series	Signatures		Seal	VG-8	F-12	VF-20	EF-40	Unc-63
330.	1891.....	Rosecrans	Nebeker	Small Red ...	$3,750.00	$7,500.00	$10,000.00	$15,000.00	—
331.	1891.....	Tillman	Morgan	Small Red ...	2,000.00	3,350.00	4,500.00	7,500.00	—
332.	1891	Bruce	Roberts	Small Red ...	2,000.00	3,350.00	4,500.00	7,500.00	—
333.	1891	Lyons	Roberts	Small Red ...	1,750.00	2,750.00	4,000.00	6,000.00	—
334.	1891	Vernon	Treat	Small Red ...	1,600.00	2,500.00	3,750.00	5,750.00	$17,000.00
335.	1891	Parker	Burke	Blue	1,450.00	2,400.00	3,400.00	5,250.00	12,000.00

Treasury or Coin Notes

Face of Note 376. Profile bust of Secretary of State (1860-1869) William H. Seward.

Back of Note 376.

No.	Series	Signatures		Seal	VG-8	F-12	VF-20	EF-40	Unc-63
376.	1891	Rosecrans	Nebeker	Small Red	$16,000.00	$37,500.00	Rare	—	—

Gold Certificates

Face of Notes 1198-1200a. Bust of Ulysses S. Grant.

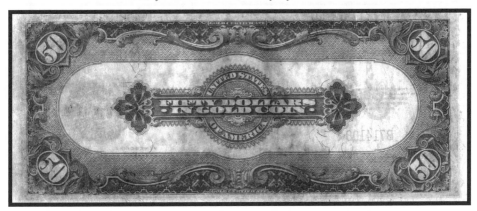

Back of Notes 1198-1200a.

No.	Series	Signatures		Seal	VG-8	F-12	VF-20	EF-40	Unc-63
1198.	1913 ...	Parker	Burke	Gold	$600.00	$700.00	$1,200.00	$1,650.00	$5,500.00
1199.	1913 ...	Teehee	Burke	Gold	650.00	750.00	1,100.00	1,450.00	4,500.00
1200.	1922 ...	Speelman	White	Gold	650.00	750.00	1,100.00	1,450.00	4,500.00
1200a.	1922 ...	Speelman	White	Gold, Small Serial Numbers	600.00	700.00	950.00	1,350.00	3,300.00

Federal Reserve Notes

Face of Notes 1012-1071. Bust of Ulysses S. Grant in center.

Back of Notes 1012-1071. Female representing Panama standing in center between the Atlantic and Pacific Oceans.

A. Series of 1914 with red seal and signatures of Burke and McAdoo
No. Issuing Bank

No.	Issuing Bank	VG-8	F-12	VF-20	EF-40	Unc-63
1012A.	Boston	$2,400.00	$4,500.00	$7,500.00	$12,000.00	—
1012B.	Boston	1,500.00	3,000.00	5,000.00	8,500.00	—
1013A.	New York	950.00	1,400.00	2,000.00	2,750.00	—
1013B.	New York	950.00	1,400.00	2,000.00	2,750.00	$5,750.00
1014A.	Philadelphia	950.00	1,400.00	2,000.00	2,750.00	5,750.00
1014B.	Philadelphia	950.00	1,400.00	2,000.00	2,750.00	—
1015A.	Cleveland	1,500.00	3,000.00	5,000.00	8,500.00	11,000.00
1015B.	Cleveland	1,500.00	3,000.00	5,000.00	7,500.00	11,000.00
1016A	Richmond	1,500.00	3,000.00	5,000.00	7,500.00	—
1016B.	Richmond	950.00	1,400.00	2,000.00	2,750.00	—
1017A.	Atlanta	950.00	1,800.00	4,000.00	—	—
1018A.	Chicago	1,500.00	3,000.00	5,000.00	8,500.00	—
1018B.	Chicago	950.00	1,400.00	2,000.00	2,750.00	—
1019A.	St. Louis	950.00	1,400.00	2,000.00	—	—
1019B.	St. Louis	950.00	1,400.00	2,750.00	4,750.00	9,000.00
1020A.	Minneapolis	1,500.00	3,000.00	5,000.00	7,500.00	—
1020B.	Mineapolis	950.00	1,400.00	2,000.00	2,750.00	—
1021A.	Kansas City	2,400.00	4,500.00	7,500.00	12,000.00	—
1021B.	Kansas City	2,400.00	4,500.00	7,500.00	12,000.00	—
1022A.	Dallas	950.00	1,400.00	2,000.00	2,750.00	—
1023A.	San Francisco	2,400.00	4,500.00	7,500.00	12,000.00	—
1023B.	San Francisco	950.00	1,400.00	2,000.00	2,750.00	8,500.00

Federal Reserve Notes

B. Series of 1914 with blue seal

No.	Issuing Bank	Signatures		VG-8	F-12	VF-20	EF-40	Unc-63
1024.	Boston	Burke	McAdoo	$220.00	$300.00	$500.00	$750.00	—
1025.	Boston	Burke	Glass	220.00	300.00	500.00	750.00	$2,000.00
1026.	Boston	Burke	Houston	450.00	750.00	1,000.00	2,250.00	—
1027.	Boston	White	Mellon	None Recorded	—	—	—	—
1028.	New York	Burke	McAdoo	200.00	275.00	425.00	575.00	1,500.00
1029.	New York	Burke	Glass	350.00	500.00	750.00	1,500.00	3,000.00
1030.	New York	Burke	Houston	200.00	275.00	425.00	575.00	1,500.00
1031A.	New York	White	Mellon	220.00	300.00	500.00	750.00	—
1031B.	New York	White	Mellon	350.00	500.00	750.00	1,500.00	—
1032.	Philadelphia	Burke	McAdoo	220.00	300.00	500.00	750.00	2,000.00
1033.	Philadelphia	Burke	Glass	350.00	500.00	750.00	1,500.00	—
1034.	Philadelphia	Burke	Houston	200.00	275.00	425.00	575.00	1,500.00
1035.	Philadelphia	White	Mellon	200.00	275.00	425.00	575.00	1,500.00
1036.	Cleveland	Burke	McAdoo	200.00	275.00	425.00	575.00	1,500.00
1037.	Cleveland	Burke	Glass	350.00	500.00	950.00	—	—
1038.	Cleveland	Burke	Houston	200.00	275.00	425.00	575.00	1,500.00
1039A.	Cleveland	White	Mellon	200.00	275.00	425.00	575.00	1,500.00
1039B.	Cleveland	White	Mellon	200.00	275.00	425.00	575.00	1,500.00
1040.	Richmond	Burke	McAdoo	220.00	300.00	500.00	750.00	2,000.00
1041.	Richmond	Burke	Glass	450.00	750.00	1,000.00	2,250.00	—
1042	Richmond	Burke	Houston	220.00	300.00	500.00	750.00	2,000.00
1043	Richmond	White	Mellon	220.00	300.00	500.00	750.00	2,500.00
1044	Atlanta	Burke	McAdoo	220.00	300.00	500.00	750.00	2,000.00
1045	Atlanta	Burke	Glass	450.00	900.00	1,750.00	—	—
1046.	Atlanta	Burke	Houston	200.00	275.00	425.00	575.00	1,500.00
1047.	Atlanta	White	Mellon	350.00	500.00	750.00	1,500.00	3,000.00
1048.	Chicago	Burke	McAdoo	200.00	275.00	425.00	575.00	1,500.00
1049.	Chicago	Burke	Glass	220.00	300.00	500.00	750.00	2,000.00
1050.	Chicago	Burke	Houston	220.00	300.00	500.00	750.00	—
1051.	Chicago	White	Mellon	220.00	300.00	500.00	750.00	2,000.00
1052.	St. Louis	Burke	McAdoo	220.00	300.00	500.00	750.00	2,000.00
1053.	St. Louis	Burke	Glass	220.00	300.00	500.00	750.00	2,000.00
1054.	St. Louis	Burke	Houston	220.00	300.00	500.00	750.00	2,000.00
1055.	St. Louis	White	Mellon	None Reported	—	—	—	—
1056.	Minneapolis	Burke	McAdoo	220.00	300.00	500.00	750.00	3,500.00
1057.	Minneapolis	Burke	Glass	None Printed	—	—	—	—
1058.	Minneapolis	Burke	Houston	400.00	600.00	1,200.00	2,000.00	—
1059.	Minneapolis	White	Mellon	1,250.00	2,000.00	3,500.00	—	—
1060.	Kansas City	Burke	McAdoo	220.00	300.00	500.00	750.00	—
1061.	Kansas City	Burke	Glass	None Printed	—	—	—	—
1062.	Kansas City	Burke	Houston	None Printed	—	—	—	—
1063.	Kansas City	White	Mellon	—	—	—	5,000.00	—
1064.	Dallas	Burke	McAdoo	250.00	325.00	550.00	850.00	2,250.00
1065.	Dallas	Burke	Glass	None Reported	—	—	—	—
1066.	Dallas	Burke	Houston	Unique	—	—	—	—
1067.	Dallas	White	Mellon	None Reported	—	—	—	—
1068.	San Francisco	Burke	McAdoo	200.00	275.00	425.00	575.00	—
1069.	San Francisco	Burke	Glass	None Printed	—	—	—	—
1070.	San Francisco	Burke	Houston	220.00	300.00	500.00	750.00	—
1071.	San Francisco	White	Mellon	225.00	300.00	500.00	750.00	—

Federal Reserve Bank Notes

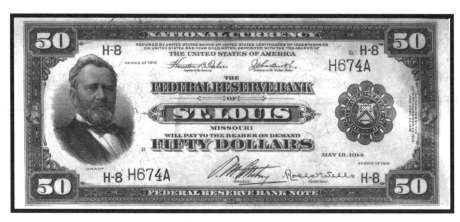

Face of Note 831. Bust of Ulysses S. Grant at left.

Back of Note 831. Female representing Panama standing in center between the Atlantic and Pacific Oceans.

No.	Issuing Bank	Series	Treasury Signatures	Bank Signatures	VG-8	F-12	VF-20	EF-40	Unc-63
831.	St. Louis	1918	Teehee Burke	Attebery Wells	$3,250.00	$6,000.00	$9,000.00	$12,500.00	$20,000.00

This is the only bank that issued a $50 Federal Reserve Bank Note.

National Bank Notes (Brown Seal)

Face of Note 1803.

Back of Note 1803.

No.		VG-8	F-12	VF-20	EF-40	Unc-63
1803-1.	Type 1	$350.00	$375.00	$395.00	$425.00	$500.00
1803-2.	Type 2	350.00	425.00	430.00	450.00	550.00

Gold Certificates (Gold Seal)

Face of Note 2404.

Back of Note 2404.

No.	Denomination	Series	Signatures	Quanity Printed	VG-8	F-12	VF-20	EF-40	Unc-63
2404.	Fifty Dollars	1928	Woods Mellon	5,520,000	$200.00	$250.00	$400.00	$600.00	$1,500.00
2404*.	Fifty Dollars	1928	Woods Mellon		1,500.00	2,200.00	3,250.00	9,500.00	12,500.00

SMALL-SIZE FIFTY DOLLAR NOTES

Federal Reserve Bank Notes (Brown Seal)

Face of Note 1880.

Back of Note 1880.

No.	Issuing Bank	Quantity Printed	VG-8	F-12	VF-20	EF-40	Unc-63
1880-B.	New York	636,000	$90.00	$95.00	$100.00	$120.00	$175.00
1880-D.	Cleveland	684,000	90.00	95.00	100.00	120.00	175.00
1880-G.	Chicago	300,000	90.00	95.00	100.00	120.00	175.00
1880-I.	Minneapolis	132,000	90.00	95.00	100.00	120.00	175.00
1880-J.	Kansas City	276,000	90.00	95.00	100.00	120.00	175.00
1880-K.	Dallas	168,000	150.00	175.00	250.00	300.00	450.00
1880-L.	San Francisco	576,000	125.00	150.00	200.00	250.00	400.00
1880*.	Most Common Districts		350.00	500.00	650.00	900.00	2,000.00

Federal Reserve Notes (Green Seal)

Face of Notes 2100-2101.

Back of Notes 2100-2101.

Federal Reserve Notes (Green Seal)
Series of 1928
Signatures of Woods and Mellon

No.	Issuing Bank	Quantity Printed	VG-8	F-12	VF-20	EF-40	Unc-63
2100-A.	Boston	265,200	$80.00	$90.00	$100.00	$250.00	$1,500.00
2100-A*.	Boston		125.00	250.00	350.00	600.00	1,800.00
2100-B.	New York	1,351,800	75.00	80.00	100.00	175.00	1,000.00
2100-B*.	New York		100.00	115.00	150.00	250.00	1,250.00
2100-C.	Philadelphia	997,056	80.00	90.00	100.00	225.00	1,300.00
2100-C*	Philadelphia		125.00	250.00	350.00	600.00	1,800.00
2100-D.	Cleveland	1,161,900	75.00	80.00	100.00	175.00	1,000.00
2100-D*.	Cleveland		125.00	250.00	350.00	600.00	1,800.00
2100-E.	Richmond	539,400	75.00	80.00	100.00	175.00	1,350.00
2100-E*.	Richmond		125.00	250.00	350.00	600.00	1,800.00
2100-F.	Atlanta	538,800	80.00	90.00	100.00	225.00	1,350.00
2100-F*.	Atlanta		125.00	250.00	350.00	600.00	1,800.00
2100-G.	Chicago	1,348,620	75.00	80.00	100.00	175.00	1,000.00
2100-G*.	Chicago		100.00	115.00	150.00	250.00	1,250.00
2100-H.	St. Louis	627,300	80.00	90.00	100.00	275.00	1,500.00
2100-H*.	St. Louis		125.00	250.00	350.00	600.00	1,800.00
2100-I.	Minneapolis	106,200	125.00	250.00	350.00	600.00	1,800.00
2100-I*.	Minneapolis		225.00	250.00	350.00	600.00	1,800.00
2100-J.	Kansas City	252,600	110.00	225.00	325.00	550.00	1,700.00
2100-J*.	Kansas City		125.00	250.00	350.00	600.00	1,800.00
2100-K.	Dallas	109,920	125.00	275.00	375.00	700.00	1,850.00
2100-K*.	Dallas		125.00	250.00	350.00	600.00	1,800.00
2100-L.	San Francisco	447,600	80.00	90.00	100.00	225.00	1,350.00
2100-L*.	San Francisco		125.00	250.00	350.00	600.00	1,800.00

Series of 1928-A
Signatures of Woods and Mellon

No.	Issuing Bank	Quantity Printed	VG-8	F-12	VF-20	Unc-63
2101-A.	Boston	1,834,989	$75.00	$80.00	$85.00	$425.00
2101-B.	New York	3,392,328	75.00	80.00	85.00	425.00
2101-C.	Philadelphia	3,078,944	75.00	80.00	85.00	425.00
2101-D.	Cleveland	2,453,364	75.00	80.00	85.00	425.00
2101-E.	Richmond	1,516,500	75.00	80.00	85.00	425.00
2101-F.	Atlanta	338,400	80.00	85.00	100.00	550.00
2101-G.	Chicago	5,263,956	75.00	80.00	85.00	425.00
2101-H.	St. Louis	880,500	75.00	80.00	85.00	425.00
2101-I.	Minneapolis	780,240	75.00	80.00	85.00	425.00
2101-J.	Kansas City	791,604	75.00	80.00	85.00	425.00
2101-K.	Dallas	701,496	75.00	80.00	85.00	425.00
2101-L.	San Francisco	1,522,620	75.00	80.00	85.00	425.00
2101*.	No Star Notes Known		—	—	—	—

Federal Reserve Notes (Green Seal)

Face of Notes 2102-2106.

Back of Notes 2102-2106.

Series of 1934
Signatures of Julian and Morgenthau

The two shades of green seals also exist in this series. The lighter variety is slightly scarcer, with star notes much more scarce.

No.	Issuing Bank	Quantity Printed	VG-8	F-12	VF-20	EF-40	Unc-63
2102-A.	Boston	2,729,400	$65.00	$70.00	$75.00	$85.00	$225.00
2102-A*.	Boston		100.00	110.00	125.00	150.00	600.00
2102-B.	New York	17,894,676	65.00	70.00	75.00	85.00	225.00
2102-B*.	New York		100.00	110.00	125.00	150.00	600.00
2102-C.	Philadelphia	5,833,200	65.00	70.00	75.00	85.00	225.00
2102-C*.	Philadelphia		100.00	110.00	125.00	150.00	600.00
2102-D.	Cleveland	8,817,720	65.00	70.00	75.00	85.00	225.00
2102-D*.	Cleveland		100.00	110.00	125.00	150.00	600.00
2102-E.	Richmond	4,826,628	65.00	70.00	75.00	85.00	225.00
2102-E*.	Richmond		100.00	125.00	150.00	175.00	650.00
2102-F.	Atlanta	3,069,348	65.00	70.00	75.00	85.00	225.00
2102-F*.	Atlanta		100.00	110.00	125.00	150.00	600.00
2102-G.	Chicago	8,675,940	65.00	70.00	75.00	85.00	225.00
2102-G*.	Chicago		100.00	110.00	125.00	150.00	600.00
2102-H.	St. Louis	1,497,144	65.00	70.00	75.00	85.00	225.00
2102-H*.	St. Louis		100.00	110.00	125.00	150.00	650.00
2102-I.	Minneapolis	539,700	65.00	70.00	75.00	85.00	225.00
2102-I*	.Minneapolis		100.00	110.00	175.00	225.00	675.00
2102-J.	Kansas City	1,133,520	65.00	70.00	75.00	85.00	225.00
2102-J*.	Kansas City		100.00	110.00	125.00	150.00	600.00
2102-K.	Dallas	1,194,876	65.00	70.00	75.00	85.00	225.00
2102-K*.	Dallas		100.00	110.00	125.00	150.00	600.00
2102-L.	San Francisco	8,101,200	65.00	70.00	75.00	85.00	225.00

Federal Reserve Notes (Green Seal)

Series of 1934-A
Signatures of Julian and Morgenthau

No.	Issuing Bank	Quantity Printed	VG-8	F-12	VF-20	EF-40	Unc-63
2103-A.	Boston	406,200	$65.00	$70.00	$75.00	$90.00	$300.00
2103-A*.	Boston		100.00	125.00	175.00	225.00	900.00
2103-B.	New York	4,710,648	65.00	70.00	75.00	90.00	275.00
2103-B*.	New York		100.00	125.00	150.00	200.00	800.00
2103-D.	Cleveland	864,168	65.00	70.00	75.00	90.00	300.00
2103-D*.	Cleveland		100.00	125.00	175.00	225.00	900.00
2103-E.	Richmond	2,235,372	65.00	70.00	75.00	90.00	275.00
2103-E*.	Richmond		100.00	125.00	175.00	225.00	900.00
2103-F.	Atlanta	416,100	60.00	65.00	70.00	90.00	300.00
2103-F*.	Atlanta		100.00	125.00	175.00	225.00	900.00
2103-G.	Chicago	1,014,600	65.00	70.00	75.00	90.00	300.00
2103-G*.	Chicago		100.00	125.00	175.00	225.00	900.00
2103-H.	St. Louis	361,944	65.00	70.00	75.00	90.00	300.00
2103-H*.	St. Louis		100.00	125.00	175.00	225.00	900.00
2103-I.	Minneapolis	93,300	65.00	70.00	85.00	90.00	400.00
2103-I*.	Minneapolis		100.00	125.00	175.00	225.00	900.00
2103-J.	Kansas City	189,300	65.00	70.00	80.00	90.00	350.00
2103-J*.	Kansas City		100.00	125.00	175.00	225.00	900.00
2103-K.	Dallas	266,700	65.00	70.00	80.00	90.00	350.00
2103-K*.	Dallas		100.00	125.00	175.00	225.00	900.00
2103-L.	San Francisco	162,000	65.00	70.00	75.00	90.00	325.00
2103-L*.	San Francisco		100.00	125.00	175.00	225.00	900.00

Series of 1934-B
Signatures of Julian and Vinson

No.	Issuing Bank	Quantity Printed	VG-8	F-12	VF-20	EF-40	Unc-63
2104-C.	Philadelphia	509,100				$80.00	$350.00
2104-C*.	Philadelphia					900.00	3,000.00
2104-D.	Cleveland	359,100				80.00	350.00
2104-D*.	Cleveland					900.00	3,000.00
2104-E.	Richmond	596,700				80.00	350.00
2104-E*.	Richmond					900.00	3,000.00
2104-F.	Atlanta	416,720				80.00	350.00
2104-G.	Chicago	306,000				80.00	350.00
2104-H.	St. Louis	306,000				80.00	350.00
2104-I.	Minneapolis	120,000				100.00	500.00
2104-J.	Kansas City	221,340				90.00	400.00
2104-J*.	Kansas City	2,500.00				900.00	3,000.00
2104-K.	Dallas	120,108				100.00	500.00
2104-L.	San Francisco	441,000				80.00	350.00

Series of 1934-C
Signatures of Julian and Snyder

No.	Issuing Bank	Quantity Printed	VG-8	F-12	VF-20	EF-40	Unc-63
2105-A.	Boston	117,600	$60.00	$65.00	$75.00	$90.00	$250.00
2105-B.	New York	1,556,400	60.00	65.00	75.00	90.00	200.00
2105-B*.	New York		125.00	200.00	450.00	700.00	1,500.00
2105-C.	Philadelphia	107,283	65.00	70.00	75.00	90.00	200.00
2105-C*.	Philadelphia		125.00	200.00	450.00	700.00	1,500.00
2105-D.	Cleveland	374,400	60.00	65.00	75.00	90.00	200.00
2105-D*.	Cleveland		125.00	200.00	450.00	700.00	1,500.00
2105-E.	Richmond	1,821,960	60.00	65.00	75.00	90.00	250.00
2105-E*.	Richmond		125.00	200.00	450.00	700.00	1,500.00
2105-F.	Atlanta	107,640	60.00	65.00	75.00	90.00	200.00
2105-G.	Chicago	294,432	60.00	65.00	75.00	90.00	225.00
2105-G*.	Chicago		125.00	200.00	450.00	700.00	1,500.00
2105-H.	St. Louis	535,200	65.00	70.00	75.00	90.00	200.00
2105-I.	Minneapolis	118,800	65.00	70.00	75.00	90.00	225.00
2105-I.	Minneapolis		125.00	200.00	450.00	700.00	1,500.00
2105-J*.	Kansas City	303,600	60.00	65.00	75.00	90.00	200.00
2105-K.	Dallas	429,900	60.00	65.00	75.00	90.00	200.00
2105-K*.	Dallas		125.00	200.00	450.00	700.00	1,500.00

SMALL-SIZE FIFTY DOLLAR NOTES

Federal Reserve Notes (Green Seal)

Series of 1934-D
Signatures of Clark and Snyder

No.	Issuing Bank	Quantity Printed	VG-8	F-12	VF-20	EF-40	Unc-63
2106-A.	Boston	279,600	$60.00	$65.00	$75.00	$100.00	$250.00
2106-A*.	Boston		350.00	700.00	950.00	1,250.00	3,000.00
2106-B.	New York	898,776	60.00	65.00	75.00	100.00	200.00
2106-B*.	New York		350.00	700.00	950.00	1,250.00	3,000.00
2106-C.	Philadelphia	699,000	60.00	65.00	75.00	100.00	200.00
2106-C*.	Philadelphia		350.00	700.00	950.00	1,250.00	3,000.00
2106-E.	Richmond	156,000	60.00	65.00	75.00	100.00	250.00
2106-F.	Atlanta	216,000	60.00	65.00	75.00	125.00	250.00
2106-F*.	Atlanta		350.00	700.00	950.00	1,250.00	3,000.00
2106-G.	Chicago	494,016	60.00	65.00	75.00	125.00	200.00
2106-G*.	Chicago		350.00	700.00	950.00	1,250.00	3,000.00
2106-I.	Minneapolis		Rare	—	—	—	—
2106-K.	Dallas	103,200	60.00	65.00	75.00	125.00	250.00
2102-L*.	San Francisco						

Face of Notes 2107-2112.

Back of Notes 2107-2112.

Series of 1950
Signatures of Clark and Snyder

No.	Issuing Bank	Quantity Printed	VG-8	F-12	VF-20	EF-40	Unc-63
2107-A.	Boston	1,248,000	$60.00	$65.00	$75.00	$125.00	$300.00
2107-A*.	Boston		100.00	125.00	150.00	250.00	775.00
2107-B.	New York	10,236,000	60.00	65.00	75.00	125.00	300.00
2107-B*.	New York		100.00	125.00	150.00	250.00	675.00
2107-C.	Philadelphia	2,352,000	60.00	65.00	95.00	125.00	300.00
2107-C*.	Philadelphia		100.00	125.00	150.00	250.00	775.00
2107-D.	Cleveland	6,180,000	60.00	65.00	75.00	125.00	300.00
2107-D*.	Cleveland		100.00	125.00	150.00	250.00	775.00
2107-E.	Richmond	5,064,000	60.00	65.00	75.00	125.00	300.00
2107-E*.	Richmond		100.00	125.00	150.00	250.00	775.00
2107-F.	Atlanta	1,812,000	60.00	65.00	75.00	125.00	300.00
2107-F*.	Atlanta		100.00	125.00	150.00	250.00	775.00
2107-G.	Chicago	4,212,000	60.00	65.00	75.00	125.00	300.00
2107-G*.	Chicago		100.00	125.00	150.00	250.00	775.00

Federal Reserve Notes (Green Seal)

No.	Issuing Bank	Quantity Printed	VG-8	F-12	VF-20	EF-40	Unc-63
2107-H.	St. Louis	892,000	$60.00	$65.00	$75.00	$125.00	$300.00
2107-H*.	St. Louis		100.00	125.00	150.00	250.00	725.00
2107-I.	Minneapolis	384,000	65.00	70.00	95.00	150.00	500.00
2107-I*.	Minneapolis		110.00	150.00	200.00	500.00	1,250.00
2107-J.	Kansas City	696,000	60.00	65.00	75.00	125.00	300.00
2107-J*	Kansas City		110.00	150.00	200.00	500.00	1,250.00
2107-K.	Dallas	1,100,000	60.00	65.00	75.00	125.00	300.00
2107-K*.	Dallas		100.00	125.00	150.00	250.00	775.00
2107-L.	San Francisco	3,996,000	60.00	65.00	75.00	150.00	300.00
2107-L*.	San Francisco		100.00	125.00	150.00	250.00	775.00

Series of 1950-A
Signatures of Priest and Humphrey

No.	Issuing Bank	Quantity Printed	VG-8	F-12	VF-20	EF-40	Unc-63
2108-A.	Boston	720,000	$60.00	$65.00	$75.00	$100.00	$200.00
2108-A*.	Boston		70.00	80.00	100.00	200.00	550.00
2108-B.	New York	6,495,000	60.00	65.00	75.00	100.00	200.00
2108-B*.	New York		70.00	80.00	100.00	200.00	550.00
2108-C.	Philadelphia	1,728,000	60.00	75.00	85.00	100.00	200.00
2108-C*.	Philadelphia		70.00	80.00	100.00	200.00	550.00
2108-D.	Cleveland	1,872,000	60.00	65.00	75.00	100.00	200.00
2108-D*.	Cleveland		70.00	80.00	100.00	200.00	550.00
2108-E.	Richmond	2,016,000	60.00	65.00	75.00	100.00	200.00
2108-E*.	Richmond		70.00	80.00	100.00	200.00	550.00
2108-F.	Atlanta	288,000	60.00	65.00	75.00	100.00	200.00
2108-F*.	Atlanta		70.00	80.00	100.00	200.00	550.00
2108-G.	Chicago	2,016,000	60.00	65.00	75.00	100.00	200.00
2108-G*.	Chicago		70.00	80.00	100.00	200.00	550.00
2108-H.	St. Louis	576,000	60.00	65.00	75.00	100.00	200.00
2108-H*.	St. Louis		70.00	80.00	100.00	200.00	550.00
2108-J.	Kansas City	144,000	60.00	70.00	85.00	110.00	300.00
2108-J*.	Kansas City		70.00	80.00	100.00	200.00	550.00
2108-K.	Dallas	864,000	60.00	65.00	75.00	100.00	200.00
2108-K*.	Dallas		70.00	80.00	100.00	200.00	550.00
2108-L.	San Francisco	576,000	60.00	65.00	75.00	100.00	200.00
2108-L*.	San Francisco		70.00	80.00	100.00	200.00	550.00

Series of 1950-B
Signatures of Priest and Anderson

No.	Issuing Bank	Quantity Printed	VG-8	F-12	VF-20	EF-40	Unc-63
2109-A.	Boston	864,000	$60.00	$65.00	$70.00	$90.00	$200.00
2109-A*.	Boston		75.00	80.00	100.00	200.00	550.00
2109-B.	New York	8,352,000	60.00	70.00	85.00	90.00	200.00
2109-B*.	New York		75.00	80.00	100.00	200.00	550.00
2109-C.	Philadelphia	2,592,000	70.00	80.00	85.00	90.00	200.00
2109-C*	Philadelphia		75.00	80.00	100.00	200.00	550.00
2109-D.	Cleveland	1,728,000	70.00	75.00	80.00	90.00	200.00
2109-D*.	Cleveland		75.00	80.00	100.00	200.00	550.00
2109-E.	Richmond	1,584,000	60.00	65.00	70.00	90.00	200.00
2109-E*.	Richmond		75.00	80.00	100.00	200.00	550.00
2109-G.	Chicago	4,320,000	60.00	65.00	70.00	90.00	200.00
2109-G*.	Chicago		75.00	80.00	100.00	200.00	550.00
2109-H.	St. Louis	576,000	60.00	65.00	70.00	90.00	200.00
2109-H*.	St. Louis		75.00	80.00	100.00	200.00	550.00
2109-J.	Kansas City	1,008,000	60.00	65.00	70.00	90.00	200.00
2109-J*	Kansas City		75.00	80.00	100.00	200.00	550.00
2109-K.	Dallas	1,008,000	60.00	65.00	70.00	90.00	200.00
2109-K*.	Dallas		75.00	80.00	100.00	200.00	550.00
2109-L.	San Francisco	1,872,000	60.00	65.00	70.00	90.00	200.00
2109-L*.	San Francisco		75.00	80.00	100.00	200.00	550.00

SMALL-SIZE FIFTY DOLLAR NOTES

Federal Reserve Notes (Green Seal)

Series of 1950-C
Signatures of Smith and Dillon

No.	Issuing Bank	Quantity Printed	VF-20	EF-40	Unc-63
2110-A.	Boston	720,000	$70.00	$100.00	$200.00
2110-A*.	Boston		100.00	125.00	550.00
2110-B.	New York	5,328,000	70.00	100.00	200.00
2110-B*.	New York		100.00	125.00	550.00
2110-C.	Philadelphia	1,296,000	70.00	100.00	200.00
2110-C*.	Philadelphia		100.00	125.00	550.00
2110-D.	Cleveland	1,296,000	70.00	100.00	200.00
2110-D*.	Cleveland		100.00	125.00	550.00
2110-E.	Richmond	1,296,000	70.00	100.00	200.00
2110-E*.	Richmond		100.00	125.00	550.00
2110-G.	Chicago	1,728,000	70.00	100.00	200.00
2110-G*.	Chicago		100.00	125.00	550.00
2110-H.	St. Louis	576,000	70.00	100.00	200.00
2110-H*.	St. Louis		100.00	125.00	550.00
2110-I.	Minneapolis	144,000	70.00	100.00	200.00
2110-I*.	Minneapolis		125.00	150.00	750.00
2110-J.	Kansas City	432,000	70.00	100.00	200.00
2110-J*.	Kansas City		100.00	125.00	550.00
2110-K.	Dallas	720,000	70.00	100.00	200.00
2110-K*.	Dallas		100.00	125.00	550.00
2110-L.	San Francisco	1,152,000	70.00	100.00	200.00
2110-L*.	San Francisco		100.00	125.00	550.00

Series of 1950-D
Signatures of Granahan and Dillon

No.	Issuing Bank	Quantity Printed	VF-20	EF-40	Unc-63
2111-A.	Boston	1,728,000	$70.00	$100.00	$200.00
2111-A*.	Boston		100.00	150.00	550.00
2111-B.	New York	7,200,000	70.00	100.00	200.00
2111-B*.	New York		100.00	150.00	550.00
2111-C.	Philadelphia	2,736,000	70.00	100.00	200.00
2111-C*.	Philadelphia		100.00	150.00	550.00
2111-D.	Cleveland	2,8125,000	70.00	100.00	200.00
2111-D*.	Cleveland		100.00	150.00	550.00
2111-E.	Richmond	2,616,000	70.00	100.00	200.00
2111-E*	Richmond		100.00	150.00	550.00
2111-F.	Atlanta	576,000	75.00	125.00	250.00
2111-F*.	Atlanta		125.00	175.00	700.00
2111-G.	Chicago	4,176,000	70.00	100.00	200.00
2111-G*.	Chicago		100.00	150.00	550.00
2111-H.	St. Louis	1,440,000	70.00	100.00	200.00
2111-H*.	St. Louis		100.00	150.00	550.00
2111-I.	Minneapolis	288,000	75.00	125.00	275.00
2111-I*	Minneapolis		125.00	175.00	700.00
2111-J.	Kansas City	720,000	75.00	110.00	250.00
2111-J*	Kansas City		125.00	175.00	700.00
2111-K.	Dallas	1,296,000	70.00	100.00	200.00
2111-K*.	Dallas		100.00	150.00	550.00
2111-L.	San Francisco	2,160,000	70.00	100.00	200.00
2111-L*.	San Francisco		100.00	150.00	550.00

Series of 1950-E
Signatures of Granahan and Fowler

No.	Issuing Bank	Quantity Printed	VF-20	EF-40	Unc-63
2112-B.	New York	3,024,000	$125.00	$175.00	$600.00
2112-B.	New York		275.00	350.00	1,000.00
2112-G.	Chicago	1,008,000	150.00	200.00	800.00
2112-G.	Chicago		400.00	600.00	2,250.00
2112-L.	San Francisco	1,296,000	175.00	225.00	750.00
2112-L*.	San Francisco		300.00	500.00	1,500.00

Federal Reserve Notes (Green Seal)

Face of Notes 2113-2125.

Back of Notes 2113-2125.

Series of 1963-A
Signatures of Granahan and Fowler

No.	Issuing Bank	Quantity Printed	VF-20	EF-40	Unc-63
2113-A.	Boston	1,536,000			$200.00
2113-A*.	Boston	320,000	$125.00	$150.00	500.00
2113-B.	New York	11,008,000			175.00
2113-B*.	New York	1,408,000	100.00	125.00	400.00
2113-C.	Philadelphia	3,328,000			200.00
2113-C*.	Philadelphia	704,000	100.00	125.00	400.00
2113-D.	Cleveland	3,584,000			200.00
2113-D*.	Cleveland	256,000	125.00	150.00	500.00
2113-E.	Richmond	3,072,000			200.00
2113-E*.	Richmond	704,000	100.00	125.00	400.00
2113-F.	Atlanta	768,000			200.00
2113-F*.	Atlanta	384,000	125.00	150.00	500.00
2113-G.	Chicago	6,912,000			200.00
2113-G*.	Chicago	768,000	100.00	125.00	400.00
2113-H.	St. Louis	512,000			200.00
2113-H*.	St. Louis	128,000	175.00	225.00	600.00
2113-I.	Minneapolis	512,000			200.00
2113-I*.	Minneapolis	128,000	175.00	225.00	600.00
2113-J.	Kansas City	512,000			200.00
2113-J*	Kansas City	64,000	225.00	300.00	900.00
2113-K.	Dallas	1,536,000			200.00
2113-K*.	Dallas	128,000	175.00	225.00	600.00
2113-L.	San Francisco	4,352,000			200.00
2113-L*.	San Francisco	704,000	125.00	150.00	500.00

SMALL-SIZE FIFTY DOLLAR NOTES

Federal Reserve Notes (Green Seal)

Series of 1969
Signatures of Elston and Kennedy. With new Treasury seal

No.	Issuing Bank	Quantity Printed	VF-20	EF-40	Unc-63
2114-A.	Boston	2,048,000			$150.00
2114-B.	New York	12,032,000			100 .00
2114-B*.	New York	384,000	$75.00	$100.00	250.00
2114-C.	Philadelphia	3,584,000			125.00
2114-C*.	Philadelphia	128,000	90.00	125.00	300.00
2114-D.	Cleveland	3,584,000			125.00
2114-D*.	Cleveland	192,000	85.00	120.00	275.00
2114-E.	Richmond	2,560,000			125.00
2114-E*.	Richmond	64,000	100.00	125.00	400.00
2114-F.	Atlanta	256,000			150.00
2114-G.	Chicago	9,728,000			125.00
2114-G*.	Chicago	256,000	75.00	100.00	250.00
2114-H.	St. Louis	256,000			150.00
2114-I.	Minneapolis	512,000			125.00
2114-J.	Kansas City	1,280,000			125.00
2114-J*.	Kansas City	64,000	100.00	125.00	400.00
2114-K.	Dallas	1,536,000			125.00
2114-K*.	Dallas	64,000	100.00	125.00	400.00
2114-L.	San Francisco	6,912,000			125.00
2114-L*.	San Francisco	256,000	75 .00	100.00	250.00

Series of 1969-A
Signatures of Kabis and Connally

No.	Issuing Bank	Quantity Printed	VF-20	EF-40	Unc-63
2115-A.	Boston	1,536,000			$150.00
2115-A*.	Boston	128,000			225.00
2115-B.	New York	9,728,000			125.00
2115-B*.	New York	704,000			200.00
2115-C.	Philadelphia	2,560,000			125.00
2115-D.	Cleveland	2,816,000			125.00
2115-E.	Richmond	2,304,000			125.00
2115-E*.	Richmond	64,000	$90.00		300.00
2115-F.	Atlanta	256,000			150.00
2115-F*.	Atlanta	64,000	95.00		350.00
2115-G.	Chicago	3,584,000			125.00
2115-G*.	Chicago	192,000			225.00
2115-H.	St. Louis	256,000			150.00
2115-I.	Minneapolis	512,000			150.00
2115-J.	Kansas City	256,000			150.00
2115-K.	Dallas	1,024,000			125.00
2115-K*.	Dallas	64,000	90.00		300.00
2115-L	San Francisco	5,120,000			125.00
2115-L*	San Francisco	256,000			225.00

Series of 1969-B
Signatures of Banuelos and Connally

No.	Issuing Bank	Quantity Printed	VF-20	EF-40	Unc-63
2116-A.	Boston	1,024,000	$450.00		$1,300.00
2116-B.	New York	2,560,000	400.00		800.00
2116-C.	Philadelphia	2,048,000	200.00		700.00
2116-E.	Richmond	1,536,000	450.00		1,300.00
2116-F.	Atlanta	512,000	550.00		1,300.00
2116-G.	Chicago	1,024,000	400.00		1,300.00
2116-K.	Dallas	1,024,000	450.00		1,000.00
2116-K*.	Dallas	128,000	1,000.00		2,500.00

Series of 1969-C
Signatures of Banuelos and Shultz

No.	Issuing Bank	Quantity Printed	Unc-63
2117-A.	Boston	1,792,000	$110.00
2117-A*.	Boston	64,000	300.00
2117-B.	New York	7,040,000	100.00
2117-B*.	New York	192,000	200.00
2117-C.	Philadelphia	3,584,000	100.00
2117-C*.	Philadelphia	256,000	200.00
2117-D.	Cleveland	5,120,000	100.00
2117-D*.	Cleveland	192,000	200.00
2117-E.	Richmond	2,304,000	100.00
2117-E*.	Richmond	64,000	300.00
2117-F.	Atlanta	256,000	125.00
2117-F*.	Atlanta	64,000	300.00
2117-G.	Chicago	6,784,000	100.00
2117-G*.	Chicago	576,000	175.00
2117-H.	St. Louis	2,688,000	100.00
2117-H*.	St. Louis	64,000	300.00
2117-I.	Minneapolis	256,000	145.00
2117-I*.	Minneapolis	64,000	300.00
2117-J.	Kansas City	1,280,000	100.00
2117-J*.	Kansas City	128,000	200.00
2117-K.	Dallas	3,456,000	100.00
2117-K*.	Dallas	64,000	300.00
2117-L.	San Francisco	4,608,000	100.00
2117-L*.	San Francisco	256,000	200.00

Series of 1974
Signatures of Neff and Simon

No.	Issuing Bank	Quantity Printed	Unc-63
2118-A.	Boston	3,840,000	$125.00
2118-A*.	Boston	256,000	200.00
2118-B.	New York	38,400,000	100.00
2118-B*.	New York	768,000	200.00
2118-C.	Philadelphia	7,040,000	100.00
2118-C*.	Philadelphia	192,000	200.00
2118-D.	Cleveland	21,200,000	100.00
2118-D*.	Cleveland	640,000	200.00
2118-E.	Richmond	14,080,000	125.00
2118-E*.	Richmond	576,000	200.00
2118-F.	Atlanta	1,280,000	125.00
2118-F*.	Atlanta	640,000	200.00
2118-G.	Chicago	30,720,000	100.00
2118-G*.	Chicago	1,536,000	200.00
2118-H.	St. Louis	1,920,000	125.00
2118-H*.	St. Louis	128,000	200.00
2118-I.	Minneapolis	3,200,000	125.00
2118-I*.	Minneapolis	192,000	200.00
2118-J.	Kansas City	4,480,000	125.00
2118-J*.	Kansas City	192,000	200.00
2118-K.	Dallas	8,320,000	125.00
2118-K*.	Dallas	128,000	200.00
2118-L.	San Francisco	7,378,000	125.00
2118-L*.	San Francisco	64,000	250.00

SMALL-SIZE FIFTY DOLLAR NOTES

Federal Reserve Notes (Green Seal)
Series of 1977
Signatures of Morton and Blumenthal

No.	Issuing Bank	Quantity Printed	Unc-63
2119-A.	Boston	16,400,000	$125.00
2119-A*.	Boston	1,088,000	200.00
2119-B.	New York	49,920,000	100.00
2119-B*.	New York	2,112,000	150.00
2119-C.	Philadelphia	5,120,000	125.00
2119-C*.	Philadelphia	128,000	250.00
2119-D.	Cleveland	23,040,000	100.00
2119-D*.	Cleveland	1,024,000	200.00
2119-E.	Richmond	19,200,000	125.00
2119-E*.	Richmond	896,000	200.00
2119-F.	Atlanta	2,560 ,000	125.00
2119-F*.	Atlanta	128,000	200.00
2119-G.	Chicago	47,360,000	100.00
2119-G*.	Chicago	2,304,000	200.00
2119-H.	St. Louis	3,840,000	125.00
2119-H*.	St. Louis	512,000	250.00
2119-I.	Minneapolis	3,840,000	125.00
2119-I*.	Minneapolis	128,000	250.00
2119-J.	Kansas City	7,680,000	125.00
2119-J*.	Kansas City	256,000	250.00
2119-K.	Dallas	14,080,000	125.00
2119-K*.	Dallas	576,000	250.00
2119-L.	San Francisco	19,200,000	100.00
2119-L*.	San Francisco	768,000	200.00

Series of 1981
Signatures of Buchanan and Regan

No.	Issuing Bank	Quantity Printed	Unc-63
2120-A.	Boston	18,560,000	$135.00
2120-B.	New York	78,080,000	135.00
2120-B*.	New York	768,000	250.00
2120-C.	Philadelphia	1,280,000	135.00
2120-D.	Cleveland	28,160,000	135.00
2120-D*.	Cleveland	256,000	250.00
2120-E.	Richmond	25,600,000	135.00
2120-F.	Atlanta	4,480,000	135.00
2120-F*.	Atlanta	768,000	250.00
2120-G.	Chicago	67,200,000	135.00
2120-G*.	Chicago	128,000	300.00
2120-H.	St. Louis	4,480,000	135.00
2120-I.	Minneapolis	5,760,000	135.00
2120-I*.	Minneapolis	128,000	300.00
2120-J.	Kansas City	18,560,000	135.00
2120-J*.	Kansas City	128,000	300.00
2120-K.	Dallas	19,840,000	135.00
2120-L.	San Francisco	35,200,000	135.00
2120-L*.	San Francisco	256,000	250.00

Series of 1981-A
Signatures of Ortega and Regan

No.	Issuing Bank	Quantity Printed	Unc-63
2121-A.	Boston	9,600,000	$150.00
2121-B.	New York	28,800,000	150.00
2121-B*.	New York	3,200,000	250.00
2121-D.	Cleveland	12,800,000	150.00
2121-E.	Richmond	12,800,000	150.00
2121-E*.	Richmond	704,000	250.00
2121-F.	Atlanta	3,200,000	150.00
2121-G.	Chicago	28,800,000	150.00
2121-H.	St. Louis	3,200,000	150.00

Federal Reserve Notes (Green Seal)

No.	Issuing Bank	Quantity Printed	Unc-63
2121-I.	Minneapolis	3,200,000	$150.00
2121-J.	Kansas City	6,400,000	150.00
2121-K.	Dallas	6,400,000	150.00
2121-L.	San Francisco	22,400,000	150.00
2121-L*.	San Francisco	640,000	250.00

Series of 1985
Signatures of Ortega and Baker

No.	Issuing Bank	Quantity Printed	Unc-63
2122-A.	Boston	51,200,000	$90.00
2122-A*.	Boston	64,000	250.00
2122-B.	New York	182,400,000	90.00
2122-B*.	New York	1,408,000	200.00
2122-C.	Philadelphia	3,200,000	90.00
2122-D.	Cleveland	57,600,000	90.00
2122-D*.	Cleveland	64,000	250.00
2122-E.	Richmond	54,400,000	90.00
2122-F.	Atlanta	9,600,000	90.00
2122-G.	Chicago	112,000,000	90.00
2122-G*.	Chicago	1,280,000	250.00
2122-H.	St. Louis	6,400,000	90.00
2122-I.	Minneapolis	12,800,000	90.00
2122-J.	Kansas City	9,600,000	90.00
2122-K.	Dallas	25,600,000	90.00
2122-L.	San Francisco	57,600,000	90.00

Series of 1988
Signatures of Ortega and Brady

No.	Issuing Bank	Quantity Printed	Unc-63
2123-A.	Boston	9,600,000	$100.00
2123-B.	New York	214,400,000	100.00
2123-B*.	New York	1,408,000	200.00
2123-D.	Cleveland	32,000,000	100.00
2123-E.	Richmond	12,800,000	100.00
2123-G.	Chicago	80,000,000	100.00
2123-J.	Kansas City	6,400,000	100.00
2123-L.	San Francisco	12,800,000	100.00

Series of 1988-A
None printed

Series of 1990
Signatures of Villalpando and Brady

No.	Issuing Bank	Quantity Printed	Unc-63
2124-A.	Boston	28,800,000	$85.00
2124-B.	New York	232,000,000	85.00
2124-B*.	New York	3,116,000	125.00
2124-C.	Philadelphia	41,600,000	85.00
2124-C*.	Philadelphia	1,280,000	125.00
2124-D.	Cleveland	92,800,000	85.00
2124-E.	Richmond	76,800,000	85.00
2124-G.	Chicago	108,800,000	85.00
2124-G*.	Chicago	1,032,000	125.00
2124-H.	St. Louis	16,000,000	85.00
2124-I.	Minneapolis	22,400,000	85.00
2124-J.	Kansas City	35,200,000	85.00
2124-J*.	Kansas City	640,000	125.00
2124-K.	Dallas	16,000,000	85.00
2124-L.	San Francisco	119,200,000	85.00

SMALL-SIZE FIFTY DOLLAR NOTES

Federal Reserve Notes (Green Seal)

Series of 1993
Signatures of Withrow and Bentsen

No.	Issuing Bank	Quantity Printed	Unc-63
2125-A.	Boston	41,600,000	$85.00
2125-B.	New York	544,000,000	85.00
2125-B*.	New York	4,224,000	100.00
2125-D.	Cleveland	60,800,000	85.00
2125-D*.	Cleveland	1,280,000	100.00
2125-E.	Richmond	35,200,000	85.00
2125-G.	Chicago	144,000,000	85.00
2125-G*.	Chicago	1,280,000	100.00
2125-H.	St. Louis	3,200,000	85.00
2125-J.	Kansas City	12,800,000	85.00
2125-K.	Dallas	9,600,000	85.00

Face of Notes 2126 -2127

Back of Notes 2126 -2127

Series of 1996
Signatures of Withrow and Rubin
Printed in Washington, DC

No.	Issuing Bank	Quantity Printed	Unc-63
2126-A.	Boston	54,400,000	$65.00
2126-B.	New York	560,800,000	65.00
2126-B*.	New York	5,120,000	80.00
2126-C.	Philadelphia	76,800,000	65.00
2126-D.	Cleveland	119,200,000	65.00
2126-E.	Richmond	106,400,000	65.00
2126-F.	Atlanta	119,200,000	65.00
2126-G.	Chicago	241,600,000	65.00
2126-G*.	Chicago	1,280,000	80.00
2126-H.	St. Louis	28,800,000	65.00
2126-I.	Minneapolis	35,200,000	65.00
2126-J.	Kansas City	57,600,000	65.00
2126-E.	Richmond	106,400,000	65.00
2126-J*.	Kansas City	1,920,000	80.00
2126-K.	Dallas	92,800,000	65.00
2126-L.	San Francisco	219,200,000	65.00
2126-L*.	San Francisco	3,200,000	80.00

Federal Reserve Notes (Green Seal)

Series of 1999
Signatures of Withrow and Summers
None printed

Series of 2001
Signatures of Marin and O'Neill
Printed in Washington, DC

No.	Issuing Bank	Quantity Printed	Unc-63
2127-A.	Boston	6,400,000	$65.00
2127-B.	New York	54,400,000	65.00
2127-B*.	New York	320,000	750.00
2127-C.	Philadelphia	19,200,000	65.00
2127-D.	Cleveland	16,000,000	65.00
2127-E.	Richmond	32,000,000	65.00
2127-E.*	Richmond	64,000	350.00
2127-F.	Atlanta	22,800,000	65.00
2127-G.	Chicago	35,200,000	65.00
2127-H.	St. Louis	3,200,000	65.00
2127-I.	Minneapolis	3,200,000	65.00
2127-J.	Kansas City	3,200,000	65.00
2127-K.	Dallas	6,400,000	65.00
2127-L.	San Francisco	32,000,000	65.00

Series of 2004

Signatures of Marin and Snow
Printed at the Western Facility (Fort Worth, Texas)

Face of Note 2128.

Back of Note 2128.

No.	Issuing Bank	Quantity Printed	Unc-63
2128-A.	Boston		Current
2128-B.	New York		Current
2128-B*.	New York		Current
2128-C.	Philadelphia		Current
2128-D.	Cleveland		Current
2128-E.	Richmond		Current
2128-F.	Atlanta		Current
2128-G.	Chicago		Current
2128-G*.	Chicago		Current
2128-H.	St. Louis		Current
2128-I.	Minneapolis		Current
2128-J.	Kansas City		Current
2128-K.	Dallas		Current
2128-K*.	Dallas		Current
2128-L.	San Francisco		Current

OF MARCH 3D.
1863. 96727

"Attractive and complex, the $100 series include many first-class rarities, as well as notes equally appealing and more readily attainable…"

$100

GOLD CERTIFICATE

100 C

TIFICATE

SER
19

D

BENTON

N2030316

ONE HUNDRED DOLLAR NOTES

Large-Size $100 Notes

Large-size currency of the $100 denomination is collected mainly by types, not varieties. Nearly all early issues are rare. Certain varieties from the late 19th and early 20th centuries are available inexpensively in relation to their elusive nature.

$100 Interest Bearing Notes, Large-Size: Interest Bearing Notes of various authorizations from 1861 through 1865 are so rare as to be non-collectable. A few stray examples exist. The designs are attractive and sometimes complex, but are best known through viewing on proof impressions (one-sided impressions, without serial numbers, made for test or presentation purposes).

$100 Legal Tender Notes, Large-Size: This series begins with the United States Notes or Legal Tender Notes of the Series of 1862 and 1863. Similar to other denominations, imprints exist with the National Bank Note Company and/or the American Bank Note Company. The design of the first note is very imposing, with a particularly powerful American eagle at the upper left, and the denomination given in three arrangements of overlapping petals (a trademark of the National Bank Note Company, which used similar designs on state-chartered bank bills).

The Series of 1869 Legal Tender bills feature Lincoln at the upper left, and an allegorical scene at the lower right titled *Reconstruction* (symbolic of the rebuilding of the South after the Civil War). The reverse is a combination of numerals, letters, and geometric designs, with ample open space, particularly at the corners. Then follow the later series from 1875 through 1880, with different styles of Treasury seal and different signatures. The face of the note remains the same with Lincoln and *Reconstruction*, but the reverse has been redesigned.

$100 Compound Interest Treasury Notes, Large-Size: Compound Interest Treasury Notes under the Act of March 3, 1863, bear an interest schedule on the back. Although these were issued to the extent of over a half million notes, only about 300 are outstanding on the Treasury books today. Just a handful are known to collectors, and any example is considered to be a first-class rarity.

$100 National Bank Notes, Large-Size: Large-size National Bank notes follow the theme of lower denominations, with the Original Series ("First Charter") coming first, then the Series of 1875. These bills depict on the face *Commodore Perry's Victory* (the official title of this scene from the Battle of Lake Erie) to the left, this being from the War of 1812. An allegorical figure, *The Union*, is at right. The reverse is a panoramic depiction of the painting by John Trumbull, *The Signing of the Declaration of Independence*. This is one of the more popular themes in American currency, among state-chartered bank issues as well as federal varieties, with its most recent use being on the $2 bill issued for the Bicentennial in 1976 and in related later series.

Series of 1882 ("Second Charter") bank notes were made in the Brown Back versions as well as the 1882-1908 Date Back, and the ONE HUNDRED DOLLARS Value Back. The Value Back bills were issued by just two institutions, the Winters National Bank of Dayton, Ohio, and the Canal-Commercial National Bank of New Orleans.

Then follow the Series of 1902 ("Third Charter") notes with three varieties: red seal and two varieties of blue seal (one with Date Back and one with Plain Back). The last are seen with some frequency, but are rare. On the face is John Jay Knox, long-time comptroller of the currency—remembered today as a financial historian, the author of the Coinage Act of 1873, and a dedicated numismatist.

Most specialists in National Bank notes consider themselves fortunate to have one or two $100 bills to illustrate the types. These cannot be systematically collected with any effectiveness, as just about all 19th-century issues range from very rare to extremely rare, and those of the 20th century are elusive. The Value Back issues are classic rarities, seldom encountered, even in the largest collections.

$100 National Gold Bank Notes, Large-Size: National Gold Bank $100 bills were issued in California by institutions in Oakland, Petaluma, Sacramento, San Jose, San Francisco, Santa Barbara, and Stockton. Although slightly more than 5,000 notes were issued, just 84 are outstanding on Treasury books, and only nine are known to exist today. Any example is a landmark rarity.

$100 Silver Certificates, Large-Size: These commence with the Series of 1878 and in the large size continue through Series of 1891. The earlier versions have the word SILVER in large letters across the back. At the upper left of each of these notes is the portrait of President James Monroe. Varieties exist of Treasury seals, signature combinations, and different back designs, through the Series of 1880 and 1891. All are scarce, and some are exceedingly rare.

$100 Treasury or Coin Notes, Large-Size: The famous "Watermelon Note"—with zeros resembling green watermelons—are famous, rare, and highly desired, one of the "trophy notes" of American currency. Depicted on the face is Admiral David G. Farragut. The Series of 1891 simplifies the reverse and replaces it with a design with large areas of open field. Although the 1891 notes are about three times rarer than those of 1890, they do not share the same glory.

$100 Gold Certificates, Large-Size: Gold Certificates issued under the Act of 1863 are extreme rarities today. Varieties include issues bearing the dates 1863, 1870, 1871, and 1875. Then follow the Series of 1882 Gold Certificates, made in different Treasury seal styles and signature combinations through the Series of 1922. While earlier varieties are rare, the later signature combinations are available on occasion and can be acquired for type. The vast majority of such notes were redeemed in the 1930s after the United States went off the gold standard.

$100 Federal Reserve Notes, Large-Size: Federal Reserve Notes of the Series of 1914, red seal and blue seal varieties, can be collected by bank varieties. The blue seals can be collected by signature varieties as well. Most of these are relatively inexpensive, although hardly common. The face value and the small supply of available notes preclude wide popularity.

Small-Size $100 Notes

All have the portrait of Benjamin Franklin on the face and a depiction of Independence Hall on the back. Among small-size $100 notes of the late 1920s and early 1930s, National Bank notes are avidly collected, and are scarce. Most others are sought only by those desiring an example of the type. Federal Reserve Notes are still being printed for, and distributed by, the 12 different banks, but they are not widely collected by varieties.

$100 Legal Tender Notes, Small-Size: These Legal Tender or United States Notes include the Series of 1966 and 1966-A, with red seal. These are anomalous among small-size issues and are the only Legal Tender Note over the $5 value. Such bills are popularly collected singly for type.

$100 National Bank Notes, Small-Size: National Bank Notes of the small size, Series of 1929, were issued in the Type 1 and Type 2 styles, similar to other denominations. The Type 2 issues are the more elusive and are significantly more expensive. Again, few were saved due to the high face value, and while those from the larger city banks turn up on occasion, there are many others that are rare or non-collectable.

$100 Gold Certificates, Small-Size: Small-size Gold Certificates with gold seal were printed for Series of 1928 and 1928-A, the latter not issued. The Series of 1928 with Woods-Mellon signatures are relatively available today.

$100 Federal Reserve Bank Notes, Small-Size: Notes of the Series of 1929, brown seal, are collectable from certain of the banks, but not all. None were printed for Boston, Philadelphia, Atlanta, St. Louis, or San Francisco.

$100 Federal Reserve Notes, Small-Size: Then follow Federal Reserve Notes of the Series of 1928, issued for the 12 districts, continuing through various signature combinations and later series designations. After the 1940s these were the highest denomination bills produced. Today, they remain in wide demand, including by overseas holders of American money.

In 1991 a plastic security strip was added to the currency paper. A makeover of the design was undertaken with the Series of 1996. The portrait of Franklin was enlarged and various security modifications were made (see related commentary in the section on small-size $50 bills). On the back the image of Independence Hall was essentially retained, but the border was altered. These notes can be collected by banks and signature combinations, although, once again, the high face value precludes a wide interest.

Proof impression of a two-subject plate finessed at the Bureau of Engraving and Printing in 1884, with a $50 and $100 Series of 1882 note for the National State Capital Bank of Concord, New Hampshire. The plate, made by the American Bank Note Co., and imprinted as such, was re-entered and also, bears the line on each note, "Printed at the Bureau of Printing & Engraving, U.S. Treasury Dept." The plate is dated in script, Jan. 3rd 1885. The bank charter number 758 is part of the border design. The inked notations on the margins are from BEP employees who have approved the details on the plate, such as the bank title, location, and date. (Courtesy of the Smithsonian Institution)

Interest Bearing Notes

Face of Note 199 (not shown) depicts a 3/4 length bust of George Washington in center with female representations of Guardian and Justice at left and right.

Back of Note 199 (not shown) depicts the denomination on left and right within ornate lathe work.

No.	Denomination	
199.	One Hundred Dollars.	Extremely Rare (3 Known)

Face of Note 204 (not shown) depicts Treasury Department building at top center; at left, men seated representing Science and Mechanics; sailors firing cannon at right.

Back of Note 204 (not shown) Two of the Roman numeral "C" at left and right.
Obligation printed on two panels in center.

No.	Denomination		
204.	One Hundred Dollars. . . . .*2005 Heritage Auction, sold for $299,000* . . . . .Extremely Rare

Face of Note 208. Bust of General Winfield Scott. Similar to below.

No.	Denomination	
208.	One Hundred Dollars.	Unknown

Face of Note 212a. Bust of General Winfield Scott.

Back of Note 212a.

No.	Denomination	
212a.	One Hundred Dollars.	3 Known

LARGE-SIZE ONE HUNDRED DOLLAR NOTES

Interest Bearing Notes

No.	Denomination	
212e.	One Hundred Dollars.	Extremely Rare

Face of Note 212e (not shown). As above.

Legal Tender Notes

Face of Notes 165-167b. Large eagle with wings spread.

Back of Notes 165-167b.

Act of 1862, with signatures of Chittenden and Spinner and red seal
First Obligation on back

No.	Series	VG-8	F-12	VF-20	EF-40	Unc-63
165.	American Bank Note Co. monogram in upper left	$9,000.00	$17,500.00	$25,000.00	$37,500.00	$80,000.00
165a.	As above, No ABNCo monogram	9,000.00	17,500.00	25,000.00	37,500.00	80,000.00

Second Obligation on back

No.	Series	Signatures		Seal	VG-8	F-12	VF-20	EF-40	Unc-63
166.	1862	Chittenden	Spinner . . .	Red	Unique	—	—	—	—
167.	1863 . . .	Chittenden	Spinner . . .	Red, One Serial No.	—	—	—	—	—

Two notes above with National Bank Note Co. and American Bank Note Co. printed at top

No.	Series	Signatures		Seal	VG-8	F-12	VF-20	EF-40	Unc-63
167a.	1863	Chittenden	Spinner	Red, Two Serial Nos.	$9,000.00	$17,500.00	$25,000.00	$37,500.00	$100,000.00
167b.	1863	Chittenden	Spinner	Red, One Serial No.	Very Rare	—	—	—	—

Legal Tender Notes

Face of Note 168. Bust of Abraham Lincoln at left; woman and child representing Architecture at right.

Back of Note 168.

No.	Series	Signatures	Seal	VG-8	F-12	VF-20	EF-40	Unc-63
168.	1869	Allison Spinner	Large Red	$10,000.00	$14,500.00	$23,000.00	$30,000.00	$75,000.00

Face of Notes 169-182. Bust of Abraham Lincoln at left; woman and child representing Architecture at right.
Red floral design at top.

Legal Tender Notes

Face of Notes 169-182. Bust of Abraham Lincoln at left; woman and child representing Architecture at right. Red floral design at top.

Back of Notes 169-182.

No.	Series	Signatures		Seal	VG-8	F-12	VF-20	EF-40	Unc-63
169.	1875 ..	Allison	New	Small Red with Rays (Series A) ..	$7,000.00	$12,000.00	$19,500.00	$30,000.00	$80,000.00
170.	1875 ..	Allison	Wyman ...	Small Red with Rays	8,000.00	14,000.00	22,500.00	35,000.00	—
171.	1878 ..	Allison	Gilfillan ...	Small Red with Rays	6,000.00	10,000.00	16,500.00	27,000.00	70,500.00

Face as above but with black floral design at top.

No.	Series	Signatures		Seal	VG-8	F-12	VF-20	EF-40	Unc-63
172.	1880 ..	Bruce	Gilfillan ..	Large Brown	$5,000.00	$9,000.00	$15,000.00	$25,500.00	$60,000.00
173.	1880 ..	Bruce	Wyman .	Large Brown	4,500.00	9,000.00	15,000.00	25,500.00	—
174.	1880 ..	Rosecrans	Jordan ..	Large Red, Plain	3,500.00	8,000.00	14,000.00	24,000.00	55,000.00
175.	1880 ..	Rosecrans	Hyatt ...	Large Red, Plain	Very Rare	—	—	—	—
176.	1880 ..	Rosecrans	Hyatt ...	Large Red, Spiked	5,000.00	9,000.00	15,000.00	25,500.00	—
177.	1880 ..	Rosecrans	Huston ..	Large Red, Spiked	4,500.00	8,000.00	14,000.00	24,000.00	—
178.	1880 ..	Rosecrans	Huston ..	Large Brown	4,500.00	8,000.00	14,000.00	24,000.00	55,000.00
179.	1880 ..	Tillman	Morgan .	Small Red, Scalloped	3,750.00	6,500.00	10,500.00	19,000.00	30,000.00
180.	1880 ..	Bruce	Roberts .	Small Red, Scalloped	4,250.00	8,000.00	12,500.00	22,000.00	—
181.	1880 ..	Lyons	Roberts .	Small Red, Scalloped	3,750.00	6,500.00	10,500.00	19,000.00	30,000.00
182.	1880 ..	Napier	McClung .	Small Red, Scalloped	Unknown	—	—	—	—

Compound Interest Treasury Notes

Face of Notes 193-193b. George Washington standing in center with females representing Guardian and Justice at left and right.

Back of Notes 193-193b.

No.	Act of	Overprint Date	Signatures		VG-8	F-12
193.	1863	June 10, 1864	Chittenden	Spinner	$14,000.00	Rare
193a.	1864	July 15, 1864	Chittenden	Spinner	Unknown	—
193b.	1864	Aug. 15, 1864 - Sep. 1, 1865 ...	Colby	Spinner	Extremely Rare	—

National Bank Notes
"First Charter Period" (Original Series and Series of 1875)

Face of Notes 452-463. Battle of Lake Erie *from the War of 1812 at left;* at right, winged Liberty seated before fasces.

"First Charter Period" (Original Series and Series of 1875)

Back of Notes 452-463. Signing of the Declaration of Independence.

No.	Series	Signatures		Seal	VG-8	F-12	VF-20
452.	Original	Chittenden	Spinner	Red, Rays	$13,000.00	$18,000.00	$24,000.00
454.	Original	Colby	Spinner	Red, Rays	13,000.00	18,000.00	24,000.00
455.	Original	Allison	Spinner	Red, Rays	13,000.00	18,000.00	24,000.00
456.	1875	Allison	New	Red, Scalloped	13,000.00	18,000.00	24,000.00
457.	1875	Allison	Wyman	Red, Scalloped	13,000.00	18,000.00	24,000.00
458.	1875	Allison	Gilfillan	Red, Scalloped	13,000.00	18,000.00	24,000.00
459.	1875	Scofield	Gilfillan	Red, Scalloped	13,000.00	18,000.00	24,000.00
460.	1875	Bruce	Gilfillan	Red, Scalloped	13,000.00	18,000.00	24,000.00
461.	1875	Bruce	Wyman	Red, Scalloped	13,000.00	18,000.00	24,000.00
462.	1875	Rosecrans	Huston	Red, Scalloped	13,000.00	18,000.00	24,000.00
462a.	1875	Rosecrans	Nebeker	Red, Scalloped	Rare	—	—
463.	1875	Tillman	Morgan	Red, Scalloped	Rare	—	—

National Bank Notes
"Second Charter Period" (Series of 1882)
Brown Backs

*Face of Notes 519-531. Battle of Lake Erie from the War of 1812 at left;
at right, winged Liberty seated before fasces.*

Back of Notes 519-531. Green bank charter numbers against ornate background of brown lathe-work.

No.	Signatures		VG-8	F-12	VF-20	EF-40	Unc-63
519.	Bruce	Gilfillan	$6,000.00	$7,800.00	$10,000.00	$13,000.00	$18,000.00
520.	Bruce	Wyman	6,000.00	7,800.00	10,000.00	13,000.00	18,000.00
521.	Bruce	Jordan	6,000.00	7,800.00	10,000.00	13,000.00	18,000.00
522.	Rosecrans	Jordan	6,000.00	7,800.00	10,000.00	13,000.00	18,000.00
523.	Rosecrans	Hyatt	6,000.00	7,800.00	10,000.00	13,000.00	18,000.00
524	Rosecrans	Huston	6,000.00	7,800.00	10,000.00	13,000.00	18,000.00
525.	Rosecrans	Nebeker	6,000.00	7,800.00	10,000.00	13,000.00	18,000.00
526.	Rosecrans	Morgan	6,000.00	7,800.00	10,000.00	13,000.00	18,000.00
527.	Tillman	Morgan	6,000.00	7,800.00	10,000.00	13,000.00	18,000.00
528.	Tillman	Roberts	6,000.00	7,800.00	10,000.00	13,000.00	18,000.00
529.	Bruce	Roberts	6,000.00	7,800.00	10,000.00	13,000.00	18,000.00
530.	Lyons	Roberts	6,000.00	7,800.00	10,000.00	13,000.00	18,000.00
531.	Vernon	Treat	6,000.00	7,800.00	10,000.00	13,000.00	18,000.00

Date Backs

Face of Notes 566-572a. Battle of Lake Erie *from the War of 1812 at left;*
at right, winged Liberty seated before fasces.

Back of Notes 566-572a.

No.	Signatures		VG-8	F-12	VF-20	EF-40	Unc-63
566.	Rosecrans	Huston	$5,500.00	$7,500.00	$9,000.00	$12,000.00	$16,000.00
567.	Rosecrans	Nebeker	5,500.00	7,500.00	9,000.00	12,000.00	16,000.00
568.	Tillman	Morgan	5,500.00	7,500.00	9,000.00	12,000.00	16,000.00
569.	Tillman	Roberts	5,500.00	7,500.00	9,000.00	12,000.00	16,000.00
570.	Bruce	Roberts	5,500.00	7,500.00	9,000.00	12,000.00	16,000.00
571.	Lyons	Roberts	5,500.00	7,500.00	9,000.00	12,000.00	16,000.00
572.	Vernon	Treat	5,500.00	7,500.00	9,000.00	12,000.00	16,000.00
572a.	Napier	McClung	5,500.00	7,500.00	9,000.00	12,000.00	16,000.00

Value Backs

Face of Note 586a (note shown) depicts Battle of Lake Erie *from the War of 1812 at left;*
at right, winged Liberty seated before fasces

Back of Note 586a (not shown) depicts value in oval panel.
Similar to the other "Value Back" notes of the Second Charter Period.

No.	Signatures				
586a.	Lyons	Roberts	Only 2 Bank Reported	Very Rare	(5 Known)

"Third Charter Period" (Series of 1902)

First Issue: Series of 1902 with Red Seal

Face of Notes 686-688. Bust of Comptroller of the Currency (1872-1884) John J. Knox.

Back of Notes 686-688.

No.	Signatures		VG-8	F-12	VF-20	EF-40	Unc-63
686.	Lyons	Roberts	$7,500.00	$9,000.00	$12,000.00	$16,000.00	$20,000.00
687.	Lyons	Treat	7,500.00	9,000.00	12,000.00	16,000.00	20,000.00
688.	Vernon	Treat	7,500.00	9,000.00	12,000.00	16,000.00	20,000.00

"Third Charter Period" (Series of 1902)

Second Issue: Series of 1902 with blue seal and with "1902-1908" on back

Face of Notes 689-699. Bust of Comptroller of the Currency (1872-1884) John J. Knox.

Back of Notes 689-697.

Second Issue: Series of 1902 with blue seal and with "1902-1908" on back

No.	Signatures		VG-8	F-12	VF-20	EF-40	Unc-63
689.	Lyons	Roberts	$1,800.00	$2,250.00	$2,750.00	$3,750.00	$6,000.00
690.	Lyons	Treat	1,800.00	2,250.00	2,750.00	3,750.00	6,000.00
691.	Vernon	Treat	1,800.00	2,250.00	2,750.00	3,750.00	6,000.00
692.	Vernon	McClung	1,800.00	2,250.00	2,750.00	3,750.00	6,000.00
693.	Napier	McClung	1,800.00	2,250.00	2,750.00	3,750.00	6,000.00
694.	Napier	Thompson	1,800.00	2,250.00	2,750.00	3,750.00	6,000.00
695.	Napier	Burke	1,800.00	2,250.00	2,750.00	3,750.00	6,000.00
696.	Parker	Burke	1,800.00	2,250.00	2,750.00	3,750.00	6,000.00
697.	Teehee	Burke	1,800.00	2,250.00	2,750.00	3,750.00	6,000.00

"Third Charter Period" (Series of 1902)

Second Issue: Series of 1902 with blue seal and without "1902-1908" on back

Face of Notes 698-707a. Bust of Comptroller of the Currency (1872-1884) John J. Knox.

Back of Notes 698-707a.

No.	Signatures		VG-8	F-12	VF-20	EF-40	Unc-63
698.	Lyons	Roberts	$1,800.00	$2,275.00	$2,750.00	$3,750.00	$6,000.00
699.	Lyons	Treat	1,800.00	2,275.00	2,750.00	3,750.00	6,000.00
700.	Vernon	Treat	1,800.00	2,275.00	2,750.00	3,750.00	6,000.00
701.	Vernon	McClung	1,800.00	2,275.00	2,750.00	3,750.00	6,000.00
702.	Napier	McClung	1,800.00	2,275.00	2,750.00	3,750.00	6,000.00
702a.	Napier	Thompson	1,800.00	2,275.00	2,750.00	3,750.00	6,000.00
702b.	Napier	Burke	1,800.00	2,275.00	2,750.00	3,750.00	6,000.00
703.	Parker	Burke	1,800.00	2,275.00	2,750.00	3,750.00	6,000.00
704.	Teehee	Burke	1,800.00	2,275.00	2,750.00	3,750.00	6,000.00
705.	Elliott	Burke	1,800.00	2,275.00	2,750.00	3,750.00	6,000.00
706.	Elliott	White	1,800.00	2,275.00	2,750.00	3,750.00	6,000.00
707.	Speelman	White	1,800.00	2,275.00	2,750.00	3,750.00	6,000.00
707a.	Woods	White	Rare	—	—	—	—

National Gold Bank Notes

Face of Notes 1162-1166 (not shown) depicts Battle of Lake Erie *from the War of 1812 at left; at right, winged Liberty seated before fasces.*

Back of Notes 1162-1166 (not shown) features an array of contemporary United States gold coins. Similar to the other National Gold Bank Notes.

No.	Date	Name of Bank	City	
1162.	1870	First National Gold Bank	San Francisco	Rare
1163.	1875	Series. First National Gold Bank	San Francisco	Rare
1164.	1873	First National Gold Bank	Santa Barbara	Unique
1165.	1874	First National Gold Bank	Petaluma	Rare
1166.	1875	Union National Gold Bank	Oakland	Rare
1166I.	1872	National Gold Bank and Trust Company	San Francisco	Unknown
1166II.	1872	National Gold Bank of D.O. Mills and Co.	Sacramento	Unknown
1166III.	1873	First National Gold Bank	Stockton	Rare
1166IV.	1874	Farmer's National Gold Bank	San Jose	Unknown

Silver Certificates

Face of Notes 336-342. Bust of President James Monroe.

Back of Notes 336-342. Countersigned notes with signatures of Scofield and Gilfillan and a large red seal. The 1878 notes countersigned lack the legend, "Series of 1878." All with engraved countersignatures except notes 337 and 337a, which are autographed.

Silver Certificates

No.	Series	Countersigned By	Payable At	
336.	1878	W.G. White	New York	Unique
336a.	1878	J.C. Hopper or T. Hillhouse	New York	Unknown
337*.	1878	R.M. Anthony	San Francisco	Unique
337a*.	1878	A.U. Wyman	Washington, DC	Unique
337b.	1878	A.U. Wyman	Washington, DC	Extremely Rare

No.	Series	Signatures		Seal	VG-8	F-12	VF-20
338.	1880	Scofield	Gilfillan	Large Brown, Rays	Unknown	—	—
339.	1880	Bruce	Gilfillan	Large Brown, Rays	Extremely Rare	—	—
340.	1880	Bruce	Wyman	Large Brown, Rays	$6,750.00	$13,500.00	$25,000.00

As above, with large "C" below. No countersigned signature

No.	Series	Signatures		Seal	VG-8	F-12	VF-20
341.	1880	Rosecrans	Huston	Large Brown, Spikes	$6,000.00	$12,000.00	$23,000.00

As above with large seal in center, no "C" or "100"

No.	Series	Signatures		Seal	VG-8	F-12	VF-20
342.	1880	Rosecrans	Nebeker	Small Red	$6,750.00	$13,500.00	$25,000.00

As above with small seal at right bottom

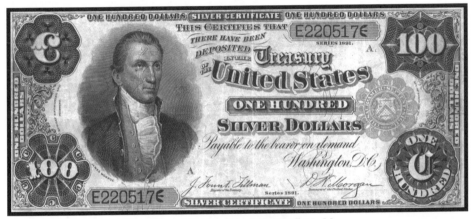

Face of Notes 343-344. Bust of President James Monroe.

Back of Notes 343-344.

No.	Series	Signatures		Seal	VG-8	F-12	VF-20	EF-40	Unc-63
343.	1891	Rosecrans	Nebeker	Small Red	$5,750.00	$9,000.00	$14,000.00	$20,000.00	$45,000.00
344.	1891	Tillman	Morgan	Small Red	5,750.00	9,000.00	14,000.00	20,000.00	45,000.00

Treasury or Coin Notes

Face of Note 377. Facing bust of Admiral David Farragut.

Back of Note 377. The style of the zeroes on the back results in this being called the "Watermelon Note."

No.	Series	Signatures	Seal	VG-8	F-12	VF-20	EF-40	Unc-63
377.	1890	Rosecrans Huston	Large Brown	$17,500.00	$50,000.00	$60,000.00	Rare	—

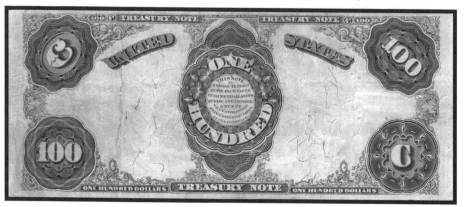

Face of Note 378 (not shown) similar to Note 377.

Back of Note 378.

No.	Series	Signatures	Seal	VG-8	F-12	VF-20	EF-40	Unc-63
378.	1891	Rosecrans Nebeker	Small Red	$25,000.00	$60,000.00	$85,000.00	Rare	—

Gold Certificates

Face of Note 1166a (not shown) depicts eagle standing on shield at left; at right right value.
Back of Note 1166c (note shown) has "One Hundred Dollars" in rectangular panel.

No.	Denomination	
1166c.	One Hundred Dollars.	Extremely Rare

Bust of Thomas Hart Benton

No.	Denomination	
1166h.	One Hundred Dollars.	Unknown

Face of Notes 1201-1215. Bust of Thomas Hart Benton.

Back of Notes 1201-1215. Eagle standing on fasces.

No.	Series	Signatures		Seal	VG-8	F-12	VF-20	EF-40	Unc-63
1201.	1882	Bruce	Gilfillan	Brown	Rare	—	—	—	—
1202.	1882	Bruce	Gilfillan	Brown	Extremely Rare	—	—	—	—

(The above note is countersigned by Thomas C. Acton, Assistant Treasurer, and payable at New York.)

No.	Series	Signatures		Seal	VG-8	F-12	VF-20	EF-40	Unc-63
1203.	1882	Bruce	Wyman ...	Brown	Extremely Rare	—	—	—	—
1204.	1882	Rosecrans	Hyatt	Large Red	Extremely Rare	—	—	—	—
1205.	1882	Rosecrans	Huston	Large Brown	Rare	—	—	—	—
1206.	1882	Lyons	Roberts ...	Small Red	$1,100.00	$2,300.00	$5,250.00	$7,000.00	$17,500.00
1207.	1882	Lyons	Treat	Small Red	2,000.00	3,750.00	6,000.00	8,500.00	17,500.00
1208.	1882	Vernon	Treat	Small Red	1,100.00	2,300.00	5,250.00	7,000.00	—
1209.	1882	Vernon	McClung ..	Small Red	700.00	1,000.00	2,000.00	3,500.00	17,500.00
1210.	1882	Napier	McClung ..	Small Red	950.00	1,800.00	3,750.00	5,000.00	—
1211.	1882	Napier	Thompson .	Small Red	700.00	1,000.00	2,000.00	3,500.00	—
1212.	1882	Napier	Burke	Small Red	700.00	1,000.00	2,000.00	3,500.00	—
1213.	1882	Parker	Burke	Small Red	700.00	1,000.00	2,000.00	3,500.00	17,500.00
1214.	1882	Teehee	Burke	Small Red	560.00	875.00	1,600.00	2,300.00	7,250.00
1215.	1922	Speelman	White	Small Red	450.00	700.00	1,000.00	1,900.00	5,500.00

Federal Reserve Notes

Face of Notes 1072-1131. Profile bust of Benjamin Franklin.

Back of Notes 1072-1131. Group of five allegorical figures.

A. Series of 1914 with red seal and signatures of Burke and McAdoo

No.	Issuing Bank	VG-8	F-12	VF-20	EF-40	Unc-63
1072A.	Boston	$1,000.00	$1,500.00	$3,000.00	$5,000.00	$9,500.00
1072B.	Boston	1,300.00	2,000.00	4,000.00	7,000.00	—
1073A.	New York	1,300.00	2,000.00	4,000.00	7,000.00	12,000.00
1073B.	New York	2,100.00	3,500.00	7,000.00	12,500.00	—
1074A.	Philadelphia	1,300.00	2,000.00	4,000.00	7,000.00	12,000.00
1074B.	Philadelphia	1,000.00	1,500.00	3,000.00	5,000.00	—
1075A.	Cleveland	2,100.00	3,500.00	7,000.00	12,500.00	—
1075B.	Cleveland	1,000.00	1,500.00	3,000.00	5,000.00	—
1076A.	Richmond	1,300.00	2,000.00	4,000.00	7,000.00	—
1076B.	Richmond	2,100.00	3,500.00	7,000.00	12,500.00	—
1077A.	Atlanta	2,100.00	3,500.00	7,000.00	12,500.00	—
1077B.	Atlanta	Extremely Rare	—	—	—	—
1078A.	Chicago	1,700.00	2,750.00	5,500.00	9,000.00	—
1078B.	Chicago	1,000.00	1,500.00	3,000.00	5,000.00	9,500.00
1079A.	St. Louis	1,300.00	2,000.00	4,000.00	7,000.00	—
1079B.	St. Louis	2,100.00	3,500.00	7,000.00	12,500.00	—
1080A.	Minneapolis	Rare	—	—	—	—
1080B.	Minneapolis	1,700.00	2,750.00	5,500.00	9,000.00	—
1081A.	Kansas City	1,700.00	2,750.00	5,500.00	9,000.00	—

Federal Reserve Notes

A. Series of 1914 with red seal and signatures of Burke and McAdoo

No.	Issuing Bank	VG-8	F-12	VF-20	EF-40	Unc-63
1081B.	Kansas City	$1,300.00	$2,000.00	$4,000.00	$7,000.00	—
1082A.	Dallas	2,100.00	3,500.00	7,000.00	—	—
1082B.	Dallas	2,100.00	3,500.00	7,000.00	12,500.00	—
1083A.	San Francisco	2,100.00	3,500.00	7,000.00	12,500.00	—
1083B.	San Francisco	1,000.00	1,500.00	3,000.00	5,000.00	$9,500.00

B. Series of 1914 with blue seal

No.	Issuing Bank	Signatures		VG-8	F-12	VF-20	EF-40	Unc-63
1084.	Boston	Burke	McAdoo	$650.00	$750.00	$850.00	$1,100.00	$3,000.00
1085.	Boston	Burke	Glass	600.00	700.00	700.00	950.00	2,500.00
1086.	Boston	Burke	Houston	600.00	700.00	700.00	950.00	2,000.00
1087.	Boston	White	Mellon	650.00	750.00	850.00	1,100.00	—
1088.	New York	Burke	McAdoo	550.00	650.00	750.00	850.00	1,700.00
1089.	New York	Burke	Glass	550.00	650.00	750.00	850.00	—
1090.	New York	Burke	Houston	550.00	650.00	750.00	850.00	1,700.00
1091.	New York	White	Mellon	600.00	700.00	800.00	950.00	2,500.00
1092.	Philadelphia	Burke	McAdoo	550.00	650.00	750.00	850.00	1,750.00
1093.	Philadelphia	Burke	Glass	None printed	—	—	—	—
1094.	Philadelphia	Burke	Houston	None printed	—	—	—	—
1095.	Philadelphia	White	Mellon	Rare	—	—	—	—
1096.	Cleveland	Burke	McAdoo	750.00	950.00	1,150.00	1,350.00	—
1097.	Cleveland	Burke	Glass	750.00	950.00	1,150.00	—	—
1098.	Cleveland	Burke	Houston	600.00	700.00	800.00	950.00	2,500.00
1099.	Cleveland	White	Mellon	750.00	950.00	1,150.00	1,350.00	2,400.00
1100.	Richmond	Burke	McAdoo	600.00	700.00	800.00	950.00	2,000.00
1101.	Richmond	Burke	Glass	750.00	950.00	1,150.00	1,350.00	—
1102.	Richmond	Burke	Houston	None printed	—	—	—	—
1103.	Richmond	White	Mellon	550.00	650.00	750.00	850.00	1,500.00
1104.	Atlanta	Burke	McAdoo	900.00	1,125.00	1,350.00	1,750.00	2,800.00
1105.	Atlanta	Burke	Glass	None printed	—	—	—	—
1106.	Atlanta	Burke	Houston	900.00	1,125.00	1,350.00	1,750.00	3,000.00
1107.	Atlanta	White	Mellon	750.00	950.00	1,150.00	1,350.00	2,400.00
1108.	Chicago	Burke	McAdoo	550.00	650.00	750.00	850.00	1,700.00
1109.	Chicago	Burke	Glass	None printed	—	—	—	—
1110.	Chicago	Burke	Houston	550.00	650.00	750.00	850.00	1,700.00
1111.	Chicago	White	Mellon	550.00	650.00	750.00	850.00	1,700.00
1112.	St. Louis	Burke	McAdoo	550.00	650.00	750.00	850.00	1,700.00
1113.	St. Louis	Burke	Glass	None printed	—	—	—	—
1114.	St. Louis	Burke	Houston	None printed	—	—	—	—
1115.	St. Louis	White	Mellon	None printed	—	—	—	—
1116.	Minneapolis	Burke	McAdoo	550.00	650.00	750.00	850.00	1,700.00
1117.	Minneapolis	Burke	Glass	None printed	—	—	—	—
1118.	Minneapolis	Burke	Houston	None printed	—	—	—	—
1119.	Minneapolis	White	Mellon	7500.00	950.00	1,150.00	1,350.00	3,200.00
1120.	Kansas City	Burke	McAdoo	550.00	650.00	750.00	850.00	1,700.00
1121.	Kansas City	Burke.	Glass	None printed	—	—	—	—
1122.	Kansas City	Burke	Houston	None printed	—	—	—	—
1123.	Kansas City	White	Mellon	600.00	700.00	800.00	950.00	3,000.00
1124.	Dallas	Burke	McAdoo	600.00	700.00	800.00	950.00	2,000.00
1125.	Dallas	Burke	Glass	None printed	—	—	—	—
1126.	Dallas	Burke	Houston	None printed	—	—	—	—
1127.	Dallas	White	Mellon	900.00	1,125.00	1,350.00	1,750.00	2,800.00
1128.	San Francisco	Burke	McAdoo	550.00	650.00	750.00	850.00	1,700.00
1129.	San Francisco	Burke	Glass	None printed	—	—	—	—
1130.	San Francisco	Burke	Houston	550.00	650.00	750.00	850.00	1,700.00
1131.	San Francisco	White	Mellon	600.00	700.00	800.00	950.00	2,000.00

A large number of F-1092 notes are suspected of being extremely high-quality counterfeits made in the 1930s—caution is advised.

SMALL-SIZE ONE HUNDRED DOLLAR NOTES

Legal Tender Notes (Red Seal)

Face of Notes 1550-1551.

Back of Notes 1550-1551.

No.	Series	Signatures		Quantity Printed	VF-20	EF-40	Unc-63
1550.	1966	Granahan	Fowler	768,000	$200.00	$225.00	$450.00
1550*.	1966	Granahan	Fowler	128,000	450.00	600.00	1,750.00
1551.	1966-A	Elston	Kennedy	512,000	250.00	325.00	1,000.00

National Bank Notes (Brown Seal)

Face of Note 1804.

Back of Note 1804.

National Bank Notes (Brown Seal)

No.		VF-20	EF-40	Unc-63
1804-1.	Type 1	$500.00	$550.00	$750.00
1804-2.	Type 2	500.00	575.00	800.00

Gold Certificates (Gold Seal)

Face of Notes 2405-2406.

Back of Notes 2405-2406.

No.	Series	Signatures		Quantity Printed	VG-8	F-12	VF-20	EF-40	Unc-63
2405.	1928	Woods	Mellon	3,240,000	$300.00	$400.00	$600.00	$800.00	$2,500.00
2405*.	1928	Woods	Mellon	1,000.00	1,600.00	2,750.00	8,000.00	11,000.00
2406.	1934	Julian	Morgenthau	120,000	Not Issued	—	—	—	—

Federal Reserve Bank Notes (Brown Seal)

Face of Note 1890.

Back of Note 1890.

SMALL-SIZE ONE HUNDRED DOLLAR NOTES

Federal Reserve Bank Notes (Brown Seal)

No.	Issuing Bank	Quantity Printed	VF-20	EF-40	Unc-63
1890-B.	New York	480,000	$175.00	$225.00	$350.00
1890-D.	Cleveland	276,000	175.00	225.00	350.00
1890-E.	Richmond	142,000	175.00	225.00	350.00
1890-G.	Chicago	384,000	175.00	225.00	350.00
1890-I.	Minneapolis	144,000	175.00	225.00	350.00
1890-J.	Kansas City	96,000	400.00	500.00	800.00
1890-K.	Dallas	36,000	300.00	350.00	700.00
1890*.	Most Common Districts		600.00	750.00	3,000.00

Federal Reserve Notes (Green Seal)

Face of Note 2150.

Back of Notes 2150.

Series of 1928
Signatures of Woods and Mellon

No.	Issuing Bank	Quantity Printed	VF-20	EF-40	Unc-63
2150-A.	Boston	376,000	$135.00	$175.00	$550.00
2150-A*.	Boston		300.00	350.00	1,250.00
2150-B.	New York	755,400	135.00	175.00	475.00
2150-B*.	New York		250.00	300.00	1,000.00
2150-C.	Philadelphia	389,100	135.00	175.00	550.00
2150-C*.	Philadelphia		300.00	350.00	1,250.00
2150-D.	Cleveland	542,400	135.00	175.00	500.00
2150-D*.	Cleveland		300.00	350.00	1,750.00
2150-E.	Richmond	364,416	135.00	175.00	550.00
2150-E*.	Richmond		300.00	350.00	1,250.00
2150-F.	Atlanta	357,000	135.00	175.00	550.00
2150-F*.	Atlanta		300.00	350.00	1,250.00
2150-G.	Chicago	783,300	135.00	175.00	475.00
2150-G*.	Chicago		250.00	350.00	1,000.00
2150-H.	St. Louis	187,200	135.00	175.00	600.00
2150-H*.	St. Louis		300.00	350.00	1,250.00
2150-I.	Minneapolis	102,000	145.00	200.00	650.00
2150-I*.	Minneapolis		300.00	375.00	1,250.00
2150-J.	Kansas City	234,612	135.00	175.00	600.00
2150-J*.	.Kansas City		300.00	375.00	1,250.00
2150-K.	Dallas	80,140	145.00	185.00	650.00
2150-K*.	Dallas		300.00	375.00	1,250.00
2150-L.	San Francisco	486,000	135.00	175.00	475.00
2150-L*.	San Francisco		250.00	325.00	950.00

Federal Reserve Notes (Green Seal)

Face of Notes 2151-2156.

Back of Notes 2151-2156.

Series of 1928-A
Signatures of Woods and Mellon

No.	Issuing Bank	Quantity Printed	VF-20	EF-40	Unc-63
2151-A.	Boston	980,400	$135.00	$175.00	$325.00
2151-B.	New York	2,938,176	135.00	175.00	300.00
2151-C.	Philadelphia	1,496,844	135.00	175.00	325.00
2151-D.	Cleveland	992,436	135.00	175.00	325.00
2151-E.	Richmond	621,364	135.00	175.00	325.00
2151-F.	Atlanta	371,400	135.00	175.00	325.00
2151-G.	Chicago	4,010,424	135.00	175.00	300.00
2151-H.	St. Louis	749,544	135.00	175.00	325.00
2151-H*.	St. Louis	24,000	Rare	—	—
2151-I.	Minneapolis	503,040	135.00	175.00	325.00
2151-J.	Kansas City	681,804	135.00	175.00	325.00
2151-K.	Dallas	594,456	135.00	175.00	325.00
2151-L.	San Francisco	1,228,032	135.00	175.00	325.00

Series of 1934
Signatures of Julian and Morgenthau
The two shades of green seals also exist in this series. Notes with the darker green seal are worth approximately 10% more.

No.	Issuing Bank	Quantity Printed	VF-20	EF-40	Unc-63
2152-A.	Boston	3,710,000	$100.00		$200.00
2152-A*.	Boston		250.00		600.00
2152-B.	New York	3,086,000	125.00	$150.00	235.00
2152-B*.	New York		200.00	250.00	800.00
2152-C.	Philadelphia	2,776,800	125.00	150.00	235.00
2152-C*.	Philadelphia		200.00	250.00	800.00
2152-D.	Cleveland	3,447,108	125.00	150.00	235.00
2152-D*.	Cleveland		200.00	250.00	800.00
2152-E.	Richmond	4,317,600	125.00	150.00	235.00
2152-E*.	Richmond		200.00	250.00	800.00
2152-F.	Atlanta	3,264,420	125.00	150.00	235.00
2152-F*.	Atlanta		200.00	250.00	800.00
2152-G.	Chicago	7,075,000	125.00	150.00	235.00

SMALL-SIZE ONE HUNDRED DOLLAR NOTES

Federal Reserve Notes (Green Seal)

No.	Issuing Bank	Quantity Printed	VF-20	EF-40	Unc-63
2152-G*.	Chicago		$200.00	$250.00	$800.00
2152-H.	St. Louis	2,106,192	125.00	150.00	235.00
2152-H*.	St. Louis		200.00	250.00	800.00
2152-I.	Minneapolis	852,600	125.00	150.00	235.00
2152-I*.	Minneapolis		200.00	250.00	800.00
2152-J.	Kansas City	1,932,900	125.00	150.00	235.00
2152-J*.	Kansas City		200.00	250.00	800.00
2152-K.	Dallas	1,506,516	125.00	150.00	235.00
2152-K*.	Dallas		200.00	250.00	800.00
2152-L.	San Francisco	6,521,940	125.00	150.00	235.00
2152-L*.	San Francisco		200.00	250.00	800.00

Series of 1934-A
Signatures of Julian and Morgenthau

No.	Issuing Bank	Quantity Printed	VF-20	EF-40	Unc-63
2153-A.	Boston	102,000	$130.00	$150.00	$250.00
2153-A*.	Boston		130.00	150.00	250.00
2153-B.	New York	15,278,892	130.00	150.00	250.00
2153-B*.	New York		130.00	150.00	250.00
2153-C.	Philadelphia	588,000	130.00	150.00	250.00
2153-C*.	Philadelphia		130.00	150.00	250.00
2153-D.	Cleveland	645,300	130.00	150.00	250.00
2153-E.	Richmond	770,000	130.00	150.00	250.00
2153-F.	Atlanta	589,886	130.00	150.00	250.00
2153-G.	Chicago	3,328,800	130.00	150.00	250.00
2153-G*.	Chicago		130.00	150.00	250.00
2153-H.	St. Louis	434,208	130.00	150.00	250.00
2153-I.	Minneapolis	153,000	130.00	150.00	250.00
2153-I*	Minneapolis		130.00	150.00	250.00
2153-J.	Kansas City	455,000	130.00	150.00	250.00
2153-J*	Kansas City		130.00	150.00	250.00
2153-K.	Dallas	226,164	130.00	150.00	250.00
2153-L.	San Francisco	1,130,400	130.00	150.00	250.00
2153-L*.	San Francisco		130.00	150.00	250.00

Series of 1934-B
Signatures Julian and Vinson

No.	Issuing Bank	Quantity Printed	VF-20	EF-40	Unc-63
2154-A.	Boston	41,400	$150.00	$200.00	$350.00
2154-C.	Philadelphia	39,600	150.00	200.00	350.00
2154-D.	Cleveland	61,200	150.00	200.00	350.00
2154-E.	Richmond	977,400	150.00	200.00	350.00
2154-E*.	Richmond		1,250.00	1,750.00	3,250.00
2154-F.	Atlanta	645,000	150.00	200.00	350.00
2154-G.	Chicago	396,000	150.00	200.00	350.00
2154-H.	St. Louis	676,200	150.00	200.00	350.00
2154-H*.	St. Louis		1,250.00	1,500.00	3,250.00
2154-I.	Minneapolis	377,000	150.00	200.00	350.00
2154-I*.	Minneapolis		1,250.00	1,500.00	3,250.00
2154-J.	Kansas City	364,500	150.00	200.00	350.00
2154-J*.	Kansas City		1,250.00	1,500.00	3,250.00
2154-K.	Dallas	392,700	150.00	200.00	350.00
2154-K*.	Dallas		1,250.00	1,500.00	3,250.00

Federal Reserve Notes (Green Seal)
Series of 1934-C
Signatures of Julian and Snyder

No.	Issuing Bank	Quantity Printed	VF-20	EF-40	Unc-63
2155-A.	Boston	13,800	$150.00	$200.00	$375.00
2155-B.	New York	1,556,400	150.00	200.00	300.00
2155-C.	Philadelphia	13,200	150.00	200.00	375.00
2155-D.	Cleveland	1,473,200	150.00	200.00	300.00
2155-E.	Richmond		175.00	225.00	450.00
2155-E*.	Richmond		900.00	1,200.00	4,500.00
2155-F.	Atlanta	493,900	150.00	200.00	300.00
2155F*.	Atlanta		900.00	1,200.00	3,250.00
2155-G.	Chicago	612,000	150.00	200.00	300.00
2155-G*.	Chicago		900.00	1,200.00	4,500.00
2155-H.	St. Louis	957,000	150.00	200.00	300.00
2155-H*.	St. Louis		900.00	1,200.00	4,500.00
2155-I.	Minneapolis	392,904	150.00	200.00	300.00
2155-I*.	Minneapolis	392,904	900.00	1,200.00	4,500.00
2155-J.	Kansas City	401,100	150.00	200.00	300.00
2155-K.	Dallas	280,700	150.00	200.00	300.00
2155-L.	San Francisco	432,600	150.00	200.00	300.00
2155-L*.	San Francisco		900.00	1,200.00	4,500.00

Series of 1934-D
Signatures of Clark and Snyder

No.	Issuing Bank	Quantity Printed	VF-20	EF-40	Unc-63
2156-B.	New York	156	Rare	—	—
2156-C.	Philadelphia	308,400	$250.00	$300.00	$450.00
2156-C*.	Philadelphia	308,400	2,000.00	2,500.00	5,500.00
2156-F.	Atlanta	260,400	250.00	300.00	450.00
2156-F*.	Atlanta		2,000.00	2,500.00	5,500.00
2156-G.	Chicago	78,000	250.00	300.00	450.00
2156-G*.	Chicago		2,000.00	2,500.00	5,500.00
2156-H.	St. Louis	166,800	250.00	300.00	450.00
2156-K.	Dallas	66,000	250.00	300.00	450.00

Face of Notes 2157-2162.

Back of Notes 2157-2162.

SMALL-SIZE ONE HUNDRED DOLLAR NOTES

Federal Reserve Notes (Green Seal)

Series of 1950
Signatures of Clark and Snyder

No.	Issuing Bank	Quantity Printed	VF-20	EF-40	Unc-63
2157-A.	Boston	768,000			$300.00
2157-A*.	Boston		$275.00	$500.00	950.00
2157-B.	New York	3,908,000			300.00
2157-B*.	New York		275.00	500.00	950.00
2157-C	Philadelphia	1,332,000			300.00
2157-C*.	Philadelphia		275.00	500.00	950.00
2157-D	Cleveland	1,632,000			300.00
2157-E.	Richmond	4,076,000			300.00
2157-E*.	Richmond	4,076,000	275.00	500.00	950.00
2157-F.	Atlanta	1,824,000			300.00
2157-G.	Chicago	4,428,000			300.00
2157-G*.	Chicago		275.00	500.00	950.00
2157-H.	St. Louis	1,284,000			300.00
2157-H*.	St. Louis		275.00	500.00	950.00
2157-I.	Minneapolis	564,000			300.00
2157-J.	Kansas City	864,000			300.00
2157-J*.	Kansas City	864,000	300.00	575.00	1,450.00
2157-K.	Dallas	1,216,000			300.00
2157-L.	San Francisco	2,524,000			300.00
2157-L*.	San Francisco	2,524,000	275.00	500.00	950.00

Series of 1950-A
Signatures of Priest and Humphrey

No.	Issuing Bank	Quantity Printed	VF-20	EF-40	Unc-63
2158-A.	Boston	1,008,000			$275.00
2158-A*.	Boston		$200.00	$225.00	600.00
2158-B.	New York	2,880,000			275.00
2158-B*.	New York		200.00	225.00	600.00
2158-C.	Philadelphia	576,000			275.00
2158-C*.	Philadelphia		200.00	225.00	600.00
2158-D.	Cleveland	288,000			275.00
2158-D*.	Cleveland	288,000	225.00	450.00	600.00
2158-E.	Richmond	2,160,000			275.00
2158-E*	Richmond		200.00	225.00	600.00
2158-F.	Atlanta	288,000			275.00
2158-G.	Chicago	864,000			275.00
2158-G*.	Chicago		200.00	225.00	600.00
2158-H.	St. Louis	432,000			275.00
2158-H*	.St. Louis		200.00	225.00	600.00
2158-I.	Minneapolis	144,000			275.00
2158-J.	Kansas City	288,000			275.00
2158-J*	Kansas City		200.00	225.00	600.00
2158-K.	Dallas	432,000			275.00
2158-K*.	Dallas		200.00	225.00	600.00
2158-L.	San Francisco	720,000			275.00
2158-L*.	San Francisco		200.00	225.00	600.00

Series of 1950-B
Signatures of Priest and Anderson

No.	Issuing Bank	Quantity Printed	VF-20	EF-40	Unc-63
2159-A.	Boston	720,000			$245.00
2159-B.	New York	6,636,000			235.00
2159-B*.	New York		$200.00	$225.00	600.00
2159-C.	Philadelphia	720,000			245.00
2159-C*.	Philadelphia		200.00	250.00	600.00
2159-D.	Cleveland	432,000			245.00
2159-D*	Cleveland		200.00	250.00	600.00
2159-E.	Richmond	1,008,000			235.00
2159-F.	Atlanta	576,000			245.00
2159-F*.	Atlanta		200.00	250.00	600.00

Federal Reserve Notes (Green Seal)

Series of 1950-B
Signatures of Priest and Anderson

No.	Issuing Bank	Quantity Printed	VF-20	EF-40	Unc-63
2159-G.	Chicago	2,592,000			$235.00
2159-G*.	Chicago		$200.00	$250.00	600.00
2159-H.	St. Louis	1,152,000			235.00
2159-H*.	St. Louis		200.00	250.00	600.00
2159-I.	Minneapolis	288,000			260.00
2159-I*.	Minneapolis		200.00	250.00	600.00
2159-J.	Kansas City	720,000			245.00
2159-J*.	Kansas City		200.00	250.00	600.00
2159-K.	Dallas	1,728,000			235.00
2159-K*.	Dallas		200.00	250.00	600.00
2159-L	.San Francisco	2,880,000			235.00
2159-L*.	San Francisco		200.00	250.00	600.00

Series of 1950-C
Signatures of Smith and Dillon

No.	Issuing Bank	Quantity Printed	VF-20	EF-40	Unc-63
2160-A.	Boston	864,000			$250.00
2160-A*.	Boston		$250.00	$300.00	700.00
2160-B.	New York	2,448,000			235.00
2160-B*.	New York		250.00	300.00	700.00
2160-C.	Philadelphia	576,000			250.00
2160-C*.	Philadelphia		250.00	300.00	700.00
2160-D.	Cleveland	576,000			250.00
2160-D*.	Cleveland		250.00	300.00	700.00
2160-E.	Richmond	1,440,000			250.00
2160-E*.	Richmond		250.00	300.00	700.00
2160-F.	Atlanta	1,296,000			250.00
2160-F*.	Atlanta		250.00	300.00	700.00
2160-G.	Chicago	1,584,000			250.00
2160-G*.	Chicago		250.00	300.00	700.00
2160-H.	St. Louis	720,000			250.00
2160-H*.	.St. Louis		250.00	300.00	700.00
2160-I.	Minneapolis	288,000			250.00
2160-I*.	Minneapolis		250.00	300.00	700.00
2160-J.	Kansas City	432,000			250.00
2160-K.	Dallas	720,000			250.00
2160-K*.	Dallas		250.00	300.00	700.00
2160-L.	San Francisco	2,160,000			235.00
2160-L*.	San Francisco		250.00	300.00	700.00

Series of 1950-D
Signatures of Granahan and Dillon

No.	Issuing Bank	Quantity Printed	VF-20	EF-40	Unc-63
2161-A.	Boston	1,872,000			$235.00
2161-A*.	Boston		$200.00	$250.00	600.00
2161-B.	New York	7,632,000			230.00
2161-B*.	New York		200.00	250.00	600.00
2161-C.	Philadelphia	1,872,000			235.00
2161-C*.	Philadelphia		200.00	250.00	600.00
2161-D.	Cleveland	1,584,000			235.00
2161-D*.	Cleveland		200.00	250.00	600.00
2161-E.	Richmond	2,880,000			235.00
2161-E*.	Richmond		200.00	250.00	600.00
2161-F.	Atlanta	1,872,000			235.00
2161-F*.	Atlanta		200.00	250.00	600.00
2161-G.	Chicago	4,608,000			230.00
2161-G*.	Chicago		200.00	250.00	600.00
2161-H.	St. Louis	1,440,000			235.00
2161-H*.	St. Louis		200.00	250.00	600.00
2161-I.	Minneapolis	432,000			245.00

Federal Reserve Notes (Green Seal)

Series of 1950-D
Signatures of Granahan and Dillon

No.	Issuing Bank	Quantity Printed	VF-20	EF-40	Unc-63
2161-I*.	Minneapolis		$200.00	$250.00	$600.00
2161-J.	Kansas City	864,000			240.00
2161-J*.	Kansas City		200.00	250.00	600.00
2161-K.	Dallas	1,728,000			235.00
2161-K*.	Dallas		200.00	250.00	600.00
2161-L.	San Francisco	3,312,000			230.00
2161-L*.	San Francisco		200.00	250.00	600.00

Series of 1950-E
Signatures of Granahan and Fowler

No.	Issuing Bank	Quantity Printed	VF-20	EF-40	Unc-63
2162-B.	New York	3,024,000	$225.00	$300.00	$750.00
2162-B*	New York		500.00	750.00	2,750.00
2162-G.	Chicago	576,000	275.00	350.00	900.00
2162-G*.	Chicago		700.00	850.00	4,000.00
2162-L.	San Francisco	2,736,000	225.00	300.00	750.00
2162-L*.	San Francisco		550.00	800.00	3,000.00

Face of Notes 2163-2167.

Back of Notes 2163-2167.

Series of 1963-A
Signatures of Granahan and Fowler

No.	Issuing Bank	Quantity Printed	VF-20	EF-40	Unc-63
2163-A.	Boston	1,536,000			$200.00
2163-A*.	Boston	128,000	$185.00	$200.00	450.00
2163-B.	New York	12,544,000			185.00
2163-B*	New York	1,536,000	185.00	200.00	450.00
2163-C.	Philadelphia	1,792,000			200.00
2163-C*.	Philadelphia	192,000	185.00	200.00	450.00
2163-D.	Cleveland	2,304,000			200.00
2163-D*.	Cleveland	192,000	185.00	200.00	450.00
2163-E.	Richmond	2,816,000			200.00

SMALL-SIZE ONE HUNDRED DOLLAR NOTES

Federal Reserve Notes (Green Seal)

Series of 1963-A
Signatures of Granahan and Fowler

No.	Issuing Bank	Quantity Printed	VF-20	EF-40	Unc-63
2163-E*.	Richmond	192,000	$185.00	$200.00	$450.00
2163-F.	Atlanta	1,280,000			200.00
2163-F*.	Atlanta	128,000	185.00	200.00	450.00
2163-G.	Chicago	4,352,000			200.00
2163-G*.	Chicago	512,000	185.00	200.00	450.00
2163-H.	St. Louis	1,536,000			200.00
2163-H*.	St. Louis	256,000	185.00	200.00	450.00
2163-I.	Minneapolis	512,000			200.00
2163-I*.	Minneapolis	128,000	185.00	200.00	450.00
2163-J.	Kansas City	1,024,000			200.00
2163-J*.	Kansas City	128,000	185.00	200.00	450.00
2163-K.	Dallas	1,536,000			200.00
2163-K*.	Dallas	192,000	185.00	200.00	450.00
2163-L.	San Francisco	6,400,000			200.00
2163-L*.	San Francisco	832,000	185.00	200.00	450.00
2164-A.	Boston	2,048,000			200.00
2164-A*.	Boston	128,000	125.00	200.00	325.00
2164-B.	New York	11,520,000			200.00

Series of 1969
Signatures of Elston and Kennedy. With new Treasury seal

No.	Issuing Bank	Quantity Printed	VF-20	EF-40	Unc-63
2164-B*.	New York	128,000			$325.00
2164-C.	Philadelphia	2,560,000	$125.00	$200.00	200.00
2164-C*.	Philadelphia	128,000			325.00
2164-D.	Cleveland	768,000			200.00
2164-D*.	Cleveland	64,000	125.00	200.00	325.00
2164-E.	Richmond	2,560,000			200.00
2164-E*.	Richmond	192,000	125.00	200.00	325.00
2164-F.	Atlanta	2,304,000			200.00
2164-F*.	Atlanta	128,000	125.00	200.00	325.00
2164-G.	Chicago	5,888,000			200.00
2164-G*.	Chicago	256,000	125.00	200.00	325.00
2164-H.	St. Louis	1,280,000			200.00
2164-H*.	St. Louis	64,000	125.00	200.00	500.00
2164-I.	Minneapolis	512,000			200.00
2164-I*.	Minneapolis	64,000	125.00	200.00	500.00
2164-J.	Kansas City	1,792,000			200.00
2164-J*.	Kansas City	384,000	125.00	200.00	325.00
2164-K.	Dallas	2,048,000			200.00
2164-K*.	Dallas	128,000	125.00	200.00	325.00
2164-L.	San Francisco	7,168,000			200.00
2164-L*.	San Francisco	320,000	125.00	200.00	325.00

Series of 1969-A
Signatures of Kabis and Connally

No.	Issuing Bank	Quantity Printed	VF-20	EF-40	Unc-63
2165-A.	Boston	1,280,000			$200.00
2165-A*.	Boston	320,000	$125.00	$150.00	400.00
2165-B.	New York	11,264,000			200.00
2165-B*.	New York	640,000	125.00	150.00	400.00
2165-C.	Philadelphia	2,048,000			200.00
2165-C*.	Philadelphia	448,000	125.00	150.00	400.00
2165-D.	Cleveland	1,280,000			200.00
2165-D*.	Cleveland	192,000	125.00	150.00	400.00
2165-E.	Richmond	2,304,000			200.00
2165-E*.	Richmond	192,000	125.00	150.00	400.00
2165-F.	Atlanta	2,304,000			200.00
2165-F*.	Atlanta	64,000	125.00	150.00	400.00
2165-G.	Chicago	5,376,000			200.00
2165-G*.	Chicago	320,000	125.00	150.00	400.00

Federal Reserve Notes (Green Seal)

Series of 1969-A
Signatures of Kabis and Connally

No.	Issuing Bank	Quantity Printed	VF-20	EF-40	Unc-63
2165-H.	St. Louis	1,024,000			$200.00
2165-H*.	St. Louis	64,000	$150.00	$150.00	450.00
2165-I.	Minneapolis	1,024,000			200.00
2165-J.	Kansas City	512,000			200.00
2165-K.	Dallas	3,328,000			200.00
2165-K*.	Dallas	128,000	125.00	150.00	400.00
2165-L.	San Francisco	4,352,000			200.00
2165-L*.	San Francisco	640,000	125.00	150.00	400.00

Series of 1969-B
None printed.

Series of 1969-C
Signatures of Banuelos and Shultz

No.	Issuing Bank	Quantity Printed	VF-20	EF-40	Unc-63
2166-A.	Boston	2,048,000			$200.00
2166-A*.	Boston	64,000	$125.00	$150.00	350.00
2166-B.	New York	15,616,000			200.00
2166-B*	New York	256,000	135.00	160.00	400.00
2166-C.	Philadelphia	2,816,000			200.00
2166-C*.	Philadelphia	64,000	135.00	160.00	400.00
2166-D.	Cleveland	3,456,000			200.00
2166-D*.	Cleveland	64,000	135.00	160.00	400.00
2166-E.	Richmond	7,296,000			200.00
2166-E*.	Richmond	128,000	125.00	150.00	350.00
2166-F.	Atlanta	2,432,000			200.00
2166-F*.	Atlanta	64,000	135.00	175.00	400.00
2166-G.	Chicago	6,016,000			200.00
2166-G*.	Chicago	320,000	125.00	160.00	350.00
2166-H.	St. Louis	5,376,000			200.00
2166-H.	St. Louis	64,000	135.00	175.00	400.00
2166-I.	Minneapolis	512,000			200.00
2166-I*.	Minneapolis	64,000	135.00	175.00	400.00
2166-J.	Kansas City	4,736,000			200.00
2166-J*.	Kansas City	192,000	135.00	175.00	400.00
2166-K.	Dallas	2,944,000			200.00
2166-K*.	Dallas	64,000	135.00	175.00	400.00
2166-L.	San Francisco	10,240,000			200.00
2166-L*.	San Francisco	512,000	135.00	175.00	400.00

Series of 1974
Signatures of Neff and Simon

No.	Issuing Bank	Quantity Printed	VF-20	EF-40	Unc-63
2167-A.	Boston	11,520,000			$175.00
2167-A*.	Boston	320,000	$135.00	$175.00	400.00
2167-B.	New York	62,720,000			175.00
2167-B*.	New York	1,728,000	135.00	175.00	400.00
2167-C.	Philadelphia	7,680,000			175.00
2167-C*.	Philadelphia	192,000	135.00	175.00	400.00
2167-D.	Cleveland	8,320,000			175.00
2167-D*.	Cleveland	256,000	135.00	175.00	400.00
2167-E.	Richmond	11,520,000			175.00
2167-E*.	Richmond	256,000	135.00	175.00	400.00
2167-F.	Atlanta	4,480,000			175.00
2167-F*.	Atlanta	128,000	135.00	175.00	400.00
2167-G.	Chicago	26,880,000			175.00
2167-G*	Chicago	1,216,000	135.00	175.00	400.00
2167-H.	St. Louis	5,760,000			175.00
2167-H*.	St. Louis	192,000	135.00	175.00	400.00
2167-I.	Minneapolis	4,480,000			175.00
2167-I*.	Minneapolis	256,000	135.00	175.00	400.00

Federal Reserve Notes (Green Seal)

Series of 1974
Signatures of Neff and Simon

No.	Issuing Bank	Quantity Printed	VF-20	EF-40	Unc-63
2167-J.	Kansas City	5,760,000			$175.00
2167-J*.	Kansas City	448,000	$135.00	$175.00	400.00
2167-K.	Dallas	10,240,000			175.00
2167-K*.	Dallas	192,000	135.00	175.00	400.00
2167-L.	San Francisco	29,440,000			175.00
2167-L*	San Francisco	896,000	135.00	175.00	400.00

Series of 1977
Signatures of Morton and Blumenthal

No.	Issuing Bank	Quantity Printed	VF-20	EF-40	Unc-63
2168-A.	Boston	19,200,000			$175.00
2168-A*.	Boston	320,000		$125.00	275.00
2168-B.	New York	166,400,000			175.00
2168-B*.	New York	1,664,000		125.00	275.00
2168-C.	Philadelphia	5,195,000			175.00
2168-C*.	Philadelphia	128,000		125.00	275.00
2168-D.	Cleveland	16,640,000			175.00
2168-D*.	Cleveland	192,000		125.00	275.00
2168-E.	Richmond	24,320,000			175.00
2168-E*.	Richmond	384,000		125.00	275.00
2168-F.	Atlanta	3,840,000			175.00
2168-F*.	Atlanta	64,000		130.00	325.00
2168-G.	Chicago	39,680,000			175.00
2168-G*.	Chicago	960,000		125.00	275.00
2168-H.	St. Louis	15,360,000			175.00
2168-H*.	St. Louis	448,000		125.00	275.00
2168-I.	Minneapolis	5,195,000			175.00
2168-I*.	Minneapolis	192,000		125.00	275.00
2168-J.	Kansas City	38,400,000			175.00
2168-J*.	Kansas City	640,000		125.00	275.00
2168-K.	Dallas	38,400,000			175.00
2168-K*.	Dallas	640,000		125.00	275.00
2168-L.	San Francisco	39,680,000			175.00
2168-L*.	San Francisco	576,000		125.00	275.00

Series of 1981
Signatures of Buchanan and Regan

No.	Issuing Bank	Quantity Printed	VF-20	EF-40	Unc-63
2169-A.	Boston	8,960,000			$200.00
2169-B.	New York	105,600,000			175.00
2169-C.	Philadelphia	12,800,000			200.00
2169-D.	Cleveland	5,760,000			200.00
2169-E.	Richmond	23,680,000			175.00
2169-E*.	Richmond	640,000	$275.00	$500.00	900.00
2169-F.	Atlanta	6,400,000			200.00
2169-G.	Chicago	33,280,000			175.00
2169-H.	St. Louis	5,760,000			200.00
2169-I.	Minneapolis	3,200,000			225.00
2169-J.	Kansas City	23,680,000			200.00
2169-K.	Dallas	23,680,000			200.00
2169-L.	San Francisco	24,960,000			200.00

Series of 1981-A
Signatures of Ortega and Regan

No.	Issuing Bank	Quantity Printed	VF-20	EF-40	Unc-63
2170-A.	Boston	16,000,000			$200.00
2170-B.	New York	64,000,000			200.00
2170-C.	Philadelphia	3,200,000			200.00
2170-D.	Cleveland	6,400,000			200.00
2170-E.	Richmond	12,800,000			200.00
2170-F.	Atlanta	12,800,000			200.00

SMALL-SIZE ONE HUNDRED DOLLAR NOTES

Federal Reserve Notes (Green Seal)

No.	Issuing Bank	Quantity Printed	VF-20	EF-40	Unc-63
2170-G.	Chicago	22,400,000			$200.00
2170-H.	St. Louis	12,800,000			200.00
2170-I.	Minneapolis	3,200,000			200.00
2170-K.	Dallas	3,200,000			200.00
2170-L.	San Francisco	19,200,000			200.00
2170-L*.	San Francisco	640,000	$300.00	$500.00	900.00

Series of 1985
Signatures of Ortega and Baker

No.	Issuing Bank	Quantity Printed	VF-20	EF-40	Unc-63
2171-A.	Boston	32,000,000			$175.00
2171-B.	New York	259,200,000			175.00
2171-C.	Philadelphia	19,200,000			175.00
2171-D.	Cleveland	28,800,000			175.00
2171-D*.	Cleveland	1,280,000			375.00
2171-E.	Richmond	54,400,000			175.00
2171-F.	Atlanta	16,000,000			175.00
2171-G.	Chicago	64,000,000			175.00
2171-H.	St. Louis	12,800,000			175.00
2171-I.	Minneapolis	12,800,000			175.00
2171-J.	Kansas City	12,800,000			175.00
2171-J*.	Kansas City	1,280,000			375.00
2171-K.	Dallas	48,000,000			175.00
2171-K*.	Dallas	3,200,000			375.00
2171-L.	San Francisco	38,400,000			100.00

Series of 1988
Signatures of Ortega and Brady

No.	Issuing Bank	Quantity Printed	VF-20	EF-40	Unc-63
2172-A.	Boston	9,600,000			$175.00
2172-B.	New York	448,000,000			175.00
2172-B*.	New York	4,480,000	$135.00	$200.00	450.00
2172-C	Philadelphia	9,600,000			175.00
2172-D.	Cleveland	35,200,000			175.00
2172-E.	Richmond	19,200,000			175.00
2172-G.	Chicago	51,200,000			175.00
2172-H.	St. Louis	9,600,000			175.00
2172-J.	Kansas City	9,600,000			175.00
2172-L.	San Francisco	10,200,000			175.00

Series of 1988-A
None Printed.

Series of 1990
Signatures of Villalpando and Brady

No.	Issuing Bank	Quantity Printed	Unc-63
2173-A.	Boston	76,800,000	$150.00
2173-B.	New York	595,200,000	150.00
2173-B*.	New York	1,880,000	200.00
2173-C.	Philadelphia	112,000,000	150.00
2173-C*.	Philadelphia	1,280,000	200.00
2173-D.	Cleveland	115,200,000	150.00
2173-E.	Richmond	108,800,000	150.00
2173-F.	Atlanta	64,000,000	150.00
2173-G.	Chicago	134,400,000	150.00
2173-G*.	Chicago	640,000	200.00
2173-H.	St. Louis	121,600,000	150.00
2173-I.	Minneapolis	48,000,000	150.00
2173-J.	Kansas City	76,800,000	150.00
2173-J*.	Kansas City	3,200,000	200.00

Federal Reserve Notes (Green Seal)

Series of 1988-A
None Printed.

Series of 1990
Signatures of Villalpando and Brady

No.	Issuing Bank	Quantity Printed	Unc-63
2173-K.	Dallas	165,400,000	$150.00
2173-K*.	Dallas	1,920,000	200.00
2173-L.	San Francisco	147,200,000	150.00
2173-L*.	San Francisco	3,200,000	200.00

Series of 1993
Signatures of Withrow and Bentsen

No.	Issuing Bank	Quantity Printed	Unc-63
2174-A.	Boston	83,200,000	$150.00
2174-B.	New York	288,,000,000	150.00
2174-B*.	New York	2,560,000	175.00
2174-C.	Philadelphia	41,600,000	150.00
2174-C*.	Philadelphia	1,280,000	175.00
2174-D.	Cleveland	9,600,000	150.00
2174-D*.	Cleveland	1,024,000	175.00
2174-E.	Richmond	64,000,000	150.00
2174-F.	Atlanta	150,400,000	150.00

Series of 1993
Signatures of Withrow and Bentsen

No.	Issuing Bank	Quantity Printed	Unc-63
2174-G.	Chicago	44,800,000	$150.00
2174-H.	St. Louis	16,000,000	150.00
2174-H*.	St. Louis	640,000	175.00
2174-I.	Minneapolis	9,600,000	150.00
2174-J.	Kansas City	9,600,000	150.00
2174-K.	Dallas	51,200,000	150.00
2174-L.	San Francisco	19,200,000	150.00

Face of Notes 2175 -

Back of Notes 2175 -

SMALL-SIZE ONE HUNDRED DOLLAR NOTES

Federal Reserve Notes (Green Seal)

Series of 1996
Signatures of Withrow and Rubin
Printed in Washington, DC

No.	Issuing Bank	Quantity Printed	Unc-63
2175-A.	Boston	125,600,000	$125.00
2175-A*.	Boston	2,560,000	165.00
2175-B.	New York	2,325,600,000	125.00
2175-B*.	New York	17,920,000	125.00
2175-C.	Philadelphia	86,400,000	125.00
2175-D.	Cleveland	176,800,000	125.00
2175-D*.	Cleveland	160,000	175.00
2175-E.	Richmond	276,800,000	125.00
2175-E*.	Richmond	3,200,000	165.00
2175-F.	Atlanta	222,400,000	125.00
2175-F*.	Atlanta	2,560,000	165.00
2175-G.	Chicago	244,800,000	125.00
2175-G*.	Chicago	1,920,000	165.00
2175-H.	St. Louis	112,800,000	125.00
2175-I.	Minneapolis	32,000,000	125.00
2175-J.	Kansas City	83,200,000	125.00
2175-K.	Dallas	144,800,000	125.00
2175-K*.	Dallas	1,920,000	165.00
2175-L.	San Francisco	406,400,000	125.00
2175-L*.	San Francisco	2,560,000	165.00

Series of 1999
Signatures of Withrow and Summers
Printed in Washington, DC

No.	Issuing Bank	Quantity Printed	Unc-63
2176-A.	Boston	48,000,000	$125.00
2176-A*.	Boston	3,520,000	145.00
2176-B.	New York	172,800,000	125.00
2176-B*	New York	3,840,000	145.00
2176-C.	Philadelphia	3,200,000	145.00
2176-D.	Cleveland	19,200,000	125.00
2176-E.	Richmond	60,800,000	125.00
2176-F.	Atlanta	16,000,000	145.00
2176-G.	Chicago	52,400,000	125.00
2176-H.	St. Louis	22,400,000	125.00
2176-I.	Minneapolis	70,400,000	125.00
2176-J.	Kansas City	25,600,000	125.00
2176-K.	Dallas	19,200,000	125.00

Series of 2001
Signatures of Marin and O'Neill
Printed in Washington, DC

No.	Issuing Bank	Quantity Printed	Unc-63
2177-A.	Boston	32,000,000	Current
2177-B.	New York	579,200,000	Current
2177-B*.	New York	320,000	Current
2177-C.	Philadelphia	32,000,000	Current
2177-D.	Cleveland	19,200,000	Current
2177-D*.	Cleveland	1,920,000	Current
2177-E.	Richmond	64,000,000	Current
2177-E*.	Richmond	1,920,000	Current
2177-F.	Atlanta	99,200,000	Current
2177-F*.	Atlanta	1,600,000	Current
2177-G.	Chicago	57,600,000	Current
2177-H.	St. Louis	25,600,000	Current
2177-I.	Minneapolis	9,600,000	Current
2177-J.	Kansas City	22,400,000	Current
2177-K.	Dallas	60,800,000	Current
2177-L.	San Francisco	147,200,000	Current

Federal Reserve Notes (Green Seal)

Series of 2003
Signatures of Marin and Snow
Printed in Washington, DC

No.	Issuing Bank	Unc-63
2178-A.	Boston	Current
2178-B.	New York	Current
2178-B*.	New York	Current
2178-C.	Philadelphia	Current
2178-D.	Cleveland	Current
2178-E.	Richmond	Current
2178-E*.	Richmond	Current
2178-F.	Atlanta	Current
2178-F*.	Atlanta	Current
2178-G.	Chicago	Current
2178-H.	St. Louis	Current
2178-I.	Minneapolis	Current
2178-J.	Kansas City	Current
2178-K.	Dallas	Current
2178-K*.	Dallas	Current
2178-L.	San Francisco	Current

Large-size $500 notes were made in several different series from the 1860s through the 1920s. Early issues range from very rare to non-existent; most later varieties are elusive. Small-size Federal Reserve Notes and Gold Certificates were issued, each depicting William McKinley on the face. These are scarce today. However, enough exist that many varieties can be gathered by the interested collector.

$500

FIVE HUNDRED DOLLAR NOTES

Interest Bearing Notes

No.	Denomination	
195d.	Five Hundred Dollars.	1 Proof Known

No.	Denomination	
200.	Five Hundred Dollars. The Ship *New Ironsides*.	Unknown

Face of Note 202a.
Bust of General Winfield Scott in center; vignettes of a wayfarer and farmer at left and right.

Back of Note 202c.

No.	Denomination	
202c.	Five Hundred Dollars.	1 Proof Known

Liberty and eagle.

No.	Denomination	
205.	Five Hundred Dollars. Liberty and Eagle.	Unknown

Face of Note 209. Head of George Washington with female representations of
Justice and Transportation at left and right.

Interest Bearing Notes

Back of Note 209.

No.	Denomination		
209.	Five Hundred Dollars. . . . . .2005 Heritage Auction, sold for $299,000 . . . . .Unique

Face of Note 212b. Bust of Alexander Hamilton with a mortar firing at left and a 3/4 bust of George Washington at right.

Back of Note 212b.

LARGE-SIZE FIVE HUNDRED DOLLAR NOTES

Interest Bearing Notes

No.	Denomination	
212b.	Five Hundred Dollars.	1 Known
212f.	Five Hundred Dollars.	1 Known

Legal Tender Notes

Most $500 Legal Tender Notes are represented by one to six notes known. Most examples are held in government institutions. When privately held notes are sold, prices from $75,000 to $200,000 are not uncommon.

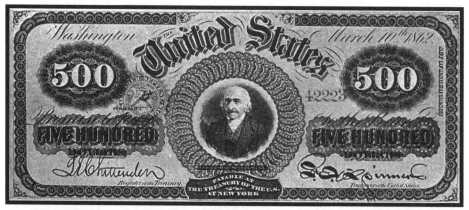

Face of Notes 183a-183d. Facing bust of Secretary of the Treasury (1801-1813) Albert Gallatin.

Back of Notes 183a -183d.

No.	Act	Signatures	Seal	
183a.	1862	Chittenden Spinner	Red. First Obligation	1 Known
183b.	1862	Chittenden Spinner	Red. Second Obligation	Unknown
183c.	1863	Chittenden Spinner	Red. Second Obligation, One Serial No. . . .	4 Known
183d.	1863	Chittenden Spinner	Red. Second Obligation, Two Serial No's. . . .	1 Known

Legal Tender Notes

Face of Note 184. Justice seated at left; at right, bust of President John Quincy Adams.

Back of Note 184.

No.	Series	Signatures		Seal		
184.	1869	Allison	Spinner	Large Red	4 Known	Extremely Rare

Legal Tender Notes

Face of Notes 185a-185n. At right, bust of Major General Joseph King Mansfield;
female representation of Victory standing at left.

Back of Notes 185a-185n.

No.	Series	Signatures		Seal	
185a.	1874	Allison	Spinner	Small Red, Rays	
185b.	1875	Allison	New	Small Red, Rays	
185c.	1875	Allison	Wyman	Small Red, Rays	
185d.	1878	Allison	Gilfillan	Small Red, Rays	
185e.	1880	Scofield	Gilfillan	Large Brown	Unknown
185f.	1880	Bruce	Wyman	Large Brown	
185g.	1880	Rosecrans	Jordan	Large Red, Plain	Unknown
185h.	1880	Rosecrans	Hyatt	Large Red, Plain	Unknown
185i.	1880	Rosecrans	Huston	Large Red, Spiked	
185j.	1880	Rosecrans	Nebeker	Small Red, Scalloped	
185k.	1880	Tillman	Morgan	Small Red, Scalloped	
185l.	1880	Bruce	Roberts	Small Red, Scalloped	
185m.	1880	Lyons	Roberts	Small Red, Scalloped	
185n.	1880	Napier	McClung	Small Red, Scalloped	Unknown

National Bank Notes
"First Charter Period" (Original Series and Series of 1875)

Face of Notes 464-464a (not shown) depicts the Spirit of the Navy *at left;*
at right, the steamship Sirius *arriving in New York City.*

Back of Notes 464-464a (not shown) depicts the surrender of General Burgoyne
to General Gates at the Battle of Saratoga.

National Bank Notes
"First Charter Period" (Original Series and Series of 1875)

No.	Series	Signatures		Seal	
464.	Original	Colby	Spinner	Red, Rays	Extremely Rare
464a.	1875	Allison	New	Red, Scalloped	Extremely Rare
	(173 pieces are still outstanding.)				

Gold Certificates

No.	Denomination	
1166-d.	Five Hundred Dollar Note.	Unknown

Head of Lincoln

No.	Denomination	
1166-l.	Five Hundred Dollar Note	Unique
1166-n.	Five Hundred Dollar Note 1875.	Unknown

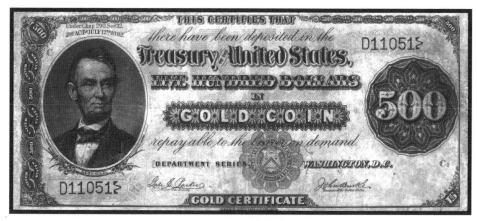

Face of Notes 1215a-1217. Bust of Abraham Lincoln.

Back of Notes 1215a-1217. Large spread-winged eagle.

LARGE-SIZE FIVE HUNDRED DOLLAR NOTES

Gold Certificates

No.	Series	Signatures		Seal		VG-8	F-12	VF-20	EF-40	Unc-63
1215a.	1882	Bruce	Gilfillan	Brown		Unique	—	—	—	—
1215b.	1882	Bruce	Gilfillan	Brown		Unknown	—	—	—	—

Above countersigned by Thomas C. Acton, Assistant. Treasurer, and payable in New York

No.	Series	Signatures		Seal		VG-8	F-12	VF-20	EF-40	Unc-63
1215c.	1882	Bruce	Wyman	Brown		Unique	—	—	—	—
1215d.	1882	Rosecrans	Hyatt	Large Red		Unique	—	—	—	—
1216.	1882	Lyons	Roberts	Small Red		$5,000.00	$9,500.00	$13,500.00	Rare	—
1216a.	1882	Parker	Burke	Small Red		5,000.00	9,500.00	13,500.00	Rare	—
1216b.	1882	Teehee	Burke	Small Red		5,000.00	9,500.00	13,500.00	Rare	—
1217.	1922	Speelman	White	Small Red		5,000.00	10,500.00	14,500.00	Rare	—

Compound Interest Treasury Notes

Face of Notes 194-194b (not shown) depicts the ship, New Ironsides.

No.	Act	Overprint Date	Signatures		
194.	1863	June 10, 1864	Chittenden	Spinner	Unknown
194a.	1864	July 15, 1864	Chittenden	Spinner	Unknown
194b.	1864	Aug. 15, 1864 - Oct. 1, 1865 . .	Colby	Spinner	Unknown

National Gold Bank Notes

Face of Note 1166a (not shown) depicts, at left, the Spirit of the Navy;
at right, the steamship Sirius *arriving in New York City.*
Back of Note 1166a (not shown) depicts an array of contemporary United States gold coins.

No.	
1166a.	This denomination was issued by three banks—two in San Francisco, and one in Sacramento.
	No specimen of these notes is now known to exist, although four notes are still outstanding.

Silver Certificates

Face of Notes 345a-345d. Profile bust of Senator Charles Sumner.
The 1878 countersigned note is without the legend "Series of 1878."

Back of Notes 345a-345d.

No.	Series	Signatures		Seal	
345a.	1878	Scofield	Gilfillan	Large Red, Rays (countersigned)	Unique
345b.	1880	Scofield	Gilfillan	Large Brown	Unknown
345c.	1880	Bruce	Gilfillan	Large Brown	Rare
345d.	1880	Bruce	Wyman	Large Brown	Extremely Rare

Treasury or Coin Notes

Face of Note 379 (not shown) depicts bust of General William T. Sherman.

No.	Series	Signatures		
379.	1891	Bruce	Roberts	Unknown

Federal Reserve Notes

Face of Notes 1132-1132b. Bust of Chief Justice John Marshall.

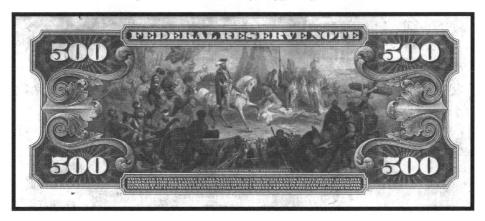

Back of Notes 1132-1132b.

Series of 1918
Different bank varieties are known

No.	Signatures		VG-8	F-12	VF-20	EF-40	Unc-63
1132.	Burke	Glass	$3,750.00	$7,500.00	$9,500.00	$14,000.00	$25,000.00
1132a.	Burke	Houston	2 Known	—	—	—	—
1132b.	White	Mellon	3 Known	—	—	—	—

SMALL SIZE FIVE HUNDRED DOLLAR NOTES

Gold Certificates (Gold Seal)

No.	Series	Signatures	Quantity Printed	VG-8	F-12	VF-20	EF-40	Unc-63
2407.	1928	Woods Mellon	.....420,000	$1,750.00	$3,000.00	$5,000.00	$7,500.00	$17,500.00

Federal Reserve Notes (Green Seal)

Face of Notes 2200-2204.

Back of Notes 2200-2204.

Series of 1928
Signatures of Woods and Mellon

No.	Issuing Bank	Quantity Printed	EF-40	Unc-63
2200-A.	Boston	69,120	$9,000.00	$14,000.00
2200-A*.	Boston		Unknown	—
2200-B.	New York	299,400	1,250.00	4,000.00
2200-B*.	New York		Unknown	—
2200-C.	Philadelphia	135,120	1,250.00	4,000.00
2200-C*.	Philadelphia		12,500.00	35,000.00
2200-D.	Cleveland	166,440	1,250.00	4,000.00
2200-D*.	San Francisco		Unknown	—
2200-E.	Richmond	84,720	1,500.00	5,250.00
2200-E*.	Richmond		Unknown	—
2200-F.	Atlanta	69,360	1,500.00	5,250.00
2200-F*.	Atlanta		Unknown	—
2200-G.	Chicago	573,600	1,100.00	3,000.00
2200-G*.	Chicago		12,500.00	35,000.00
2200-H.	St. Louis	66,180	1,100.00	3,000.00
2200-I.	Minneapolis	34,680	1,500.00	5,250.00
2200-I*.	Minneapolis		Unknown	—
2200-J.	Kansas City	510,720	1,500.00	5,250.00
2200-J*.	Kansas City		Unknown	—
2200-K.	Dallas	70,56	1,500.00	5,250.00
2200-K*.	Dallas		Unknown	—
2200-L.	San Francisco	64,080	1,500.00	5,250.00
2200-L*.	San Francisco		Unknown	—

Federal Reserve Notes (Green Seal)
Series of 1934

No.	Issuing Bank	Quantity Printed	EF-40	Unc-63
2201-A.	Boston	56,628	$950.00	$1,750.00
2201-B.	New York	288,000	950.00	1,500.00
2201-B*.	New York		2,500.00	6,500.00
2201-C.	Philadelphia	31,200	950.00	1,750.00
2201-C*.	Philadelphia		2,500.00	6,500.00
2201-D.	Cleveland	39,000	950.00	1,750.00
2201-D*.			2,500.00	6,500.00
2201-E.	Richmond	40,800	950.00	1,750.00
2201-E*.	Richmond		2,500.00	6,500.00
2201-F.	Atlanta	46,200	950.00	1,750.00
2201-F*.	Atlanta		2,500.00	6,500.00
2201-G.	Chicago	212,400	950.00	1,500.00
2201-G*.	Chicago		2,500.00	6,500.00
2201-H.	St. Louis	24,000	950.00	1,750.00
2201-H*.	St. Louis		2,500.00	6,500.00
2201-I.	Minneapolis	24,000	1,100.00	2,000.00
2201-I*.	Minneapolis		3,500.00	8,500.00
2201-J.	Kansas City	40,800	950.00	1,750.00
2201-J*.	Kansas City		2,500.00	6,500.00
2201-K.	Dallas	31,200	950.00	2,000.00
2201-K*.	Dallas		3,500.00	8,500.00
2201-L.	San Francisco	83,400	950.00	1,750.00
2201-L*.	San Francisco		2,500.00	6,500.00

Series of 1934-A
Signatures of Julian and Morgenthau

No.	Issuing Bank	Quantity Printed	EF-40	Unc-63
2202-B.	New York	276,000	$950.00	$1,750.00
2202-B*.	New York		4,500.00	10,000.00
2202-C.	Philadelphia	45,300	950.00	1,750.00
2202-D.	Cleveland	28,800	950.00	1,750.00
2202-E.	Richmond	36,000	950.00	1,750.00
2202-E*.	Richmond		4,500.00	10,000.00
2202-F.	Atlanta	incl. above	950.00	1,750.00
2202-G.	Chicago	214,800	950.00	1,750.00
2202-G*.	Chicago		4,500.00	10,000.00
2202-H.	St. Louis	57,600	950.00	1,750.00
2202-I.	Minneapolis	14,400	1,200.00	2,000.00
2202-J.	Kansas City	55,200	950.00	1,750.00
2202-J*.	Kansas City		4,500.00	10,000.00
2202-K.	Dallas	34,800	1,200.00	2,000.00
2202-L.	San Francisco	93,000	950.00	1,750.00
2202-L*.	San Francisco		4,500.00	10,000.00

Series of 1934-B
Signatures of Julian and Vinson
Although these two series (1934-B and 1934-C) are reported, none are known.

No.	Issuing Bank	Quantity Printed	
2203-F.	Atlanta	2,472	Rare

Series of 1934-C
Signatures of Julian and Snyder
The Bureau of Engraving and Printing records indicate the existence of these notes although none have been seen.

No.	Issuing Bank	Quantity Printed	
2204-A.	Boston	1,440	Rare
2204-B.	New York	204	Very Rare

Large-size $1,000 notes were made in several series from the 1860s through the 1920s. Some early varieties no longer survive, and those that do are exceedingly rare. Most later varieties are elusive. Small-size Federal Reserve Notes and Gold Certificates were issued, each depicting Grover Cleveland on the face. These are scarce today. However, enough exist that varieties can be collected.

$1,000

Interest Bearing Notes

No.	Denomination	
201.	One Thousand Dollars.	Unknown

 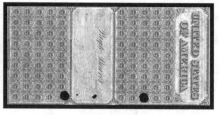

Face of Note 202d. *Back of Note 202d.*

No.	Denomination	
202d.	One Thousand Dollars.	1 Proof Known
206.	One Thousand Dollars.	Unknown
210.	One Thousand Dollars.	Unknown
212c.	One Thousand Dollars. Probably Issued.	Unknown
212g.	One Thousand Dollars.	3 Known

Legal Tender Notes

All $1,000 Legal Tender Notes are either unknown, unique, or only a few are known. The exception is F-187j, of which slightly over 10 are known. In today's market an example should bring $75,000 to $200,000 depending on condition.

Face of Notes 186a-186e (not shown) depict facing bust of Robert Morris.

No.	Act	Signatures	Seal	
186a.	1862	Chittenden Spinner	Red. First Obligation	Unknown
186b.	1862	Chittenden Spinner	Red. Second Obligation	Unknown
186c.	1863	Chittenden Spinner	Red. Second Obligation, One Serial No.	
	American Bank Note Co. at right, National Bank Note Co. at left			Unique
186d.	1863	Chittenden Spinner	Red. Second Obligation, One Serial No.	
	American Bank Note Co. at right only		....	2 Known
186e.	1863	Chittenden Spinner	Red. Second Obligation, Two Serial Nos.	
	American Bank Note Co. at right only		....	Unique

Face of Note 186f. Bust of DeWitt Clinton in center; Christopher Columbus seated at left.

Legal Tender Notes

Back of Note 186f.

No.	Act	Signatures		Seal		
186f.	1869	Allison	Spinner	Large Red		2 Known

Face of Notes 187a-187f. Bust of DeWitt Clinton in center; Christopher Columbus seated at left.

Back of Notes 187a-187f.

LARGE-SIZE ONE THOUSAND DOLLAR NOTES

Legal Tender Notes

No.	Series	Signatures		Seal
187a.	1878	Allison	Gilfillan	Small Red, Rays
187b.	1880	Bruce	Wyman	Large Brown
187c.	1880	Rosecrans	Jordan	Large Red, Plain
187d.	1880	Rosecrans	Hyatt	Large Red, Spiked
187e.	1880	Rosecrans	Huston	Large Red, Spiked
187f.	1880	Rosecrans	Nebeker	Large Brown
187g.	1880	Tillman	Morgan	Small Red, Scalloped
187h.	1880	Tillman	Roberts	Small Red, Scalloped
187i.	1880	Bruce	Roberts	Small Red, Scalloped
187j.	1880	Lyons	Roberts	Small Red, Scalloped
187k.	1880	Vernon	Trent	Small Red, Scalloped
187l.	1880	Napler	McClung	Small Red, Scalloped

All these are extremely rare.

Compound Interest Treasury Notes

No.	Act	Overprint Date	Signatures			
195.	1864	July 15, 1864	Chittenden	Spinner		Unknown
195a.	1864	Aug. 15, 1864 - Sep. 15, 1865	Colby	Spinner		Unknown

National Bank Notes

Face of Note 465 (not shown) depicts General Winfield Scott at left; U.S. Capitol at right.
Back of Note 465 (not shown) depicts Washington Resigning His Commission.

No.	Denomination	
465.	One Thousand Dollars.	(Unknown, although 21 pieces are still outstanding.)

Silver Certificates

Face of Notes 346a-346d. Bust of William L. Marcy.

Silver Certificates

Back of Notes 346a-346d.

The 1878 countersigned note is without the legend "Series of 1878."

No.	Series	Signatures		Seal	
346a.	1878	Scofield	Gilfillan	Large Red, Rays (countersigned)	Unknown
346b.	1880	Scofield	Gilfillan	Large Brown	Unknown
346c.	1880	Bruce	Gilfillan	Large Brown	Unknown
346d.	1880	Bruce	Wyman	Large Brown	Extremely Rare

Face of Note 346e. Bust of William L. Marcy at right; at left, female leaning on shield.

Back of Note 346e.

Silver Certificates

No.	Series	Signatures		Seal	
346e.	1891	Tillman	Morgan	Small Red	Extremely Rare

Treasury Notes

Face of Notes 379a-379b.

Profile bust of General George Gordon Meade.

Back of Notes 379a-379b.

No.	Series	Signatures		Seal	
379a.	1890	Rosecrans	Huston	Large Brown	Extremely Rare
379b.	1890	Rosecrans	Nebeker	Small Red	2 Known

The nicer of two known F-379a notes in AU sold in 1998 by Lyn Knight Currency Auctions for $792,000.

Treasury Notes

Back of Notes 379c-379d (not shown). Face is similar to Notes 379a and 379b.

No.	Series	Signatures		Seal	
379c.	1891	Tillman	Morgan	Small Red	Unique
379d.	1891	Rosecrans	Nebeker	Small Red	Unique

Gold Certificates

No.	Denomination	Series	
1166e.	One Thousand Dollars.		Unique
1166j.	One Thousand Dollars.		Unique
1166o.	One Thousand Dollars.	1875	Unknown

Face of 1218 (not shown) features a bust of Alexander Hamilton.

Back of Note 1218 (not shown) depicts large eagle; Roman numeral "M" at left.

No.	Series	Signatures		Seal	
1218.	1882	Bruce	Gilfillan	Brown	Unknown
1218a.	1882	Bruce	Gilfillan	Brown	Extremely Rare

Countersigned by Thomas C. Acton, Assistant Treasurer, payable at New York.

No.	Series	Signatures		Seal	
1218b.	1882	Bruce	Wyman	Brown	Unique
1218c.	1882	Rosecrans	Hyatt	Large Red	Unique
1218d.	1882	Rosecrans	Huston	Large Brown	Extremely Rare
1218e.	1882	Rosecrans	Nebeker	Small Red	Extremely Rare
1218f.	1882	Lyons	Roberts	Small Red	Rare
1218g.	1882	Lyons	Treat	Small Red	Rare

Gold Certificates

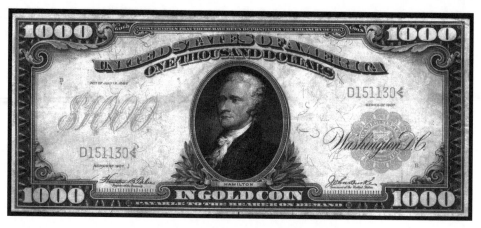

Face of Notes 1219-1220. Bust of Alexander Hamilton.

Back of Notes 1219- 1220.

No.	Series	Signatures		Seal	VG-8	F-12	VF-20	EF-40	Unc-63
1219.	1907	Vernon	Treat	Gold	Rare	—	—	—	—
1219a.	1907	Vernon	McClung	Gold	Unknown	—	—	—	—
1219b.	1907	Napier	McClung	Gold	Unique	—	—	—	—
1219c.	1907	Napier	Burke	Gold	Extremely Rare	—	—	—	—
1219d.	1907	Parker	Burke	Gold	$9,000.00	$10,500.00	$20,000.00	—	—
1219e.	1907	Teehee	Burke	Gold	6,500.00	9,500.00	18,000.00	—	—
1220.	1922	Speelman	White	Gold	9,000.00	10,500.00	20,000.00	—	—

Federal Reserve Notes

Face of Notes 1133-1133b. Bust of Alexander Hamilton.

Back of Notes 1133-1133b.

Series of 1918
Different bank varieties are known.

No.	Signatures		VG-8	F-12	VF-20	EF-40	Unc-63
1133	Burke	Glass	$4,000.00	$7,000.00	$12,500.00	$17,000.00	$37,500.00
1133a.	Burke	Houston	5,500.00	8,500.00	15,000.00	—	—
1133b.	White	Mellon	5,500.00	9,500.00	15,000.00	—	—

Gold Certificates (Gold Seal)

The design (not shown) is identical to that of the Federal Reserve Notes to follow, except for different wording to indicate "Gold Certificate" and the use of a gold-colored seal and serial numbers.

No.	Denomination	Series	Signatures	Quantity Printed	VG-8	F-12	VF-20	EF-40	Unc-63
2408	One Thou. Dollars	1928	Woods Mellon	28,800	$4,500.00	$6,000.00	$8,500.00	$11,500.00	$25,000.00
2409	One Thou. Dollars	1934	Julian Morgenthau	84,000	For bank use only			Rare	—

Federal Reserve Notes (Green Seal)

Face of Notes 2210-2213.

Back of Notes 2210-2213.

Series of 1928
Signatures of Woods and Mellon

No.	Issuing Bank	Quantity Printed	VF-20	EF-40	Unc-63
2210-A.	Boston	58,320	$10,000.00	$12,500.00	$20,000.00
2210-A*.	Boston		Unknown	—	—
2210-B.	New York	139,200	1,800.00	2,100.00	4,000.00
2210-B*.	New York		17,500.00	—	—
2210-C.	Philadelphia	96,708	2,000.00	2,500.00	5,250.00
2210-C*.	Philadelphia		17,500.00	—	—
2210-D.	Cleveland	79,680	2,000.00	2,500.00	5,250.00
2210-D*.	Cleveland		17,500.00	—	—
2210-E.	Richmond	66,840	2,000.00	2,500.00	5,250.00
2210-E*.	Richmond		17,500.00	—	—
2210-F.	Atlanta	47,400	2,000.00	2,500.00	5,250.00
2210-F*.	Atlanta		Unknown	—	—
2210-G.	Chicago	355,800	1,800.00	2,100.00	4,000.00
2210-G*.	Chicago		17,500.00	—	—
2210-H.	St. Louis	60,000	1,800.00	2,100.00	4,000.00
2210-H*.	St. Louis		Unknown	—	—
2210-I.	Minneapolis	26,640	2,250.00	2,750.00	15,000.00
2210-I*.	Minneapolis		Unknown	—	—
2210-J.	Kansas City	62,172	2,000.00	2,500.00	5,250.00
2210-J*.	Kansas City		Unknown	—	—
2210-K.	Dallas	42,960	2,250.00	2,750.00	15,000.00

Federal Reserve Notes (Green Seal)

No.	Issuing Bank	Quantity Printed	VF-20	EF-40	Unc-63
2210-K*.	Dallas	Unknown	—	—	
2210-L.	San Francisco	67,920	$2,000.00	$2,500.00	$5,250.00
2210-L*.	San Francisco	Unknown	—	—	

Series of 1934
Signatures of Julian and Morgenthau

No.	Issuing Bank	Quantity Printed	VF-20	EF-40	Unc-63
2211-A.	Boston	46,200	$1,800.00	$2,100.00	$3,000.00
2211-A*.	Boston		15,000.00	20,000.00	—
2211-B.	New York	322,784	1,800.00	2,100.00	3,000.00
2211-B*.	New York		15,000.00	20,000.00	—
2211-C.	Philadelphia	33,000	1,800.00	2,100.00	3,000.00
2211-C*.	Philadelphia		5,000.00	7,500.00	15,000.00
2211-D.	Cleveland	35,400	1,800.00	2,100.00	3,000.00
2211-D*.	Cleveland		5,000.00	7,500.00	15,000.00
2211-E.	Richmond	19,560	1,800.00	2,100.00	3,000.00
2211-E*.	Richmond		15,000.00	20,000.00	—
2211-F.	Atlanta	67,800	1,800.00	2,100.00	3,000.00
2211-F*.	Atlanta		5,000.00	7,500.00	15,000.00
2211-G.	Chicago	167,040	1,800.00	2,100.00	3,000.00
2211-G*.	Chicago		5,000.00	7,500.00	15,000.00
2211-H.	St. Louis	22,400	1,800.00	2,100.00	3,000.00
2211-H*.	St. Louis		5,000.00	7,500.00	15,000.00
2211-I.	Minneapolis	12,000	2,000.00	2,300.00	5,000.00
2211-I*.	Minneapolis		5,000.00	7,500.00	15,000.00
2211-J.	Kansas City	51,840	1,800.00	2,100.00	3,000.00
2211-J*.	Kansas City		5,000.00	7,500.00	15,000.00
2211-K.	Dallas	46,800	2,000.00	2,300.00	5,000.00
2211-K*.	Dallas		5,000.00	7,500.00	15,000.00
2211-L.	San Francisco	90,600	1,800.00	2,100.00	3,000.00
2211-L*.	San Francisco		5,000.00	7,500.00	15,000.00

Series of 1934-A
Signatures of Julian and Morgenthau

No.	Issuing Bank	Quantity Printed	VF-20	EF-40	Unc-63
2212-A.	Boston	30,000	$1,800.00	$2,100.00	$3,000.00
2212-B.	New York	174,348	1,800.00	2,100.00	3,000.00
2212-B*.	New York		8,500.00	12,500.00	Rare
2212-C.	Philadelphia	78,000	1,800.00	2,100.00	3,000.00
2212-D.	Cleveland	28,800	1,800.00	2,100.00	3,000.00
2212-E.	Richmond	16,800	1,800.00	2,100.00	3,000.00
2212-F.	Atlanta	80,964	1,800.00	2,100.00	3,000.00
2212-F*.	Atlanta		Unknown	—	—
2212-G.	Chicago	134,400	1,800.00	2,100.00	3,000.00
2212-G*.	Chicago		8,500.00	12,500.00	Rare
2212-H.	St. Louis	39,600	1,800.00	2,100.00	3,000.00
2212-I.	Minneapolis	4,800	2,100.00	2,500.00	12,500.00
2212-J.	Kansas City	21,600	1,800.00	2,100.00	3,000.00
2212-L.	San Francisco	36,600	1,800.00	2,100.00	3,000.00

Series of 1934-C
Signatures of Julian and Snyder
Although reported, none of the notes below are known.

No.	Issuing Bank	Quantity Printed	VF-20
2213-A.	Boston	1,200	Rare
2213-B.	New York	168	Very Rare

Large-size $5,000 notes were made in several different series from the 1860s through the 1920s. Early issues are mainly known to us through proof impressions. Most later varieties are exceedingly rare. Small-size Federal Reserve Notes and Silver Certificates were issued, each depicting James Madison on the face. These are scarce today-even scarcer than the higher-denomination $10,000 bills.

$5,000

FIVE THOUSAND DOLLAR NOTES

LARGE-SIZE FIVE THOUSAND DOLLAR NOTES

Interest Bearing Notes

No.	Denomination	
202.	Five Thousand Dollars.	Unknown
211.	Five Thousand Dollars.	Unknown

Legal Tender Notes

Face of Note 188. Facing bust of President James Madison.

Back of Note 188. Eagle standing on shield.

No.	Series	Signatures		Seal
188.	1878	Scofield	Gilfillan	Large Brown

Gold Certificates

No.	Denomination	
1166f.	Five Thousand Dollars.	Unique
1166k.	Five Thousand Dollars.	Unknown

Gold Certificates

Face of Notes 1221-1222b. Facing bust of James Madison.

Back of Notes 1221-1222b.

No.	Series	Signatures		Seal	
1221.	1882	Bruce	Gilfillan	Brown	Unknown
1221a.	1882	Bruce	Gilfillan	Brown	Unknown

The above note is countersigned by Thomas C. Acton, Assistant Treasurer, and payable at New York.

No.	Series	Signatures		Seal	
1221b.	1882	Bruce	Wyman	Brown	Unknown
1221c.	1882	Rosecrans	Hyatt	Large Red	Unknown
1221d.	1882	Rosecrans	Nebeker	Small Red	Unknown
1221e.	1882	Lyons	Roberts	Small Red	Unknown
1221f.	1882	Vernon	Treat	Small Red	Unknown
1221g.	1882	Vernon	McClung	Small Red	Unknown
1221h.	1882	Napier	McClung	Small Red	Unknown
1221i.	1882	Parker	Burke	Small Red	Unknown
1221j.	1882	Teehee	Burke	Small Red	Extremely Rare (2 Known)
1222.	1888	Rosecrans	Hyatt	Large Red	All Redeemed, None Outstanding
1222a.	1888	Rosecrans	Nebeker	Small Red	All Redeemed, None Outstanding
1222b.	1888	Lyons	Roberts	Small Red	All Redeemed, None Outstanding

LARGE-SIZE FIVE THOUSAND DOLLAR NOTES

Federal Reserve Notes

Face of Note 1134 (not shown) features a bust of James Madison, as on the following small-size note.

Back of Note 1134 (not shown) shows Washington resigning his commission.

No.	Denomination	Series
1134.	Five Thousand Dollars	Series of 1918. Different bank varieties were issued. ....8 Known

SMALL SIZE FIVE THOUSAND DOLLAR NOTES

Gold Certificates (Gold Seal)

The design (not shown) is identical to that of the Federal Reserve Notes to follow except for different wording to indicate "Gold Certificate" and the use of a gold-colored seal and serial numbers.

No.	Denomination	Signatures	Design No.	Quantity Printed
2410.	Five Thousand Dollars 1928	Woods Mellon	234	.24,000 ....Rare

Federal Reserve Notes (Green Seal)

Face of Notes 2220-2223.

Back of Notes 2220-2223.

Federal Reserve Notes (Green Seal)
Series of 1928
Signatures of Woods and Mellon

No.	Issuing Bank	Quantity Printed	VF-20	EF-40	Unc-63
2220-A.	Boston	1,320	$45,000.00	$55,000.00	$85,000.00
2220-B.	New York	2,640	Unknown	—	—
2220-D.	Cleveland	3,000	Unknown	—	—
2220-E.	Richmond	3,984	45,000.00	55,000.00	85,000.00
2220-F.	Atlanta	1,440	45,000.00	55,000.00	85,000.00
2220-G.	Chicago	3,480	45,000.00	55,000.00	85,000.00
2220-J.	Kansas City	720	Unknown	—	—
2220-K.	Dallas	360	Unknown	—	—
2220-L.	San Francisco	1,300	Unknown	—	—

Series of 1934
Signatures of Julian and Morgenthau

No.	Issuing Bank	Quantity Printed	VF-20	EF-40	Unc-63
2221-A.	Boston	9,480	$37,500.00	$42,500.00	$60,000.00
2221-B.	New York	11,520	37,500.00	42,500.00	60,000.00
2221-C.	Philadelphia	3,000	37,500.00	42,500.00	60,000.00
2221-D.	Cleveland	1,680	37,500.00	42,500.00	60,000.00
2221-E.	Richmond	2,400	37,500.00	42,500.00	60,000.00
2221-F.	Atlanta	3,600	37,500.00	42,500.00	60,000.00
2221-G.	Chicago	6,600	37,500.00	42,500.00	60,000.00
2221-H.	St. Louis	2,400	37,500.00	42,500.00	60,000.00
2221-J.	Kansas City	2,400	37,500.00	42,500.00	60,000.00
2221-K.	Dallas	2,400	37,500.00	42,500.00	60,000.00
2221-L.	San Francisco	6,000	37,500.00	42,500.00	60,000.00

Series of 1934-A
Signatures of Julian and Morgenthau

No.	Issuing Bank	Quantity Printed
2222-H.	St. Louis	1,440

Series of 1934-B
Signatures of Julian and Vinson

Although Bureau of Engraving and Printing records indicate that these two notes exist, none are known.

No.	Issuing Bank	Quantity Printed
2223-A.	Boston	1,200
2223-B.	New York	12

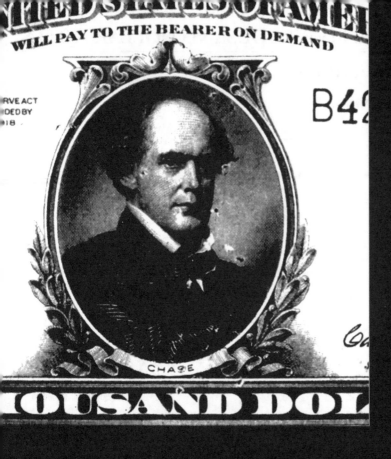

Large-size $10,000 notes were made in several series from the 1860s through the 1920s. Today such bills range from non-existent to extremely rare. Small-size Federal Reserve Notes and Gold Certificates, each depicting Salmon P. Chase on the face (the same portrait as featured on the $1 Legal Tender Notes of 1862, among other places), were issued. These are scarce today, but enough exist that they have achieved popularity as "trophy notes."

$10,000

ACT OF MARCH 14, 1900

JACKSON

M59655✦

SERIES OF 1900

10,000 GOLD CERTIFICATE 10,000

TEN THOUSAND DOLLAR NOTES

Legal Tender Notes

Face of Note 189. Bust of Andrew Jackson.

Back of Note 189. Illustration is of a Bureau of Engraving and Printing sample.

No.	Series	Signatures		Seal	
189.	1878	Scofield	Gilfillan	Large Brown	Unknown

Gold Certificates

No.	Denomination	Series		
1166g.	Ten Thousand Dollars.	....		Unknown
1166-I.	Ten Thousand Dollars.	....		Unknown
1166q.	Ten Thousand Dollars.	....	1875	Unique

Face of Notes 1223-1225. Bust of Andrew Jackson.

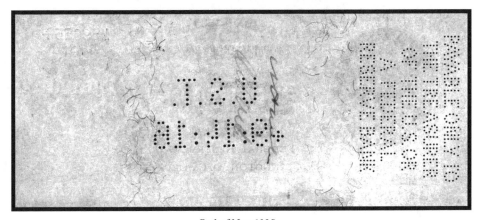

Back of Note 1225.

No.	Series	Signatures		Seal	
1223.	1882	Bruce	Gilfillan	Brown	Unknown
1223a.	1882	Bruce	Gilfillan	Brown	Unknown

The above note is countersigned by Thomas C. Acton, Assistant Treasurer, and payable at New York.

No.	Series	Signatures		Seal	
1223b.	1882	Bruce	Wyman	Brown	Unknown
1223c.	1882	Rosecrans	Hyatt	Large Red	Unknown
1223d.	1882	Rosecrans	Nebeker	Small Red	Unknown
1223e.	1882	Lyons	Roberts	Small Red	Unknown
1223f.	1882	Vernon	Treat	Small Red	Unknown
1223g.	1882	Teehee	Burke	Small Red	Extremely Rare (2 Known)
1224.	1888	Rosecrans	Hyatt	Large Red	All Redeemed, None Outstanding
1224a.	1888	Rosecrans	Nebeker	Small Red	All Redeemed, None Outstanding
1224b.	1888	Lyons	Roberts	Small Red	All Redeemed, None Outstanding
1225.	1900	All known notes are canceled—not redeemable.			

Federal Reserve Notes

Face of Note 1135. Bust of Salmon P. Chase.

Back of Note 1135. The Embarkation of the Pilgrims.

No.	Denomination	Series		
1135.	Ten Thousand Dollars.	1918	Different bank varieties were issued	5 Known

SMALL-SIZE TEN THOUSAND DOLLAR NOTES

Gold Certificates (Gold Seal)

The design (not shown) is identical to that of the Federal Reserve Notes to follow, except for different wording to indicate "Gold Certificate" and the use of a gold-colored seal and serial number.

No.	Series	Signatures		Quantity Printed	
2411.	1928	Woods	Mellon	48,000	Unknown
2412.	1934	Julian	Morgenthau	36,000	—

Federal Reserve Notes (Green Seal)

Face of Notes 2230-2233.

Federal Reserve Notes (Green Seal)

Back of Notes 2230-2233.

Series of 1928
Signatures of Woods and Mellon

No.	Issuing Bank	Quantity Printed	VF-20	EF-40	Unc-63
2230-A.	Boston	1,320	Unknown	—	—
2230-B.	New York	4,680	Unknown	—	—
2230-D.	Cleveland	960	$75,000.00	$95,000.00	$150,000.00
2230-E.	Richmond	3,024	75,000.00	95,000.00	150,000.00
2230-F.	Atlanta	1,440	75,000.00	95,000.00	150,000.00
2230-G.	Chicago	1,800	Unknown	—	—
2230-H.	St. Louis	480	Unknown	—	—
2230-I.	Minneapolis	480	Unknown	—	—
2230-J.	Kansas City	480	Unknown	—	—
2230-K.	Dallas	360	Unknown	—	—
2230-L.	San Francisco	1,824	75,000.00	95,000.00	150,000.00

Series of 1934
Signatures of Julian and Morgenthau

No.	Issuing Bank	Quantity Printed	VF-20	EF-40	Unc-63
2231-A.	Boston	9,720	$55,000.00	$65,000.00	$85,000.00
2231-B.	New York	11,520	50,000.00	60,000.00	75,000.00
2231-C.	Philadelphia	6,000	55,000.00	65,000.00	85,000.00
2231-D.	Cleveland	1,480	Unknown	—	—
2231-E.	Richmond	1,200	55,000.00	65,000.00	85,000.00
2231-F.	Atlanta	2,400	55,000.00	65,000.00	85,000.00
2231-G.	Chicago	3,840	55,000.00	65,000.00	85,000.00
2231-H.	St. Louis	2,040	55,000.00	65,000.00	85,000.00
2231-J.	Kansas City	1,200	55,000.00	65,000.00	85,000.00
2231-K.	Dallas	1,200	55,000.00	65,000.00	85,000.00
2231-L.	San Francisco	3,600	55,000.00	65,000.00	85,000.00

Series of 1934-A
Signatures of Julian and Morgenthau

No.	Issuing Bank	Quantity Printed
2232-G.	Chicago	1,560

Series of 1934-B
Signatures of Julian and Vinson

No.	Issuing Bank	Quantity Printed
2233-B.	New York	24

DEXTER, SECY TREASY 1801.

OF MARCH 3ᴿᴰ 1863

FRACTIONAL CURRENCY

FRACT

FRACTIONAL CURRENCY

3¢ Notes
Third Issue: December 5, 1864 - February 23, 1867

Face of Notes 1226-1227.
Bust of George Washington.

Back of Notes 1226-1227.

No.	Variety	VG-8	F-12	VF-20	EF-40	Unc-63
1226.	Light background behind portrait	$40.00	$50.00	$60.00	$70.00	$120.00
1227.	Dark background behind portrait	45.50	55.00	70.00	110.00	250.00

5¢ Notes
First Issue: August 21, 1862 - May 27, 1863

Face of Notes 1228-1231.
Back of Notes 1228-1231.
Engraving of 5¢ postage stamp with bust of Thomas Jefferson.

No.	Variety	VG-8	F-12	VF-20	EF-40	Unc-63
1228.	Perforated edges; monogram (ABNCo) of American Bank Note Co. on back	$40.00	$55.00	$65.00	$80.00	$275.00
1229.	Perforated edges; no monogram.	45.00	60.00	75.00	100.00	375.00
1230.	Straight edges; with monogram.	30.00	40.00	50.00	70.00	125.00
1231.	Straight edges; no monogram.	40.00	50.00	60.00	100.00	350.00

Second Issue: October 10, 1863 - February 23, 1867

Face of Notes 1232-1235.
Back of Notes 1232-1235.
Bust of George Washington in oval, bronze-colored frame.

No.	Variety	VG-8	F-12	VF-20	EF-40	Unc-63
1232.	No figures on corners of back.	$25.00	$30.00	$40.00	$55.00	$100.00
1233.	With surcharge figures "18-63" on corners of back........	25.00	30.00	45.00	60.00	125.00
1234.	With surcharge figures "18-63" and "S."	25.00	30.00	60.00	70.00	200.00
1235.	With surcharge figures "18-63" and "R-1." Fiber paper.	35.00	55.00	85.00	120.00	600.00

5¢ Notes
Third Issue: December 5, 1864 - February 23, 1867

Face of Notes 1236-1239. *Back of Notes 1236-1239.*

Bust of Spencer M. Clark, superintendent of the National Currency Bureau.

No.	Variety	VG-8	F-12	VF-20	EF-40	Unc-63
1236.	Red back.	$35.00	$45.00	$70.00	$85.00	$250.00
1237.	Red back; with design letter "a" at extreme left on face.	40.00	50.00	75.00	100.00	400.00
1238.	Green back.	25.00	35.00	45.00	65.00	125.00
1239.	Green back; with design letter "a" at extreme left on face.	25.00	40.00	50.00	75.00	180.00

10¢ Notes
First Issue: August 21, 1862 - May 27, 1863

Face of Notes 1240-1243. *Back of Notes 1240-1243.*

Engraving of 10¢ postage stamp with bust of George Washington.

No.	Variety	VG-8	F-12	VF-20	EF-40	Unc-63
1240.	Perforated edges; with monogram (ABNCo) of American Bank Note Co. on back.	$40.00	$55.00	$65.00	$80.00	$275.00
1241.	Perforated edges; no monogram.	45.00	60.00	75.00	100.00	375.00
1242.	Straight edges; with monogram.	30.00	40.00	50.00	60.00	100.00
1243.	Straight edges; no monogram.	40.00	55.00	70.00	100.00	350.00

Second Issue: October 10, 1863 - February 23, 1867

Face of Notes 1244-1249. *Back of Notes 1244-1249.*

Bust of George Washington in oval, bronze-colored frame.

No.	Variety	VG-8	F-12	VF-20	EF-40	Unc-63
1244.	Without small surcharged figures on corners of back.	$25.00	$30.00	$40.00	$55.00	$100.00
1245.	With surcharge "18-63".	25.00	30.00	40.00	60.00	120.00
1246.	With surcharge "18-63" and "S".	30.00	40.00	50.00	75.00	200.00
1247.	With surcharge "18-63" and "I".	50.00	60.00	80.00	110.00	375.00
1248.	With surcharge "0-63".	500.00	675.00	1,300.00	1,800.00	3,800.00
1249.	With surcharge "18-63" and "T-1". Fiber paper	35.00	55.00	85.00	120.00	600.00

FRACTIONAL CURRENCY

10¢ Notes
Third Issue: December 5, 1864 - February 23, 1867

Face of Notes 1251-1256.   Back of Notes 1251-1256.

Bust of George Washington.

No.	Variety	VG-8	F-12	VF-20	EF-40	Unc-63
1251.	Red back.	$30.00	$40.00	$60.00	$75.00	$225.00
1252.	Red back with design numeral "1" on face.	40.00	45.00	75.00	95.00	270.00
1253.	Red back with autographed signatures of Colby and Spinner.	55.00	80.00	95.00	120.00	325.00
1254.	Red back with autographed signatures of Jeffries and Spinner	70.00	100.00	135.00	175.00	500.00
1255.	Green back.	25.00	30.00	40.00	55.00	100.00
1255a.	Green back with autographed signatures of Colby and Spinner	Extremely Rare†	—	—	—	—
1256.	Green back with design numeral "1" on face.	25.00	35.00	45.00	60.00	125.00

†Last time this sold was 1997 CAA/Friedberg auction, for $39,000. Only two are known.

Fourth Issue: July 14, 1869 - February 16, 1875

Face of Notes 1257-1261.   Back of Notes 1257-1261.

Head of Liberty.

No.	Variety	VG-8	F-12	VF-20	EF-40	Unc-63
1257.	Large red seal; watermarked paper with pink silk fibers	$25.00	$35.00	$45.00	$60.00	$100.00
1258.	Large red seal; unwatermarked paper with pink silk fibers ..	25.00	35.00	45.00	60.00	120.00
1259.	Large red seal; paper with violet silk fibers and blue end right on face.	25.00	35.00	45.00	60.00	100.00
1261.	Smaller red seal; paper with violet silk fibers and blue end right on face.	25.00	35.00	45.00	60.00	100.00

Fifth Issue: February 26, 1874 - February 15, 1876

Face of Notes 1264-1266a.   Back of Notes 1264-1266a.

Bust of Treasury Secretary (1849-1850) William M. Meredith.

10¢ Notes

Fifth Issue: February 26, 1874 - February 15, 1876

No.	Variety	VG-8	F-12	VF-20	EF-40	Unc-63
1264.	Green seal.	$30.00	$40.00	$60.00	$75.00	$150.00
1265.	Red seal with long, thin key.	22.00	28.00	35.00	45.00	70.00
1266.	Red seal with short, thick key.	22.00	28.00	35.00	45.00	70.00

15¢ Notes

Fourth Issue

Face of Notes 1267-1271.   *Back of Notes 1267-1271.*

Bust of Columbia in oval frame above faces.

No.	Variety	VG-8	F-12	VF-20	EF-40	Unc-63
1267.	Large red seal; watermarked paper with pink silk fibers.	$55.00	$75.00	$90.00	$120.00	$175.00
1268.	Large red seal; unwatermarked paper with pink silk fibers†	300.00	500.00	800.00	1,000.00	—
1269.	Large red seal; paper with violet fibers and blue right on end face.	55.00	75.00	90.00	120.00	195.00
1271.	Smaller red seal; paper with violet fibers and blue right on end face.	55.00	75.00	90.00	120.00	225.00

†Scarce note; check carefully for watermarks (cf.-1267)

25¢ Notes

First Issue

Face of Notes 1279-1282.   *Back of Notes 1279-1282.*

Five overlapping 5¢ postage stamps with bust of George Washington.

No.	Variety	VG-8	F-12	VF-20	EF-40	Unc-63
1279.	Perforated edges; with monogram (ABNCo) of American Bank Note Co. on back.	$35.00	$50.00	$60.00	$80.00	$400.00
1280.	Perforated edges; no monogram.	35.00	55.00	70.00	130.00	475.00
1281.	Straight edges; with monogram.	30.00	40.00	45.00	65.00	175.00
1282.	Straight edges; no monogram.	40.00	60.00	95.00	135.00	475.00

Second Issue

Face of Notes 1283-1290.   *Back of Notes 1283-1290.*

Bust of George Washington in bronze-colored oval frame.

FRACTIONAL CURRENCY

25¢ Notes
Second Issue

No.	Variety	VG-8	F-12	VF-20	EF-40	Unc-63
1283.	No small surcharged figures on corners of back.	$30.00	$40.00	$50.00	$70.00	$250.00
1284.	Surcharge "18-63".	30.00	45.00	60.00	80.00	280.00
1285.	Surcharge "18-63" and "A".	30.00	50.00	70.00	85.00	280.00
1286.	Surcharge "18-63" and "S".	30.00	40.00	50.00	70.00	250.00
1288.	Surcharge "18-63" and "2".	30.00	45.00	60.00	80.00	280.00
1289.	Surcharge "18-63" and "T-1"; fiber paper.	45.00	60.00	75.00	160.00	500.00
1290.	Surcharge "18-63" and "T-2"; fiber paper.	45.00	60.00	85.00	150.00	425.00

Third Issue

Face of Notes 1291-1300.   *Back of Notes 1291-1300.*

Bust of Treasury Secretary (1864-1865) William P. Fessenden.

No.	Variety	VG-8	F-12	VF-20	EF-40	Unc-63
1291.	Red back.	$30.00	$45.00	$65.00	$90.00	$300.00
1292.	Red back with small design letter "a" on face.	30.00	50.00	75.00	110.00	375.00
1294.	Green back.	20.00	30.00	40.00	50.00	125.00
1295.	Green back with small design letter "a" on face.	20.00	35.00	45.00	55.00	180.00
1296.	Green back with large design letter "a" on face, 7 mm. the to lower right of the normal location.	750.00	1,000.00	2,000.00	2,400.00	5,000.00
1297.	Green back with surcharge "M-2-6-5"; fiber paper.	35.00	50.00	70.00	95.00	425.00
1298.	Same as above but with design letter "a" on face.	45.00	70.00	95.00	150.00	525.00
1299.	Green back with surcharge "M-2-6-5"; the two ornamental designs on face surcharged in heavy solid bronze, and not merely outlined as on previous issues; fiber paper.	200.00	350.00	700.00	1,250.00	2,700.00
1300.	Same as above but with design letter "a" on face.	600.00	875.00	1,850.00	2,750.00	5,750.00

Fourth Issue

Face of Notes 1301-1307.   *Back of Notes 1301-1307.*

Bust of George Washington.

No.	Variety	VG-8	F-12	VF-20	EF-40	Unc-63
1301.	Large red seal; watermarked paper with pink silk fibers.	$25.00	$30.00	$45.00	$65.00	$140.00
1302.	Large red seal; unwatermarked paper with pink silk fibers.	25.00	30.00	45.00	65.00	150.00
1303.	Large red seal; paper with violet fibers and blue right on end face.	25.00	35.00	50.00	85.00	200.00
1307.	Smaller red seal; paper with violet fibers and blue right on end face.	25.00	30.00	45.00	65.00	170.00

25¢ Notes
Fifth Issue

Face of Notes 1308-1309. *Back of Notes 1308-1309.*

Bust of Treasury Secretary (1845-1849) Robert J. Walker.

No.	Variety	VG-8	F-12	VF-20	EF-40	Unc-63
1308.	With long, thin key in Treasury seal (5 mm).	$22.00	$28.00	$35.00	$45.00	$80.00
1309.	With short, thick key in Treasury seal (4 mm).	22.00	28.00	35.00	45.00	80.00

50¢ Notes
First Issue

Face of Notes 1310-1313. *Back of Notes 1310-1313.*

Five overlapping ten-cent stamps with portrait of George Washington.

No.	Variety	VG-8	F-12	VF-20	EF-40	Unc-63
1310.	Perforated edges; with monogram of American Bank Note Co. (ABNCo) on back.	$40.00	$50.00	$60.00	$90.00	$400.00
1310a.	Same, but 14 perforations per 20 mm instead of 12	Rare	—	—	2,500.00	3,750.00
1311.	Perforated edges; no monogram.	50.00	70.00	100.00	160.00	600.00
1312.	Plain edges; monogram.	35.00	45.00	55.00	75.00	200.00
1313.	Plain edges; no monogram.	50.00	70.00	125.00	200.00	800.00

Second Issue

Face of Notes 1314-1322. *Back of Notes 1314-1322.*

Head of George Washington within bronze oval frame.

FRACTIONAL CURRENCY

50¢ Notes
Second Issue (see images, previous page)

No.	Variety	VG-8	F-12	VF-20	EF-40	Unc-63
1314.	No surcharge figures on corners of back.	Only known as a specimen				
1316.	Surcharge "18-63".	$30.00	$50.00	$65.00	$80.00	$300.00
1317.	Surcharge "18-63" and "A".	30.00	50.00	65.00	80.00	300.00
1318.	Surcharge "18-63" and "1".	30.00	50.00	65.00	80.00	300.00
1320.	Surcharge "18-63" and "0-1"; fiber paper.	40.00	60.00	85.00	120.00	475.00
1321.	Surcharge "18-63" and "R-2"; fiber paper.	45.00	65.00	160.00	275.00	675.00
1322.	Surcharge "18-63" and "T-1"; fiber paper.	45.00	70.00	95.00	110.00	425.00

Third Issue

Face of Notes 1324-1330. Bust of Treasurer of the U.S. (1861-1875) General F.E. Spinner.

Back of Notes 1324-1330. Red Back, Surcharge "A-2-6-5."

No.	Variety	VG-8	F-12	VF-20	EF-40	Unc-63
1324.	No design figures on face.	$75.00	$95.00	$110.00	$135.00	$350.00
1325.	Figures "1" and "a" on face.	100.00	125.00	175.00	350.00	1,000.00
1326.	Figure "1" only on face.	75.00	100.00	120.00	150.00	450.00
1327.	Figure "a" only on face.	75.00	100.00	125.00	170.00	500.00
1328.	Autographed signatures of Colby and Spinner.	85.00	135.00	140.00	190.00	500.00
1329.	Autographed signatures of Allison and Spinner.	95.00	100.00	150.00	200.00	750.00
1330.	Autographed signatures of Allison and New.	750.00	1,200.00	1,950.00	2,700.00	5,000.00

Green Back, No Surcharge.

No.	Variety	VG-8	F-12	VF-20	EF-40	Unc-63
1331.	No design figures on face.	$45.00	$75.00	$90.00	$110.00	$325.00
1332.	Figures "1" and "a" on face.	90.00	110.00	125.00	150.00	625.00
1333.	Figure "1" only on face.	45.00	85.00	100.00	125.00	400.00
1334.	Figure "a" only on face.	45.00	85.00	100.00	125.00	400.00

Green Back and Surcharge "A-2-6-5."

No.	Variety	VG-8	F-12	VF-20	EF-40	Unc-63
1335.	Without design figures on face.	$75.00	$100.00	$125.00	$150.00	$400.00
1336.	Figures "1" and "a" on face.	325.00	600.00	1,000.00	1,750.00	4,000.00
1337.	Figure "1" only on face.	90.00	110.00	135.00	150.00	650.00
1338.	Figure "a" only on face.	90.00	110.00	140.00	170.00	800.00

50¢ Notes
Third Issue

Back of Notes 1339-1342. (Face similar to Notes 1324-1338.)

No.	Variety	VG-8	F-12	VF-20	EF-40	Unc-63
1339.	Green back; no surcharges and design figures.	$45.00	$75.00	$90.00	$135.00	$400.00
1340.	Green back; figures "1" and "a" on face.	110.00	170.00	225.00	290.00	1,000.00
1341.	Green back; figure "1" only on face.	60.00	80.00	100.00	145.00	500.00
1342.	Green back; figure "a" only on face.	60.00	80.00	120.00	160.00	550.00

Face of Notes 1343-1346. Justice seated with arm on shield.

Back of Notes 1343-1346. Red back, no surcharge.

No.	Variety	VG-8	F-12	VF-20	EF-40	Unc-63
1343.	No design figures on face.	$80.00	$95.00	$120.00	$170.00	$500.00
1344.	Design figures "1" and "a" on face.	200.00	400.00	900.00	1,250.00	3,800.00
1345.	Design figure "1" only on face.	85.00	110.00	135.00	200.00	600.00
1346.	Design figure "a" only on face.	85.00	110.00	135.00	200.00	600.00

FRACTIONAL CURRENCY

50¢ Notes
Third Issue (continued)

Red back and surcharge "A-2-6-5" (not shown).

No.	Variety	VG-8	F-12	VF-20	EF-40	Unc-63
1347.	No design figures on face............................	$80.00	$95.00	$120.00	$170.00	$500.00
1348.	Design figures "1" and "a" on face......................	275.00	600.00	1,200.00	1,400.00	3,500.00
1349.	Design figure "1" only on face........................	80.00	95.00	135.00	200.00	750.00
1350.	Design figure "a" only on face.......................	80.00	95.00	135.00	200.00	950.00

Red back and surcharge "S-2-6-4"; printed signatures (not shown).

No.	Variety	VG-8	F-12	VF-20	EF-40	Unc-63
1351.	No design figures on face; fiber paper.	$2,500.00	$4,000.00	$8,000.00	$10,500.00	$22,000.00
1352.	Design figures "1" and "a" on face; fiber paper†		Extremely Rare			
1353.	Design figure "1" only on face; fiber paper	3,000.00	5,500.00	12,500.00	16,000.00	21,000.00
1354.	Design figure "a" only on face; fiber paper..............	3,250.00	5,500.00	13,000.00	17,000.00	23,000.00

†Three known. A Choice AU in Stacks-Ford sale (5/04) brought $115,000

Red back; autographed signatures of Colby and Spinner (not shown).

No.	Variety	VG-8	F-12	VF-20	EF-40	Unc-63
1355.	No surcharges and design figures.	$85.00	$110.00	$160.00	$225.00	$525.00
1356.	Surcharge "A-2-6-5" on back........................	85.00	125.00	225.00	275.00	600.00
1357.	Surcharge "S-2-6-4"; fiber paper.	200.00	300.00	450.00	675.00	2,000.00

Green back, no surcharge (not shown).

No.	Variety	VG-8	F-12	VF-20	EF-40	Unc-63
1358.	No design figures on face............................	$45.00	$75.00	$90.00	$110.00	$400.00
1359.	Design figures "1" and "a" on face.....................	300.00	500.00	1,000.00	1,450.00	3,500.00
1360.	Design figure "1" only on face........................	50.00	80.00	100.00	135.00	500.00
1361.	Design figure "a" only on face........................	50.00	80.00	100.00	140.00	600.00

Green back and surcharge "A-2-6-5" compactly spaced (not shown).

No.	Variety	VG-8	F-12	VF-20	EF-40	Unc-63
1362.	No design figures on face............................	$45.00	$75.00	$90.00	$110.00	$450.00
1363.	Design figures "1" and "a" on face.	125.00	175.00	275.00	400.00	1,000.00
1364.	Design figure "1" only on face........................	50.00	80.00	100.00	150.00	500.00
1365.	Design figure "a" only on face........................	50.00	80.00	100.00	175.00	525.00

Green back and surcharge "A-2-6-5" widely spaced (not shown).

No.	Variety	VG-8	F-12	VF-20	EF-40	Unc-63
1366.	No design figures on face............................	$45.00	$75.00	$130.00	$225.00	$500.00
1367.	Design figures "1" and "a" on face.	450.00	900.00	1,400.00	2,000.00	6,000.00
1368.	Design figure "1" only on face........................	55.00	100.00	140.00	350.00	750.00
1369.	Design figure "a" only on face........................	65.00	130.00	200.00	450.00	1,000.00

Green back with surcharge "A-2-6-5"; fiber paper (not shown).

No.	Variety	VG-8	F-12	VF-20	EF-40	Unc-63
1370.	No design figures on face............................	$80.00	$100.00	$170.00	$300.00	$1,000.00
1371.	Design figures "1" and "a" on face.....................	450.00	600.00	1,500.00	2,000.00	5,000.00
1372.	Design figure "1" only on face........................	90.00	120.00	200.00	350.00	1,000.00
1373.	Design figure "a" only on face.	100.00	135.00	220.00	380.00	1,200.00
1373-a.	Green back with surcharge "S-2-6-4"; fiber paper; printed signatures; no design figure or letter.	7,500.00	10,000.00	15,000.00	23,000.00	—

50¢ Notes
Fourth Issue

Face of Notes 1374-1375. Bust of Abraham Lincoln.

Back of Notes 1374-1375.

No.	Variety	VG-8	F-12	VF-20	EF-40	Unc-63
1374.	Large seal; watermarked paper with pink silk fibers........	$50.00	$80.00	$120.00	$180.00	$650.00

Face of Note 1376. Bust of Secretary of War Edwin M. Stanton.

Back of Note 1376.

No.	Variety	VG-8	F-12	VF-20	EF-40	Unc-63
1376.	Small red seal; paper with violet fibers and blue right on end face.	$35.00	$50.00	$70.00	$110.00	$300.00

50¢ Notes
Fourth Issue

Face of Note 1379.   Back of Note 1379.

Bust of War and Treasury Secretary (1800-1801) Samuel Dexter.

No.	Variety	VG-8	F-12	VF-20	EF-40	Unc-63
1379.	Green seal; paper with light violet fibers and blue right on endface.	$35.00	$50.00	$65.00	$95.00	$200.00

Fifth Issue

Face of Notes 1380-1381.

Bust of War and Treasury Secretary (1815-1825) William H. Crawford.

Back of Notes 1380-1381.

No.	Variety	VG-8	F-12	VF-20	EF-40	Unc-63
1380.	Red seal; paper on obverse a light pink color with silk fibers	$26.00	$36.00	$45.00	$60.00	$100.00
1381.	Red seal; white paper with silk fibers and blue right on endface.	26.00	36.00	45.00	60.00	100.00

No.	Variety	
1382.	Fractional Currency Shield. With gray background	$4,500.00
1383.	Fractional Currency Shield. With pink background	10,000.00
1383a.	Fractional Currency Shield. With green background	13,000.00

Inverted Backs

Some notes of the first three issues are known with inverted backs or surcharges. Notes of the Second and Third Issues are known with surcharges partially or entirely missing. All such notes are very rare.

STAMPS

ENCASED POSTAGE STAMPS

ENCASED POSTAGE STAMPS

The outbreak of the Civil War in 1861 led to a host of economic problems including, but not limited to, a shortage of coinage, as most money was hoarded with the outcome of the war so uncertain. By 1862, the situation became dire, and postage stamps were used in lieu of coins. However, this was only a short-term solution, as the stamps were damaged through repeated commercial transactions. Fortunately, in 1862, John Gault patented a special round encasement that protected postage stamps; it had a solid metal backing and a transparent mica lid, so the stamps could be easily viewed.

Merchants purchased these encasements from Gault for a fee of two to three cents over the cost of the postage stamps. At the time, there were 1¢, 3¢, 5¢, 10¢, 12¢, 24¢, 30¢, and 90¢ stamps. Merchants often offset the encasement surcharge by using the metallic backing as an advertising medium and embossed their company messages on them.

Although the encased postage stamps helped a country in need of a way to make small change, there were few complaints when, in 1863, the government ordered the stamps to be redeemed and issued Fractional Currency in its place.

Today, both stamp and coin collectors appreciate the rarity of the encased postage stamps. They use three primary criteria for evaluating this special "situational currency": the quality of the stamp enclosed; the condition of the metallic casing; and the clarity of the mica covering. As might be expected, Uncirculated encased postage stamps are extremely rare and command premium prices.

1¢ STAMPS

No.	Issued By	Value
EP-1.	Aerated Bread Co., New York	$4,500.00
EP-2.	Ayer's Cathartic Pills	375.00
EP-3.	"Take Ayer's Pills"	275.00
EP4.	Ayer's Sarsaparilla Small "Ayer's"	650.00
EP4a.	As above but medium "Ayer's"	250.00
EP-5.	Bailey & Co., Philadelphia	700.00
EP-6.	Bates, Joseph L., Boston "Fancy Goods"	300.00
EP-6a.	As above but "Fancygoods" in one word	275.00
EP-7.	Brown's Bronchial Troches	1,000.00
EP-8.	Buhl, F. & Co., Detroit	750.00
EP-9.	Burnett's Cocoaine Kalliston	500.00
EP-10.	Burnett's Cooking Extracts	400.00
EP-11.	Claflin, A.M., Hopkinton, R.I.	4,500.00
EP-12.	Dougan, New York	1,750.00
EP-13.	Drake's Plantation Bitters	225.00
EP-13a.	Ellis, McAlpin & Co., Cincinnati	1,200.00
EP-14.	Evans, G.G	1,000.00

1¢ STAMPS

No.	Issued By	Value
EP-15.	Gage Brothers & Drake, Chicago	$750.00
EP-16.	Gault, J., Plain frame	350.00
EP-17.	Gault, J., Ribbed frame	700.00
EP-17a.	Hopkins, L.C. & Co., Cincinnati	1,500.00
EP-18.	Hunt & Nash, Irving House, N.Y.	600.00
EP-19.	Kirkpatrick & Gault, N.Y.	450.00
EP-20.	Lord and Taylor, N.Y.	2,750.00
EP-21.	Mendum's Family Wine Emporium, N.Y.	650.00
EP-22.	Miles, B.F. John W., Chicago	12,500.00
EP-23.	Norris, John W., Chicago	2,500.00
EP-24.	North American Life Insurance Co., N.Y., straight inscr.	300.00
EP-24a.	As above but curved inscr.	350.00
EP-24b.	Pearce, Tolle & Holton, Cincinnati	2,750.00
EP-25.	Schapker & Bussing, Evansville, Ind	875.00
EP-26.	Shillito, John & Co., Cincinnati	1,000.00
EP-27.	Steinfeld, S., N.Y.	2,250.00
EP-28.	Taylor N.G. & Co., Philadelphia	2,250.00
EP-29.	Weir & Larminie, Montreal, Canada	2,500.00
EP-30.	White the Hatter, N.Y.	2,500.00

2¢ STAMPS

No.	Issued By	Value
EP-31.	Gault, J., Very Rare, not a regular issue	$9,000.00

3¢ STAMPS

No.	Issued By	Value
EP-32.	Ayer's Cathartic Pills	$250.00
EP-32a.	As above but with longer arrows	300.00
EP-33.	"Take Ayer's Pills"	275.00
EP-34.	Ayer's Sarsaparilla, Plain frame	550.00
EP-34a.	As above but medium "Ayer's" (EP-34 is small)	225.00
EP-34b.	As above but large "Ayer's"	275.00
EP-35.	Ayer's Sarsaparilla, Ribbed frame	1,350.00
EP-36.	Bailey & Co., Philadelphia	650.00
EP-37.	Bates, Joseph L., Boston "Fancy Goods"	475.00
EP-37a.	Same, "Fancygoods" in one word	450.00
EP-38.	Brown's Bronchial Troches	1,500.00
EP-38a.	Buhl, F. & Co., Detroit	4,000.00
EP-39.	Burnett's Cocoaine Kalliston	300.00
EP-40.	Burnett's Cooking Extracts	300.00
EP-40a.	Claflin, A.M., Hopkinton, R.I.	4,500.00
EP-41.	Dougan, N.Y.	1,750.00
EP-42.	Drake's Plantation Bitters	350.00
EP-43.	Ellis, McAlpin & Co., Cincinnati	1,750.00
EP-44.	Evans, G.G.	1,250.00
EP-45.	Gage Brothers & Drake, Chicago	500.00
EP-46.	Gault, J., Plain frame	200.00
EP-47.	Gault, J., Ribbed frame	950.00
EP-48.	Hopkins, L.C. & Co., Cincinnati	3,000.00
EP-49.	Hunt & Nash, Irving House, N.Y.	700.00
EP-49a.	Same, but with ribbed frame	1,000.00
EP-50.	Kirkpatrick & Gault, N.Y.	375.00
EP-51.	Lord & Taylor, N.Y.	850.00
EP-52.	Mendum's Family Wine Emporium, N.Y.	550.00

ENCASED POSTAGE STAMPS

3¢ STAMPS

No.	Issued By	Value
EP-52a.	Norris, John W., Chicago	$1,500.00
EP-53.	North American Life Insurance Co., N.Y.	350.00
EP-53a.	As above, but curved inscr.	1,500.00
EP-54.	Pearce, Tolle & Holton, Cincinnati	1,850.00
EP-55.	Schapker & Bussing, Evansville, Ind.	900.00
EP-56.	Shillito, John & Co., Cincinnati	475.00
EP-57.	Taylor, N.G. & Co., Philadelphia	1,250.00
EP-58.	Weir & Larminie, Montreal, Canada	8,000.00
EP-59.	White the Hatter, N.Y.	1,500.00

5¢ STAMPS

No.	Issued By	Value
EP-60.	Ayer's Cathartic Pills	$725.00
EP-60a.	As above but with longer arrows	475.00
EP-61.	"Take Ayer's Pills", Plain frame	1,250.00
EP-62.	"Take Ayer's Pills", Ribbed frame	2,750.00
EP-63.	Ayer's Sarsaparilla, Medium "Ayer's"	275.00
EP-63a.	Ayer's Sarsaparilla, large "Ayer's"	1,750.00
EP-64.	Bailey & Co., Philadelphia	950.00
EP-65.	Bates, Joseph L., Boston, Plain frame	350.00
EP-66.	Bates, Joseph L., Boston, Ribbed frame	2,000.00
EP-66a.	Same, "Fancygoods" in one word, Plain	2,000.00
EP-67.	Brown's Bronchial Troches	350.00
EP-68.	Buhl, F. & Co., Detroit	850.00
EP-69.	Burnett's Cocoaine Kalliston	250.00
EP-70.	Burnett's Cooking Extracts	200.00
EP-71.	Claflin, A.M., Hopkinton, R.I.	9,500.00
EP-72.	Cook, H.A., Evansville, Ind.	2,000.00
EP-73.	Dougan, N.Y.	2,500.00
EP-74.	Drake's Plantation Bitters, Plain frame	350.00
EP-75.	Drake's Plantation Bitters, Ribbed frame	950.00
EP-76.	Ellis, McAlpin & Co., Cincinnati	650.00
EP-76a.	Evans, G.G.	600.00
EP-77.	Gage Brothers & Drake, Chicago	375.00
EP-78.	Gault, J., Plain frame	300.00
EP-79.	Gault, J., Ribbed frame	400.00
EP-80.	Hopkins, L.C. & Co., Cincinnati	3,250.00
EP-81.	Hunt & Nash, Irving House, N.Y., Plain frame	800.00
EP-82.	Hunt & Nash, Irving House, N.Y., Ribbed frame	475.00

5¢ STAMPS

No.	Issued By	Value
EP-83.	Kirkpatrick & Gault, N.Y	$450.00
EP-84.	Lord & Taylor, N.Y	850.00
EP-85.	Mendum's Family Wine Emporium, N.Y	750.00
EP-86.	Miles, B.F., Peoria	9,500.00
EP-87.	Norris, John W., Chicago	1,500.00
EP-88.	North American Life Insurance Co., N.Y., Plain frame, straight inscr.	600.00
EP-88a.	North American Life Ins. Co., N.Y., Ribbed frame	950.00
EP-89.	Pearce, Tolle & Holton, Cincinnati	2,000.00
EP-90.	Sands Ale	5,000.00
EP-91.	Schapker & Bussing, Evansville, Ind.	400.00
EP-92.	Shillito, John & Co., Cincinnati	350.00
EP-93.	Steinfeld, S., N.Y.	4,000.00
EP-93a.	Taylor, N.G. & Co., Philadelphia	1,450.00
EP-94.	Weir & Larminie, Montreal, Canada	1,400.00
EP-95.	White the Hatter, N.Y.	2,500.00

9¢ STRIPS

No.	Issued By	Value
EP-95a.	Three 3¢ stamps in a brass, rectangular frame, sometimes referred to as having a Feuchtwanger back. Of doubtful origin	$2,250.00

10¢ STAMPS

No.	Issued By	Value
EP-96.	Ayer's Cathartic Pills. Short arrows	$500.00
EP-96a.	As above, but long arrows	950.00
EP-97.	"Take Ayer's Pills"	950.00
EP-98.	Ayer's Sarsaparilla, Plain frame	1,200.00
EP-98a.	As above, but medium "Ayer's" (EP-98 is small)	500.00
EP-98b.	As above, but large "Ayer's"	1,000.00
EP-99.	Ayer's Sarsaparilla, Ribbed frame	1,250.00
EP-100.	Bailey & Co., Philadelphia	450.00
EP-101.	Bates, Joseph L., Boston, Plain frame	2,000.00
EP-102.	Bates, Joseph L., Boston, Ribbed frame	700.00
EP-102a.	Same, "Fancygoods" in one word. Plain.	600.00
EP-103.	Brown's Bronchial Troches	500.00
EP-104.	Buhl, F. & Co., Detroit	950.00
EP-105.	Burnett's Cocoaine Kalliston	375.00
EP-106.	Burnett's Cooking Extracts, Plain frame	325.00
EP-107.	Burnett's Cooking Extracts, Ribbed frame	2,500.00
EP-108.	Cook, H.A., Evansville, Ind	2,250.00
EP-108a.	Claflin, A.M., Hopkinton, R.I.	5,250.00
EP-109.	Dougan, N.Y.	1,850.00
EP-110.	Drake's Plantation Bitters, Plain frame	675.00
EP-111.	Drake's Plantation Bitters, Ribbed frame	1,250.00
EP-112.	Ellis,McAlpin & Co., Cincinnati	575.00
EP-113.	Evans, G.G.	2,500.00
EP-114.	Gage Brothers & Drake, Chicago, Plain frame	350.00
EP-115.	Gage Brother & Drake, Chicago, Ribbed frame	2,000.00
EP-116.	Gault, J., Plain frame	225.00

ENCASED POSTAGE STAMPS

10¢ STAMPS

No.	Issued By	Value
EP-117.	Gault, J., Ribbed frame	$325.00
EP-117a.	Hopkins, L.C. & Co., Cincinnati	3,500.00
EP-118.	Hunt & Nash, Irving House, N.Y., Plain frame	475.00
EP-119.	Hunt & Nash, Irving House, N.Y., Ribbed frame	650.00
EP-120.	Kirkpatrick & Gault, N.Y.	375.00
EP-121.	Lord & Taylor, N.Y.	900.00
EP-122.	Mendum's Family Wine Emporium, N.Y., Plain frame	1,100.00
EP-123.	Mendum's Family Wine Emporium, N.Y., Ribbed frame	2,750.00
EP-124.	Norris, John W., Chicago	2,000.00
EP-125.	North American Life Insurance Co., N.Y., Plain frame, straight inscr.	700.00
EP-125a.	As above, but curved inscr.	800.00
EP-126.	North American Life Insurance Co., N.Y., Ribbed frame, curved inscr.	1,500.00
EP-127.	Pearce, Tolle & Holton, Cincinnati	3,000.00
EP-128.	Sands Ale	2,500.00
EP-129.	Schapker & Bussing, Evansville, Ind.	325.00
EP-130.	Shillito, John & Co., Cincinnati	800.00
EP-131.	Steinfeld, S., N.Y.	3,500.00
EP-132.	Taylor, N. & Co., Philadelphia	1,750.00
EP-133	Weir & Larminie, Montreal, Canada	1,500.00
EP-134.	White the Hatter, N.Y.	1,500.00

12¢ STAMPS

No.	Issued By	Value
EP-135.	Ayer's Cathartic Pills	$1,250.00
EP-136.	"Take Ayer's Pills"	1,500.00
EP-137.	Ayer's Sarsaparilla, Medium "Ayer's"	1,750.00
EP-137a.	As above, but small "Ayer's"	1,500.00
EP-138.	Bailey & Co., Philadelphia	1,750.00
EP-139.	Bates, Joseph L., Boston	2,500.00
EP-140.	Brown's Bronchial Troches	2,500.00
EP-141.	Buhl, F. & Co., Detroit	2,500.00
EP-142.	Burnett's Cocoaine Kalliston	1,250.00
EP-143.	Burnett's Cooking Extracts	1,250.00
EP-144.	Claflin, A.M., Hopkinton, R.I.	10,000.00
EP-145.	Drake's Plantation Bitters	1,250.00
EP-146.	Ellis, McAlpin & Co., Cincinnati	2,000.00
EP-147.	Gage Brothers & Drake, Chicago	2,000.00
EP-148.	Gault, J., Plain frame	750.00
EP-149.	Gault, J., Ribbed frame	1,450.00
EP-150.	Hunt & Nash, Irving House, N.Y., Plain frame	1,500.00
EP-151.	Hunt & Nash, Irving House, N.Y., Ribbed frame	2,000.00
EP-152.	Kirkpatrick & Gault, N.Y.	700.00
EP-153.	Lord & Taylor, N.Y.	1,750.00
EP-154.	Mendum's Family Wine Emporium, N.Y.	1,250.00
EP-155.	North American Life Insurance Co., N.Y.	1,500.00
EP-156.	Pearce, Tolle & Holton, Cincinnati	1,500.00
EP-156a.	Sands Ale	3,500.00
EP-157.	Schapker & Bussing, Evansville, Ind.	2,250.00
EP-158.	Shillito, John & Co., Cincinnati	3,250.00
EP-159.	Steinfeld, S., N.Y.	2,750.00
EP-159a.	Taylor, N.G. & Co., Philadelphia	2,250.00

24¢ STAMPS

No.	Issued By	Value
EP-159b.	Ayer's Cathartic Pills	$2,700.00
EP-160.	Ayer's Sarsaparilla	2,000.00
EP-160a.	Bates, Joseph L., Boston	Unique
EP-161.	Brown's Bronchial Troches	2,500.00
EP-162.	Buhl, F. & Co., Detroit	2,500.00
EP-163.	Burnett's Cocoaine Kalliston	2,250.00
EP-164.	Burnett's Cooking Extracts	1,950.00
EP-165.	Drake's Plantation Bitters	2,000.00
EP-166.	Ellis, McAlpin & Co., Cincinnati	875.00
EP-167.	Gault, J., Plain frame	1,150.00
EP-168.	Gault, J., Ribbed frame	1,500.00
EP-169.	Hunt & Nash, Irving House, N.Y., Plain frame	1,250.00
EP-170.	Hunt & Nash, Irving House, N.Y., Ribbed frame	2,250.00
EP-171.	Kirkpatrick & Gault, N.Y.	1,500.00
EP-172.	Lord & Taylor, N.Y.	2,000.00
EP-172a.	Pearce, Tolle & Holton, Cincinnati	2,750.00

30¢ STAMPS

No.	Issued By	Value
EP-172b.	Ayer's Cathartic Pills	$2,750.00
EP-173.	Ayer's Sarsaparilla	2,750.00
EP-174.	Brown's Bronchial Troches	3,500.00
EP-175.	Burnett's Cocoaine Kalliston	3,000.00
EP-176.	Burnett's Cooking Extracts	3,000.00
EP-177.	Drake's Plantation Bitters	1,250.00
EP-178.	Gault, J., Plain frame	2,250.00
EP-179.	Gault, J., Ribbed frame	2,750.00
EP-180.	Hunt & Nash, Irving House, N.Y.	3,350.00
EP-181.	Kirkpatrick & Gault, N.Y.	2,000.00
EP-182.	Lord & Taylor, N.Y.	2,950.00
EP-183.	Sands Ale	3,850.00

90¢ STAMPS

No.	Issued By	Value
EP-183a.	"Take Ayer's Pills"	$5,250.00
EP-183b.	Ayer's Sarsaparilla	5,000.00
EP-184.	Burnett's Cocoaine Kalliston	8,250.00
EP-184a.	Burnett's Cooking Extracts	Unique
EP-185.	Drake's Plantation Bitters	3,000.00
EP-186.	Gault, J.	4,000.00
EP-187.	Kirkpatrick & Gault, N.Y	5,750.00
EP-188.	Lord & Taylor, N.Y.	5,500.00

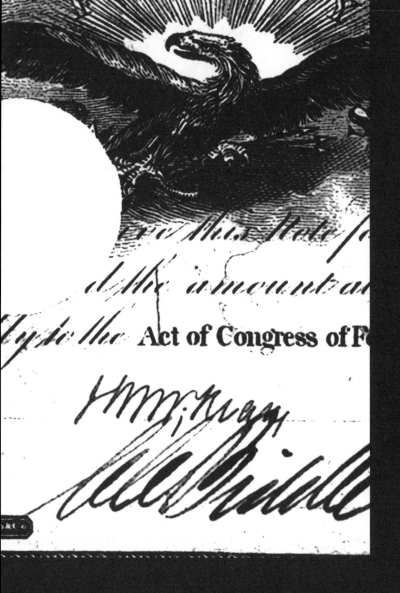

e this Note

of the amount a

ly to the **Act of Congress of F**

$

e United S

v at _____

rest from th

r ann. in conf

HUNDRED DO

THE TREASURY NOTES OF THE WAR OF 1812

Some say that the first circulating currency issued by the United States did not appear in 1861 as commonly believed, but in 1815—46 years earlier than the first Demand Notes. These Treasury Notes were issued following the outbreak of war with Great Britain in June of 1812. With the demise of the First Bank of the United States and no provision for internal revenue taxes, only loans and these innovative notes which bore interest at 1/2 cents a day per $100 (except for the "Small Notes" of 1815) were left to provide revenue to prosecute the war.

There were five issues between 1812 and 1815 totalling $36 million in denominations of $3 to $1,000. The notes were extremely successful and were fully subscribed and accepted by banks and merchants.

First Issue

Originally suggested in 1810 by then-Secretary of the Treasury Albert Gallatin, Treasury Notes as a resource for raising government revenue were first authorized by Congress on June 30, 1812. A total of $15,000,000 in denominations of $100 and $1,000 was authorized and by December, 1812 were fully subscribed by the banks. They bore interest at 5.4% or 1/2 cents a day per $100.

Subsequent issues followed a pattern in which Congress first attempted to raise funds by floating long-term loans and then making up the difference with Treasury Notes. Congress therefore authorized a second issue of $5,000,000 in Treasury Notes on February 25, 1813.

The third issue on March 4, 1814 authorized another $10,000,000 of Treasury Notes. Unlike the first two issues, which only authorized $100 and $1,000 notes, this issue and the next included $20 notes.

The fourth issue on December 26, 1814, authorized an additional $10,500,000 of Treasury Notes, but for the first time not all were fully subscribed ($8,318,400). Only $100 and $20 notes are believed to have been printed.

Small-Size Treasury Notes

With new loans and fiscal revenues far from adequate, a new monetary expedient was necessary. Specifically, the Chairman of the House Ways and Means Committee argued for a circulating currency of small denominations payable to bearer, transferable by delivery and receivable in all payments for public lands and taxes.

On February 24, 1815, Congress authorized 25,000,000 of these "Small" Treasury Notes. A few days later, the war ended and only $4,969,400 of $100 notes bearing interest at 5.4% and $3,392.994 of "Small" $3, $5, $10, $20, and $50 denominations were actually issued (although a total of $9,070,386 worth were reissued). The latter bore no interest by circulating as money.

All Treasury Notes were made by Murray, Draper, Fairman, and Co. and are one-sided. The first two issues were signed by Timothy Matlock and Charles Biddle while the latter three were signed by Earnest Fox and Samuel Clarke. The last issue was alternately signed by F. W. McGeary and C. A. Colville. Some were countersigned by William White (first two issues), T.D.T. Tucker (last two issues), or Joseph Nourse (the register on the last issue only).

The "Small Treasury Notes" of $3 to $50 were used to purchase goods and services by individuals, pay customs duties by merchants, and act as cash reserves for banks, thus preventing them from being discounted. As a result, they became the first circulating currency issued by the United States.

All these series are extremely rare in any form, and nearly all of the few known are specimens, proofs, or remainders, with most cancelled in some way. Fully signed, dated, numbered, and uncancelled notes are virtually non-existent.

Our thanks to Donald H. Kagin for his contribution in the preparation of this section.

A. Act of June 30, 1812

1-year notes of this issue bore interest at 5.4%. 100 notes outstanding.

No.	Denomination	VF-20	Unc-63
TN-1.	One Thousand Dollars. Unsigned Remainder. Two known. (2,000 issued)	$20,000.00	$30,000.00

Eagle on branch at upper right. Shield and cannon at lower center.

No.	Denomination	VF-20	Unc-63
TN-2.	One Hundred Dollars. Unsigned Remainder. Two known. (15,000 issued)	$15,000.00	$25,000.00

B. Act of February 25, 1813

1-year notes of this issue bore interest at 5.4%. 900 notes outstanding.

No.	Denomination	VF-20	Unc-63
TN-3.	One Thousand Dollars. (4000 issued).	No notes known.	
TN-4.	One Hundred Dollars. (5000 issued).	No notes known.	

THE TREASURY NOTES OF THE WAR OF 1812

C. Act of March 4, 1814

1-year notes bore interest at 5.4%. 43,160 outstanding.

No.	Denomination	VF-20	Unc-63
TN-5.	One Thousand Dollars. (6000 issued, est.).	No notes known.	
TN-6.	One Hundred Dollars. Signed by Earnest Fox & Samuel Clarke.		
	Signed Remainder dated 1/15/15. Three known. (24,000 issued, est.)	$20,000.00	$30,000.00
TN-7.	Twenty Dollars. . . . . No notes known. (8000 issued, est.).		

D. Act of December 26, 1814

1-year notes bore interest at 5.4%. 41,030 outstanding.

Eagle on branch at upper right corner. Shield and cannon below center.
Signed by Earnest Fox and Samuel Clarke.

No.	Denomination	VF-20	Unc-63
TN-8.	One Hundred Dollars. Unsigned but dated 2/11/15. Two known.	$15,000.00	$25,000.00
TN-8a.	One Hundred Dollars. Signed undated Remainder (most cancelled). Three known.	12,500.00	17,500.00
	(One proof known)		

D. Act of December 26, 1814

Spread eagle on shield at upper left. "20" surrounded by cornucopia in lower center.

Eagle on branch at upper right. Shield at lower center.

No.	Denomination	VF-20	Unc-20
TN-9.	Twenty Dollars. Unsigned. One known. (Three Proofs known.)	—	—
TN-9a.	Signed Remainder.	$8,000.00	$12,500.00

E. Act of February 24, 1815

$100 notes bore interest at 5.4%. Unknown outstanding for $100; $2,061 for "Small Notes."

Spread eagle on branch at upper right.
Signed by F. W. McGeary and C. A. Colville. Countersigned by Joseph Nourse.

No.	Denomination	VF-20	Unc-63
TN-10.	One Hundred Dollars. Unsigned Remainder.		
	Three known. (Three Proofs known) (49,694 issued)	$8,000.00	$12,500.00
TN-10a.	One Hundred Dollars. Signed.	Unconfirmed	—
TN-11.	Fifty Dollars. Unsigned Remainder. (Three Proofs known)	Unconfirmed	—
TN-11a.	Fifty Dollars. Signed. All known specimens are cancelled.	6,000.00	9,000.00
	Spread eagle at upper left.		
TN-12.	Twenty Dollars. Unsigned Remainder. (One Proof known)	6,500.00	10,000.00
TN-12a.	Twenty Dollars. Signed Remainder.	Unconfirmed	—

Similar to above. No text on right. Signed by Samuel Clarke and Earnest Fox.
Spread eagle with shield at upper left.

Text at right. Signed by F. W. McGeary and C. A. Colville.

No.	Denomination		VF-20	Unc-63
TN-13.	Ten Dollars.	Unsigned	$3,500.00	$5,500.00

Spread eagle with shield at upper right.
Illustration is of an uncut proof sheet courtesy of Donald H. Kagin.

No.	Denomination	VF-20	Unc-63
TN-15.	Five Dollars. Unsigned Remainder. (Four Proofs known)	$ 5,000.00	$ 7,500.00
TN-15a	Five Dollars. Signed Remainder.	10,000.00	15,000.00
	Shield with motto in upper center.		
TN-16.	Three Dollars. Unsigned Remainder.	5,500.00	8,500.00
TN-16a.	Signed Remainder.	7,000.00	15,500.00

ERROR NOTES

ERROR NOTES

Although errors have occurred in all sizes and types of U.S. currency since the nation first started printing paper money, error note collecting has historically been a very limited pursuit. In the past thirty years, however, errors have grown into a widely collected part of the hobby.

Error notes can be inexpensive or very costly, depending on what you collect. A double denomination (the "king of errors" in the banknote field) is the rarest of the rare—for example, a 1934-D note with a $5 face and a $10 back is worth $12,500 in Very Fine or $20,000 in Uncirculated. Other errors can be easily obtained for $10 to $15 over face value.

Mistakes on large-size notes are mostly very rare. Errors have also been found on National Bank Notes and are extremely rare.

These images depict just a few examples of different types of paper money errors.

Gutters or creases

The value of such an error will depend on size and severity: for a minor crease, the note will be worth about $10 more than face value in Very Fine condition, or $15 over face value in Uncirculated. A larger or more severe crease increases the value to $25 over face value in VF-20, or $50+ in Unc-63.

Offset transfers

A note that exhibits the face design on the back will bring prices according to how bold the transfer is. A partial or faint image will bring $25 over face value in VF or $50 in Unc. If the transfer is complete and strong, collectors will pay $100 and $200 over face value in VF and Unc.

Back on face

A complete and dark view of the back design on the note's face will increase its value by $150 to $200, in grades ranging from VF to Unc.

Ink smears

A minor ink smear (from the printing process, not from a leaky fountain pen!) will increase a note's worth by $10 over face value in VF, or $20 in Unc.

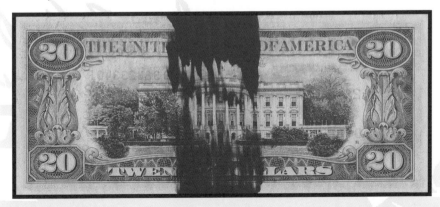

ERROR NOTES

Shifts or misaligned overprints

While minor shifts are easily found in circulation, major displacements are more rare and thus more valuable to collectors.

A shifted overprint will fetch $50 to $100 over face value, depending on the grade (VF or Unc.). A shifted overprint appearing on a star note (a replacement for a damaged note or error caught in the production process), such as the Series 1935-E Silver Certificate pictured, is more valuable.

Mismatched serial numbers

These mistakes are much sought after by error note collectors. The $1 note pictured, with one mismatched digit in the serial number, is worth $100 in VF and $200 in Unc. For the $2 note with a mismatched prefix, a collector would pay $200 in VF or $450 in Unc.

Inverted serial numbers/seals

A note printed with upside-down serial numbers and seals is worth $150 to $250 over face value, in grades ranging from VF to Unc. The $20 note pictured here also exhibits selvage, or part of an adjacent note.

ERROR NOTES

Inverted face

A typical note has its face and back aligned in the same up-down position. In the Series of 1935 $1 note pictured, the face is printed upside down. This error increases its value to $300 in VF or $650 in Unc.

Seals and serial numbers on back

With its seals and serial numbers printed on the back instead of the front, a collector would pay $150 (VF) to $300 (Unc.) for this $10 note. If they were also printed upside down, the value would increase to $350 and $750, respectively.

Third printing missing

A $5 note such as this one, with its seals and serial numbers missing, is worth $100 in VF and $300 in Unc.

Printed folds

This $10 note, with its large, attractively printed-over fold, would bring $400 in VF or $600 in Unc.

ERROR NOTES

Second printing missing

A $1 note that is missing its second printing—that is, which bears its serial numbers and seals, but is otherwise missing the back design—is worth $300 to $500 to a collector, in VF to Unc. condition. The dramatic and eye-catching $100 note of this type (pictured) is worth $600 in VF or $1,250 in Unc.

Blank back

A note with a blank back gives a collector only half the design, while increasing its value considerably—a good example of "less is more." A $20 note made this way is worth $150 in VF or $300 in Unc.

Double denomination

The most famous and desirable type of error is the "double denomination" note, with one value on the face and another on the back. These were produced in two main ways:

For small-size bills, a sheet printed on one side with $5 designs and information, but blank on the other, was then mistakenly put with one-sided $10 bills and imprinted on the other side with $10 information. A famous Series of 1934-D Silver Certificate, printed circa 1960, is of this type—with a $5 face and $10 back. Nearly a dozen of these were found by Omaha, Nebraska dealer Aubrey Bebee. Today an example is worth about $12,500 in VF-20 grade, and $20,000 in Unc.-63.

For large-size bills with more than one denomination per sheet, such an error could occur when the correct sheet was printed on the back, but upside down. A $50-$100 two-subject sheet might be printed correctly on one side, then printed on the other with the sheet misaligned so as to give the $50 the imprint intended for the $100, and vice versa.

In March 1909, *The Numismatist* reported on a batch of misprinted notes from the First National Bank of Albuquerque, New Mexico. One of these notes was mentioned in a story that made the rounds of the American Bankers' Association Convention held in Denver the preceding autumn. A hotel cashier (who was working overtime because of the convention) counted his cash, and in turning it over counted it again, but found a $50 discrepancy. According to the story, three more days (!) were spent in counting the cash, driving the cashier to the point of distraction. Finally the bill of the $100/$50 combination was found.

Photos courtesy of Harry E. Jones, Middleburg Heights, Ohio.

APPENDIX A

I. THE SIGNATURES OF UNITED STATES CURRENCY

The following table shows the exact period of time during which each two of the various signers of our currency were in office concurrently.

Register of the Treasury	Treasurer of the U.S.	Combined Tenure		Length of Time		
		Began	Ended	Years	Months	Days
Lucius E. Chittenden	F. E. Spinner	04-17-1861	8-10-1864	3	3	23
S. B. Colby	F. E. Spinner	08-11-1864	9-21-I867	3	1	10
Noah L. Jeffries	F. E. Spinner	10-05-1867	03-15-1869	1	5	10
John Allison	F. E. Spinner	04-03-1869	06-30-1877	6	2	27
John Allison	John C. New	06-30-1875	07-01-1876	1	—	1
John Allison	A.U. Wyman	07-01-1876	06-30-1877	—	11	29
John Allison	James Gilfillan	07-01-1877	03-23-1878	—	8	22
Glenni W. Scofield	James Gilfillan	04-01-1878	05-20-1881	3	1	19
Blanche K. Bruce	James Gilfillan	05-21-1881	03-31-1883	1	10	10
Blanche K. Bruce	A.U. Wyman	04-01-1883	04-30-1885	2	—	29
Blanche K. Bruce	Conrad N. Jordan	05-01-1885	06-05-1885	—	1	4
William S. Rosecrans	Conrad N. Jordan	06-08-1885	05-23-1887	1	11	15
William S. Rosecrans	James W. Hyatt	05-24-1887	05-10-1889	1	11	16
William S. Rosecrans	J.N. Huston	05-11-1889	04-21-1891	1	11	13
William S. Rosecrans	Enos H. Nebeker	04-25-1891	05-31-1893	2	1	6
William S. Rosecrans	Daniel N. Morgan	06-01-1893	06-19-1893	—	—	18
James F. Tillman	Daniel N. Morgan	07-01-1893	06-30-1897	3	11	29
James F. Tillman	Ellis H. Roberts	07-01-1897	12-02-1897	—	5	1
Blanche K. Bruce	Ellis H. Roberts	12-03-1898	05-17-1898	—	3	14
Judson W. Lyons	Ellis H. Roberts	04-07-1898	06-30-1905	7	2	23
Judson W. Lyons	Charles H. Treat	07-01-1905	04-01-1906	—	10	—
William T. Vernon	Charles H. Treat	06-12-1906	10-30-1909	3	9	18
William T. Vernon	Lee McClung	11-01-1909	03-14-1911	1	4	13
James C. Napier	Lee McClung	08-15-1911	11-21-1912	1	4	6
James C. Napier	Carmi A. Thompson	11-22-1912	03-31-1913	—	8	9
James C. Napier	John Burke	04-01-1913	09-30-1913	—	4	29
Gabe E. Parker	John Burke	10-01-1913	12-31-1914	1	5	30
Houston B.Teehee	John Burke	03-24-1915	11-20-1919	4	2	26
William S. Elliott	John Burke	11-21-1919	01-05-1921	1	7	14
William S. Elliott	Frank White	05-02-1921	01-26-1922	—	1	22
Harley V. Speelman	Frank White	01-25-1922	09-30-1927	5	8	5
Walter O. Woods	Frank White	10-01-1927	05-01-1928	—	7	—
Walter O. Woods	H.T. Tate	05-31-1928	01-17-1929	—	7	16
Edward E. Jones	Walter O. Woods	01-22-1929	05-31-1933	4	4	9

Secretary of the Treasury	Treasurer of the U.S.	Combined Tenure		Length of Time		
		Began	Ended	Years	Months	Days
William G. McAdoo	John Burke	04-01-1913	12-15-1918	5	8	14
Carter Glass	John Burke	12-18-1918	02-01-1920	1	1	15
D. F. Houston	John Burke	02-02-1920	01-05-1921	—	11	3
A. W. Mellon	Frank White	05-02-1921	05-01-1928	6	11	29
A. W. Mellon	H.T. Tate	04-30-1928	01-17-1929	—	8	16
A. W. Mellon	Walter O. Woods	01-18-1929	02-12-1932	3	—	25
Ogden L. Mills	Walter O. Woods	02-13-1932	03-03-1933	1	—	18
W. H. Woodin	Walter O. Woods	03-04-1933	05-31-1933	—	2	27
W. H. Woodin	W.A. Julian	06-01-1933	12-31-1933	—	7	—
Henry Morgenthau, Jr.	W.A. Julian	01-01-1934	07-22-1945	11	6	22
Fred M. Vinson	W.A. Julian	07-23-1945	07-23-1946	1	—	—
John W. Snyder	W.A. Julian	01-25-1946	05-29-1949	2	10	4
John W. Snyder	Georgia Neese Clark	06-21-1949	01-20-1953	3	7	—
George M. Humphrey	Ivy Baker Priest	01-28-1953	07-28-1957	4	6	—
Robert B. Anderson	Ivy Baker Priest	07-29-1957	01-20-1961	3	5	23

Secretary of the Treasury	Treasurer of the U.S.	Combined Tenure		Length of Time		
		Began	Ended	Years	Months	Days
C. Douglas Dillon	Elizabeth Rudel Smith	01-30-1961	04-13-1962	1	3	14
C. Douglas Dillon	Kathryn O'Hay Granahan	01-03-1963	03-01-1965	2	2	28
Henry Fowler	Kathryn O'Hay Granahan	04-01-1965	10-13-1966	1	6	13
Joseph Barr	Kathryn O'Hay Granahan* . . .	12-23-1968	01-20-1969	—	—	28
David Kennedy	Dorothy Andrews Elston‡	05-08-1969	09-16-1970	1	4	8
David Kennedy	Dorothy Andrews Kabis	09-17-1970	02-01-1971	1	4	8
John B. Connally	Dorothy Andrews Kabis	02-08-1971	07-03-1971	—	44	25
John B. Connally	Romana Acosta Banuelos	12-17-1971	06-12-1973	—	5	26
George P. Shultz	Romana Acosta Banuelos	06-12-1972	02-14-1974	1	8	2
William E. Simon	Francine I. Neff	06-21-1974	01-19-1977	2	6	28
W. Michael Blumenthal	Azie Taylor Morton	09-12-1977	08-04-1979	1	10	24
G. William Miller	Azie Taylor Morton	08-06-1979	01-20-1981	1	5	15
Donald T. Regan	Angela Marie Buchanan	03-17-1981	07-05-1983	2	3	18
Donald T. Regan	Katherine Davalos Ortega	09-22-1983	02-03-1985	1	4	12
James A. Baker	Katherine Davalos Ortega	02-04-1985	08-18-1988	3	6	13
Nicholas F. Brady	Katherine Davalos Ortega	09-15-1988	06-30-1989	—	9	15
Nicholas F. Brady	Catalina Vasquez Villapando . .	11-20-1989	01-20-1993	3	2	1
Lloyd M. Bentsen	Mary Ellen Withrow	03-01-1994	12-22-1994	—	9	22
Robert E. Rubin	Mary Ellen Withrow	10-01-1995	07-02-1999	3	9	1
Lawrence F. Summers	Mary Ellen Withrow	07-02-1999	01-20-2001	1	6	18
Paul H. O'Neill	Rosario Marin	08-16-2001	12-31-2002	1	4	15
John W. Snow	Rosario Marin	02-03-2003	06-30-2003	0	4	27

* Although no longer treasurer, Kathryn Granahan's signature continued in use until Dorothy Elston was named to replace her.

‡ When Dorothy Elston married Walter Kabis on September 17, 1970, it was the first time the signature of a treasurer was changed during the term of office.

APPENDIX B

Friedberg No.	Page No.
F-1 to F-5a	108
F-6 to F-10a	157
F-11 to F-15	213
F-16 to F-40	56-59
F-41 to F-60	88-90
F-61 to F-92	109-111
F-93 to F-123	158-163
F-124 to F-147	214-217
F-148 to F-164	267-269
F-165 to F-182	308-310
F-183a to F-185n	344-346
F-186a to F-187l	356-358
F-188	368
F-189	374
F-190 to F-190b	164
F-191 and F191a	217
F-192 to F-192b	270
F-193 to F-193b	311
F-194 to F-194b	348
F-195 and F-195a	358
F-195d	342
F-196 and F-196a	156
F-197 and F-197a	212
F-198	263
F-199	307
F-200	342
F-201	356
F-202	368
F-202a	264
F-202c	342
F-202d	356
F-203	265

Friedberg No.	Page No.
F-204	307
F-205	342
F-206	356
F-207	265
F-208	307
F-209	343
F-210	356
F-211	368
F-212 and F-212d	266
F-212a	307
F-212b and F-212f	343-344
F-212c and F-212g	356
F-212e	308
F-213 and F-214	176-177
F-215 to F-239	61-64
F-240 to F-258	92-94
F-259 to F-282	119-122
F-283 to F-304	173-175
F-305 to F-322	226-229
F-323 to F-335	281-282
F-336 to F-344	318-319
F-345a to F-345d	350
F-346a to F-346e	358-360
F-347 to F-352	65-66
F-353 to F-358	95-96
F-359 to F-365	123-124
F-366 to F-371	178
F-372 to F-375a	230-231
F-376	282
F-377 and F-378	320
F-379	350
F-379a to F-379d	360-361

Friedberg No.	Page No.	Friedberg No.	Page No.
F-380 to F-386	60	F-781 to F-809a	125
F-387 to F-393	91	F-810 to F-821	180
F-394 to F-408a	112	F-822 to F-830	236
F-409 to F-423a	165	F-831	286
F-424 to F-439	218	F-832A to F-891C	126-128
F-440 to F-451	271-272	F-892A to F-951C	181-182
F-452 to F-463	312	F-952A to F-1011C	234-235
F-464 and F-464a	347	F-1012A to F-1071	284-285
F-465	358	F-1072A to F-1131	322-323
F-466 to F-478	113	F-1132 to F-1132b	351
F-479 to F-492	166	F-1133 to F-1133b	363
F-493 to F-506	219	F-1134	370
F-507 to F-518a	272-273	F-1135	376
F-519 to F-531	313	F-1136 to F-1141	119
F-532 to F-538b	114	F-1142 to F-1151a	172
F-539 to F-548	167	F-1152 to F-1159b	225
F-549 to F-557	220	F-1160 to F-1161f	280
F-558 to F-565	273-274	F-1162 to F-1166IV	318
F-566 to F-572a	314	F-1166a	348
F-573 to F-575b	115	F-1166b	231
F-576 to F-579b	168	F-1166c and F-1166h	321
F-580 to F-585	221	F-1166d, l, and n	347
F-586	274-275	F-1166e, j, and o	361
F-586a	314	F-1166f and F-1166k	368
F-587 to F-597a	116	F-1166g, l, and q	374
F-598 to F-612	118	F-1167 to F-1173a	179
F-613 to F-638	169-171	F-1174 to F-1187	232-233
F-639 to F-663a	222-224	F-1188 to F-1197	278
F-664 to F-685a	275-277	F-1198 to F-1200a	283
F-686 to F-707a	315-317	F-1201 to F-1215	321
F-708 to F-746	67	F-1215 to F-1217	347-348
F-747 to F-780	97	F-1218 to F-1220	361-362

APPENDIX B

Friedberg No.	Page No.
F-1221 to F-1222b	369
F-1223 to F-1225	375
F-1226 to F-1235	380
F-1236 to F-1249	381
F-1251 to F-1261	382
F-1264 to F-1282	382-383
F-1283 to F-1307	383-384
F-1308 to F-1313	385
F-1314 to F-1338	385-386
F-1339 to F-1346	387
F-1347 to F-1373a	388
F-1374 and F-1376	389
F-1379 to F-1381	390
F-1382 to F-1383a	391
F-1500	68
F-1501 to F-1514	97-99
F-1525 to F-1536	128-129
F-1550 to F-1551	324
F-1600 to F-1610	68-70
F-1611 to F-1621	71
F-1650 to F-1651	130
F-1652 to F-1658	131
F-1700 to F-1708	184-185
F-1917-A to F-1920-C	80
F-1800-1 and F-1800-2	129
F-1801-1 and F-1801-2	183
F-1802-1 and F-1802-2	237
F-1803-1 and F-1803-2	287
F-1804-1 and F-1804-2	325
F-1850	131
F-1870-A to F-1870-L	238
F-1860-A to F-1860-L	187

Friedberg No.	Page No.
F-1880-B to F-1880-L	288
F-1890-B to F-1890-K	326
F-1900-A to F-1929-L	72-83
F-1935-A to F-1937-L	99-100
F-1950-A to F-1990-L	132-149
F-2000-A to F-2037-L	187-205
F-2050-A to F-2090-L	239-256
F-2100-A to F-2128-L	289-301
F-2150-A to F-2178-L	326-339
F-2200-A to F-2200-L	352
F-2201-A to F-2204-B	353
F-2210-A to F-2213-B	364-365
F-2220-A to F-2223-B	370-371
F-2230-A to F-2233-B	377
F-2300	70
F-2301 to F-2302	135
F-2303	191
F-2304 to F-2305	241-242
F-2306	71
F-2307	130
F-2308 and F-2309	130
F-2400 and F-2401	185
F-2402 and F-2403	237
F-2404	287
F-2405 to F-2406	325
F-2407	351
F-2408 and F-2409	364
F-2410	370
F-2411 to F-2412	376
EP-1 to EP-188	394-399
TN-1 to TN-16a	403-407

A Selection of Terms for the Paper Money Collector

ace • Numismatic nickname for a $1 bill, particularly a $1 National Bank Note of the Original Series or the Series of 1875.

American Bank Note Company • Firm founded in 1858 in New York City. Provider by contract of certain federal currency and Fractional Currency notes in the 1860s through the mid-1870s. Sometimes one private firm would print the face of a note and another would print the back. In all instances, the Treasury seal and serial numbers were separately imprinted by the Treasury Department in Washington, DC. The ABNCo monogram appears on certain Fractional Currency. This firm was the prime contractor and did more such printing than did the National Bank Note Co., the Continental Bank Note Co., or the Columbian Bank Note Co.

back • The reverse side of a note, usually called the *back*, is the paper money equivalent of *reverse* used for coins. The other side of a note is called the *face*. • In Treasury records, sometimes *obverse* and *reverse* are used, but *face* and *back* are preferred by numismatists today.

Bank Note Reporter • A newspaper issued monthly by Krause Publications (Iola, Wisconsin), devoted to the collecting of paper money.

Battleship Note • Numismatic nickname for a Series of 1918 $2 Federal Reserve Bank Note with a battleship printed in green on the back.

bill • A piece of paper money of $1 face value or higher. • Synonym: *note*.

Bison Note • Numismatic nickname for the $10 Series of 1901 Legal Tender Notes depicting Black Diamond, a resident of the Central Park Zoo (New York City). The same quadruped was featured on the 1913 Buffalo nickel and on certain modern coins.

black charter • Describes a rare variety of $5 National Bank note issued in the 1870s, with the bank charter number printed in black (instead of the normal red overprint) as part of the printing plate.

Black Eagle Note • Numismatic nickname for the $1 Series of 1899 Silver Certificates depicting a bold eagle printed in black on the center of the face of the note.

Bureau of Engraving and Printing • Federal bureau in charge of printing paper money and certain other security items. Successor to the National Currency Bureau (see below). First housed in the Treasury Building in Washington, DC, then moved to its own building in July 1880, in the same city. Today the BEP maintains a strong outreach to numismatists, including displays at conventions and the sale of sheets and souvenirs. A branch printing facility is maintained in Fort Worth, Texas.

charter number • Beginning in 1863, thousands of National Banks were chartered by the Treasury Department and were given charter numbers which were printed on the face of each note (beginning in the early 1870s, but not on the earlier National Bank Notes of the 1860s), in addition to the serial numbers. Charters for the earlier banks were for 19 years. Charters for later banks, 1864 to the early 1920s, were for 20 years and could be extended for a further 20 years, and extended again beyond that. Later, charters were made perpetual. • Sometimes when a bank changed its name or even its geographical location, the same charter number was retained.

circulation (of a National Bank) • The total face value of a given National Bank's bills in circulation in commerce (not including notes held in the bank's vault or not yet issued). From 1863 to 1900, banks could issue bills up to 90% of their paid-in capital, with appropriate bonds or other acceptable securities given as collateral. From 1900 to 1935, banks could issue up to 100% of their capital. The collateral bonds earned interest.

Coin Note • Note from $1 to $1,000 issued in the Series of 1890 and 1891, redeemable in coins (silver or gold, at the option of the Treasury Department, but in practice the bearer could make the selection). One of several distinct United States currency series (see listings under individual denominations). These are called Treasury Notes or Coin Notes interchangeably. The backs of the Series of 1890 issues are particularly ornate.

Columbian Bank Note Company • Firm located in Washington, DC, which undertook contract printing for the backs of $5 National Bank Notes in 1877.

Compound Interest Treasury Note • Note from $10 to $1,000 issued in the early 1860s yielding interest to the bearer. One of several distinct United States currency series (see listings under individual denominations).

Comptroller of the Currency • Treasury Department appointed official in charge of paper money distribution, the granting of National Bank charters, and related matters.

Continental Bank Note Company • Firm founded in 1862 in New York City. Provider by contract of certain federal currency and Fractional Currency notes in the 1860s through the mid-1870s. Sometimes one private firm would print the face of a note and another would print the back. In all instances, the Treasury seal and serial numbers were separately imprinted by the Treasury Department in Washington, DC.

counterfeit • A bill in imitation of an original design, but printed from false plates, by someone not authorized by the Treasury Department.

Date Back • Describes certain Series of 1882 National Bank Notes with the dates 1882-1908 printed prominently on the back, or certain blue-seal Series of 1902 National Bank Notes with the dates 1902 and 1908 printed on the back (in addition to other motifs).

Demand Note • Note from $5 to $20 issued in 1861. One of several distinct United States currency series (see listings under individual denominations).

denomination • The face or stated value printed on a bill, this being the amount for which the bill could be redeemed in specie or exchanged for other bills. • Denominations of federal bills in use in commerce include $1, $2, $5, $10, $20, $50, $100, $500, $1,000, $5,000, and $10,000. Denominations of Fractional Currency include 3¢, 5¢, 10¢, 15¢, 25¢, and 50¢.

deuce • Numismatic nickname for a $2 bill.

Educational Note • Name for any one of the $1, $2, and $5 Series of 1896 Silver Certificates with ornately engraved designs, among the most famous of all United States currency issues.

encased postage stamp • A regular federal postage stamp of a denomination from 1¢ to 90¢, enclosed within a brass frame with clear mica face. On the back of most, embossed in raised letters in brass, is the name of an advertiser. Patented by John Gault, and popular as a money substitute in 1862 and 1863. Often collected along with Fractional Currency. Encased postage stamps are listed in the present text.

face • The front side of a note, usually called the *face*, is the paper money equivalent of *obverse* used for coins. The other side of a note is called the *back*. • In Treasury records, sometimes *obverse* and *reverse* are used, but *face* and *back* are preferred by numismatists today.

Federal Reserve Bank Note • Note from $1 to $50 (Series of 1915 and 1918, large- size) and $5 to $100 (Series of 1929, small-size). Each bears the name of a Federal Reserve Bank (bolding imprinted across the center of the face on large-size notes) and a letter designating its district. One of several distinct series of United States currency (see listings under individual denominations).

Federal Reserve Note • Note from $1 to $10,000 issued in large-size and small-size formats, Series of 1914 to the present day (the standard imprint on all of today's notes). Each bears the name of a Federal Reserve Bank and a letter designating its district. One of several distinct series of United States currency (see listings under individual denominations).

First Charter Note • Numismatic nickname, with no basis in Treasury documents, for Original Series and Series of 1875 National Bank Notes.

Franklin • Nickname for a small-size $100 bill, from the portrait depicted.

Gold Certificate • Note from $10 to $10,000 issued in large-size and small-size formats, redeemable in gold coins. The backs of large-size notes were printed in gold color (and in green for small-size notes). One of several distinct series of United States currency (see listings under individual denominations).

grade • Designation assigned by numismatists to signify the amount of wear or circulation a note has experienced and its condition today (see the Introduction for more information). Grading can be expressed by adjectives (such as Good, Extremely Fine, and Uncirculated), or by abbreviations in combination with numbers from 1 to 70 (adapted from the ANA coin grading system), such as EF-40 or Unc-63.

Grand Watermelon Note • Numismatic nickname for the $1,000 Series of 1890 Treasury Notes (Coin Notes), with two zeros on the back in the form, fancifully, of watermelons. Also see *Watermelon Note*.

Green Eagle Note • Numismatic nickname for a Series of 1918 $1 Federal Reserve Bank Note with an eagle printed in green on the back.

greenback • Piece of paper money of $1 face value or higher with the back printed in green. Unofficial popular term for United States paper money in general, popularized by the Legal Tender Notes of the 1860s with their green backs (though these were not the first to be printed in this color), and widely used since.

Hawaii Note • Numismatic nickname for certain $1 Silver Certificates and $5, $10, and $20 Federal Reserve Notes with brown seals and HAWAII overprinted on both sides, issued in Hawaii during World War II.

Indian Chief Note • Numismatic nickname for the $5 Series of 1899 Silver Certificates depicting Indian Chief Running Antelope on the face.

Interest Bearing Note • A note from $10 to $5,000 issued in the early 1860s, yielding interest to the bearer. One of several distinct series of United States currency (see listings under individual denominations).

Jackass Note • Numismatic nickname for the $10 Series of 1869 Legal Tender Notes showing an eagle which, if turned upside down, resembles a jackass. This eagle motif was also used on certain other denominations and on Fractional Currency Shields.

launder • Term, often used in a derogatory sense, referring to the cleaning of paper money to enhance its appearance. In fact, careful cleaning, such as to remove grease or grime, can be beneficial, but should be done only by experts.

Legal Tender Note • Note from $1 to $10,000 issued in large-size and small-size formats. For a long time Legal Tender Notes were the basic mainstay of the federal paper money system. One of several distinct series of United States currency (see listings under individual denominations). • Synonym: *United States Note*.

legal tender status • A.k.a. *obligation*. Information given in the lettered inscriptions on the back of a note, describing its exchangeability. As an example, certain early Legal Tender Notes have this inscription: "This note is a legal tender for all debts, public and private, except duties on imports and interest on the public debt, and is receivable in payment of all loans made to the United States." • In addition, but not stated (Gold Certificates and National Gold Bank Notes), most early federal currency of 1862 to 1878 could not be exchanged at par for silver or gold coins.

margin • The blank area at the border of a note beyond the design or printed information. The width or amount of white space on a bill can affect its value. Generally, National Bank Notes of the 1863 to 1935 era were sent to banks in the form of uncut sheets, to be cut apart at their destination. Sometimes, especially in the 19th century, such cutting was done carelessly, resulting in uneven trimming or cutting into the border or design. The margins on Original Series and Series of 1875 $5 bills were very small, as printed on the plates, and these never have wide top and bottom margins. In contrast, many Legal Tender Notes and Silver Certificates of the 19th century have wide margins all around. There are no general rules.

Martha Washington Note • Numismatic nickname for the $1 Series of 1886 and 1891 Silver Certificates depicting the first of the nation's first ladies. • *Synonym:* Martha Note.

National Bank • Commercial bank incorporated under the laws of the federal government and given a federal charter number, pursuant to the National Banking Act of 1863 and its amendments. Such banks were regulated by the comptroller of the currency, an officer of the Treasury Department.

National Bank Note • Note bearing the imprint of a specific National Bank and its location, plus the signature of bank officers, in addition to federal signatures and information. • Original Series and Series of 1875 (nickname: "First Charter"), issued in denominations from $1 to $1,000. Large size. • Series of 1882 (nickname: "Second Charter"), issued in denominations $5 to $100. Large size. • Series of 1902 (nickname: "Third Charter"), issued in denominations $5 to $100. Large size. • Series of 1929, issued in denominations $5 to $100, Type 1 and Type 2. Small size.

National Bank Note Company • Firm founded in 1859 in New York City; a provider by contract of certain federal currency and Fractional Currency notes in the 1860s through the mid-1870s. Sometimes one private firm would print the face of a note and another would print the back. In all instances, the Treasury seal and serial numbers were separately imprinted by the Treasury Department in Washington, DC

National Bank Note regional letter • From about 1902 to 1924, each National Bank Note had a large capital letter printed on the face to designate the region in which it was issued. This was to help Treasury Department personnel sort the notes when they were redeemed at a later date. The letters: N (New England banks); E (East); S (South); M (Midwest); W (West); P (Pacific district).

National Currency Bureau • In 1862, with Spencer M. Clark as its first director, the National Currency Bureau began operations in the attic of the west wing of the Treasury Building in Washington, DC. In time, its facilities were expanded there, including to the basement. The bureau's operations consisted of adding serial numbers and Treasury seals to bills printed by private contractors; later, the printing of certain Fractional Currency; and still later, the printing of currency of all denominations. It was succeeded by the Bureau of Engraving and Printing (see above) in the 1870s.

National Gold Bank Note • A note bearing the imprint of a specific National Bank and its location, plus the signature of bank officers, in addition to federal signatures and information. Issued in the early 1870s (in denominations of $5 to $100) by National Gold Banks located in the state of California. The reverse illustrates various gold coins (the same image used on all denominations).

note • A piece of paper money of $1 face value or higher. • Synonym: *bill.*

obligation • See *legal tender status.*

***Paper Money* magazine** • A magazine issued six times per year by the non-profit Society of Paper Money Collectors.

pinhole • In the 19th century it was common practice to stitch several notes together for safekeeping or for hiding within a coat's lining. Today, when certain notes are held to the light, tiny pinholes can be seen.

Plain Back • A description of certain blue-seal Series of 1902 National Bank Notes *without* the dates 1902 and 1908 printed on the back (such notes have other motifs, however).

plate information (letters and numbers) • *National Bank Notes:* These were printed on plates with two or four subjects (and, from 1929 and later, six subjects). Although there are exceptions, generally the first note *of a given denomination* is given the plate letter A, the second note, B, etc. Thus, if a plate had a $1-$1-$1-$2 arrangement, $1 notes would be printed with plate letters A, B, and C, sometimes with the same serial number, and other times with different serial numbers. In instances in which the same serial number was used (as in Original Series National Bank Notes), there would be three $1 notes with the same serial, differing only by plate letter A, B, or C, while the single $2 note would have the same serial as well, and plate letter A. Small-size National Bank Notes have a combination letter and number on the face, such as K124. Beginning with the Series of 1882, most (but not all) National Bank Notes bore a tiny number on the back plate. • *Other Notes:* All federal notes from $1 to $10,000 bear a plate letter on the front. Small-size notes have a letter plus a number. Beginning in the late 19th century, back plates were given numbers. • *Numismatic notations:* Plate information for a given note with just a plate letter on the face can be given as A, B, C, etc. For notes with back plate numbers, the notation can be: "Plate information: A/20," as an example. For a small-size note, an example is: "C73/278."

plate information (serial numbers) • On all federal notes $1 to $10,000, a Treasury Department serial number is printed once or twice on the face. On early notes this can be a number or a number in combination with one or more letters. For small-size notes, a combination of numbers and letters is used. On a four-subject sheet of federal notes, it was common practice to give all the notes the same serial number. Accordingly, a Legal Tender note of 1862, printed from a four-subject plate with plate letters A, B, C, and D, would have each of the four notes with the same serial number, 123 for example, but differentiated by the plate letters. The same serial numbers were used on different series and varieties of notes in the same era. Accordingly, the numbering system of Series of 1886 $5 Silver Certificates was independent of numbers used on Gold Certificates or National Bank notes, etc. • *National Bank Notes:* On a 19th-century large-size National Bank Note, one of two numbers printed on the note is the Treasury Department serial. The other (usually lower and often in the range from 1 to 10,000) is the number in a sequence for the specific bank and denomination of a given bank note type. An example is provided by a $10 Series of 1902, Date Back note from the First National Bank of West Derry (NH). Records show that these bills were issued with serial numbers 1 to 1570 on plates arranged $10-$10-$10-$20, meaning that each plate had three $10 notes with the same serial plus one $20 note. The total number of $10 bills made was 4,710 (three times 1,570). Today, a bill in a private collection bears plate information E/74, bank serial number 275, and Treasury Department serial number H765723.

Porthole Note • Numismatic nickname for the $5 Series of 1923 Silver Certificates with the portrait of Abraham Lincoln in a heavy frame fancifully resembling a ship's porthole.

Professional Currency Dealers Association • A trade group, commonly known as PCDA, composed of paper money dealers in the field.

proof note • A proof (not capitalized in usage) note is an impression for test or other purposes, from a complete or partially complete plate, to illustrate its appearance. Such notes usually bear no serial numbers, or else just zeroes, and may be missing other elements, such as the Treasury seal and signatures. Proof notes are usually printed on only one side, and show either the front or back, but not both. Such proof notes are highly prized today. • Synonym: *Specimen note* (usually capitalized as such). • Specimen Fractional Currency notes, denominations 3¢ to 50¢, are sometimes called proof notes.

Refunding Certificate • Interest bearing $10 certificate, not a currency note, issued in 1879 (see the listing under $10 notes).

Second Charter Note • Numismatic nickname, with no basis in Treasury documents, for Series of 1882 National Bank Notes.

security features • Aspects of the design or printing of a note intended to deter copying and counterfeiting. In early times this consisted of minute design elements expertly engraved, as well as printing on special paper (often with silk fibers embedded) ordered by the Treasury Department. In recent years other features have included watermark designs; color-shifting ink (which changes when a note is viewed from different angles); micro-printing; and the embedment of plastic strips.

sheet of notes • An uncut group of notes, as printed, usually four subjects for large-size notes of 1861 to 1929; 12 subjects (cut apart into two six-subject sheets) for early small-size notes of the late 1920s and early 1930s; later 12 subjects; and today 36 subjects.

signatures on notes, Federal Reserve Bank officials • Federal Reserve Bank Notes bear the printed signatures of two Federal Reserve Bank officials, usually the cashier and governor, in addition to two Treasury officials.

signatures on notes, National Bank Notes • National Bank Notes of 1863 to 1935 bear the printed signatures of two Treasury Department officials plus signatures of the cashier and president of the National Bank. All early notes, to the 1890s, were required to be hand-signed in ink by the bank officials. Later, rubber-stamped signatures were permitted. In a very few instances later in the large-size note era, banks paid an extra amount and had the names of officials added to the printing plate. However, most 20th-century bills were hand-signed or rubber-stamped. Small-size National Bank Notes of 1929 to 1935 bear printed signatures of bank officials. In some instances another official signed for one or another bank position, such as assistant or acting cashier and vice president, noting this with an abbreviation such as "Asst." in front of the printed word Cashier, or "V" before the printed word President, etc.

signatures on notes, Treasury officials • Most federal currency of 1861 to date includes the signatures of two Treasury Department officials. Certainly very early notes were hand-signed by the officials or designated assistants. All others, constituting the vast majority, bear printed signatures. • *Register of the Treasury and treasurer:* The first combination is of Lucius E. Chittenden, register of the Treasury, and F.E. Spinner, treasurer of the United States, who were in office jointly from April 17, 1861, to August 10, 1864. The last combination printed on notes was Edward E. Jones and Walter O. Woods, who served together from January 22, 1929, to May 31, 1933. • *Secretary of the Treasury and treasurer:* In time, with some overlapping of use, notes bore the imprint of these two officials, the practice in use today. The first combination printed on currency was William G. McAdoo, register, and John Burke, treasurer, in office from April 1, 1913, to December 15, 1918.

Silver Certificate • A note from $1 to $1,000 issued in large-size and small-size formats, redeemable first in silver dollars, and later in silver bullion. One of several distinct series of United States currency (see listings under individual denominations).

Silver Dollar Note • Numismatic nickname for the $5 Series of 1886 Silver Certificates depicting five Morgan silver dollars in a row on the back (four reverses and the center coin showing the obverse of an 1886 dollar), printed in green.

Society of Paper Money Collectors • A non-profit organization, founded in 1961, devoted to the study and appreciation of currency. Publisher of *Paper Money*, a magazine issued six times per year.

Specimen note • Same as proof note (see above). • Specimen Fractional Currency note: general term for a Fractional Currency bill printed on one side only, face or back, and made for distribution to collectors, these being popular in the era in which they were made, the 1860s and 1870s. Usually capitalized, as Specimen.

stamp • Derisive nickname used by the public in the 1860s and 1870s for Fractional Currency notes.

star note • A large-size or small-size note from circa 1908 to date with a star next to the serial number is a replacement note, made after the first note with this number was found to be defective and then destroyed. "Star notes" form a collecting specialty, especially for small-size notes.

Technicolor Note • Later numismatic nickname (employed from the 1930s to date) for the Series of 1905 large-size Gold Certificates. The face of these notes is colorful, with part of the inscription in gold ink and with gold tint to part of the paper, and red seal and serial numbers. Nickname from a patented process for color motion picture film.

Third Charter Note • Numismatic nickname, with no basis in Treasury documents, for Series of 1902 National Bank Notes.

tinted paper • While most notes were printed on white paper, exceptions included certain issues of the late 1860s ("Rainbow Notes" in the Series of 1869 Legal Tender series, certain National Bank notes of the era), with an area of blue tint in the paper; National Gold Bank Notes of the early 1870s, on yellow-tinted paper; and the Series of 1905 Gold Certificates.

Tombstone Note • Numismatic nickname for the $1 Series of 1886, 1891, and 1908 Silver Certificates with the portrait of the recently deceased Vice President Thomas A. Hendricks in a frame resembling the outline of a tombstone, perhaps created unintentionally.

Treasury Note • Same as *Coin Note* (see below).

Treasury seal • Emblem of the Treasury Department; circular, sometimes with an ornate border, and varying in size and color, as used on the face of all federal currency $1 upward from 1862 to the present, as well as the fourth and fifth issues of Fractional Currency. The basic motif is of a pair of scales above and a key below, with inscription surrounding. The style of the Treasury seal can determine a collectable variety. Example: Series of 1886 Silver Certificates with Rosecrans-Nebeker Treasury signatures exist with a large brown Treasury seal (Friedberg-220) and a small red scalloped Treasury seal (F-221).

United States Note • Same as *Legal Tender Note* (see above).

Value Back • Describes certain Series of 1882 National Bank Notes on which the denomination is printed in green on the back, spelled out, as FIVE DOLLARS.

vignette • An ornamental or illustrative element of a bank note, such as a portrait, allegorical scene, or motif from history. For example, the Series of 1902 $100 National Bank Note bears a vignette of John J. Knox on its face and another of two men, a shield, and an eagle on the back.

Watermelon Note • Numismatic nickname for the $100 Series of 1890 Treasury Notes (Coin Notes) with two zeros on the back in the form, fancifully, of watermelons. Also see *Grand Watermelon Note*.

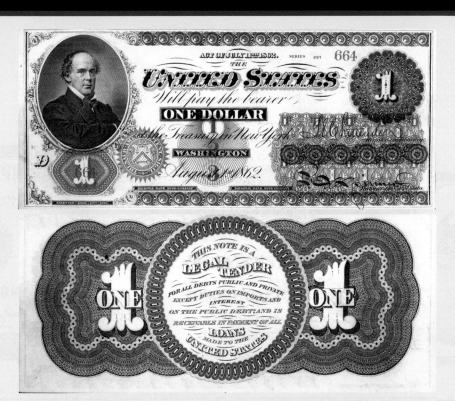

$1 Legal Tender Note (United States Note) • Series of 1862 • Friedberg-16 •
Bearing the date of August 1st 1862, these "greenback" bills were circulated in large quantities early in the Civil War, at a time when silver and gold coins were hoarded and not seen in commerce.

$1 National Bank Note • Original Series • Friedberg-280 • This note was issued by the First National Bank of Gonic, New Hampshire (charter number 938). It has the printed signatures of Treasury officials Colby and Spinner and the inked signatures of the bank's cashier and president.

$1 Treasury or Coin Note • Series of 1890 • Friedberg-347 • This is the back design, very ornate, of a Series of 1890 bill, called a Treasury Note or Coin Note. These are a special favorite of numismatists today.

$1 Silver Certificate • Series of 1896 "Educational Note" • Friedberg-224 • One of the most famous and ornate of all 19th-century federal bills is the $1 "Educational Note" of 1896. Depicted on the face is the vignette *History Instructing Youth*, with a panorama of the Potomac River and the national capital in the distance. The back of the note depicts Martha and George Washington, the only instance of an American president and first lady appearing on the same currency issue.

$2 Silver Certificate • Series of 1896 "Educational Note" • Friedberg-247 •
This $2 Silver Certificate of 1896 bears the face vignette imaginatively titled *Science Presenting Steam and Electricity to Commerce and Manufacture*. The back shows inventors Robert Fulton and Samuel F.B. Morse.

$2 National Bank Note • Series of 1875, "Lazy 2" • Friedberg-292 • This note was issued by the Laconia (NH) National Bank (charter number 1645). Bills with serial number 1, as here, are especially desirable. The design is the same as the Original Series bills, but with SERIES 1875 overprinted vertically in red toward the left.

$5 Silver Certificate • Series of 1886 "Silver Dollar Note" • Friedberg-263 •
One of the most "numismatic" of all large-size bills is the well-known Series of 1886
$5, with an array of Morgan silver dollars across the back.

$5 Silver Certificate • Series of 1899 "Indian Chief Note" • Friedberg-272 •
The $5 denomination includes many artistic, interesting, and widely collected series,
and the Series of 1899 is among the most popular. These were issued with 11 different
signature combinations, but are usually collected singly as a type.

$5 Silver Certificate • Series of 1896 "Educational Note" • Friedberg-270 •
Depicted is *Electricity as the Dominant Force in the World*. The back of the $5 note illustrates Ulysses S. Grant and Philip Sheridan, both of whom were generals in the Civil War.

$5 National Bank Note • Series of 1875 • Friedberg-404 • Issued by the Mechanicks National Bank of Concord, New Hampshire (charter 2447), this note bears bank serial number 1 at the lower left. Bills of this style also had a Treasury serial number at the upper right, above the charter number.

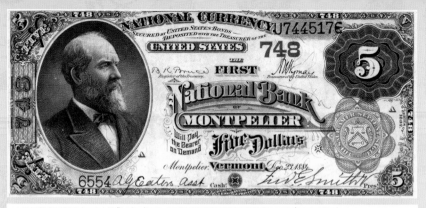

$5 National Bank Note • Series of 1882, Brown Back • Friedberg-467 •
A bill from First National Bank, Montpelier, Vermont (charter number 748) is particularly elaborate and is known as the "circus poster style." Also interesting are the signatures, quite unusual. The *assistant* cashier and *vice* president have each signed their names.

$10 Legal Tender or United States Note • Series of 1901 "Bison Note" •
Friedberg-122 • Black Diamond, a bison at the Central Park Zoo in New York City, is depicted on this popular $10 bill, a style issued through the mid-1920s. The same animal modeled the 1913 Indian Head/Buffalo nickel.

$10 National Gold Bank Note • Friedberg-1142 • Issued by the First National Gold Bank of San Francisco, this bill is one in a series that depicts a collage of actual gold coins on the back. Notes of this type, issued in the 1870s and later quickly retired, were exchangeable at par with gold coins and were backed by such, a different arrangement from that used for other National Bank Notes which were exchangeable at par only for other paper money. National Gold Bank Notes are rare today. When seen they are usually in lower grades.

$20 Gold Certificate • Series of 1905 "Technicolor Note" • Friedberg-1180 • With its red seal and gold printing this style of Gold Certificate, issued in Series 1905 through 1922, was later dubbed the "Technicolor Note" by collectors, from a film process popularized in the 1930s.

$100 Legal Tender or United States Note • Friedberg-167 • Depicting the national bird in a particularly imposing manner, the $100 Legal Tender Note of this design was widely used in large transactions in the 1860s.

$1000 Treasury or Coin Note • Series of 1890 "Grand Watermelon Note" • Friedberg-379a • One of the great trophy notes in the American series is the "Grand Watermelon Note," named for the appearance of the bright green zeroes on the back.